*Sephardi Lives*

Divergent/overlapping identities —
sources 65,

STANFORD STUDIES IN JEWISH HISTORY AND CULTURE

EDITED BY *Aron Rodrigue and Steven J. Zipperstein*

# Sephardi Lives

*A Documentary History, 1700–1950*

*Edited by Julia Phillips Cohen
and Sarah Abrevaya Stein*

STANFORD UNIVERSITY PRESS
STANFORD, CALIFORNIA

Stanford University Press
Stanford, California

Printed in the United States of America on acid-free, archival-quality paper

Library of Congress Cataloging-in-Publication Data

Sephardi lives : a documentary history, 1700-1950 / edited by Julia Phillips Cohen and Sarah Abrevaya Stein.
        pages cm--(Stanford studies in Jewish history and culture)
  Includes bibliographical references and index.
  Selections originally written in: Ladino, Hebrew, Ottoman Turkish, Modern Turkish, French, Greek, Serbian, Croatian, Bulgarian, Italian, Spanish, Portuguese, German, Yiddish, and English.
  ISBN 978-0-8047-7165-8 (cloth : alk. paper)--
  ISBN 978-0-8047-9143-4 (pbk. : alk. paper)
   1. Sephardim--History--Sources. 2. Jewish diaspora--History--Sources. 3. Jews--History--Sources. I. Cohen, Julia Phillips, editor. II. Stein, Sarah Abrevaya, editor. III. Series: Stanford studies in Jewish history and culture.
  DS134.S378 2014
  909'.0492408--dc23
                                              2014018280
  ISBN 978-0-8047-9191-5 (electronic)

Typeset by Bruce Lundquist in 10.5/15 Galliard

*To Aron Rodrigue, teacher, mentor, friend*
Kien en buen arvol se arima, buena solombra lo kuvija
*(Whoever leans against a good tree is covered in good shade)*

# Contents

( ) Publication Date
[ ] Composition Date
{ } Time period referenced

## PART II. VIOLENCE, WAR, AND REGIONAL TRANSFORMATION

# PART III. POLITICAL MOVEMENTS AND IDEOLOGIES

## PART IV. THE SECOND WORLD WAR AND ITS AFTERMATH

## PART V. DIASPORIC AND ÉMIGRÉ CIRCLES

PART VI. THE EMERGENCE OF SEPHARDI STUDIES

# List of Maps

## Acknowledgments

Despite the existence of pioneering scholarship, the study of Sephardi history is still in its infancy with many chapters still unwritten. Producing the first overarching documentary history on the modern Judeo-Spanish cultural world has hinged on the generosity of many colleagues.

Our first debt is to those who were most tireless with their aid. Olga Borovaya read every page of this book and commented with sophistication and meticulousness, identifying errors as well as conceptual problems. She is also responsible for helping identify, translate, and annotate a number of sources. Devin E. Naar and Paris Papamichos Chronakis (who, like Olga, served as ongoing consultants) were immensely helpful at every stage of this project, not only sharing the fruits of their own research, but helping us think through the broad and complex sweep of Sephardi history. For many years Rachel Deblinger served indefatigably as our editorial assistant and digital humanities guru, handling with aplomb a vast and unruly body of data and facilitating our collaboration, always with wisdom and good cheer.

Many others were generous with their own research findings, guiding us to fascinating documents of the Sephardi past, sharing their expertise in various fields, and helping us appreciate more fully the immensity of this project. Matt Goldish, Emil Kerenji, Devi Mays, and Isaac Nehama were exceedingly generous with their time, not only by translating but also by providing crucial historical insights and answers to countless queries. Thanks in this vein are also due to Kürşad Akpınar, Michael Alpert, Roumen Avramov, Yaron Ayalon, Marc Baer, Rıfat Bali, Valery Bazarov, Yuval Ben-Bassat, Yaron Ben-Naeh, Aviva Ben-Ur, Adriana Brodsky, Michelle Campos, Holly Case, Mark Cohen, Gaëlle Collin, Paula Daccarett, Dina Danon, Rachel Deblinger, Ramajana Hidić Demirović,

Howard Eissenstat, Lerna Ekmekcioglu, Louis Fishman, Miriam Frenkel, Eyal Ginio, Allyson Gonzalez, Emily Greble, Corry Guttstadt, Yali Hashash, Hilit Surowitz-Israel, Elizabeth Imber, Ethan Katz, Zvi Keren, Arthur Kiron, Maureen Jackson, Matthias Lehmann, Dario Miccoli, Leon Nar, Eliezer Papo, Hannah Pressman, Nir Shafir, Yehuda Sharim, Onur Şar, Michael Silber, Rita Spathi, Darin Stephanov, Francesca Trivellato, Dimitrios Varvaritis, and Carole Woodall. Though many sources these colleagues helped identify could not be included in this volume owing to considerations of space, their aid was nonetheless essential.

Over many years we have discussed this project with many colleagues and friends who kindly forgave our obsession and offered insights. Thanks especially are due to Jessica Marglin, David Myers, and Joshua Schreier. We are indebted to Daniel Schroeter for providing an insightful reading of an earlier draft of the entire manuscript. Ari Joskowicz, Fred Zimmerman, and Ira and Julius Zimmerman also lived with this book for many years; we are grateful for all the discussions they endured, collaborative meetings they tolerated, and insights they provided. Ever an astute witness, Julius deserves special mention, by Sarah, for helping her observe the lives of others in all their richness and poignancy.

The names of forty translators are cited in the pages that follow; we are deeply indebted to each one. Additional help with tricky questions of transliteration and translation came from Phillip I. Ackerman-Lieberman, Sebouh Aslanian, Joan Biella, Olga Borovaya, Ra'anan Boustan, David M. Bunis, Celso Castilho, Paris Papamichos Chronakis, Idit Dobbs-Weinstein, Lerna Ekmekcioglu, Geri Joskowicz, Emil Kerenji, Selim Kuru, Alan Mikhail, Devin E. Naar, Isaac Nehama, Avner Perez, Allison Schachter, Vered Shemtov, and Abdullah Uğur. Heidi Lerner in particular deserves our thanks for sharing her expertise on countless occasions.

Richard Stein kindly reviewed and commented upon many of our source introductions. Abdullah Uğur, Shoshi Joskowicz, and Darin Stephanov trekked to institutions in Istanbul, Tel Aviv, and Sofia, respectively, in order to help us secure permissions to reprint materials. Ramajana Hidić Demirović, Ethan Katz, Emil Kerenji, Devi Mays, Isaac Nehama, and Vadim Altskan made phone calls and pursued lengthy e-mail correspondence with museums and archives in Sarajevo, Marseille, Belgrade, Mexico City, Athens, and Lviv to the same ends.

Many archives, libraries, publishing houses, and holders of private papers granted us permission to translate and/or publish the material in this volume. In the pages that follow, each source bears a citation acknowledging its provenance; here, we wish to thank in particular those individuals who gave us permission to use materials from their personal collections, reprint the publications of their family members, or who fleshed out our knowledge of their ancestors: Ricardo Djaen; Lisa Hasday and Joshua Tate; Sami Kohen; Clara E. Lida; Isaac Molho; Albert Nadjary and Nelly Linda Nadjary; Solita Saltiel; Esme Solomons (née Michael); Eugénie, Florence, Laurent, and Sabbetaï Soulam; and Sivan Toledo.

Crucial financial assistance for this project came in the form of a National Endowment for the Humanities Collaborative Research Grant and two Hadassah-Brandeis Institute Research Awards as well as support from the Maurice Amado Chair at the University of California, Los Angeles; the UCLA Academic Senate; the Program in Jewish Studies at Vanderbilt University; and the Mediterranean Studies Program at Stanford University. For help in overseeing these funds we thank Diana Fonseca, Tammy Von Wagoner, and Pam Reid at UCLA, and Susan Kuyper, Lynne Perler, and Lindsey Bunt at Vanderbilt University.

Both editors of this volume are graduates of the doctoral program in Jewish History at Stanford University, and we are delighted that our work is being published as part of the Studies in Jewish History and Culture series by Stanford University Press. Warm appreciation is due to Aron Rodrigue and Steven J. Zipperstein, editors of this series, former teachers, life-long mentors, and friends, for their support. Thanks are also owed Norris Pope, who initially handled this project for the press, Stacy Wagner, who assumed editorial oversight of it after Norris's retirement, and Kate Wahl, who kindly stepped in to usher us through production at a later stage. All three editors were a pleasure to work with. Mariana Raykov was a superb production editor, while Charles Trumbull's thorough copyediting caught countless irregularities. Finally, Bill Nelson provided us with the book's historical maps, kindly tolerating our many meticulous demands.

For both of us, Aron Rodrigue has been a principal guide to and through the richness of Sephardi history. From the outset, he supported the project in myriad ways, helping us conceptualize it in all its breadth and fine-tune many nuances. His intellectual watermark is evident on every page. We dedicate the volume to him, aware that (with a small number of colleagues) he is responsible for opening up the Ottoman Judeo-Spanish world to scholars, to mentoring a new generation of researchers in the field, and to sharing his infectious love of ideas, Sephardi history, and conversation with us and so many others.

*Note on Translation and Transliteration*

This documentary history contains sources originally written in fifteen languages: Ladino, Hebrew, Ottoman Turkish and modern Turkish, French, Greek, Serbian, Croatian, Bulgarian, Italian, Spanish, Portuguese, German, Yiddish, and English. Many of these sources are plurilingual, containing a variety of languages within a given text. The polyglossic environment that Ottoman Sephardim inhabited presents complex challenges of translation and transliteration.

The Judeo-Spanish heartland was a multilingual environment in which individuals and places could be known by myriad names. For example Istanbul—historical Byzantium, which became the Ottoman capital in 1453—has been rendered variously as Stambul, İstanbul, İslambol, Kostantiniyye, Konstantiniyye, Dersaadet, Deraliye, Bab-ı Ali, Payitaht, and Asitane in Ottoman Turkish; Al-Qustantiniyah in Arabic; Konstantinopolis in Greek; Bolis in Armenian; Tsarigrad or Carigrad in various South Slavic languages (including Serbian, Croatian, Bosnian, Bulgarian, and Macedonian); different iterations of Constantinople in West and Central European languages; and in Ladino- and Hebrew-language sources alternately as Konstantinopla, Kosple, Kostan, Kushtandina, Kushta, and Stambul. The contemporary Greek city of Thessaloniki was also known historically by many names, including Saloniki in vernacular Greek, Hebrew, and German; Selânik in Ottoman and modern Turkish; Salonicco in Italian; Salonique in French; Solun in South Slavic languages; Sãrunã in Aromanian (Vlach); and variously as Saloniki, Salonika, Saloniko, Salonik, Selanik, Tesaloniki, and Thesaloniki in Ladino.

We have sought to preserve the historical integrity of our sources by employing place names as they appear in the original. In the editor's introduction and in the introductions to individual sources we use the historic name of a city with its current name in brackets the first time a place is mentioned. In four exceptional cases we use city names commonly employed in contemporary English-language scholarship, i.e.: Edirne, Istanbul, and Izmir, rather than their historical variants Adrianople, Constantinople, and Smyrna. Throughout we refer to Thessaloniki as Salonica.

Like the cities they inhabited, Sephardi Jews also went by many names. A Jewish man given the biblical name Moses at birth, for example, might be called Moshe in Hebrew, Musa in Turkish and Arabic, Moïse in French, and either Moshe, Musa, or Moise in Ladino, yet he could also be known by different iterations of the non-Jewish correlate of his Hebrew name, as Morris, Moritz, Maurizio, Mauricio, or Maurice in English, German, Italian, Spanish, and French, respectively. A name might also change in the context of a person's life history, whether they converted, as their political predilections evolved, if they migrated, or in compliance with the trajectory of their professional career. One author featured in this volume, Laura (Luna) Levi Papo of Sarajevo, for example, was known by the Ladino name Luna as a child but adopted the European name Laura after attending a French Jewish Alliance Israélite Universelle school in Istanbul. She also used other names: among family and close friends she was known by the nickname "Buka," while, in literary contexts, she used the pen name Bohoreta—a feminine version of the Hebrew *behor*, indicating that she was the firstborn child in her family.

For the sake of clarity and consistency, we standardize names in this volume. When possible, we employ names as they appear in *The Encyclopedia of Jews in the Islamic World*, ed. Norman Stillman, 5 vols. (Leiden and Boston: Brill, 2010), with diacritics removed. For individuals not included in that volume, biblical names are rendered in their standard English versions (Isaac, not Isak or Yitzhak). In exceptional cases we use the transliteration system required by the language of the source (e.g., in the case of a text in Serbian, Moric Štajner rather than Morris or Moritz Steiner).

In transliterating Ladino, we employ the Aki Yerushalayim system, which approximates a phonetic representation. Other languages that do not use the Roman alphabet are transliterated according to the systems of the Library of Congress with diacritics removed (e.g., Bulgarian, Greek, Hebrew, Russian); Library of Congress with diacritics (Serbian); modern Turkish orthography (Ottoman Turkish); and the YIVO Institute for Jewish Research (Yiddish).

Sources originally written or published in English are left unchanged; in these, readers may find antiquated terminology or spelling (e.g., Moslem instead of Muslim) that differs from our standards in the rest of the book.

When a date appears in the original according to the Jewish, Islamic, Julian, or Ottoman fiscal calendars, we include the equivalent Gregorian date in square brackets.

Biblical citations, excepting those that appear in English-language originals, are from *Tanakh: The Holy Scriptures—The New JPS Translation According to the Traditional Hebrew Text* (Philadelphia: Jewish Publication Society, 1985).

*Sephardi Lives*

# Sephardi Lives: An Introduction

"Let our wise men rise up, let each one search in his own place or
town of residence for the memories of his brothers and neighbors.
Let them call to the hidden manuscripts: come out!"

*Yosef-Da'at/El Progreso*, March 13, 1888

"History is not only the chronological narration of remarkable
events . . . [but] much more: it is the study of life, the search for
truth, the analytical description of traditions and customs according
to the manner in which they present themselves before the eyes of
the observer, and according to the manner in which they are painted
in the imagination of the historian."

Morris Isaac Cohen, 1911

"All that we have done so far is but a drop in the ocean."

Letter from Esther Michael (née Salem) in Salonica
to her brother Jacques Salem in Manchester, August 23–28, 1917

In 1749, Jews in Salonica attempt to evade a communal tax meant to
support the Jewish community of Jerusalem; in 1778 a merchant in
Livorno writes a Ladino-language guide to modern living; in 1840
eyewitnesses report on the siege of the Jewish quarter of Rhodes in
the wake of a blood libel; a rabbi of Sarajevo, writing three decades
later, lauds the virtues of the printing press; in 1895 a teacher petitions
the Ottoman government to open a school for girls in Istanbul; in the
midst of the First World War a young woman sends a letter to her
brother in Manchester, offering an eyewitness account of the horrific
fire that had just destroyed Salonica; a scholar in the fledgling Turkish
Republic, writing in 1927, defends the Arabic alphabet against attempts
to introduce the Latin script; a Greek survivor of Auschwitz gives an
interview in a displaced persons camp; in 1948 a man writes of his journey to the Belgian Congo.

What do these sources, penned in different languages, centuries,
continents, genres, states, and social contexts, have in common? The
simplest answer is that they were all produced by Jews who traced their

roots back to medieval Iberia (modern-day Spain and Portugal). These Jews have come to be known as Sephardim because of a linkage Jewish authors in the Middle Ages made between the Iberian Peninsula and a biblical land referred to in Obadiah 1:20 as Sepharad. Although Sephardi communities have historically existed in locales around the globe, the individuals, families, social groups, and institutions treated in this book formed part of the largest Judeo-Spanish cultural sphere to exist outside the Iberian Peninsula—one that reconstituted itself in the Balkans and eastern Mediterranean after the late fifteenth century.

And yet, the answer to the question of what unifies the documents described above, and the many others that fill this book, is infinitely more complicated than any terse demographic accounting can convey. The people who populate the pages of this book did not always identify themselves foremost as Sephardim, or even as Jews. Sometimes they organized themselves according to city, regional, national, imperial, religious, class, professional, and gender affiliations. In the face of this cacophony, this Introduction proposes a series of answers to the question of what unified the diverse experiences of modern Sephardim and what justifies the book you hold before you.

This sourcebook documents the history of the Judeo-Spanish heartland of Southeastern Europe, Anatolia, and the Levant as it existed in dynamic engagement with its diasporic centers on five continents over roughly two hundred and fifty years. We have chosen to begin the volume at the turn of the eighteenth century, a period of cultural stabilization for Ottoman Jewry. Our endpoint is the years immediately following the destruction of the Judeo-Spanish heartland of Southeastern Europe during the Second World War, after which the global geography of Sephardi communities assumed radically new form. Assembled here are roughly 150 sources gathered from archives and libraries all over the world, both in their English original and translated from Bulgarian, Croatian, French, German, Greek, Hebrew, Italian, Ladino, Portuguese, Serbian, Spanish, Ottoman and modern Turkish, and Yiddish.

The pages that follow offer a broad historical introduction to the modern Judeo-Spanish heartland and of the Sephardi culture it produced in dialogue with a variety of Ottoman and post-Ottoman societies in the Balkans and the Levant, with non-Jewish cultures, global Jewry, and Sephardi émigré centers.

# THE OTTOMAN JUDEO-SPANISH WORLD
# AND ITS DIASPORA, 1700–1950

The modern Sephardi communities examined in this book were constituted after 1492, when the Jews of the Iberian Peninsula were forced to choose between conversion to Christianity and exile. In the years that followed, a relatively small number of Iberian Jewish converts made their way across the Atlantic and settled in Portuguese and Spanish America, where the watchful eye of the Inquisition made impossible the public expression of Judaism. A portion of those who desired to maintain their Judaism, or return to it, settled in Amsterdam and Dutch colonial holdings in the New World, where they were free to practice their religion. Some fled to southern France and lived as secret Jews until they were finally given free rein to acknowledge their Judaism. Others migrated to North Africa to join existing communities of Arabic- and Berber-speaking Jews long settled in the region. The largest numbers of Iberian Jewish exiles, however, found their way across the Mediterranean (some by way of Italy), to the Ottoman Empire, where they were permitted to settle and practice their Judaism openly. This community is the principal subject of the present volume.

These Iberian Jewish exiles became the most demographically significant Jewish immigrant community in the Ottoman Empire. Other sizable Jewish populations had lived in the region for many centuries. Together these Jewish communities became subjects of an empire that reached, at its height, from the Bosphorus to the Danube in Europe, across the Eastern Mediterranean and North Africa, and into the Arabic-speaking Middle East as far as the western borders of modern-day Iran. Over the next four hundred and fifty years the Sephardim would prove to be an integral element in Ottoman and post-Ottoman societies, particularly in those cities in which they were most densely concentrated, such as Salonica, Istanbul, Izmir, Edirne, Sarajevo, Sofia, and Jerusalem (see Map 1).

Like most Ottoman subjects and Jews the world over, Sephardi families in the eighteenth and nineteenth centuries were typically poor and, later, working-class. Many worked as small-time peddlers or shopkeepers. Others engaged in specialized crafts and occupations, such

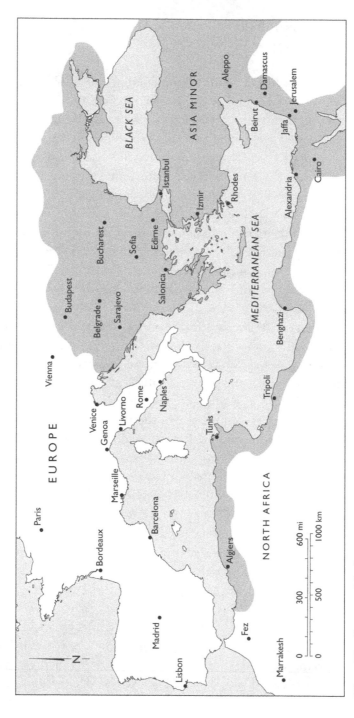

*Map 1* The Ottoman Mediterranean, ca. 1683

as Salonica's famous male porters (*hamals*) or the women who rolled cigarettes in their homes or in factories. The voices of the Jewish lower and working classes resound frequently in this book. One example is a petition drawn up in 1847 by impoverished Jews in Izmir who complained that the elites of their community were burdening them disproportionately with taxes and abusing them "much more" than the ancient Egyptians had abused the Hebrews during their enslavement. Another is a letter penned by a mid-nineteenth-century widow in Jerusalem requesting financial support. At times, poverty became a catalyst for politicization. This book also features the Ladino manifesto of a socialist federation of Salonica that was run and supported largely by Sephardi Jews: its authors used this platform to demand proper working conditions and an eight-hour workday.

In addition to poverty, questions surrounding religious observance regularly emerged in Ottoman Jewish life. One voice readers will discover in this volume is that of a Salonican rabbi who in 1755 answered a query as to whether the Dönme—descendants of those Jews who followed the self-proclaimed messiah Shabbetay Sevi into Islam after he converted in 1666—could be considered Jews. A second responsum (singular of responsa, or rabbinic answers to religious queries), penned in 1763, discusses the phenomenon of Jewish men who broke with the prohibition against cutting their *peot*, or sidelocks. Although some tested the boundaries of Judaism, until well into the twentieth century most Ottoman Sephardim were practicing Jews who as a matter of course hewed to religious institutions that structured their everyday lives. Even those who openly disregarded Jewish law or came to identify themselves as freethinkers or atheists continued to be associated with the religious community into which they had been born. In this sense, Ottoman Sephardim were products of their local environment, where religious traditions and communal boundaries remained powerful even after the empire's collapse in the wake of the First World War. Similar patterns prevailed among other Ottoman Jewish communities as well as among Ottoman Muslims and Christians across the empire.

The denominations that emerged among European and American Jews did not take root in the Sephardi world. The Jewish Reform movement, however, did capture the attention of Sephardi authors. One such response appears in this volume in the form of a mid-nineteenth century text issued by the chief rabbi of Izmir condemning the attempts of Jews in Paris and London to alter their liturgy. During the same period Isaac Akrish, a rabbi of Istanbul, denounced innovations closer to home; when reform-minded Jewish elites opened a new-style Jewish school in 1856, Akrish warned of the grave dangers that the teaching of foreign languages and "knowledge of the nations of the world" posed to traditional Jewish life. Other religious thinkers responded differently to the challenges of their age by seeking to demonstrate how their religion was compatible with modernity. In 1870 Judah Papo (d. 1873), a Sephardi rabbi in Jerusalem, praised the printing press for its ability to spread knowledge about Judaism and to give voice to rabbinical scholars like himself.

Identification with a religious body remained a given well into the twentieth century, but there were many other ways according to which Ottoman subjects identified and grouped themselves. Sephardi women and men also lived in constant dialogue with imperial and, later, national authorities, their non-Jewish neighbors, Jews of other backgrounds, and other individuals and communities across the globe. This dialogue took many forms. Jews and non-Jews shopped in the same markets, cooked similar foods, engaged in neighborly relations, made music together, experienced the same natural and man-made disasters, and appeared before the same courts. One document included in this book records the petition of a Jew who brought a case against his Muslim business partner to the Islamic law court of mid-nineteenth-century Izmir. In later periods Jews attended the same schools, adopted the same fashions, read the same newspapers and books, co-authored scholarship, participated in joint political projects, and socialized in clubs and dance halls with neighbors of other faiths.

Ottoman Sephardim were similarly intertwined with Jews of other backgrounds, including Romaniots (Greek-speaking Jews who lived in portions of the western Ottoman Empire), Mizrahim (Arabic-speaking Jews in the Middle Eastern regions of the empire), Karaites (followers of the Bible who rejected rabbinical Judaism), and Ashkenazi Jews (Jews who traced their roots to medieval Ashkenaz, aka the German Rhineland), many of whom entered the empire from Central and Eastern Europe during the modern period. Even among Sephardim, significant differences in status and class existed, such as those between

Ottoman Sephardim and the *Livornese*—a group that included Sephardi Jews who had settled in Livorno, Italy, following the Iberian expulsion of 1492 and subsequently established extensive global trading networks. The Livornese retained their Italian identity even after they had been settled in Ottoman lands for many decades. Their continued identification with Europe distinguished them from other Ottoman Jews and earned them the moniker of *francos*, *efrenji*, and *ifrangi*, terms meaning "Europeans" in Ladino, Ottoman Turkish, and Arabic respectively.

Modern Sephardim also took part in global developments. A great number resided in port cities that served as a meeting place for people of various nationalities. Many also traveled abroad, had foreign commercial contacts, and encountered travelers and officials hailing from diverse parts of the world. They read foreign publications and participated in political movements both local and international. They corresponded with friends and family who had emigrated, purchased imported goods, and kept up with the latest fashions. In the nineteenth and twentieth centuries Ottoman Jews also caught the attention of global Jewish philanthropic organizations whose leaders perceived their "Eastern" coreligionists to be in need of cultural regeneration and economic uplift.

For all these points of contact, Ottoman Sephardim also maintained their own traditions—religious, culinary, familial, and ephemeral. Perhaps the best marker of this can be found in the realm of language. During more than four centuries following their expulsion from the Iberian Peninsula, Sephardi Jews spoke and wrote in Ladino (also known as Judeo-Spanish and Judezmo), an Ibero-Romance language grammatically similar to fifteenth-century Castilian but encompassing loan words from other Romance languages as well as from Hebrew, Aramaic, and various languages Sephardim encountered in their new homes, principally Greek, Turkish, and South Slavic languages. Until the early twentieth century Ladino was printed in a semi-cursive Hebrew typeface known as the Rashi script and penned in a Sephardi style of handwriting known as *soletreo*. Well into the twentieth century the majority of Sephardi Jews in Ottoman lands claimed Ladino as their mother tongue.

The advent of the printing press changed the fabric of their everyday lives, connecting and politicizing modern Sephardi communities.

Sephardi Jews soon cultivated a rich Ladino print culture, publishing scores of periodicals and translating world literature into the language. They also used Ladino to organize politically and to create theatrical productions. As was true in the Yiddish-speaking world, sources printed in Ladino reflected a range of regional, local, and class-based variations that distinguished Sephardim from one another even as they united them.

While Jews were always a minority in the Judeo-Spanish heartland of Southeastern Europe and the Levant, there were times at which Sephardi culture—and Ladino in particular—held great sway (see Map 2). In the early twentieth century one was more likely to hear Ladino spoken on the streets of Salonica (one of the few urban communities ever to boast a majority Jewish population) than any other language; many non-Jews even learned Ladino at school or for business. There were

*Map 2* Sephardi centers in southeastern Europe, ca. 1908

also cities such as Salonica, Izmir, Edirne, and Istanbul in which Jewish journalists and authors contributed to local publications in French and Ottoman Turkish. By the nineteenth century both languages helped foster communication among elites from different ethno-religious communities in the empire.

Other changes were introduced by the state. Beginning in the early nineteenth century, the Ottoman authorities introduced a series of reforms known collectively as the Tanzimat ("Reorganization"). Among the legal changes Ottoman statesmen announced during this period was the declaration of the civic equality of Ottoman non-Muslims, a move that broke with earlier arrangements based on the state's recognition of Christians and Jews as protected peoples—*dhimmi*s in Arabic or *zimmi*s in Turkish—in exchange for their recognition of the superiority of their Islamic rulers. As part of this reform, the religious establishments of the non-Muslim communities lost much of their former sway as they were forced to compete with a lay elite that increasingly took charge of communal affairs and made alliances with the state. Beginning in the nineteenth century, Jewish educational norms, which traditionally emphasized religious learning for boys but offered no formal education for girls, were challenged both from within and without.

Many of the most radical transformations in Ottoman Jewish education followed the introduction of Jewish schools run by a Franco-Jewish philanthropy, the Alliance Israélite Universelle, established in Paris in 1860. Alliance schools offered instruction in French according to a largely secular curriculum. In such institutions generations of Jewish girls and boys received a French-inspired education. Many Alliance graduates, including some whose words are included in this volume, went on to become prominent teachers, public intellectuals, and journalists in their communities.

During the same period the Ottoman state opened new imperial schools to non-Muslims, many of whom gained entry to positions in the Tanzimat bureaucracy as a result of their training. Although the number of Jews who passed through these state schools paled in comparison with those who attended traditional Jewish schools (*meldar*s and *talmude torah*) or, later, those of the Alliance Israélite Universelle, those Jews who could boast an imperial education profoundly shaped the development of Jewish communal life in the late Ottoman era. Such individuals came to be regarded as paragons of Jewish integration who could serve as intermediaries between Jewish communities and the government.

Constant transformations and dramatic ruptures marked the two and a half centuries represented in this volume. Because fires were endemic to the dense cities of the Ottoman Balkans where wooden architecture predominated, various Ottoman Jewish sources provide a window into lives constantly threatened by such disasters. Among these sources is a Ladino editorial of 1846 portraying the damage wrought by a major conflagration in 1841 in Izmir. Another describes the devastating effect the 1917 fire in Salonica had on Jewish lives and infrastructure. Earthquakes too were a constant threat. The first source featured in this book offers the ruminations of a rabbi of Izmir about a calamitous earthquake that hit his city in the late seventeenth century.

Wars also led to border adjustments and the birth of new countries across Southeastern Europe and the Middle East. The theme of "Violence, War, and Regional Transformation" thus lends this book one of its organizing motifs. Nationally inflected revolts in the European territories of the Ottoman Empire resulted in the establishment in 1830 of an autonomous state called Serbia and in 1832 in the independence of another new state, the Kingdom of Greece. The Russo-Ottoman War of 1877–1878 (also known as the Russo-Turkish War) precipitated further Ottoman territorial losses and led to the creation of an autonomous Bulgaria under Russian protection. The war also prompted the exodus of thousands of Jews, who joined hundreds of thousands of Muslims in their retreat into the shrinking borders of the empire. While most of these Jewish refugees returned to their erstwhile homes after hostilities ceased, others chose to settle permanently in the Ottoman cities in which they had taken refuge. Some three decades later, the Italo-Ottoman War of 1911–1912 (also known as the Italo-Turkish War) and the Balkan Wars of 1912 and 1913 again ended in Ottoman defeats and resulted in the empire's loss of Libya as well as nearly all of its remaining territories in Southeastern Europe.

These conflicts represented a turning point for the Sephardi Jews in a number of respects. The Italo-Ottoman War marked the first time that Ottoman Christians and Jews fought as conscripts for the imperial army, under a universal conscription law introduced just two years earlier. It also prompted the flight of many long-time Italian Jewish residents. The Balkan Wars, which shifted Ottoman officials' attention away from North Africa and back to the empire's European territories, saw Jews fighting on all sides. Those from Serbia, Greece, and Bulgaria were among the descendants of Jewish families that had remained in these new nation-states, many of whom went to great lengths to integrate and prove their allegiance to their new homelands. These wars also precipitated the flight of many Ottoman subjects to countries far from the conflicts, including destinations in Western Europe and the Americas.

Despite the many ruptures Sephardim experienced in the modern era, it was the transfer of the historic Jewish center of Salonica from Ottoman to Greek hands in 1912 that marked the single most dramatic development for Sephardi Jewry during this period, both symbolically and practically. Up to this point the vast majority of Sephardim remained under Ottoman rule, a situation that had facilitated travel and communication among different communities. Within a period of only a few years, increasingly torn by political violence and displacement, the erstwhile Judeo-Spanish heartland was divided between enemy camps. The Ottoman Empire's entrance into the First World War on the side of the Central Powers accelerated this process and precipitated the loss of the remaining Ottoman territories in the Middle East.

The massacres and population transfers that resulted from a decade of incessant war—including the extermination of as many as a million Armenians in eastern Anatolia and the population exchange orchestrated in 1923 between Greece and the new Republic of Turkey—further homogenized the national polities that emerged after the Ottoman collapse. These events are described by eyewitnesses in the pages that follow. Indeed, due to high rates of literacy and the availability of new technologies, the interwar period witnessed an intense flurry of publications by Sephardi Jews in the empire, its successor states, and émigré centers. Jews were now being directed into state schools, where they were educated in national languages; historic Jewish neighborhoods were displaced in the interest of state-sponsored urban planning; and religious authorities lost much of what remained of their former secular functions. As elsewhere, local nationalist sentiment was accompanied by a rise in antisemitism. Both trends pressured Jews to assimilate into national cultures that showed little tolerance for linguistic, religious, or cultural differences.

All of these dramatic transformations drove Jews and non-Jews alike to novel forms of political expression and activism, the subject of another chapter. Ottomanism (imperial state patriotism), socialism, Zionism, anti-Zionism, Sephardism, feminism, and nationalism of various forms (including Serbian, Greek, Bulgarian, Turkish and other national affiliations) animated Jewish men and women in the Judeo-Spanish cultural zone, prompting endless debate and cultural output. No formula could predict an individual's political predilections, and for some, political allegiances changed fluidly with time and in step with world events.

Among those who became politicized in the era of imperial reorganization, secularization, nationalism, and increasingly frequent contact with ideas from abroad were Sephardi intellectuals and scholars. Indeed, by the last decades of the nineteenth century, increasing numbers of Sephardim began producing scholarly work on the history and traditions of their communities, impelled as much by their commitment to science as by the sense that the world of Judeo-Spanish culture they knew so intimately was poised to disappear. Wars and disasters accelerated their enterprise. These pioneers of Sephardi studies, to whom we devote another chapter of this volume, drew from many sources as well as their personal knowledge of the societies they described.

Well before the devastation of the Second World War, mass emigration disrupted the Sephardi heartland. During the final decades of the nineteenth century, many Ottoman Jews began moving intra-regionally, from smaller cities to bigger ones and especially into cultural and economic centers such as Salonica and Istanbul. By the early years of the twentieth century, Jews began leaving the Ottoman lands for Egypt, Europe, and the United States. Some were prompted by the desire to avoid conscription. Others migrated in search of economic betterment. Later waves of emigration would expand these communities and create new ones in Palestine, Rhodesia, the Belgian Congo, South Africa, Brazil, Cuba, Argentina, and Mexico, among other places (see Map 3). Many of those who survived the Second World War, including many of the Turkish and most of the Bulgarian Jews, emigrated, either to large cities in the region or to the new state of Israel. Wherever they relocated, Sephardi émigrés remained in touch with

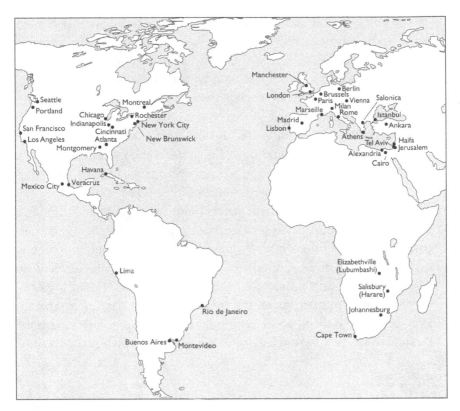

*Map 3* Sephardi émigré centers of the twentieth century

their former homes, sending letters and money to those left behind, communicating with friends and family, collaborating on the publication of books and periodicals, and helping others to emigrate in their wake. These sustained connections to the Sephardi heartland, along with the pleasures and challenges Sephardim encountered in their new homes, are the subject of the penultimate chapter of the book.

Although the cultural world of Sephardim had already begun to disintegrate even before the Second World War, the Holocaust sounded the death knell for the Judeo-Spanish heartland. While the Sephardi communities of Bulgaria and Turkey remained largely intact at the end of the war, the vast majority of Sephardim elsewhere in the region perished at the hands of the Nazis and their local accomplices. With them were destroyed homes, libraries, synagogues, neighborhoods, cemeteries, and an unimaginable quantity of objects and sources of popular culture. Even the memory of these communities was whitewashed, as gravestones from Salonica's Jewish cemetery were used as building material to pave walkways, rebuild churches, and construct the walls of city plazas, while the bones of the dead remain covered over by Aristotle University. Elsewhere, too, the former vibrancy of Sephardi life—in Macedonia, Serbia, Croatia, Bosnia, Bulgaria, and other parts of Greece—has been forgotten, as the last generation of inhabitants who remember having Jewish neighbors passed. Even in scholarly realms the history of the Holocaust is written largely in the absence of its Sephardi dimension.

In addition to the Sephardi communities in Turkey and Bulgaria, émigrés outside Europe, as well as those Jews who hid, fought as partisans, or lived through camps, did survive the war. Our sourcebook extends until the mid-twentieth century in order to document the manner in which those who survived the war reconstituted their lives and communities. And yet, given the book's focus on the Judeo-Spanish heartland, it is difficult to frame the postwar period as anything but a shadow of the rich, centuries-long Sephardi history that preceded it.


## SEPHARDI LIVES

How does one define or identify a "Sephardi life"? The boundaries of Judeo-Spanish communities were always porous, and, as Sephardim were the demographic and cultural Jewish majority in Southeastern Europe and Western Anatolia, Sephardi communities absorbed others—Jews and non-Jews—over time. Many of the sources included in this documentary history illustrate that much of what appears "Judeo-Spanish" was constituted by individuals with diverse origins and thus cannot be understood according to the principle of descent. Though in certain respects the inheritance of medieval Iberia, Sephardi culture as it was shaped in Southeastern Europe, Anatolia, and the Levant in the early modern and modern eras was unquestionably a byproduct of various local developments and multiple influences.

This dynamic is evident for example in the history of the Gabbay family of nineteenth-century Istanbul. Born into the Jewish community of Baghdad during the second half of the eighteenth century, the patriarch of this family, Bağdatlı Yehezkel Gabbay (d. 1823), served both as the personal banker of Sultan Mahmud II (r. 1808–1839) and as a communal leader of Baghdad's Jewish community before he ran afoul of the sultan and met a violent end. After his death his family remained in the imperial capital, and within just two generations his grandson Yehezkel Gabbay II (1825–1898) founded what would prove the first long-lived Ladino newspaper. A decade later, in 1871, his great-granddaughter Rosa Gabbay published a Ladino-language etiquette handbook for Jewish women, an excerpt of which is included in this volume. Members of this Arabophone Jewish family from one of the empire's most important centers of Judeo-Arabic culture thus became, within a few decades, eminent figures in Sephardi communal life and pioneers of the Judeo-Spanish newspaper industry in the Ottoman capital.

Similar examples may be found among Sephardi Jews with family ties to Ashkenazi communities, such as the influential Salonican family of printers headed for much of the nineteenth century by Sa'adi Besalel Ashkenazi a-Levi (1820–1903), whose name bears witness to his Ashkenazi origins. Sa'adi's father's family had come to the empire from Amsterdam in the early eighteenth century: his writings as well as those of his son Sam Lévy and great-granddaughter Esther Michael (née Salem) are included in the pages that follow. These figures may be said to have lived "Sephardi lives," though their origins and names point to family trees with widespread roots. Despite this they became thoroughly integrated into the Sephardi milieus in which they lived, as did other families with surnames that suggest Ashkenazi origins, such as Polako ("Polish"), or Tedeschi and Aleman ("German").

The family name of another individual featured in this volume points to the Romaniot, or Greek-Jewish, origins of certain "Sephardi" Jews. Jamila Kolonomos, whose recollections of her time as a Macedonian partisan during the Second World War are included in this book, hailed on her father's side from a Judeo-Greek family from Ioannina in present-day Greece. As Romaniot Jews the Kolonomos family had likely resided in the area under Roman and later Byzantine rule long before the Ottoman conquest of the region. Yet in the early twentieth century, three brothers from the Kolonomos family settled in Monastir, present-day Bitola, Macedonia, a city that was home to an active Sephardi community. Over time they appear to have integrated into the local Sephardi milieu. As Kolonomos recalled later in life, her childhood was filled almost exclusively with Ladino. It was the language spoken in her home, the language her father used for his correspondence, the only language she knew as a child, and the one she chose to study systematically as an adult, after the last speakers of the Macedonian Ladino she grew up with had been all but destroyed during the Holocaust.

The magnetic draw of certain geographic and cultural centers also played a role in diversifying the Judeo-Spanish community. Around the turn of the eighteenth century a man by the name of Abraham made his way into the Sephardi community of Salonica. Abraham was a Jewish slave of unknown origins who had been sold by a man from Kilis, in the Aleppo vilayet of the Ottoman Empire (in present-day southeastern Turkey near the Syrian border), to another man by the name of Mürtaza Beşe ibn-i Hasan, from Crimea. Abraham arrived in Salonica after fleeing his owner and was granted his freedom there. Both because Sephardim dominated Jewish life in Salonica and because there were few options for an existence outside of a religious community in the Ottoman setting, if Abraham chose to settle in Salonica after his manumission, it is safe to assume that he too became Sephardi in time.

Conversion and other forms of purposeful boundary crossing also altered the fabric of the Sephardi heartland. An Ashkenazi man by the name of Moric Štajner married a Sephardi woman of Belgrade, his native city, in 1900. In the years that followed he attended Belgrade's Sephardi synagogue and raised his children within that community before applying, more than two decades later, for official recognition as a member of Belgrade's Sephardi congregation. After a year of extensive deliberations between local Ashkenazi and Sephardi representatives, Štajner's wish was finally granted, and his registration into the Sephardi community complete. A parallel process unfolded twenty-five years later, when a man named Lazar Tinčević applied to the Jewish community of Salonica to convert to Judaism. After being assigned the name Abraham, he asked, instead, to be registered as Alberto—a name commonly adopted by Ladino-speaking men of the period—thus making explicit his intention to convert not only to Judaism but also to the Sephardi rite and culture of Judaism that had prevailed in his city for centuries.

The different trajectories pursued by Sephardi individuals during the modern era were similarly diverse. Few ended their lives in the same city or state in which they or their parents were born. One example is Graziella Benghiat, a graduate of an Alliance Israélite Universelle school in Izmir whose father moved to that city from the nearby town of Aydın. Benghiat, whose lecture on feminism is included in this volume, lived most of her early life in Izmir, where she ran a French-language journal in 1914. It was also in that city that she married Alexander Benghiat, a Sephardi journalist whose recollections of his education in a traditional Jewish school, or *meldar*, are also featured in this book. In the midst of the wars that plagued the region during the early twentieth century, the family dispersed: Alexander Benghiat died in Salonica, Graziella made her way to Paris with her son, while her brother-in-law spent time living in Cairo before settling in Buenos Aires. The Benghiats' diverse connections and homes were hardly an exception in the Sephardi cultural world.

Abraham Galante, another author whose writings are included in this book, spent his life between his native Bodrum, on the southern Aegean coast; the island of Rhodes, where he attended school and later became a teacher; Izmir, where he was both a teacher and a journalist; Cairo, where he fled the regime of Abdülhamid II (r. 1876–1909) and ran a Ladino newspaper for three years; London, where he attempted to gain support for his plan to settle Jews in the Sudan; and finally, Istanbul, where he lived out the final decades of his life under Ottoman and later Turkish rule. Although Galante chose to settle in Istanbul and became an ardent Turkish nationalist, his scholarly and family connections were global and linked him to the United States, Europe, Rhodesia, Palestine, and Israel, as attested by two letters included in this volume.

The story of Abraham Benaroya, a Bulgarian Sephardi labor leader and socialist whose life is documented below, is similarly dizzying. Born in Vidin in northwestern Bulgaria to a family of petty merchants, Benaroya later spent time studying at the Faculty of Law at the University of Belgrade, teaching in Plovdiv, Bulgaria, and leading a socialist federation in Salonica—whence he was exiled to Serbia by the Ottoman government and later to Naxos by the Greek state—before he was deported by the Germans during the Second World War. Surviving the war, he returned to Salonica until 1953, when he moved to Holon, Israel. There he ran a newspaper kiosk and spent the final years of his life in dire poverty, embittered and alone.

Those who ended their days in their native cities often did so only circuitously. Such was the experience of Joseph Nehama, a historian and Alliance Israélite Universelle schoolteacher from Ottoman, and later Greek, Salonica. After the Nazi occupation of his city, Nehama evacuated to Italian-occupied Athens. Fleeing that city after its occupation by German troops, Nehama attempted to make his way to Spain but was caught and deported to the Bergen-Belsen camp in 1944. It was only after his liberation the following year that Nehama made his way back to the city of his birth, now forever changed and with few traces of its once vibrant Jewish community.

Others crossed oceans never to return. This was true of Emma Adatto Schlesinger, whose family came to Seattle from Istanbul in the early twentieth century. Far from the city and empire in which she was born, Adatto lived, together with her family members and other Sephardi émigrés in Seattle, in a transplanted Ottoman Judeo-Spanish world, which she later preserved in her writings. These included one of the first master's theses written for an American university on a Sephardi theme. Her brother, Albert Adatto, soon followed in her footsteps, producing in 1939 a thesis on the history of Seattle's Sephardi community, selections of which are included in this volume. It is in homage to the Adattos' commitment to Sephardi Studies, as well as in recognition of their families' diasporic past, that we choose to feature a 1910 photograph of Emma and Albert as young children, taken in their adopted city of Seattle, on the cover of this book. Emma's later recollections of growing up in the Sephardi community of the Pacific Northwest are also featured in this volume.

As these examples suggest, Judeo-Spanish culture in the Ottoman heartland was far from homogenous, insular, or static. Above all, the boundaries of Sephardi communities were elastic: their human geography reflected the effervescence of the multicultural society in which they took shape. The permeability of Sephardi communal and cultural boundaries proved even greater in the various émigré centers in which Sephardim settled over the course of the twentieth century, especially after the Judeo-Spanish heartland all but ceased to exist.

## A DOCUMENTARY HISTORY

*Sephardi Lives* is the first wide-ranging documentary history of the modern Judeo-Spanish world. It features the voices of women and men of various classes, cities, regions, religious and political affiliations, and eras. This book contains personal correspondences and court briefs, rabbinic responsa and political manifestos; articles from the Ladino press and works of scholarship; excerpts of memoirs, diaries, and oral histories; parliamentary records and documents of state; eyewitness accounts of war, massacres, and everyday violence; etiquette manuals; as well as intimate glimpses of childhood, friendship, marriage, and political comings of age.

The sea of material from which we have drawn is vast and, for the most part, unplumbed. Because they are so often neglected, documents that illustrate day-to-day Jewish lives receive special attention. These sources record the experiences of Jewish women and children. They explore relations between family members and religious questions. They document individual responses to war and natural disasters, emigration, and meditate on the interactions between Sephardim, other Jews, and non-Jews. While the book cannot cover every dimension of Sephardi life everywhere, it paints as rich a landscape as possible, given available resources.

*Sephardi Lives* is divided into six chapters designed to reflect spheres of life that shaped the quotidian experiences of Sephardi women, men, and children along with those of their neighbors. We acknowledge that this organizational structure is something of a conceit: the world of scholarship was never distinct from "everyday life" (or vice versa), while both realms coursed with the dramas of "violence, war, and regional transformation," the shaping of "political movements and ideologies," "diasporic and émigré circles," and, in time, the trauma of the "Second World War." Readers should consider these section headings as guides rather than strictures and are encouraged to utilize the index to pursue particular themes or the lives of particular authors across chapters.

Readers may not find certain categories they expect in this book. Despite a commitment to foregrounding sources about gender and by and about women, we have chosen to integrate such sources into the various chapters rather than to create separate chapters structured around "Gender" or "Women's Lives." The delineation of material on antisemitism, another category readers might expect, was a strategy we rejected as ill-fitting the geographic context. Anti-Jewish sentiment in Southeastern Europe and the Ottoman Levant did not develop into a clearly articulated political position until the final half-century covered by this volume. Nonetheless, examples of both anti-Jewish violence and ideological expressions of resentment against Jews can be found in different chapters of the book, particularly "Violence, War, and Regional Transformation," and "The Second World War," but also in "The Emergence of Sephardi Scholarship." We have similarly refrained from developing a separate chapter covering Jewish/non-Jewish relations, although this theme also pulses through the book, which includes the voices not only of Jews but of Christians and Muslims as well.

Certain of the section headings we have chosen could command sourcebooks of their own. In particular we wish to draw attention to the fact that this book does not claim to offer comprehensive coverage of Sephardi life in émigré centers. In keeping with our focus on the Ottoman Judeo-Spanish world, this survey of the Sephardi diaspora seeks to emphasize the challenges and opportunities new émigrés encountered on new shores and the bonds that sutured the historic Sephardi heartland to various diasporic centers, indelibly imprinting both.

Wherever and whenever they lived in the Judeo-Spanish culture sphere or in diaspora, Sephardim were always highly integrated. For this reason documenting a discrete Sephardi history is impossible. We have not attempted it here. What is arguably more interesting, though also immeasurably harder, is to represent Sephardi culture as one that maintained distinct elements while remaining deeply connected to multiple other worlds.

This returns us to the question raised at the outset of this Introduction. What do the approximately 150 sources that appear in this book—written in over a dozen languages, spanning centuries, continents, genres, political and social contexts—have in common? We propose the following answers: the sources collected in this volume have in common their engagement with the diverse modern worlds of Sephardi Jews or those who identified and came into contact with their worlds.

The documents that follow should be read as disparate glimpses into the past, moments that can be understood fully only with a complete recounting of the several contexts in which they unfurled. At the same time they can be read as chapters in a larger, Sephardi story that remains coherent despite its internal dissonance. The cacophony may be daunting, but it is what makes the study of the Sephardi past endlessly engaging. Acknowledging that (to borrow from one of our epigraphs) "all that we have done so far is but a drop in the ocean," we are eager to introduce students, teachers, and scholars to lives that have been overlooked for too long.

JULIA PHILLIPS COHEN

SARAH ABREVAYA STEIN

# I. EVERYDAY LIFE
On the Street and in the Synagogue,
from Court to Courtyard

# 1. A CALAMITOUS EARTHQUAKE HITS IZMIR {1688}

*Although less common than fires, epidemics, or harsh weather, earthquakes regularly unleashed tremendous devastation in Ottoman lands. To many, the fate people experienced during natural disasters was a clear sign of God's wrath or favor. Among those who held this view was Rabbi Elijah HaCohen (ca. 1659–1729), who lived through a massive earthquake that hit Izmir in 1688. His account told of the great— but unequal—suffering wrought by the earthquake, which killed thousands and left all of the mosques and churches of the city in ruins. Although some 400 Jews died and two synagogues were damaged, HaCohen believed that divine providence had spared the Jews. Writing many months after the earthquake, having witnessed six months of ongoing destruction (including fires, an epidemic, aftershocks, and lawlessness), HaCohen chose to write of the miracles he witnessed at the time of the quake, demonstrating his unshaken belief that God had shown mercy to his Jewish believers.*

*[handwritten margin note: could've easily argued the opposite]*

And I shall tell you of the miracles that occurred to the Jews during this earthquake. The first is that it happened on Shabbat, and they were at home, and not scattered about in the markets and the streets . . . as the devastation occurred mainly in the quarters of the non-Jews . . . and all the nations [i.e. non-Jews] attested to this miracle. And another is that it occurred during the midday meal while they were all at home and not outdoors visiting relatives and friends. Another is that it happened in the summer and not during the winter. Another is that the dead were [found and] buried. Another is that the fire did not reach the Jewish neighborhood, so they all managed to salvage things from their houses. Another is that God drove those who were destined to be saved from the houses that collapsed to other places where they were not harmed. And a great and unparalleled miracle happened to me, the author: the place where I found myself during the earthquake was a narrow place surrounded by four high walls that fell on top of me, and it became dark from the dust caused by the collapse. I did not now what to do. There was no spirit left in me and I was trembling and confused. I rose to my feet and said "God is the King, God has ruled, God will rule forever . . ." about ten times, as was customary on such occasions, and yet the tremors did not cease, so I recited "Hear, O Israel" . . . and other verses. And when [the earthquake] did not subside I almost died and was silent. As soon as the moment of anger ceased and the darkness cleared I found myself in a pit of stones consisting of the four walls [that had collapsed] . . . and I was not hurt at all. Blessed be He that does *annoyingly glass-half-full*

good to those who are undeserving! And you should also know that during this period a plague broke out in the city, and many died, non-Jews and Jews alike, more than the number of those who died during the earthquake. And as I write there are still people dying. . . .

Elijah ben Solomon Abraham HaCohen, "Inyan ha-Ra'ash," in *Ve-Lo 'Od Ela* (Izmir, 1853), 167b–168b. Translated from Hebrew and introduced by Yaron Ben-Naeh.

## 2. A WILL FROM RASHID, EGYPT [1695]

*Wills and testaments illuminate various aspects of past lives for which no other written trace may remain, offering insights into material culture, family relations and, above all, the values of those who drafted them. Here we find a will left by Abraham ben Natan, a wealthy Salonican Jewish merchant living in Rashid, a port city in Ottoman Egypt that attracted merchants from across the Mediterranean. Although the will allocated a limited portion of ben Natan's fortune to relatives, it was primarily filled with elaborate instructions for the establishment of a yeshiva[1] in his name. The will also bears testimony to the centrality of Jerusalem and the Land of Israel more generally to the religious universe of its author. In accordance with Jewish practice, ben Natan's will clarified that he wished to be buried in Jerusalem or another of the Four Holy Cities of Jewish tradition. Although it presents the Land of Israel as a pivot of the author's religious devotion, the will also highlights ben Natan's international ties: the funds to support his project would come from Livorno, Venice, and Amsterdam—centers that housed thriving Sephardi communities during the period—thus pointing to ben Natan's participation in a network that was at once economic, familial, and cultural.*

[I], Abraham, son of Hayim Natan, . . . give all of my property to said persons for the endowment I am establishing in order to provide for a house of study for *hakhamim*,[2] as is written and explained in a separate writ. . . . [I hereby state] that if I have any living descendants they will be given 5,000 arayot[3] each and no more; moreover, if God allows me to ascend to Jerusalem and be buried there, or in Hebron or Safed, or anywhere in the Land of Israel where I may die, the local holy community shall be given 200 kuruş and any other necessities

---

1. A traditional Jewish academy for the advanced study of Talmud (Jewish oral law), written commentary, and other rabbinic texts.

2. Literally, "wise men"; rabbinic scholars.

3. Literally, "lions"; Dutch lion thalers, known variously as arslanlı or esedi kuruş in Turkish.

for my burial and a tombstone that befits my honor. If the *hesger*[4] is already established, the *hakhamim* who are chosen shall study Torah each Thursday night for a whole year following my death, as is the custom, and they shall receive a special bonus of ten silver coins each per night. And if the *hesger* is not yet established, ten *hakhamim* shall be chosen to study Torah from among the best in the town. They will receive a bonus of ten silver coins for each of the seven days of my mourning, and they shall perform the *veilada*[5] every Thursday night, and they shall also study on the night of the seventh day of *Pesah* [Passover] and on the night of *Shavu'ot* [Pentacost] and on the night of Rosh Hashanah and on the night of Yom Kippur and on the night of *Hoshana Raba* and on the night of my *yahrzeit*.[6] They will be accorded the aforementioned sum each night; and they will also be given all expenses required for their nightly study, such as oil and candles, etc. I also request that every year 1,000 silver coins shall be given from my estate so that these *hakhamim* can perform a nightly study vigil at the tomb of Rachel or the Prophet Samuel. A yearly sum of one hundred arayot [should be put aside] for my mother's expenses as long as she lives, and after her death, one hundred arayot will be given for her burial expenses, including a tombstone and all that might be needed as befits her honor. And my wife shall be given one hundred arayot a year as long as she remains unmarried to honor my memory. All other inheritors shall share a total of 500 arayot.

Manuscript ARC.4° 1271/511, Archive of Ya'akov Shaul Elyashar, Department of Archives, National Library of Israel. Translated from Hebrew and introduced by Yaron Ben-Naeh.

## 3. MANUMISSION OF A JEWISH SLAVE IN SALONICA
### [1700]

*Documents generated by the courts of eighteenth-century Ottoman Salonica provide a window into the lives of ordinary people who lived and labored in or traveled through the city. The following document records a legal compromise brokered in Salonica's Islamic law court by a Muslim slave owner and his fugitive Jewish slave. Having traveled great distances after fleeing servitude, the slave, identified only as*

4. Study house, or type of yeshiva.
5. Nightly study vigil.
6. *Lel ptirati* in the original; the anniversary of a death date.

*Abraham, successfully rebuffed his former master's claims of ownership by buying his independence. Although his ingenuity and tenaciousness may have been unusual, Abraham's path from the Crimean Peninsula to Salonica, and from slavery to freedom, demonstrates the extraordinary personal transformations that were sometimes available even to the most marginal figures in Ottoman society.*

The individual named Mürtaza Beşe ibn-i Hasan was originally an inhabitant of the protected city of Akmescit[7] in the Crimean Peninsula, which is situated in the Tatar region. He is currently staying in the secured city of Salonica as a traveler. Of his own will he confirmed and gave a declaration in the *şeriat*[8] court in the presence of a tall and black-eyed Jew by origin, who is the subject of this legal document; a young man whose beard had not yet grown named Abraham: "I purchased the abovementioned Abraham a year and a half prior to the registration of this document from someone called Kasab, who lives in the city of Kilis, in return for 125 esedi kuruş.[9] Afterwards, about a year ago, the abovementioned Abraham ran away from me. Now I found him in the abovementioned secured city. When I submitted a claim of servitude [against him], he rejected [my claim]. Consequently many disputes erupted between us. At the present time, the abovementioned Abraham paid and gave me 60 esedi kuruş. I likewise took and received the mentioned sum of money. In return I manumitted him." Following his declaration that from this day onwards the abovementioned Abraham is a free man like other people who were born free, these events were registered . . . on 25 Şevval of the year IIII [April 15, 1700].

Sicil vol. 6, p. 113, 25 Şevval IIII (15 April 1700), held in the collections of the Historical Archives of Macedonia (Thessaloniki, Greece). Translated from Ottoman Turkish by Eyal Ginio.

## 4. A RABBI IN ISTANBUL INTERPRETS THE BIBLE FOR LADINO READERS (1730)

*A popular biblical commentary in Ladino consisting of eighteen volumes produced by a dozen authors between the years 1730 and 1899, the* Me'am Lo'ez *was designed to be broadly accessible to all Ottoman Sephardim. Its title, literally "from a foreign*

7. Today Simferopol, Crimea.
8. Turkish equivalent of the Arabic *shari'a*, or Islamic law.
9. A Dutch currency circulating within the Ottoman Empire, also known as arslanlı kuruş in Turkish.

*people," indicates that it was written in a language other than Hebrew. Although the volumes of the* Me'am Lo'ez *differed from each other in scope, style, and worldview, they shared a single pedagogical agenda shaped by Rabbi Jacob Huli (1689–1732) of Istanbul, who authored the first two volumes of the series. Driven by the belief that most Ottoman Sephardim knew little about Judaism and barely understood Hebrew, Huli sought to create an educational tool that could teach his coreligionists the rabbinic tradition, offer interpretations of the Bible, and replace the complex ethical works of earlier centuries with straightforward guidance. He also aimed to provide his readers with suitable secular knowledge and entertainment so as to shield them from the influence of books written by non-Jews. In the introduction to the work, Huli stated that his goal was to explain the Torah to the "foolish and ignorant masses," including "men and women and the youth of Israel." Judging by the number of their reprints, Huli's volumes enjoyed great popularity, becoming classics of Ladino literature.*

Now, because of our sins, the world has changed and declined and degenerated to such a degree that very few people are able to read a biblical verse correctly. And such hunger overcame [the people] that all the preparations made by the men we mentioned above and the tables they laid are not enough to sate it and to enable people to read two words of the Law,[10] because they do not understand the holy tongue, and even those who know the words do not understand what they are saying. And every day [the scriptures] are studied less and less, and the Law of the people [of Israel] and the precepts of Judaism are forgotten. And when on the Sabbath the cantor reads the weekly Torah portion, many people have no idea of its content or what it means. And at the time of judgment—the great and terrible day of judgment—one will be asked, "What have you learned during all these years in that world? Tell us what you have learned and understood from the weekly Torah portion and *haftarah*"[11]—because one is obliged to read and understand them. And, of course, [the ignorant] will be very embarassed not to know what to answer, and will have to say, "Oh, what shame. Oh, what ignominy!" And they will be greatly distressed.

As for the precepts of Judaism, nobody is able to read a ruling from the *Shulhan Arukh* because people do not know Hebrew, and thus no-

---

10. Among the works referenced here is Joseph Caro's *Shulhan Arukh* (literally, "set table") (1565), the most authoritative legal code of Judaism, which appeared in an abridged Ladino version in 1568.

11. Weekly portion from the books of the Prophets that accompany the reading of the Torah portion.

body knows the rulings one is obliged to follow. Praise God, blessed be He, that Jews, being children of a good father, are great friends of the Law and are eager to learn new things from it, because the sanctity of Abraham, Isaac, and Jacob is upon them. But when one returns from his shop, he has nothing to read, because if he takes a *midrash*,[12] or *'En Ya'akov*,[13] or *Shulhan Arukh*, or other books, even if it is *agadah*,[14] they are very difficult and [too] profound for him. And since he does not understand anything, he falls asleep. And on winter nights, he gets up early but does not find anything to study before dawn, and thus, not knowing what to do, he spends this time of clarity in mundane conversations.

Long ago there was a sage who translated the *Shulhan Arukh* into Ladino and even printed it in square letters with vowel points, so that everybody could understand it.[15] And the same was done with the book called *Hovot ha-Levavot*.[16] But for many reasons this did not help much either, due to the fact that he [the translator] wrote it in his idiom, in Spanish words that are very difficult and incomprehensible for people in these parts of Turkey, Anatolia, and Arabistan, and therefore most people have nothing to study. And [this is] particularly [true of] the book written by our master and teacher Moses Almosnino of blessed memory, called *Regimiento de la vida*,[17] which is a very lucid book, but its idiom is incomprehensible. And the manner of writing used in those books is also different, and though of course it is correct and genuine, because the people in these parts do not understand it they cannot benefit from it.[18] And besides, to understand what [Almosnino] wanted to say one has to know how to study, as he intended to be brief in order to convey much knowledge in few words. This is not useful for the common people because they cannot spend a whole day trying to understand one thing, and on every passage they try to read, sometimes

---

12. Collection of rabbinical interpretations of biblical stories.

13. A collection of rabbinic stories compiled by Jacob ibn Habib de Zamora, first published in Salonica in 1515 and reprinted numerous times.

14. Rabbinic writings that do not deal with the law.

15. Huli refers here to *merubah*, or square Hebrew letters, accompanied by vowel signs, which were used to make reading easier for those who did not know Hebrew well.

16. Bahya ibn Paquda's *Hovot ha-Levavot* (Duties of the Heart), a major work of Jewish ethics. A Ladino translation appeared in 1569.

17. Moses Almosnino's 1564 *Regimiento de la vida* (Regimen of Living), the first Ladino ethical treatise, based on Aristotle's *Nicomachean Ethics*.

18. Huli refers here to sixteenth-century works written in a register of Ladino that was close to Castilian Spanish and had become incomprehensible to most Ladino readers by the eighteenth century.

having to stop because they do not comprehend the words to which they are not accustomed, sometimes because of the manner of writing and sometimes in order to understand the meaning of the sentences which, being very short, require much study. Also, [Almosnino's] book is small and will be finished quickly, and then one will have nothing else to do. And [this is] particularly [true for] old or sick people who are locked in their homes and do not have anything from which to learn. And some people have many books inherited from their fathers, but they do not touch them because they do not understand their idiom, so these books are lying around [neglected] in their shops. And thus everything people hear from a rabbi, even if it is a simple biblical verse, is new to them because they do not read the Bible or the *Shulhan Arukh* and they know nothing, neither the positive commandments, which the Law requires us to perform, nor the negative commandments, which are the things one should avoid; and they do not know about what happened to our ancestors or about the miracles God performed for them; and this leads one to forget the Law of Israel, God forbid.

"Hakdamah," *Me'am Lo'ez: Bereshit* (Istanbul: R. Yona ben Yaakov Ashkenazi, 1730). Translated from Ladino and introduced by Olga Borovaya.

## 5. ARE THE DÖNME JEWISH? A RABBINICAL REFLECTION (1755)

*Born in the Ottoman port city of Izmir, Shabbetay Sevi (1626–1676) was a Jewish ascetic and mystic who gained fame across the Jewish world after declaring himself the Messiah. Sevi's open challenges to Jewish and Ottoman authorities drew the ire of individuals within the rabbinical establishment and also of Sultan Mehmed IV (r. 1648–1687), who presented Sevi with the choice of conversion to Islam or death. Sevi's conversion sent shockwaves across the Jewish world. Most Jews who had supported his messianic claims publicly renounced their position. A small portion of Sevi's disciples followed him into Islam. The descendants of these converts, referred to in Turkish as Dönme ("those who turned"), maintained a distinct ethno-religious identity for centuries, even as they became part of the elite in Salonica, where the majority of the community had settled. The Dönme functioned as a separate community and maintained their own mosques, cemeteries, and schools. The following query sent to a Salonican rabbi nearly a century after Sevi's followers began to form a breakaway religion, suggests that Dönme and Jews remained in contact after their schism. Yet as this rabbi's response suggests, the Dönme's uncertain status threatened the rabbinical elite, including this writer, who argued without equivocation that the Dönme were not Jews.*

They came to ask whether it is permissible to write an amulet for those apostates living among us, the ones who abandoned the words of God [Torah] a long time ago and today still cling to their impurity. They publicly transgress the Sabbath and eat carcasses and torn animals.[19] [Yet] they do have the opportunity to flee for their lives [back to Judaism]. Many of them have done so and hold fast to the laws of Moses and Israel to this day.

Response:

It would appear that it is forbidden; for even with reference to someone who is completely Jewish, Rashba[20] of blessed memory goes to great lengths to explain that it is improper to write [amulets][21]. . . . From the generality of these considerations we must judge our situation and conclude that although these apostates in our time did not originally leave the Jewish community out of a desire to antagonize [God], but rather for a reason that is known to them . . . they are still called apostates who intend to antagonize[22]. . . . If so, in our situation, with reference to those apostates who live among us Jews in the diaspora and transgress all the laws of the Torah even in private, despite the fact that their ancestors turned renegade and forsook the Torah of Moses (of blessed memory) for reasons known to them, and despite the fact that they considered themselves part of Israel, they overturned the basin.[23] We now see that their descendants have defected altogether, to the point that there is no difference at all between them and the gentiles. They transgress everything that is written in the Torah. They are thus certainly considered non-Jews in every way. That being the case, it would be improper to grant permission to write for them holy names [of God] or passages from the Torah intended for healing. . . .

Isaac ben Elijah ibn Sangi, *Beerot Ha-mayim* (Salonica: Refael Yeudah Kala'i ve . . . Mordekhai Nahman, 1755), Question 4, p. 113v. Translated from Hebrew by Matt Goldish.

---

19. A reference to meat forbidden by Jewish law.

20. Thirteenth-century Rabbi Solomon ben Adret.

21. In a section omitted here Ibn Sangi discusses precedents for dealing with apostates who abandon Judaism for various reasons.

22. Here he cites references to rabbinic decisions concerning conversos, or Jews who converted to Catholicism.

23. That is, misconstrued their obligations as Jews.

## 6. AN INCIDENT IN A BARBERSHOP (1763)

*While there were always Jews who transgressed Jewish law as a matter of convenience, the man portrayed here appears to have challenged Jewish law as a matter of principle. The site of his transgression was a barbershop, where the rebel convinced his friend to cut the "corners" of his beard (peot) with a blade (an act prohibited in Leviticus 19:27), while simultaneously denouncing rigorous observers of Jewish law as "hamorim"—a Hebrew term meaning both "strict observers" and "asses." While he railed against the strictures of Jewish law and the rabbis who enforced them in general terms, the rebellious man's target was carefully chosen, for removing one's sidelocks was a highly visible indication of a Jewish male's assimilation into Muslim or Christian culture, suggesting that he may have hoped to erode the various legal stringencies that separated Jews from their non-Jewish neighbors.*

The following event occurred. A Jewish man entered the barbershop to have his hair cut and there found his friend, an iniquitous man. When this Jew uncovered his head, the wicked man saw it and became furious because the corners of this Jew's hair were long. He opened his mouth and said thus to the Jew, "Why do you do this, to leave a blessing and let your side-curls grow unnecessarily long on your head? You are nothing but one of those who is overly stringent with himself, like those asses!" The man accepted the rebuke of this scoundrel inadvertently [by listening to him] and did not leave the place until he had ruined and shaved the corners of his head with a blade. He left only a small fingerbreadth, more or less. Now on the day of the Sabbath when this Jew came to me as was his custom, and I saw how he looked, that his face was not as it had always been, I confronted him and spoke harshly with him. When he heard this he raised his voice and wept. He said, "That snake, the iniquitous man, tricked me!"[24] The shaved man has now come to ask the word of God: What is his sin? Has he seriously transgressed a negative commandment or committed a forbidden act? Or has he not actually committed a sin, since he did leave some [hair]? . . . [Montequio and his colleagues determine that the man committed a grave transgression even though he did not entirely shave his sidelocks.]

Joseph ben Isaac Montequio, *Sefer Ketonet Yosef* (Salonica: Refael Yeudah Kal'ai va-havero Mordekhai Nahman, 1763), Yoreh De'ah, Question 1, pp. 25v–27v. Translated from Hebrew and introduced by Matt Goldish.

---

24. A reference to Genesis 3:13.

## 7. LESSONS FOR A CHILD: A LADINO GUIDE TO MODERN LIVING (1778)

*The eighteenth century produced a large outpouring of rabbinic writings in Ladino, but only one work of secular Ladino literature,* La guerta de oro *(The Golden Garden), published in the Tuscan port of Livorno in 1778. Its author, David Attias, was a well-read Ottoman Jewish merchant born in Sarajevo who spent many years in Livorno. Written as an anthology of useful knowledge,* La guerta *included writings that ranged from an introduction to the Italian language and the Greek alphabet to a treatise on physiognomy and a description of cures for infertility. At a time when Ottoman rabbis actively promoted religious education, Attias was the only Sephardi author to advocate secular education, the study of European languages, and practical knowledge. He argued that Ottoman Jews needed to overcome their backwardness if they wished to successfully compete with Europeans in business. What follows is excerpted from* La guerta's *"Sixth Treatise," which contains a number of lessons that Attias believed children should receive from their mothers, presented in the form of an imaginary "letter written by a young man in the north to his mother in the east." Attias's conviction that his Ottoman coreligionists needed to learn from the West foreshadowed the nineteenth-century project of Sephardi reformers who turned to Europe in search of models of secular education.*

[Young man in the north to his mother in the east]: In this letter I want to tell you that I returned to your letters because I missed you, but I stopped because certain words in them inflamed my heart and mind and require a response. You reproachfully remind me that you nurtured me and struggled when I was a child.

Of course I have to respond to these words, but first of all I ask you to forgive me for my way of speaking, for you will see that what I say is true. Then I will tell you that, if you struggled when I was a child, you did not do more than you were obliged, because wishing to have pleasures one also has to have displeasures. We see the same in animals who, upon giving birth, nurse their little ones and look lovingly at them until they are big enough to find food on their own. And when they can feed themselves and look for food on their own, the mother goes in one direction and the children in another, and they will never ask each other for help or reproach one another as you reproach me. You know that, thank God, you do not lack anything and that I never have and never will leave you without help, but I do not want you to think that I am doing this to pay you back for giving birth to me, because if you believe that you have done me a favor by giving birth to me, I will tell you that you are wrong. I would be more grateful if you had left me in nothingness, which is where I was before you conceived me, instead of bringing me into this world full of all kinds of dangers, fears, and sorrows. And if this were not enough, one lives in fear expecting that in the other world there will be more suffering, and one will go either to Gehenna or to the Garden of Eden, depending on whether he is good or bad. As we are born in pain and start our lives crying and weeping, it is clear how the end will be, because, as the saying goes, the morning foretells the rest of the day. And the great sage, the poet Metastasio, talks about man as follows, "When a person is born, he enters a sea of so much suffering that he learns to bear all sorts of worries."[25] And the wise King Solomon also said in Ecclesiastes that the one who has not been born is happier than those who are living and those who are dead, because they have not yet experienced what happens under the sun.[26] I am saying this so that you will understand that you have not done me a favor by giving birth to me, because if you created me from nothingness, to nothingness I will have to return. But our fortitude is in understanding and learning how to govern oneself and navigate this path on earth during the few years of our life. This is the true wisdom and law, which the wise King Solomon proclaimed when he said, "My son, heed the discipline of your father, and do not forsake the instruction of your mother."[27] And I will tell you what this teaching should be, but it seems that because of our sins nobody wants to understand it and so far nobody has explained it. If you had taught it to me, you would have the right to reproach me, because it is not the same as conceiving me or struggling to nurture me. Then you could say that you have indeed given me life and rightly remind me of the commandment "Honor your father and your mother, that you may long endure."[28] In that case the mother's law would have been explained, and it would be wrong for the son to speak to her this way.

---

25. A quote from the Italian poet Metastasio (1698–1782), which appeared in Attias's text in the original Italian in Latin characters.

26. A free rendering of Ecclesiastes 4:2–3: "Then I accounted those who died long since more fortunate than those who are still living; and happier than either are those who have not yet come into being and have never witnessed the miseries that go on under the sun."

27. Proverbs 1:8.

28. Exodus 20:12.

[The lessons a mother should give her son]: My son, you should know that before your body looked the way it does now, it was nothing. You were formed in my belly from the drops of fertility that came from me and your father, and thus you grew in my belly, and nine months later I gave birth to you and delivered you into this world. But you should know that this body of yours has grown because it consists of the following four things: the earth on which you walk, the heat that you feel, which is sent to you by the sun, water, and air. My son, you would not have been born or grown up if we did not eat the things that come from the earth, nor would you live if your body did not receive the heat sent to the earth and to all of us by the sun. You would not exist if from time to time you did not counter this heat and fire that you feel through thirst with water used to cook our food. We could not even breathe if we did not have air, which also refreshes our bodies. And all the birds you see flying and all the animals you see walking on four legs on earth are made of these things. All of this, as I told you, is the image of God, who is One and his name is One.

My son, do not get sad or upset when you learn that someone has died. For the reason I have explained, you should not be frightened or saddened by death, because before you were conceived you were nothing and dead. And from the moment I conceived you, you began to die, and every hour of your life was deadly. And thus at the moment I gave birth to you, time—or rather, God—condemned you to death and to return to your original place, which was nothingness, where you will soon be again. So do not be surprised or afraid of this path that will take you to nothingness because, whether you like it or not, time is pushing you and years will fly by until you reach the point where you will have to pay back what time has lent you so that you could live. Why should you get angry and upset about something that you never owned? If someone lends you something why should you get angry when you have to return it? Thirty or forty years ago you did not exist in this world. Time lent you these years and the world lent itself to you so that you could live and die in it. So why do you get angry when you have to pay it back, knowing that none of this is yours? And thus you will give back everything. Time will take back the years that passed; the earth will take back your life; the sun will take back its heat from your body and will absorb its humidity to return it to the water in clouds; the air will take back your breath; God will take back your true holy and wise soul; and fortune or people will take back the clothes and garments they gave you. And thus, having returned everything, you will rest in that place where you had been before you were born, which is nothingness. So you should live in peace and not worry about anything because things are going as they should and cannot go any better. And if you want to understand this better, look at a new candle. What is it before it is lit? It does not do anything, and it is nothing and darkness. But when it is lit, it begins to shine and shrivel, killing itself, and eventually this candle becomes what it had been before it was lit, which is nothing and darkness. The same is true of human beings before and after they are born, when they live and die, and even when they are dead. There is only one difference: we have to make sure that the light of our lives is bright and full in our existence, both in what we do and how we live, and that it shines both before God and people. And as for the fear of Gehenna, if you want to free yourself from this fear, follow what reason tells you and, above all, know that God is neither cruel nor vindictive like people, but merciful and forgiving. In addition, he will see that you used the soul he gave you to do good.

My son, do not lie, because otherwise, even when you tell the truth, nobody will believe you. But I do not recommend that you tell the truth that can hurt you. Keep silent and, rather than lying or telling the truth, say, "I do not know," and thus you will not do good to anybody or hurt anybody.

My son, to make a living learn a profession that is indispensable for the world, thus you will not depend on fortune. And try to be useful to people and the world, which will make people and the world useful to you. The shop said to the merchant, "If you maintain me and take care of me, I will maintain you and take care of you. But if you do not do this for me, I will not do anything for you either."

My son, stay close to wise people in order to refine your mind. And when this is not possible, be with yourself and enjoy it. And from time to time get to know the wicked and the lost and all sorts of people and talk to them, but be careful not to make them your friends, because eventually they will damage or hurt you. Keep your eyes open and observe their ways and the evils that befall them, and thus you will learn to avoid their ways. All of this will help you to refine your mind.

My son, if you want to have a long life, live like the poor, which means eat little, just enough to sate the hunger, but not too much. This way you will cure yourself of all diseases.

My son, study as much as possible and day and night ask God to give you wisdom and understanding in the matters you must handle as well as courage and patience in misfortunes and humility in prosperity and wealth.

David Attias, *La guerta de oro* (Livorno: Giovanni Vincenzo Falorni, 1778). Translated from Ladino and introduced by Olga Borovaya.

## 8. HOPING FOR REDEMPTION: ANTICIPATING THE MESSIANIC YEAR 5600 (1840)

*For many centuries Jewish authors predicted that the Hebrew year 5600 (1839/1840) would bring about the coming of the Messiah. Among those who expected redemption at this time was Judah ben Solomon Hai Alkalay (1798–1878), a Sephardi author who was born in Sarajevo and educated in Jerusalem, but spent most of his life in Zemun (Semlin, now a suburb of Belgrade), where he served as a Hebrew teacher and rabbi. Alkalay also traveled to various European cities to propagate the idea of Jewish settlement in Palestine and raise funds for the Jewish community of Jerusalem. In his 1840 Ladino work* Shalom Yerushalayim *(The Peace of Jerusalem), a portion of which is excerpted here, Alkalay responds to the traditional Jewish critique of "forcing the end" by moving to the Holy Land before the end of days. He urges readers to hasten the redemption by promoting Jewish unity, fulfilling their religious duties, and repenting. It has been suggested that Alkalay may have influenced Theodor Herzl (1860–1904)—widely regarded as the founder of political Zionism— because Herzl's grandfather was a member of Alkalay's congregation and owned one of Alkalay's works. Yet, although he proposed that Jews stop waiting passively for the coming of the Messiah before returning to their ancestral homeland in Palestine, Alkalay's deeply religious and mystical approach was distinct from that of the largely secular Jewish nationalists of the later nineteenth century.*

"And this he said of Judah: Hear, O Lord, the voice of Judah, and restore him to his people. Though his own hands strive for him, help him against his foes."[29]

Since the days when the truth of "our land yields its produce"[30]

29. Deuteronomy 33:7.
30. Psalm 85:13.

are approaching, I do not need to excuse myself for speaking out to announce the anguish I feel as I enter a great sea and a raging river. It is well known that the *hakhme ha-musar*[31] say: A preacher or herald who refrains from saying what is in his heart for fear of people cannot be called a preacher or a herald. And [yet] here one cannot say what he wishes. And it is better not to enter here as Israel usually does. But he is the Holy One, and "by Him actions are measured."[32] And he did not make it clear, so that it would be hard for me to start speaking. "God, the Lord God! He knows, and Israel too shall know!"[33] That for a long time my heart feared that this year, 5600 of the creation, would not be good, because much has been said about it. Therefore I admonished my community on the day of Rosh Hashanah before the sound of the shofar as is the custom.[34] Today, in the year 5600 of the creation, today justice will be meted to all creatures in the universe. And who will be able to withstand this judgment? King David implored: "Do not enter into judgment with Your servant."[35]

For our great sins, a few days later we received the news of the terrible fire, which God caused to happen on the night of Rosh Hashanah in Salonica, city and mother of Israel. . . . Before Tishri was over, we received more bad news: the beacon of Israel went out; we lost God's luminous ark of our diaspora . . . our teacher Moses Sofer . . . may his memory live in the world to come, [and] may his merits protect us. It is written in Genesis that "God said, 'Let there be light', and there was light."[36] He saw that we are unable to enlighten ourselves with this great light and he saved it for the righteous ones. . . .[37] When I saw these troubles related to one another, fear and terror overcame me. And I said in my mind that it is time to awaken [people] with my words [and] penetrate their hearts. And it happened that precisely in those days I took my book to a printing

---

31. The ethical works produced by sixteenth-century kabbalists who predicted that the messianic age would begin in 5600.

32. 1 Samuel 2:3.

33. Joshua 22:22.

34. The Jewish new year, Rosh Hashanah, begins on the first day of the month of Tishri and is announced by the blowing of a ram's horn called the shofar.

35. Psalm 143:2.

36. Genesis 1:3.

37. According to the Talmud, righteous men are endowed with special privileges and obligations.

house in Belgrade: it was *Kuntres darkhe no'am*, a book on grammar. And I wrote in the introduction a few words regarding three things on which the universe is founded. And in order to explain that what is said about the year 5600 is not empty talk, I described some signs concerning its number, 600,[38] in reasonable, pleasant, and truthful words so that we could prepare our hearts for repentance and so that we would not, God forbid, return to falsehood.[39] As our sages say, if Israel does not repent every year in the opportune time, its time will become inopportune. . . .

Pilar Romeu, ed., *Yehudá Alcalay y su obra La paz de Jerusalén (Ofen, 1840): En los orígenes del sionismo y en lengua sefardí* (Barcelona: Tirocinio, 2011), 65–66. Translated from Ladino and introduced by Olga Borovaya.

## 9.  THE SINS THAT STARTED THE FIRE: A JOURNALIST'S VIEW FROM IZMIR (1846)

*In December 1845 the first known Ladino periodical was launched in the Ottoman port city of Izmir under the editorship of Raphael Uziel. The following editorial, published on the fifth anniversary of a major fire in Izmir and three days before the commemoration of the destruction of the Temple of Jerusalem, draws a parallel between the events and suggests that the sins of the local Jewish community, namely a conflict that had arisen between rich and poor Jews over the communal tax on meat, were to blame for the fire. Here Uziel urges his readers, and the rabbis who regulated the taxation of ritually slaughtered meat in particular, to end this dispute in order to prevent greater catastrophe.*

Gentlemen, having recieved incorrect information in the last column of the previous issue, we reported that the discords in our community had been settled. We also promised to give a detailed account of this much-desired peace, which is what we hoped for. "We hoped for good fortune," etc.,[40] "when they heard how I was sighing."[41] As if it were not enough that we endure afflictions everywhere else, now we suffer seeing the disarray and poor administration in the Jewish community

---

38. An abbreviated reference to the Hebrew year 5600.

39. Alkalay uses the Hebrew word *sheker*, whose numeric value is 600. Interpretation of events based on the numeric value of respective Hebrew words is a common kabbalistic device.

40. Jeremiah 8:15a. The full verse reads: "We hoped for good fortune, but no happiness came; For a time of relief--instead there is terror!"

41. Lamentations 1:21a.

of Izmir. . . . "Because of this our hearts are sick, because of these our eyes are dimmed."[42]

The same controversy and nearly the same disputes that we see today occurred in our community in 5599 [1839]. Everybody already knows about the great harm they caused as well as about the two parties' mutual insults and resentment, and especially about the amount of money both parties spent [to further their cause]. But the worst thing was the great desecration of God to which it led: we were scorned and shamed by the nations.[43] And so many storms have erupted around us that it is impossible to recount even one percent of those troubles. Finally, after two years of continuous controversies, on 11 Av 5601 [July 29, 1841], great fire descended from heaven and burned down two thirds of Izmir, our beautiful and illustrious city. Two thirds, I tell you. Ninety percent of Jewish houses were destroyed in this great disaster. Within sixteen hours the city of Izmir was destroyed and desolate. All people, men and women, young and old, were crying out loudly and bitterly, weeping, and begging God for mercy. Those who had died of hunger and thirst were lying in the middle of the streets, as the prophet said [of those] "who faint for hunger at every street corner."[44] Day and night we pray to the great and merciful God that this shall not happen to us again. "Nevermore shall you be called 'Forsaken,' nor shall your land be called 'Desolate.'"[45]

What was the cause of the disaster that befell us? The great animosity that reigned among us, the great hatred between us. Why was our Temple destroyed? Why was our Jerusalem desolate? "Fair Jerusalem; 'Is this the city that was called perfect in beauty?'"[46] "The crown has fallen from our head; Woe to us that we have sinned!"[47] Why did we become slaves among the nations? Why are we in this sad and despondent condition? Finally, why do we live in such misery? All of this is because of our terrible crimes, unwarranted hatred, speaking evil of others, desecration of God, and murder. May he who in his mercy and grace forgives crimes and absolves sins forgive us our crimes and

---

42. Lamentations 5:17.
43. Non-Jews.
44. Lamentations 2:19.
45. Isaiah 62:4.
46. Lamentations 2:15.
47. Lamentations 5:16.

absolve us and all sinners in his great name. . . . "Turn from Your blazing anger, and renounce the plan to punish Your people."[48] "Look and save the sheep of your flock,"[49] "because you are a compassionate and merciful king."[50]

After all these troubles and misfortunes had passed, "and the land had peace for four years."[51] For about four years there was some peace in the city. Three or four months ago, one could notice that a new upheaval threatened to emerge in the community, but nobody tried to prevent it from spreading. A great fire inflamed the Jewish community in all parts of the city. Thus the controversy of 5599 [1839] returned. As we explained in the previous issue, the community is split into two parties: one seems to have forgotten what that infamous controversy led to four years ago; the other does not remember the past [at all]. After two years of upheaval, neither of the parties gained anything, [and] there was no improvement. And thus one party lost as much as the other. There was no time of healing,[52] and the upper classes lost the reputation and influence they had enjoyed in the community. And nothing has been gained. Brothers, "Let us search and examine our ways, and turn back to the Lord."[53] Now we are humbly begging our esteemed rabbis, highly revered shepherds of this flock, filled with zeal and love of God and the people, to embrace peace[54] and step in between the two parties. Gentlemen, take on the work of Aaron, the High Priest. Find a reasonable agreement that would suit both parties. Let peace and love dwell in our community. Wake up, gentlemen, act like fathers toward their children. "He cares about the poor and the needy; He brings the needy deliverance. He redeems them from fraud and lawlesness; the shedding of their blood weighs heavily upon him."[55] Help the people to achieve abundance and prosperity. All our misery is caused by these terrible controversies, hatred, and animosity. Therefore, do your best to conciliate them, so that a worse disaster

---

48. Exodus 32:12b.
49. From the *Tahanun*, or supplication, which forms part of the morning and afternoon prayers.
50. From the *'Arvit le-Shabat* prayer.
51. Judges 3:11, but replacing "forty" with "four," a reckoning that better suited Uziel's account.
52. A paraphrase of Jeremiah 8:15a.
53. Lamentations 3:40.
54. Paraphrase of Psalms 132:9a: "Your priests are clothed in triumph."
55. Psalm 72:13–14.

may not occur. We are sure that in the next issue, with God's help, we will report on the agreement and complete peace that will [soon] reign in our community.

"May the Lord grant strength to His people! May the Lord bestow on His people wellbeing!"[56]

"Sovre las diferensias de la nasion israelit[a] de Izmir," *Sha'are mizrah/Puertas de oriente*, 6 Av 5606 (July 29, 1846), 89–90. Translated from Ladino and introduced by Olga Borovaya.

## 10.  CLASS CONFLICT AMIDST THE JEWS OF IZMIR: A REBELLION OF THE JEWISH POOR (1847)

*The following is an excerpt from an anonymous booklet published in 1847 chronicling the plight of Izmir's lower and working classes. Speaking in the name of the poor of the city, the document describes injustices in communal administration, particularly with respect to taxation. Traditionally Jewish communities levied a sales tax on kosher goods such as wine, meat, and cheese to be able to provide for the indigent, pay rabbinic salaries, and maintain institutions such as the communal cemetery. In Ottoman communities these taxes were known as gabela taxes, and, given their essentially regressive nature, often disproportionately burdened the poor. The booklet describes frustration both with this traditional arrangement and with the overall governance of the community's leaders.*

With God's help, hear the cry of the poor, hear the plea of the impoverished, and save him:

We, the poor of Israel, inhabitants of the city of Izmir, may God protect it, slaves of our lord and king, Sultan Abdülmecid, may his name be praised and long live his reign, [are] oppressed and humiliated by the wealthy communal leaders, may God protect and keep them, many of whom are *francos*.[57] For many years we have been dishonored and abused by their governance and rule over the city, which has always been in their hands. If a poor or middle-class person rejects their rule, no matter how minor the issue, he is excommunicated, or turned over to the authorities and arrested or beaten. When one of them violates the law, he is never brought to justice. The poor,

---

56. Psalm 29:11.

57. The Ladino term *franco* tended to refer to the families of Tuscan and Livornese Jewish merchants who resided in Ottoman lands as European protégés.

believing that it was [the leaders] who were covering the expenses of the community, such as the sums due to the government, [as well as] those for charitable institutions and those dedicated to caring for the sick and the cemetery, tolerated this, as one who relies on another becomes subservient to him.

Now the poor and middle classes have realized that as a result of the *Tanzimat-ı Hayriye* [Beneficial Reforms] that our merciful king has applied to all of his reign, there are no longer any additional taxes or fines apart from the poll tax and the profit tax that each person must pay individually. All of the expenses of the city, [including the cost of the] Society for Visiting and Tending to the Sick, the Burial Society, the Society for Clothing the Poor, the Talmud Torah [school],[58] the *'asara batlanim*,[59] the chief rabbi, and the rabbinic court are covered by the *gabela* on wine, meat, and cheese. Of the 25,000 arayot yielded every year by the wine *gabela*, the poor and middle classes pay twenty thousand arayot, while the wealthy communal leaders pay five thousand. The same is true for meat. The poor cover the payments that are due to the ritual slaughterers along with additional sums for the expenses of the city, nearing forty thousand arayot. The ritual slaughterer receives his payment right away, [which means that] the poor pay double the price for meat while the rich eat meat with no tax or payment to the ritual slaughterers. As has been made known across the whole city, of the ninety thousand [arayot] yielded by the meat *gabela* per year, the poor and middle classes pay at least seventy thousand. Such is the administration and rule of the wealthy communal leaders, who treat the poor as slaves, taking no pity on them and abusing them much more than [we were abused during] our enslavement in Egypt.

"Shav'at 'Aniyim" (Izmir, 1847), © British Library Board (London) (1938.g.2). Translated from Ladino and introduced by Dina Danon.

---

58. Principal house of worship and Jewish school.
59. A group of ten men paid to study and pray on behalf of the community.

## 11. "A LONE JEW AMONG ALL THOSE CHRISTIANS": A BULGARIAN JEWISH DEVOTEE OF CLASSICAL GREEK {1851–1856}

*Abraham ben Israel Rosanes (1838–1879) was born in the town of Rusçuk (now Ruse) in the Ottoman Danube province, which became part of autonomous Bulgaria during the final years of his life. An early site of Ottoman reforms, Rusçuk provided a fertile intellectual environment to progressive thinkers at the mid-century. Rosanes was among them. In the 1860s he founded a Jewish school, where he employed local Jewish intellectuals to teach Hebrew using modern methods. It was also during this period that Rosanes began to keep a record of his life, explaining that he had been inspired after seeing that "many of the most able contributors" to the Hebrew press of his day "were recording their memoirs and chronicles of events from their youth until old age." In his first entry, penned on 17 Heshvan 5626 (November 16, 1864), he explained that he planned to write of all that befell him and that which occurred to him for the rest of his days. The following passage, excerpted from Rosanes's private journal, offers a reflection on his life as a young man, when he elected to attend a local Bulgarian school in order to learn ancient Greek.*

In the year 5612 [1851–1852] I heard that about five Jewish students were attending the school of the Bulgarians in order to learn Greek. Now a spirit of tradition gripped me, which I could not ignore. I determined not to walk in the path of sin or bring pain to the faces of my family any longer.[60] I would instead return to the path of good and go to study diligently at the above-mentioned school along with those students. I begged my father (of blessed memory) that he enroll me in this school and here is what he answered me.

"My son, I am aware of how much my disappointment has weighed on you. I tried with you innumerable times and in innumerable ways, but you would not return from your ways. Now therefore if I place you in the school you will last three days there and not want to continue. It will embarrass me in front of the non-Jews. Would it not be better for me not to enroll you there at all?"

Finally I feared God and He had mercy. I began to cry and plead with [my father], swearing to him that from that day forward I would take myself in hand and walk along the good path, never abandoning

---

60. In earlier passages, Rosanes described a period in which he did not pursue his studies in a serious manner.

it, if he would only place me in that school to learn Greek as those other students did.

In the month of Tevet of the same year I entered that school and began studying Greek with tremendous dedication. I repented of all my previous actions and habits, just as I had promised my father (of blessed memory) that I would. My desire to learn that language was immense, so much so that I turned night into day, sleeping only very little and reviewing my lessons. I would rise early in the morning and go immediately to school after prayers, staying there until nightfall. It was a long distance from my house to the school and bitter cold that winter, but none of it impeded my attendance every single day. My Jewish friends on the other hand were often absent because of these impediments.

At lunchtime one day, after I had been there about four months, my friends began to converse with some of the Armenian students there concerning their messiah [Jesus]. Over the course of their conversation they began to mock and curse each other until they became embroiled in a full-blown fight. They brought the matter before the teacher, who informed the school principal. A decision was made to expel the Jewish children, and I alone would remain because I had not spoken a word. This was the truth and this was what those students told the principal. It was extremely difficult to be the lone Jew among all those Christians in addition to the long distance I needed to travel every morning and evening and the other distractions. My enthusiasm, however, overcame them all, and I never missed a day of attendance for an entire year. In this manner I acquired an excellent knowledge of that language.

When this period had passed, I was no longer able to attend the school. This is because a war raged in those days[61] . . . so that most days the shops in our city were shuttered, because the townspeople were called to the duty of the king. Another issue was that they would bring cattle through the marketplaces and I was scared of them. I therefore requested of my father (may his soul dwell in Eden) that he hire a tutor who would come to our house every day and teach me. Now my father (may his soul dwell in Eden), having seen that I kept

---

61. The Crimean War (1853–56).

my promise to give up my wayward life, did not refuse me in this matter. At great expense he hired for me the very same teacher with whom I had studied at the school! He would come each day for about an hour, by which means I continued my studies for about another eight months. I almost completed my studies of that modern language, and I therefore began to learn the ancient language called *Ellin-nana*,[62] but after a short time the teacher did not wish to come any more and I did not learn more.

In the month of Sivan 5615 [June 1855], my father (may his soul dwell in Eden) brought me to Vienna (may God preserve it) along with my mother (may God preserve her forever) and my sister, and we stayed through the whole summer in the village of Baden. I then commenced studying the German language with *Hakham* Jacob Ashkenazi, but after two months he left me to travel to Belgrade, and I could find no other Jew to instruct me in this language.

In the month of Rahamim [Elul, in early fall] of that year my brother Isaac (may his light shine) also came there because he had decided to divorce his first wife. We remained in Baden until after the holiday of Sukkot, at which time we returned to Vienna. In the month of Marheshvan in the year 5716 [late fall of 1855], after my father (may his soul dwell in Eden) had opened a store in Vienna, he decided to place it in the hands of my brother Isaac (may his lamp shine) while he, my mother (may she be blessed above all the women of the tent), I, and my sister would return to our city. When I heard this my face fell and I was deeply saddened, for I wanted to remain there to learn German as well as ancient Greek. I spoke about this with my honored mother and begged her to intercede with my father (may his soul dwell in Eden), [asking] that he leave me there with my brother. My father (may his soul dwell in Eden), being very anxious to see me successfully educated, did not refuse my request even though it caused him to incur great expense. He put out the costs of clothing and other needs with a glad heart, knowing with certainty that my mind was made up to search out and pursue wisdom. I would not even mention my past deeds of three [wasted] years, let alone repeat them.

---

62. Most likely *Ellinika*, i.e., Greek.

Now since no one could be found who knew the Greek language to instruct me—for I preferred it to the German tongue—[my father] was compelled to entreat the principal and Greek [Orthodox] priest who were there to accept me into their school and add me to the list of students. They acceded to his request and promised to receive me on certain conditions. My father (may his soul dwell in Eden) placed me in the charge of friends he had there and of my brother, and he returned to our city.

In the month of Kislev I began to attend that school with great joy, and I studied with devotion. To my enormous sorrow, however, I was not able to continue there for long, for the teacher was a man who hated the religion [of Judaism] and did not supervise me properly. He would show me the anger in his face in order that I leave and never return. At first I thought he might be doing this to me because he was being forced to teach me for free under instructions of the principals, and I therefore tried to appease him in a different way. One day I said to him, "Sir, if you are interested in teaching me the German language during the afternoon when you are free I will pay you as much money for it as you require." He replied, "But you should know that I will take a florin every day." I answered him, "Fine, I will pay you as you wish."

He did begin to teach me every day, and as soon as we finished learning, I would give him the florin. None of this helped me though, for my real desire was to learn Greek, that to which my soul aspired. But it was not long until I saw that this was also in vain; I was paying him this enormous sum every day and yet his evil attitude did not change. I then fully understood that he harbored nothing but profound hatred for the [Jewish] religion. He could not even look me in the face. I was therefore forced to leave that school and move on.

In the month of Tevet [winter 1856], I hired a German teacher whom I would visit every day in his home for about five hours before noon and another two hours in the afternoon. Within three months I was able to read and speak that language well. I read with him and translated two books as well as learning German grammar. If I could have remained to study with him for a full year I would certainly have mastered that language entirely, but I was called on by my father (may his soul dwell in Eden) to return to my city, for he wanted to train me in the operation of his merchant house. In those days his business was quite large because it was a time of rising values and he needed to bring me back, for there was nobody in his business upon whom he could rely. I was therefore compelled, again against my will, to return to my city. . . .

Excerpts from an unpublished memoir of Abraham Rosanes of Rusçuk, Private Collection of Sivan Toledo. Transcribed from *soletreo* by Zvi Keren and translated from Hebrew by Matt Goldish.


## 12.  A COMMERCIAL SUIT BY A JEW AGAINST
##      A MUSLIM [1854]

*Multiple, overlapping legal systems coexisted in the Ottoman Empire. By the nineteenth century, Jewish, Christian, and Muslim courts competed with and complemented Ottoman and foreign consular courts. As elsewhere in Muslim lands, Ottoman rabbinic authorities tried to discourage Jews from applying to Islamic courts for legal assistance, but Jews nonetheless frequently appeared before Islamic judges. In some instances Jews did so voluntarily, when bypassing the Jewish court would serve their personal interests. In other instances Jews (as well as Christians) had little choice but to appear in the Islamic courts, the default site for the adjudication of cases involving Muslims and non-Muslims. The following document offers an example of the latter scenario. The case involves a Jewish man by the name of Isaac who brought a suit against Hacı[63] Mustafa Efendi, a Muslim merchant whom he charged with improper business practices. As the following record makes clear, Isaac ultimately proved unsuccessful in his suit owing to the fact that by Islamic law the burden of proof lies with the plaintiff. In this instance, the Jewish plaintiff was unable to garner sufficient proof to make his case, allowing the defendant to swear an oath testifying to his innocence, and thus to clear his name.*

Isaac the Jew, son of Judah, resident of Manisa, came to Izmir's *kadı* court.[64] Together with him Hacı Mustafa Efendi, son of Abdullah, from Menemen, was also present.

Isaac reported the following: "Eight years ago, I left my dry goods worth 902 kuruş to Hacı Mustafa Efendi, allowing him to sell them with a ratio of one-eighth. To do this, I appointed him my commissioner with a written contract. He then approved the deal and took my goods

---

63. *Hacı* is the Turkish version of Arabic *hajji*, or one who completes the pilgrimage to Mecca, a religious duty of able-bodied Muslims.

64. Islamic court, here named after the *kadı*, or Islamic judge.

in exchange for a written receipt. Afterwards, he sold the dry goods worth 902 kuruş, with a profit ratio of one-eighth. However, instead of sharing the one-eighth of the profit with me, he used it for his own personal needs. Therefore I am requesting my 902 kuruş from him."

When asked about Isaac's arguments, Hacı Mustafa Efendi responded, "[It is true that] he came to my store in the district of Menemen on the day he claimed. He left me dry goods worth only 307 kuruş and 30 para. I took them in exchange for a receipt, and kept them in my closet in the store. During the year 1262 [1846] the great fire took place in our district. Together with my own goods, the dry goods with which he entrusted me were completely destroyed before I could take them out of the fire. Hence I do not accept his accusations. I did not sell his dry goods to anyone."

As a result Isaac the plaintiff was asked to present proof of his accusations. As he was unable to do so, he instead asked to take an oath. In response Hacı Mustafa Efendi consented once again that he had taken Isaac's dry goods but maintained that they were all destroyed in the fire. In the presence of the *kadı*, he also made a pledge in the name of Allah the Almighty. Ultimately, because Isaac the Jew was unable to prove his accusations, he was prohibited from bringing charges against Hacı Mustafa Efendi without any proof.

Jacob Barnai and Haim Gerber, eds., *The Jews in Izmir in the 19th Century: Ottoman Documents from the Shar'i Court* (Jerusalem: Misgav Yerushalayim, 1984), 74. We thank Prof. Yaron Ben-Naeh, director of the Misgav Yerushalayim Center for the Study of Sephardi Jewry at the Hebrew University of Jerusalem, for permission to reprint this source. Translated from Ottoman Turkish by Onur Şar.

## 13. A PETITION FOR AID: A SEPHARDI COLLECTIVE IN JERUSALEM APPEALS TO THE BRITISH CONSUL [1854]

*Bilateral agreements (known as capitulations) brokered between the Ottoman Empire and various European powers conferred certain rights and privileges on subjects of foreign states living or conducting business in Ottoman territory. Those who could not acquire foreign protection, including the Jewish poor, were nonetheless aware that consuls in the empire had considerable political clout and financial resources. In this document, a group of poor Jews in Jerusalem appeals to the British consul in search of financial support, building their petition on a labyrinth of biblical quotations that they presumably hoped would resonate with their Anglican interlocutor.*

His Highness the Minister and Honorable Sir Jacob Finn, Consul of Britain . . . in Jerusalem, who has mercy upon the poor.

Before we begin, there are many peace offerings [to be offered]—public peace offerings and obligatory peace offerings.[65] We pray for the Lord who has chosen Zion,[66] [that He] will keep you alive and well, in abundance of riches and honor,[67] with children and children's children,[68] settled and secure[69] . . .

We have come to inform you on high that we constitute one hundred and fifty families wandering about [searching for] for bread.[70] And no one takes pity on us, and we have no prop nor support[71] but for our Lord that is in Heaven, the God of Israel, and our Lordship the Minister, to keep an eye on us for the good, as God's hand is good upon him, and to be of aid to us in several matters, both in the matter of dispatching missives to cities abroad [with the aid] of our Lord the Minister, and in the matter of the response to the missives that arrive to us, so that they will not be handed to anyone but us. For if perhaps the ministers of Israel will have mercy on us and their spirits will be made willing to dispatch to us anything, it is our wish that our Lord will guide us and at his command we will make camp and at his command we will break camp . . . in order to cure our diseases and save our lives and the lives of our infants. . . . Just as the Minister and Officer in Constantinople [Istanbul] was a shield and aid to the poor, we put our trust in your great compassion for the poor so as to save us from those who wish to harm us, with no malice on our part. This is a profoundly good deed and the Lord will repay him for his actions[72] and his recompense from the Lord will be full[73] in plenty of strength and peace.

---

65. See Talmud, Mas. Betsah 20a.
66. Psalm 132:13.
67. Proverbs 3:16.
68. Deuteronomy 4:25.
69. Jeremiah 48:11.
70. Job 15:23.
71. Isaiah 3:1.
72. Job 34:11.
73. Ruth 2:12.

We came to sign this,
The company of the poor and humble city dwellers

A group of poor Jewish city dwellers in Jerusalem to James Finn, the British consul of Jerusalem, 1854, Inv/724, The Central Archives for the History of the Jewish People (Jerusalem). Cited from Yali Hashash, "Shifting Social Attitudes and Economic Change in the Sephardic Community in Palestine, 1841–1880" (Ph.D. dissertation, Haifa University, 2011) (Hebrew), 216–19. Translated from Hebrew by Yali Hashash.

## 14. A MUSLIM INTELLECTUAL RECOUNTS A JEWISH COMMUNAL CONFLICT IN ISTANBUL (1862)

*Tensions between conservative and reformist factions in the Jewish community of Istanbul erupted in 1862. At this time Yehezkel Gabbay II (1825–1898) published an article sympathetic to Freemasonry in his Ladino periodical El Djurnal Israelit, causing an uproar among Jewish traditionalists in the capital. When the influential Jewish lay leader Abraham Camondo (1781–1873) summoned a rabbi from the conservative camp to discuss the matter, the rabbi excommunicated him. Receiving the support of the Ottoman government as well as Jewish reformers in the empire, Camondo survived this event unscathed, a sign of the waning reach of rabbinic power among elite and official circles in the empire at this time. The conservative faction's popular support was significant, however. When Sultan Abdülaziz (r. 1861–1876) arrested the rabbi, thousands of Jews marched through the Ottoman capital, opposing—and eventually preventing—his continued imprisonment. The following source, an article written by the renowned Young Ottoman[74] poet, journalist, and translator İbrahim Şinasi (1826–1871) offers the perspective of an Ottoman Muslim intellectual on the split in the Jewish community.*

There has been conflict and disagreement among Jews for quite a long time. Many of these individuals came to the Sublime Porte and the Palace a few days ago to present their complaints. It is convenient to write down the details of these events to the extent that we are permitted.

European Jews have begun imitating the traditions and ways of life of the French and thus are becoming part of modern civilization. After [the French] became more numerous in the Orient, they tried to make Oriental Jews become like them. And some of the latter began to imi-

---

74. Secret Ottoman organization founded in Istanbul in 1865. The Young Ottomans opposed the regime of Abdülaziz (r. 1861–1876) and advocated for a constitutional government within the empire.

tate them. Furthermore [a number of Jewish lay notables] constituted a communal assembly. This is the primary reason for the current strife.

According to reports by certain reliable informants, Yehezkel [Gabbay] Bağdatlı[75] is the secretary of the assembly and at the same time the chamberlain of the chief rabbinate. He is also a journalist. We do not know how, but he gained a certain influence over the assembly. [Yet] his actions offended the majority of people. Moreover, because he is a freethinker, he is the target of the chief rabbi and the conservatives, who constitute the majority of the Jewish community.

Previously, a number of rabbis complained about Yehezkel to Mr. Camondo, a notable Austrian merchant and president of the assembly, because Yehezkel had written an article promoting Freemasonry. Yet, because Camondo is one of Yehezkel's protectors, he remained undisturbed. The frustrated rabbis, who were disappointed by Camondo's decision, excommunicated him. He [Camondo] responded by having one of them beaten and sent into exile to İplikhane[76]. . . .

In response thousands of Jews presented petitions of complaint to Sultan Abdülaziz as he made his way to visit Eyüp.[77] Consequently, the [Jewish communal] assembly was temporarily closed and the issue was carried to the Supreme Court for Judicial Ordinances.[78] The majority [of the complaints] emphasize that the president [Camondo] is a foreign subject and opposes the community's general opinion. Therefore, they suggest, both Camondo and the chief rabbi who supported him should be removed from their positions.

On the other hand another group argues that rabbis misuse their power within the community and thereby harm the overall well being of the community. Moreover, they conclude, Jews will gradually face extinction because the rabbis make the observance of religious life very difficult.

Ultimately the Supreme Court left the matter of excommunication to the chief rabbis of Selânik [Salonica], Izmir, and Siroz [Serres]. They were summoned via telegraph. Two of them showed up. The rabbi of Salonica, who is not an Ottoman subject, did not come.

---

75. A nickname meaning "from Baghdad" in reference to the family's Baghdadi roots.
76. İplikhane ("spinning mill"), a building used as a jail in Istanbul.
77. A district of Istanbul.
78. *Meclis-i Vala.*

We do not know why. Because he did not appear, the rabbi of Filibe [Plovdiv] was brought in his place.

Yehezkel has recently announced that the rabbis have decided in favor of the chief rabbi. The present conflict was the result of this verdict. It is rumored that the case will be left in the hands of the provincial rabbis.

Since ancient times Jews have been divided into two groups with regard to religious belief. Those who oppose the majority are called Karaites.[79] Now the separation extends to politics as well: those who left the community are called "civilized."[80]

It is quite a mystery to know what the result of these developments will be.

İbrahim Şinasi, *Tasvir-i Efkar*, no. 52, 4 Receb 1279/14 Kanunievvel 1278 (December 26, 1862). Translated from Ottoman Turkish by Onur Şar.

## 15.  ON THE POSSIBILITIES OF SYNAGOGUE REFORM: AN OTTOMAN RABBI'S ANSWER TO A QUERY FROM PARIS (1869)

*Haim ben Jacob Palache (1788–1868), chief rabbi of Izmir from 1855 until his death, was one of the most influential Sephardi leaders of the nineteenth-century Ottoman world. As the following document makes clear, Palache's reputation reached as far as Paris, where Jews sought his legal opinion on matters of controversy in Europe. The case questioned both the permissibility of introducing organ music performed by non-Jews into the synagogue and the elimination of liturgical poems and psalms from certain services. Proponents of these changes argued that they made Judaism compatible with the modern era and thereby helped to integrate Jews into non-Jewish society; critics considered such forms of acculturation an existential threat to Judaism. It is possible that members of the reformist camp in Paris imagined that a Sephardi rabbi from the Ottoman Empire would be so isolated from the West as to be immune to these religious storms or that a Sephardi scholar might take a more lenient approach to changing traditions than his Ashkenazi counterparts. If so, they were disappointed. In response to their query Palache not only made clear that he was aware*

---

79. A Jewish group that recognizes only the Bible as a source of authority.

80. During the nineteenth century, Jewish reformers in the Ottoman capital borrowed from the language of the Ottoman Armenian community, which was undergoing similar conflicts between self-declared conservative and progressive factions, calling themselves *lusavorial* ("enlightened") and labeling their detractors *khavarial* ("obscurantist").

*of the new schisms facing European Jews, he also adamantly opposed any changes to*
*Jewish liturgy or synagogue ritual.*

Question:

I was asked to respond to a question from the great men, those who
fear God and care for His name, from the great city. They are mighty
men, kings and princes, wise and insightful persons[81] . . . of the ten
overseers from the royal city of Paris, may God preserve it . . .

They ask the law concerning a new group that has appeared and cast
doubt [on current practices], wishing to change the original order—
the proper traditions and traditions of the elders—in order to reduce
the order of liturgical poems and psalms customarily read in the prayer
services. A new voice has appeared wishing to bring musicians into the
house of God to perform on Sabbaths and holy days—inappropriate
musicians who are non-Jews who [nonetheless] could perform because
they are not members of our covenant. This is something our ancestors never envisioned, for to do this—to change their traditions, to
add and subtract—was evil and bitter in their eyes. It is an insult to the
holy men, the mighty ones of the earth, who are still alive [in spirit]
and among whom are kings. [What they are discussing represents] a
change from the opinions of the holy ones, our ancestors and teachers of previous generations, of blessed memory, as well as our aged
[teachers] who are still alive. It is rather an obligation incumbent on
every member of the People of Israel, from old to young, to hold fast
to the deeds of our ancestors and not to change practices that are very
ancient, having existed for so many years. These were great people—
the *Urim* and *Tummim*.[82]

In their letter to me, they [the French Jews] begged me with their
pens in pleading language, saying that I should hurry and rush to
send them a detailed response addressing the issues, for they fear that
an even greater breach may occur [if there is a delay in sending] the
words of the earlier and later rabbis. They [the new group] will break
through the fence and change all kinds of traditions. That is what led
[the questioners] to come to me with pleading and requests. According to the law, should they prevent these innovations in the manner

---

81. A reference to great rabbis.
82. Prophetic luminaries.

that they are occurring all over the world? Should they continue to practice and follow their ways as they have been since ancient times with no breach? Or, perhaps it is appropriate to adopt innovations, and their additions and subtractions [from earlier practice] would have the support of the rabbis. Perhaps the law allows new practices that were never known before. This is the gist of their words. May God be upon them, may they live a good life, and live out their days; so may it be God's will, amen.

Response:

. . . I will answer by saying that in order to respond to this question we must explore three areas. The first [question to] study is the order of prayer. Is it possible to change the tradition practiced by the community concerning what is said [in prayer]? May a community add something to its traditional order of prayer or remove some liturgical poem or other such passage without aspects of the law preventing it? The second study concerns whether a community may add something to the traditional order of the prayer service [such as] bringing musicians to perform during the service [on] what is called an organ, something that was not previously the practice. The third question concerns whether it is permissible to invite non-Jewish musicians into the synagogue on the Sabbath in order to play the organ. Is it a desecration of the Sabbath when one tells the non-Jew [to play]? And so on. . . .

All the more so, and by an argument of *ad minori ad majus*, the law would dictate that one must not nullify a good and virtuous tradition, one that is habitual in the prayers of every mouth; it must not be abolished. Can it be there for no reason? And where have we ever found our hands or feet in a situation like this, that we should stand up as if in the beginning, to come and to annul righteous practices and true doctrines practiced by the community, as now? . . . Who is it that has the authority to abolish publicly a tradition that is proper, virtuous, and well established by our ancient teachers? This is something that would never be permitted nor even mentioned; no justification or grounds exist in any book. This is a very simple matter about which they need not have even written to ask.

Nevertheless, in order to accede to the request of this quorum of excellent men who asked me to voice my opinion on the matter and write a legal decision with multiple proofs, I decided to assent to their will. I know that their query is intended for the sake of Heaven, for they fear that a disaster may result—a questioning of the words of the Sages. . . . Now if I were to attempt to cite here everything stated about the laws of traditional practices—that which is written in the Bible, the Talmud, the Sages, the earlier authorities and the later authorities—where it says not to change any traditional practice, each person following the traditions of his ancestors as they did since ancient times, scrolls upon endless, innumerable scrolls would not suffice. For this reason I will limit myself to citing a few proofs that one must not alter traditional practices in the order of the prayer service based on what is written in the Talmud and legal authorities—all true statutes and teachings. . . .

Aside from the very transgression of nullifying a tradition of the ancestors, another evil occurs: that of "one evil deed leads to another."[83] For as soon as the strap has been loosened, allowing a tradition to be abolished, they will soon come to abolish something that is forbidden according to the words of the Torah or the Sages. When the power to annul has been handed to them, they will make no distinction between tradition and law. It is as those who sent the question informed me; they fear that this matter, the change in an ancestral tradition, will become an excuse to go out and break down the barriers created by the words of the Sages, as they wrote in their letter. Furthermore, this entire matter of changing traditional practices and building a platform[84] for himself is all with the intention that he will thereby become separate and disconnected from the community of our congregation, [and] that which was practiced by our fathers and grandfathers.

This is the first reason that their authority should not be accepted. [We must not] listen to the voices of rebellious people by coming to them with appeasements and thus assenting to their desire and will, which is to throw the yoke of the Torah and commandments off of themselves. If the commandment of building a synagogue is to establish a place with a Torah scroll where people can pray with a quorum of ten [men]—a law about which the legal scholars were extremely emphatic—then one who seeks to prevent them and annul them is

_[handwritten marginal note: theme: importance of tradition]_

---

83. Mishnah Avot 4:2.
84. From the Hebrew *bamah*, literally "a high place." It is used in the Bible to refer to private altars usually used for idolatry.

preventing the community from performing a commandment. He is liable to the punishment of excommunication. . . .

Even in a situation where [a change in practice] is for the fulfillment of an excellent commandment, if our eyes see that it will cause division and baseless hatred, we prevent people from doing it. It is all the more so when someone comes to change a practice of our ancestors, for it is a transgression in itself (since the one who does it is trying to build a platform for himself and to breed dissent), but also because it causes concern about the future. We fear that they will come to throw off the yoke of Torah and the commandments; it is certain that they will not leave these in place. . . . They clearly come to show that their wisdom is superior to that of [their] predecessors and to change ancient practices. They also hold themselves to be very learned in knowledge and insightful in perception—more so than those came before them [and] whose traditions they seek to abolish. They proclaim, "We have the upper hand." There is no arrogance greater than this! . . . The essential transgression of arrogance is that the one who makes a change causes strife, and the change is itself the arrogance, which is the thing that is forbidden. . . .

There were great sages in every generation since the destruction of the Temple—thousands and tens of thousands of wise men and rabbis—who generation by generation did not bring organ players into the synagogue during prayer services. This should be sufficient to teach us that the aspiration to renew this practice comes from a desire to resemble the non-Jews. For this is *their* practice, to play exactly these musical instruments, called organs, in their places of worship. God forbid that this should become a stumbling block of sin for us. It is forbidden to follow in their ways. . . .

Just now there arrived in my hands a prayer book published in 1840 [in London]. In the introduction it states:

> Here now, entirely new, we have seen the printing of a book of prayers called *Seder Tefilot*, which will clearly appear to anyone who can see the sun to be a version of the prayers and blessings containing strange things and omissions. It is ordered in a manner at odds with our holy oral Torah passed down to us by the sages of blessed memory.[85] Without the oral Torah none of us can understand the written Torah; and anyone

---

85. The rabbinic tradition of Talmud and Midrash.

who does not believe in the words of [the Talmudic Sages] is a denier of our holy Torah given to us at Mount Sinai through our teacher Moses, the servant of God. When we saw this great evil we rose up and took encouragement with the help of God, to improve matters and remove a stumbling block from the path of our nation, our brothers, the Children of Israel. We warned all who are called by the name of Israel and in whose heart the fear of God resides that he not buy this prayer book, nor bring it into his house, and especially not pray from it. . . .

I conclude by noting that there is also no way to allow the new practice they wish to introduce of bringing non-Jewish musicians to the synagogue to play music during the service on the Sabbath. According to the law, the opponents have the upper hand, as I have explained. These are the words of the one who has signed here in our city of Izmir (may God preserve it), the eleventh day of the month of mercy [Elul] in the year [5]620 [July 30, 1860].

Haim Palache, *Sefer Lev Hayim*, vol. 2 (Izmir, 1869), Question 9, pp. 3r–11r. Translated from Hebrew and introduced by Matt Goldish.

## 16. "THE SORROWS OF A WOMAN": A JEWISH WIDOW FACES EVICTION [1866]

*After making a fortune on the stock exchange, the British Jewish banker Moses Montefiore (1784–1885) became one of the most celebrated philanthropists of his time, offering financial support and humanitarian assistance to Jews throughout Eastern Europe, the Americas, and the Middle East. Montefiore was an avid traveler and enjoyed face-to-face giving, which in turn encouraged many poor Jews to seek his favor, as did the widow whose words appear here. Her plea reflects the reverence felt for Montefiore across the Sephardi and Ashkenazi worlds, while also pointing to the extreme penury experienced by many Ottoman Sephardim of the period.*

To Sir Moses Montefiore, from Oro, the widow of Hayim Arieh, 1866

[Oh] one who gives light to the earth and to them that dwell thereon, who is full of good deeds, the father of orphans, the champion of widows,[86] the poor and needy,[87] Moses, the faithful shepherd, the doer of good deeds, the minister and officer, his great lordship . . . our

86. Psalm 68:6.
87. Isaiah 41:17.

*over-the-top praise*

teacher and rabbi Sir Moses Montefiore, may his candle shine on forever . . . and in our times and in his days, Judah shall be delivered and Israel shall dwell secure.[88] He shall come as redeemer to Zion, amen.[89]

I come to his highness bowing low with a prayer, that he shall live long to reign upon his kingdom. . . . I come begging, in tears, to inform his royal highness of the magnitude of my oppression and sorrows, the sorrows of a woman. For it has been some two years since my husband died and I was left a widow with three children, two nursing twin boys and one five-year-old daughter, naked and destitute, wandering about [searching] for bread and water. My cry has risen to the very skies, and my eyes, my eyes run with tears over my misfortune, the dire straits of the poor.[90] What is more, I owe the rent of the house and I am being pressed every day in these times of disturbances, and there is no one to save me. And so I go unto the king[91] to beg him and ask that he will keep his compassionate eye on us. Act for the orphans and widows. Act for the nursing infants. Act for the sake of the weaned babes.[92] As a father has compassion for his children, so have compassion upon[93] . . . as is becoming of his good virtue, his hand as good as a king's hand. For it is a great deed to revive four souls from Israel. Indeed it is like reviving the dead. And for that his glory shall live forever. Great is the charity that brings salvation closer. . . .

Institute of Microfilmed Hebrew Manuscripts, F-6159, The National Library of Israel (Jerusalem). Cited from Yali Hashash, "Shifting Social Attitudes and Economic Change in the Sephardic Community in Palestine, 1841–1880" (Ph.D. dissertation, Haifa University, 2011) (Hebrew), 222–25. Translated from Hebrew by Yali Hashash.

## 17.  IS THE PRINTING PRESS HARMFUL?
## A RABBI FROM SARAJEVO RESPONDS (1870)

*Between 1845 and 1939, approximately 300 Sephardi periodicals were published in the Ottoman Empire and its former territories. The vast majority of these newspapers were published in Ladino, with smaller numbers appearing in French, Hebrew, and*

---

88. Jeremiah 23:6.
89. Isaiah 59:20.
90. Lamentations 1:16.
91. Esther 4:16.
92. Avinu Malkenu.
93. Psalm 103:13.

*Ottoman Turkish. Popular newspapers in Ladino exposed readers to the day's news, brought them serialized translations of European fiction, and taught them about new trends in scholarship, science, and fashion. They tended to preach a reformist political and cultural agenda. Many rabbis perceived the Ladino popular press as a threat because newspapers contained information they deemed un-Jewish and inappropriate and because a new generation of editors presented themselves as a source of alternative authority to the religious leadership. Among the rabbis who added their voices to these debates was Rabbi Judah Papo of Jerusalem (d. 1873), who presented his reflections on the topic in an 1870 Ladino edition of his father Eli'ezer Papo's Hebrew-language* Pele Yo'ets, *a classic of rabbinic ethical, or* musar, *literature. Rather than offering a direct translation of his father's work, Judah Papo adapted the book for a broad reading public by writing in Ladino, shortening parts of the original book, and including new chapters that responded to some of the changes Ottoman Jewry had experienced since the publication of his father's edition in 1826. In this source, Papo offers an optimistic reading of technological innovation as he reflects on the impact printed matter could have for the popularization of rabbinic writings, including his own work.*

How great is the benefit of the printing houses, for thanks to the power of the printing press, the Torah is enhanced everywhere in the world. The rabbis are certainly making the effort to produce books, but nothing is gained because for the most part they do not have the means to have them printed. It is appropriate for the notables to support them in this [endeavor], and by virtue [of their support] they become the partners of the rabbi and gain most of [the benefit], for the one who enables [Torah study] is greater than the one who engages [in Torah study himself]. . . . When we consider this, we find that there is no better use of money than [supporting the publication of rabbinic books], for all expenses in fulfillment of a religious commandment are temporary, while this [act] lasts for generations. Furthermore, [the sponsor] is considered to be the one who sustains the hand of the rabbi, especially when his is a book of [religious] law or ethics, for its virtue is very great, as in each generation all those who acquire virtue on account of this book, [the sponsor] will share [in their merit]. The merit of the masses is dependent on him and will give him much enjoyment in the world to come, where he is sure to receive gifts. . . .

Furthermore, there is [another] great benefit from printing in that it enables the enhancement of understanding and perfection in the entire world. The newspapers that are printed, even though they carry much information that is of no importance, still have useful things in them that allow a person to educate himself. All the sciences and all kinds of knowledge and all the arts come off the printing press, and there is always a piece of wisdom or knowledge or art that one would not find elsewhere. If someone gathers all the wisdom from all of them, he surely will become a wise person, affirming what it says in the verse: "I have more understanding than my teachers."[94] For the person who is learning from everyone educates himself, and this is what benefited people in Europe, where the sciences and knowledge and perfection continue to advance. Thank God that printing presses are now available everywhere and that there is [thus] a way for the Jewish people to derive much good from this.

*more*
*forward*
*looking*
*rabbinical*
*analysis*

Judah Papo, *Pele Yo'ets* (Vienna: Estamparia de Ya'akov HaKohen Shlosberg, 1870), 177–79. Translated from Ladino and introduced by Matthias Lehmann.

## 18.  AN ETIQUETTE HANDBOOK FOR SEPHARDI WOMEN (1871)

*This Ladino book, penned by a Sephardi woman of Istanbul, offers her female coreligionists lessons on how to become part of polite society by conveying to them bourgeois and Western-inspired rules of behavior and courtesy. The author, Rosa Gabbay (ca. 1850–ca. 1936), was the daughter of Yehezkel Gabbay II (1825–1898), a senior judge descended from an influential Baghdadi Jewish family long resident in the Ottoman capital and himself the founder of the Istanbul-based Ladino newspaper El Djurnal Israelit. Rosa Gabbay's father, a scholar, likely attended to the religious education of his daughter, which would account for Rosa Gabbay's erudition on religious matters as well as her reliance on Hebrew in her writing. As a woman Gabbay operated independently from the traditional centers of intellectual power in the Ottoman Jewish milieu, a circumstance that surely enabled her critique of existing formal educational options for Jewish girls.*

Praised be the Creator and exalted our Protector, who created this world . . . for the needs of the people, and who, at the end of his acts of creation, made man in the image of God, handed this world into his care, and gave him the intelligence to search for and understand things each in their turn, so that the more he studies, the more he understands the power and marvel of God's creation of the world and

94. Psalms 119:99.

everything that is in it. He also gave speech to the human being so that he could do everything his mind encompasses and apply reason to everything. Though man was created after everything else, He gave him power over all. But then He created woman, saying about her that it was not good [for man to be] without her. And if He placed obligations on men, He gave many more to women, and our wise sages lightened women's religious obligations, seeing that their material obligations were heavy and demanding. They instructed men to honor their wives and in return enriched them. Men without vision take these words literally and often say, "I have honored my wife but I am not rich." But if they took the trouble they would understand that the saying of our ancient masters is that the household is itself [a form of] wealth and that a man's family is entrusted to the care of his wife, so you should honor her and love her so that she in her turn may love you and strive for your wellbeing, for this is the greatest wealth and happiness a man can have. Happy is the banker whose cashier is loyal.

As I write these words it occurs to me that, since it is the woman who runs the household, she must have wide knowledge and be a good manager. For many centuries our nation ignored women's education but the nation itself did not progress.[95] Until now our leaders did not concern themselves about our women and, while they strove to advance men's education, they achieved nothing and there was no way to achieve it. But today we cannot deny that our leaders are exerting themselves to expand schools. The gentleman who occupies the presidency of the honorable Communal Council is not concentrating [any longer] on pointless business but rather on the development of schools, for here lies the prosperity of our nation. On his initiative a girls' school has been opened, as has been needed for many years. Finally the school has been opened, but there is not even a book in our language to begin teaching the youngest girls in order to give them some sort of start: at least five years are necessary to learn French and begin one's education, and it is not as easy for girls to learn foreign languages because there is no time for study.

We must concentrate on girls and educate them as soon as possible. On the basis of all these ideas and also as a reminder to my female

---

95. Here Gabbay appears to refer not to the Jewish people as a whole but rather to the Ottoman Jewish community in particular.

coreligionists and perhaps also to the men who may read this book or hear it read, I have undertaken this task and collected these ideas from some books that discuss French manners. I have added some of what is appropriate for Jews and I have shown that most good manners are already required by our Holy Law, but unfortunately women are lacking in knowledge of that law. We hope that reading this book will heal the wound of ignorance and replace it with a desire for knowledge and civilization and that they will [consequently] read more advanced books than this one, since our book is no more than a door and entrance to education and manners.

And because this is the first time, we have taken a great deal of trouble to abandon proper Spanish in order that it should not be a hindrance to those who do not understand it. [Instead] we have sought to use Oriental Spanish [Ladino] in the hope that our work will find acceptance by ladies and gentlemen and that it will be, for me and other women, an encouragement to continue to translate and publish books for the progress of our nation, for this was the desire of my youth and that is what I have learned from my dear parents.[96] My female friends! Let us awaken from the sleep in which we have been made to live! Let us seek our own advancement! Let us show that God created woman equal to men in cleverness and intelligence, and in a short time let us demonstrate our worth and put to shame those who do not appreciate women, and the God of Heaven will aid us. May all our knowledge and understanding be added to our fear and love of our Creator! . . .

The rules of good behavior and civilization are known by the word "courtesy." And since courtesy teaches the way in which young ladies should behave towards people, both in speech and actions, it should be an important part of girls' education.

In our world, women, who are half the human race, have to carry out tasks that form the basis of all human life. Do they not have to run a household? Do they not have to make their husbands happy? Or bring up children properly?

Women are children's first teachers before they are given into other hands for their education. Fénelon, a wise Frenchman, said, "Women can ruin or sustain a household, and part of the human race thus depends on

---

96. The reference here may be to the fact that Yehezkel Gabbay II, the author's father, translated two major legal works from Turkish to Ladino.

them. For this reason, what is bad or good in the world depends principally on them."

In another place the same sage said, "as good comes from women when they are well-educated, so also they inculcate evil when they lack good education."[97] It is well-proven that women's bad upbringing causes more evil than men's, given that men's bad behavior comes mostly from their being raised badly by their mothers. . . .

This is enough to prove that it is very important to educate girls well. The most important part of education is "courtesy," since real courtesy properly understood is no more than the application of the holy commands of our religion. It is well known that the whole of our Law can be summed up in one of its commandments: "Love your neighbor as yourself."

Courtesy took its first principles from our holy religion, which is the basis of civilization. It also grants us divine and human favor by inculcating good feelings in our hearts. It eradicates all those vices caused by a bad character or a savage nature. It helps us to remedy our faults.

Courtesy requires us to behave well, even those who are uncivilized and uncouth, so that we may expect that they will also become civilized. We must start by behaving well towards them.

Courtesy teaches us to behave well towards the aged, children and [all] our fellow human beings.

Rosa Gabbay, *La kortezia, o reglas del komportamiento* (Istanbul: Estamparia del Djurnal Israelit, 1871). Translated from Ladino by Michael Alpert.

## 19. IN A CITY OF GREEK CHRISTIANS: A JEWISH MAN'S QUANDARY (1874)

*Moses ben Raphael Pardo (d. 1888) lived much of his life in Jerusalem before assuming a rabbinical position in Alexandria, Egypt, in 1871. This document is derived from a collection of Pardo's responsa. It describes a married man who, after being lost at sea and stranded in a remote location, took a new wife out of the conviction that he had neither an alternative means of survival nor a viable way home. Once his circumstances changed and he was able to return to his previous life, the man*

---

97. These quotations are drawn from *De l'education des filles* (1687) by the French Roman Catholic poet, writer, theologian, and archbishop François de Salignac de la Mothe-Fénelon (1651–1715).

*asked whether he was permitted to remain married to his new wife and what his*
*obligations were to the wife he left behind. As is sometimes the case with such com-*
*pendia, it is difficult to ascertain the extent of its historical accuracy. It is certainly*
*possible—indeed, likely—that the man who sent his query to Pardo exaggerated the*
*gravity of his quandary in order to help his case.*

An event occurred in which a certain man traveled to conduct business and his ship sank in the sea. Thank God he knew how to swim
and was saved. He ended up in a city in which all the residents were
Greek Christians. He had nothing at all with him but his body and
had no place to sleep until a certain Christian who had a hut took pity
and allowed him to sleep there for two or three nights. [The Jew] did
not even have means to buy a crust of bread. He went out to beg but
nobody sympathized or pitied him when they saw that he was a Jew.
They did tell him that if he would convert they would feed him, give
him to drink, and clothe him. He did not eat for three days, going
hungry and with no clothes to protect him from the cold.

On the third day the owner of the hut said to him, "I see the distress in your face. Tell me what you do, whence you come, and from
what nation you derive."[98] He told him everything that had happened,
and [the hut owner] said to him, "Look, there is one Jew with his
household living here in this town. Come with me and I will show you
his shop. Maybe he will like you and take care of you. You should not
think that that there is any hope at this time for your future and that
you will return home, for the sea is growing more stormy before the
anger of the oppressor right now, when vortices are common in the
narrow sea and there is no governor or judge overseeing us. No ship at
all will pass through here because of the fear of wars; each person will
go to take care of his own plunder."

When the poor man heard this he wept. The hut owner took him
to the shop of the [only] Jewish man [in town] and he fell at his feet
crying and beseeching him, "Please, take care of me, [at least as you
would] a dog and you will keep me alive, for we are brothers!" This
man then said to him, "Know and understand that I have a daughter
who is long since grown up. I am here in exile in this city, which I am
unable to escape in any way because of the terror of the sea. Not even

---

98. See Jonah 1:8.

a bird has been able to fly here for the past seven years. I speak out of fear lest, God forbid, she end up prostituting herself with one of these Christians. Even at night my heart is not still for she is already advanced in years, over twenty. How happy is your fate, young man, if she should become your wife! I would take care of all your needs, my son—you will eat to your satisfaction and you will oversee my household like a son for his father."

*plot twist*

The poor man responded to him, "Sir, how can I do this? First of all, I am bound by an oath that I took to my wife that I would never marry an additional wife during her lifetime. Furthermore, there are no [Jewish] witnesses to perform the wedding. How can I sleep with her in the absence of matrimony, which cannot be performed with fewer than two [Jews]?" The man answered him that despite all this, if he did not marry her he would not give him anything at all.

This poor man was starving to death, but he suffered fasting for two more days, at which point he saw that he could not take any more. Under this duress he permitted himself [the marriage], acceded to the wishes of the old man, and married the woman. After some time the danger abated and he returned to settled lands along with his aforementioned second wife. He came [to the rabbis] to ask whether he had done the proper thing, whether he must divorce her and remain with his first wife, whether he needed a writ of divorce in light of the fact that there were no witnesses there, and even though she had given birth to two children who were products of an improper union, whether the oath [to his first wife] was void because it was broken. He also asked whether, if he were allowed to stay with [the second wife], he should hold a betrothal ceremony. His heart was constricted and troubled because of the love he had for her and her two children. The issue of providing [for her] was also weighing on him, because his [second] father-in-law had passed away, leaving him a great deal of money. She [the first wife] herself was crying and weeping over the husband of her youth. He also asked whether, if he were forced to divorce his first wife, he could remain with the new one.

Moses ben Raphael Pardo, *Sefer Shemo Moshe* (Izmir, 1874), Question 9, pp. 60r–65v. Translated from Hebrew by Matt Goldish.

## 20. AN UNREPENTANT WIFE: A DIVORCE
## IN IZMIR (1878)

*Whether undertaken for romantic, religious, or financial reasons, conversion was rare but possible for Ottoman Jews. Although rabbinic authorities did all they could to prevent apostasy within their communities, a small but steady number of Jews converted to Islam over the many centuries of Ottoman rule and, after the government legalized conversion to religions other than Islam in the nineteenth century, to various Christian denominations as well. For men the choice might allow them to rise in the ranks of the Ottoman administration or flee enemies within the Jewish community or a wife who refused a divorce. For women the reasons were often social or pecuniary: conversion could offer a means of escaping the social stigma of prostitution or adultery or the hardships of poverty. In the following source we learn of a divorce case involving a Jewish woman charged with engaging in illicit sexual relations with non-Jews. Such women were considered by rabbinic authorities to be at risk of apostasy. Having already converted once before, this woman, identified only as Rusha, had apparently returned to Judaism following her husband's intervention, a process so expensive it had pauperized him. The case, which mandated the divorce of the couple in question, points to the potentially fluid nature of the religious boundary dividing Ottoman Jews and non-Jews.*

On the first day of the week, the fourth day of the month of Nisan in the year 5637 [1877] from the creation of the world, Solomon, son of Moses (Zani), presented a certificate of divorce of his own free will to the hand of his wife, Rusha, daughter of David, who is known as Bekhor (Mosagi). The matter was urgent because the eighth hour had already arrived when we commenced and it could not be left even for the next day. The reason for this [rush] was that we feared that she would go and apostatize, as she had done the previous year. She had converted and her husband had to spend more than a thousand kuruş on her to return her to her nation and to her God. The husband furthermore is now such a poor man that he is unable to pay the fee of a scribe,[99] so [the certificate] was drawn up for him free of charge.

We only composed one certificate of divorce, with no points.[100] We constructed it according to the formulation of Rabbi Solomon ben Hasson of blessed memory, and [the husband] placed it in her hand with neither points nor a signature. It was afterward conveyed to a scribe in order that he fill in the details. [He] commanded the wit-

---

99. Babylonian Talmud, Bava Metsi'a 17r.
100. That is, details of date and place were not completed.

nesses to sign it, which they did. They then gave it to [the wife], telling her, "He has already divorced you, etc."

The reason for this divorce was that it had become known to those who assess fines that she had conducted illicit sexual relations multiple times with non-Jews, may God have mercy. At this time she is in her fifth month of pregnancy. We made them swear that they would never remarry each other. The signatories, along with me, were Rabbi Isaac Nissim al-Granati (may God preserve him), and Rabbi Isaac Crispin (may God preserve him), who served as the witnesses and the scribe mentioned above.

[Postscript:] She gave birth to a son on the ninth day of Sivan and his mother [i.e. Rusha] did not want to nurse him. The baby was immediately taken to the home of her divorced husband about whom we spoke. Now this man, upon seeing his troubles and [understanding] that he did not have the money to hire a wet nurse, went and enlisted under the flag of the military, may God return him in peace.[101] Three days later he regretted what he had done and returned home, where the charities of the city assumed responsibility for the child (may they see God's mercy on Zion).

Nissim Haim Moda'i, *Meimar Hayim*, vol. 2: *Even ha-Ezer* (Izmir: Hayim Abraham de Segura, 1878), Question 39, part 41, 66r–66v. Translated from Hebrew by Matt Goldish.

## 21. TURKISH MUSIC IN THE SYNAGOGUE: THE OBJECTIONS OF A RABBI [1881–1902]

*This memoir, the first known in the Ladino language, was written by one of the pillars of modern secular Ladino letters, Sa'adi Besalel a-Levi (1820–1903). Sa'adi, as he was known by contemporaries, was the founding editor of Salonica's longest-running Ladino newspaper,* La Epoka, *as well as the city's most popular French-language newspaper,* Le Journal de Salonique. *Sa'adi's memoir was published by his sons in installments in* La Epoka *shortly after his death. Later, in the 1930s, excerpts of the memoir were issued again by the Ladino journal* La Aksion *of Salonica, demonstrating a sustained interest in the life of this pioneer of Salonican Jewish publishing. Although by profession a printer, Sa'adi was by passion a musician, composer, and performer. Distinguished Jewish composers like Sa'adi were an integral and highly integrated*

---

101. That is, the husband voluntarily conscripted himself for service in the Ottoman military, which was then involved in a war with Russia.

*part of the Ottoman musical landscape: they trained and practiced with non-Jewish masters; the most distinguished of them in turn trained both Jewish and non-Jewish apprentices. In this passage, Sa'adi recounts the opposition of members of the Salonican rabbinic establishment to his performance, in the synagogue, of a traditional Hebrew prayer set in a Turkish musical mode. This episode was one of many that pitted the reformist-minded publisher against Salonica's religious authorities, ultimately resulting in his excommunication, an event that haunted him for the rest of his life.*

The *sinyor Rav h"r*[102] Shaul had a strong aversion to the Turkish language to the extent that he would excommunicate anyone singing Turkish songs. Not only Turkish songs, but even a Jewish liturgical poem chanted in a Turkish mode or copying a known Turkish song.

Let me tell you a story, my dear readers! I did tell you earlier that I, the author of this account, lost my father at the age of five or six and my mother at the age of sixteen or seventeen and that I was left with a ten- or twelve-year-old brother who had kidney disease. Under these circumstances I dedicated myself body and soul to my printing business, but my income was pitiful. I had a great love of the art of singing given my promising voice.

Among Jews we had a certain *maestro* who knew many Hebrew songs. He knew some twenty *fasıls* in varying *makams*, with three *peşrevs*, *bestes*, *kiyares*, *samayis*, etc. etc.[103] He also knew the chants of the Days of Awe. His name was *h"r* Aaron Barzilay. In a previous celebration he had heard me sing a couple of Turkish songs I was taught by the Turkish master singer Murteza İzeddinoğlu, who had an extraordinary voice. This *maestro* liked me almost as if I was his own son and used to ask me to sing with him in various festivities. *Maestro*, *h"r* Aaron Barzilay also took me under his wing, teaching me all that he knew.

At that time a certain rich and scholarly *sinyor hakham*[104] had to marry his son. This *hakham* was *h"r* Yeuda Alkalay [d. 1849],[105] who ran the Great *Yeshiva* of *rabanim* in his house, called the Alkalay Yeshiva.

---

102. Hebrew acronym for *hakham ribi*, indicating that the man in question was a rabbi and scholar of Jewish law.
103. The Hebrew songs in question are set to these Ottoman modes. A *fasıl* is a concert program; *peşrev* is the best known Ottoman musical form played as prelude; *bestes* are the words of a musical composition; a *kiyare* is a piece sung after a *peşrev*; and *samayi* is a Turkish musical rhythmic pattern.
104. Sephardi rabbi.
105. Alkalay was a publisher of rabbinic works, including a commentary on the *Zohar*, and was reputed to have a very large private library.

Twice a year, he held a reception for the *hakhamim*,[106] with me and my young brother as singers.

A day before the wedding, he invited me to sing in his house for the eight days, on condition that I arrange a new song for the *kidush*[107] chanted during wedding ceremony. I composed a melody based on the *kadish*,[108] while I also asked four to five handsome young men to join me for rehearsals to prepare them to sing it. The synagogue was filled with *rabanim*,[109] *hakhamim*, and the entire aristocracy of Salonica before the arrival of the groom. When the time for the singing of the *kadish* came, my colleagues and I ascended the *bima*[110] to sing the *kadish* in the *hüzzam* mode.[111] The multitude of people in the synagogue attending this wedding were overwhelmed with this *kadish* they were hearing for the first time in this brand new melody. All of them congratulated me for my skillful rendition of this *kadish*, except for the *sinyor Rav h"r* Shaul, who paid no attention to my singing the *kadish*, having never in his lifetime enjoyed any singing. When he went home accompanied by eight to ten of his friends, he removed his cape and sat on his elevated cushion for some rest; he was asked if he had enjoyed the *kadish* that Sa'adi had arranged based on a Turkish melody. The *sinyor rav* hit the roof when he heard this question, saying, "What a wicked person to sing a Turkish melody inside the synagogue! Immediately, go and tell *h"r* Yeuda that he cannot employ such a wicked one for his celebration."

When *h"r* Yeuda heard the words of the beadle, he became incensed and turned red like a beet. He said, "Is he also trying now to order us around to do this and not that?" All those important people who had been invited to this wedding were equally infuriated to hear such talk. But *sinyor Rav h"r* Shelomo Pipano begged *h"r* Yeuda not to get too upset, because he would be able to convince the *Rav h"r* Shaul to retract the message he sent. He went at once to see the *rav* and to demand a satisfactory explanation, telling him, "By what right did you send a message asking him not to hire this singer for his celebration?"

106. Hebrew masculine plural of *hakham*.
107. Sanctification.
108. An Aramaic doxology recited between different parts of the Jewish liturgy or after a study session.
109. Rabbis.
110. Raised platform in a synagogue from which the Torah is read.
111. Makam or musical mode.

His response to *h"r* Yeuda was that "this singer is a wicked person because he sings in the Turkish style and sang the *kadish* in synagogue according to the Turkish style." To these words *h"r* Shelomo retorted, "Aren't all of our liturgical poems written in our sacred tongue chanted in the Turkish style? Please, refer yourself to the book composed by the Rav Nadjara,[112] and you will notice that every one of them bears the mention of a Turkish mode.[113] Rabbi Yeuda a-Levi[114] composed his liturgical poems for the Days of Awe, specifically those of the Day of Atonement, based on Arabic modes." Having never known anything about music his entire life, *Rav* Shaul was utterly surprised to hear *h"r* Shelomo's words. He was finally convinced! He sent word to *h"r* Yeuda that this was an involuntary mistake, that what he heard had misled him, and that now he was free to do as he pleased, on condition that there be no Turkish-style songs.

Aron Rodrigue and Sarah Abrevaya Stein, eds., *A Jewish Voice from Ottoman Salonica: The Ladino Memoir of Sa'adi Besalel a-Levi*, with a transliteration, translation, and Glossary by Isaac Jerusalmi (Stanford, CA: Stanford University Press, 2012), 24–26.

## 22. AMBIVALENT RECOLLECTIONS OF A JEWISH BOARDER IN AN OTTOMAN IMPERIAL HIGH SCHOOL {1880s}

*Sam Lévy (né Shemuel Sa'adi a-Levi, 1870–1959) published the most popular French- and Ladino-language newspapers in Salonica (*Le Journal du Salonique *and* La Epoka, *respectively), from the late 1890s until 1911. He came from a long line of Jewish printers that included his father, Sa'adi Besalel a-Levi, the founder of the aforementioned journals. Lévy pursued multiple paths of politicization. Early in his life he defended Ladino against those Ottoman Jewish intellectuals who advocated abandoning the language in favor of French, Hebrew, or Ottoman Turkish. He also promoted the idea that Ottoman Jews should begin to acquire fluency in Ottoman Turkish, a language the majority of Jews did not read. He himself learned Ottoman while at-*

---

112. Israel ben Moses Nadjara (ca. 1555–1625) was a famous poet, kabbalist, and musician. Born in Damascus, he died in Gaza.

113. Because there existed a controversy about using Ottoman musical modes in liturgical texts as part of a Jewish prayer service, the *maftirim* (or special repertoire of Ottoman Jewish hymns) are considered paraliturgical. While various pieces in the traditional liturgy were composed according to Arabic prosody, full awareness of their origin disappeared over time.

114. Judah Ha-Levi (ca. 1075-1141) was a renowned philosopher and poet of medieval Muslim Spain.

*tending an imperial high school in Salonica, to which he was admitted with the help
of his brother, Daut Efendi, a prominent government official. While still a young
man, Lévy spent time in Paris, where he witnessed firsthand the political strife of the
Dreyfus affair, an experience that further politicized him as a Jew. (For more on Lévy
see sources 67, 89, and 125; on his father, Sa'adi Besalel a-Levi, see sources 21 and 33.)*

My older brother, Daut Efendi, who was director of the Bureau of Passports, was also the personal secretary of Rauf Pasha, governor-general
of the province, and was very close with all the high officials. He campaigned on my behalf to Director of Public Education Emrullah Efendi,
who had received the order to create an imperial high school in Salonica.
I was one of the first to be enrolled in this new establishment as a resi-
dential student.

The high school was housed in two enormous villas . . . surrounded
by vast courtyards and beautiful Andalusian gardens, all donated to
the state by an old and extremely rich pasha who lived in Istanbul. Its
position at the top of the hill . . . was idyllic.

Often on starry nights or nights when you could not see the moon,
some of my bunkmates and I would spend hours promenading along
the old ramparts, reciting poems of Fuzuli's *Gülistan*[115] or entire pages
of Namık Kemal's adaptations of *Télémaque*.[116] Namık Kemal was the
most illustrious Turkish writer of the nineteenth century. His work
was to the then burgeoning Ottoman sentimental literature what
Fénelon[117] was to the Romanticism of his day.

My studies at the high school lasted three years. I was baptized
Kemal. It is almost embarrassing for me to report, [but] I learned clas-
sical Turkish literature better than my Muslim peers. My deep knowledge of Hebrew roots, which had the same origin as those of Arabic,
and the inflections and flexibility of the Latin languages—Spanish, Italian, and French—which were all familiar to me, all made more comprehensible and palatable the vocabulary and turns of phrase of the
Turkish-Arabic-Persian amalgam that formed the composite [Otto-
man] Turkish language.

---

115. Lévy appears to refer here to the collection entitled *Gülistan*, which was composed in 1259
by the Persian poet Sadi, not the Ottoman author Fuzuli (ca. 1483–1556).

116. It was in fact not Namık Kemal but rather Yusuf Kamil Pasha, grand vizier during the
reign of Sultan Abdülaziz, who in 1861 translated François Fénelon's 1699 novel *Les aventures de
Télémaque* into Ottoman Turkish.

117. François Fénelon (1651–1715), French Roman Catholic author and theologian.

This impressed the entire school. Teachers and students alike demonstrated a special sympathy for me. The director of public education
informed my brother, saying, "Daut, if things continue this way we're
going to make Kemal into a professor of Turkish literature."

This sympathy, or rather the clear affection of which I was the object, had a hidden goal (as I was to realize a bit too late). Teachers
and students, especially the Arabic professor . . . and General Director
Abdullah Efendi, were wont to speak with praise of the religion of
Islam that was destined to conquer the world. They secretly dreamt
of bringing me into the mosque and, who knows, perhaps making me
accomplish the sacred pilgrimage to the Ka'aba, the famous rock carefully preserved in the great mosque of Mecca! It was a great glory for
each of them to spare an infidel soul from perdition. . . .

Yet the seeds of religious skepticism had already been planted in me.
. . . I should also say that I did not always comport myself: I had an
impulsive and argumentative character. Thus these attempts at shaping me made me angry. At this moment the charm [of the school] was
broken. . . .

[At this point one of the Qur'anic instructors at the school approached him]: "Kemal, if you adopt Islam . . . I will give you a present
of this Qur'an, richly composed and copied entirely by my own hand."

I responded innocently that Judaism was older and superior to all
other religions and even it could not hold me captive. . . .

As he heard these words Abdullah Efendi flew into a rage; he in-
sulted me and sent other students after me. This was a bad sign. I was
the only Jew among 300 boarders. Frankly I was terrified.

From that night on no one tried to convert me: the students
changed their tactics. The sympathetic interest they had shown me—to
the level of hypocrisy—changed overnight into a ferocious jealousy and
a profound aversion animated by the famous doctor Nazım Bey. . . .

The open hostility to which I became subject and which was announced constantly became a reason to live. My classmates still acknowledged my superiority in the physical and natural sciences. But
they could not pardon me for being stronger than they in their own
language. They could never swallow what for them was such a bitter
pill. Two events, rather insignificant in themselves, brought their rage to
its height and were the cause of the intractable hatred they felt for me.

One day a commission came unannounced from Istanbul along with the minister of public education. They halted classes and instead began to interview the students spontaneously about the material they studied. They also came to our class. One of these men proceeded to take a piece of chalk and trace an Arabic phrase, which I cannot erase from my memory, on the board. After doing so he turned towards the students and said with authority, "Translate this for me. He who gives the proper answer will be rewarded."

The students remained in awe, dumbstruck. No one broke the deep silence. I timidly raised my hand. Invited to come up to the chalkboard, I wrote the following translation: "I love pacifists and I am one myself because Allah nourishes me with peace."

"Wonderful [the man responded]! What is your name, my son?"

"Kemal, sir."

"Kemal what?"

"Kemal Levi, sir."

"Are you Turkish?"

"Yes, sir."

"Muslim?"

"No sir, I am from the Jewish *millet*."[118]

"And are there other Jews here?"

"Among the boarders no, but there are five day students."

"Do they know Turkish as well as you?"

"I don't think so, sir."

"Where have you learned our national language?"

"At the Alliance Israélite [Universelle] school, sir."

"Thank you, my son."

Emrullah Efendi intervened and said to the inspector, "This young man is the brother of the director of the Bureau of Passports, Daut Efendi, an esteemed high official."

"I would like to make his acquaintance in order to congratulate him." Then, addressing the students, the inspector remarked, "I urge you to pursue your studies as your classmate Kemal Levi does."

*Sam Lévy, "Mes memoires: Salonique à la fin du XIXe siècle," in Isaac Rafael Molho, ed., Tesoro de los judíos sefardíes: Estudios sobre la historia de los judíos sefardíes y su cultura, vol. 6 (Jerusalem: Ahva, 1959), lviii–lxii. Translated from French by Julia Phillips Cohen.*

---

118. Officially recognized religious community within the Ottoman Empire.

## 23.  JEWISH WOMEN VISIT A DERVISH LODGE (1897)

*Jewish journalists in the Ottoman Empire frequently used the pages of Ladino news-*
*papers to advocate for reforms within their communities. At times they urged local*
*leaders to reform communal administrations, support novel educational efforts, or re-*
*linquish power in order to create more democratic institutions. Just as frequently they*
*called upon their coreligionists to modify their public behavior. Among the practices*
*the Ladino press decried were Jews' habits of praying aloud on city streets, promenad-*
*ing and getting drunk in public, and begging for money from non-Jewish neighbors.*
*In nearly all cases Ladino-language editorials criticized Jews for refusing to abide*
*by the rules of public propriety, particularly when their transgressions exposed them*
*to the ridicule or contempt of non-Jews. In addition to addressing their coreligionists*
*directly through the medium of the newspaper, Ottoman Jewish journalists regularly*
*called upon the police and local rabbis to use their power to end transgressive behav-*
*ior. The following source, which appeared in the Ladino serial* El Meseret *of Izmir,*
*is typical in this respect, though its subject matter is more unusual. Here we find*
*middle-class Jewish housewives frequenting the local lodge of a Sufi Muslim ascetic*
*group known as the dervish order. Their actions reflect the porous nature of relations*
*between members of different religious communities in the Ottoman Empire, where*
*men and women of different religions often studied together, played music together,*
*and visited one another's house of worship. It is possible that in this case the Jewish*
*women who gathered at Izmir's dervish lodge got caught up in the ecstatic nature*
*of the ceremonies they watched and drew unwanted attention to themselves in the*
*process. Given the gendered and religious dimensions of this scenario, it is hardly sur-*
*prising that their activities offended the bourgeois sensibilities of the Jewish journalists*
*who made it their mission to stop them.*

We have already spoken on another occasion of the scandals that occur
during public promenades [Jews take] in the summertime. The chief
rabbi has responded to our pleas and has issued a directive [to preach-
ers in the synagogues of the city] to preach that meetings in said places
should be halted immediately, and that [violators] will be subject to
punishment by the police.

Now [we are compelled to discuss] something even more delicate
and shameful: the visits our Jewish housewives of various classes make
on Sundays to the dervish lodge. [On these occasions] some one hundred, two hundred, or possibly more women, girls, children, and even
a few elderly ladies gather together in this place. They go there to yell
and interrupt the prayers of the dervishes and at times even close off
the passage to the men who come [to the lodge] until they are finally
thrown out.

We therefore feel obliged to bring this issue to the attention of our venerable chief rabbi. We ask that he arrange for announcements to be made in the synagogues tomorrow, on Shabbat, that our women should stop visiting the dervish lodges and making us look ridiculous in the eyes of the nations.[119]

"En la tekiye del bazariko," *El Meseret*, May 7, 1897, 2. Translated from Ladino by Julia Phillips Cohen.

## 24.  A LADINO JOURNAL CONDEMNS WOMEN'S SINGING IN CAFÉS ON THE SABBATH (1900)

*The Ottoman musical world was inherently multi-sectarian, multilingual, and multiethnic, with Muslims, Christians, and Jews sharing a repertoire, creating music together, and learning at the feet of the same masters. During the late Ottoman era some women and girls became public singers—in violation of Talmudic injunction—out of economic necessity. Even when they willingly chose the profession, they often faced familial and social censure for taking up what was broadly considered a disreputable profession. The following editorial, drawn from the Ladino newspaper* La Epoka *of Salonica in 1900, conveys the scorn female performers regularly encountered, as it denounces the activities of two young Jewish women who had taken to giving concerts along Salonica's waterfront. The author's principal targets were the girls' mothers, as he believed they were to blame for supporting and possibly even organizing their daughters' performances. More troubling still, he reasoned, was the fact that they sang on the Sabbath and sought profit for their performances, thereby desecrating the Jews' day of rest. This source not only documents how dramatically gender norms were shifting within the Ottoman Jewish community at the turn of the twentieth century; it also illustrates how these changes took shape in tandem with the evolution of public space.*

Along the quay, near the White Tower, there is a café where two young Jewish girls from Salonica sing every day, including Shabbat. In truth we do not find their behavior as low as that of other young women, since [in this case] it is driven by pure necessity. What we cannot tolerate is the presence of their mothers in their *kofyas*, *antares*, and *devantales* at their daughters' concerts.[120]

Let us explain our position. It is not enough that these women, who

---

119. Here the Ladino *nasiones* refers to the other religious communities of Izmir.
120. The author refers here to the traditional clothing of Sephardi women.

call themselves Jews, take great pleasure in permitting their daughters' shameful performances. By asking them to work on Shabbat they also commit a thousand base deeds that bring no honor whatsoever to our nation [the Jews].

We felt it was our duty to call the attention of the authorities to this matter. We ask that they do everything in their power to protect us from condemnation. We have been informed that there exists a group of young men willing to present themselves to the chief rabbinate in order to bring forward further information about this issue so as to prevent a great desecration of God's name and of the name of our people.

Yeremiah (el yoron), "El repozo de Shabat," *La Epoka*, August 10, 1900, 5. Translated from Ladino by Julia Phillips Cohen.

## 25. "A SPANISH ATTITUDE": ELIAS CANETTI'S CHILDHOOD REMINISCENCES OF BULGARIA {1905–1911}

*Winner of the Nobel Prize in Literature in 1991 and many other distinguished literary awards, Elias Canetti (1905–1994) spent the first six years of his life in Rusçuk (Ruse, Bulgaria), a port town on the Danube River. Canetti's family, which counted among its members the earliest founders of Rusçuk's Jewish community, left Bulgaria in 1911, moving first to England and subsequently to Austria, where Canetti studied chemistry at the University of Vienna, gravitated toward leftist politics, and began a career as a writer, publishing four memoirs, multiple novels and plays, and various influential works of nonfiction. Though Canetti spoke many languages, including Ladino, his mother tongue, he always wrote in German, repeatedly revisiting his own childhood and youth in autobiographical works. In the following selection Canetti looks back with ambivalence on the formative years of his life. Although he fondly recalls the multiethnic and multi-religious life of the city, composed, as he remembers it, of Albanians, Armenians, Circassians, Greeks, Jews, Roma (Gypsies), Romanians, and Russians, he recoils from the parochialism and haughty pride he believed his mother exhibited in her attachment to the family's Spanish Jewish identity.*

Ruschuk, on the lower Danube, where I came into the world, was a marvelous city for a child, and if I say that Ruschuk is in Bulgaria, then I am giving an inadequate picture of it. For people of the most varied backgrounds lived there, on anyone day you could hear seven or eight languages. Aside from the Bulgarians, who often came from the countryside, there were many Turks, who lived in their own neighborhood, and next to it was the neighborhood of the Sephardim, the Spanish Jews—our neighborhood. There were Greeks, Albanians, Armenians, Gypsies. From the opposite side of the Danube came Rumanians; my wet nurse, whom I no longer remember, was Rumanian. There were also Russians here and there.

As a child, I had no real grasp of this variety, but I never stopped feeling its effects. Some people have stuck in my memory only because they belonged to a particular ethnic group and wore a different costume from the others. Among the servants that we had in our home during the course of six years, there was once a Circassian and later on an Armenian. My mother's best friend was Olga, a Russian woman. Once every week, Gypsies came into our courtyard, so many that they seemed like an entire nation; the terrors they struck in me will be discussed below.

Ruschuk was an old port on the Danube, which made it fairly significant. As a port, it had attracted people from all over, and the Danube was a constant topic of discussion. There were stories about the extraordinary years when the Danube froze over; about sleigh rides all the way across the ice to Rumania; about starving wolves at the heels of the sleigh horses.

Wolves were the first wild animals I heard about. In the fairy tales that the Bulgarian peasant girls told me, there were werewolves, and one night, my father terrorized me with a wolf mask on his face.

It would be hard to give a full picture of the colorful time of those early years in Ruschuk, the passions and the terrors. Anything I subsequently experienced had already happened in Ruschuk. There, the rest of the world was known as "Europe," and if someone sailed up the Danube to Vienna, people said he was going to Europe. Europe began where the Turkish Empire had once ended. Most of the Sephardim were still Turkish subjects. Life had always been good for them under the Turks, better than for the Christian Slavs in the Balkans. But since many Sephardim were well-to-do merchants, the new Bulgarian regime maintained good relations with them, and King Ferdinand, who ruled for a long time, was said to be a friend of the Jews.

The loyalties of the Sephardim were fairly complicated. They were pious Jews, for whom the life of their religious community was rather important. But they considered themselves a special brand of Jews, and that was because of their Spanish background. Through the centuries since their expulsion from Spain, the Spanish they spoke with one another had changed little. A few Turkish words had been absorbed, but they were recognizable as Turkish, and there were nearly always Spanish words for them. The first children's songs I heard were Spanish, I heard old Spanish *romances*; but the thing that was most powerful, and irresistible for a child, was a Spanish attitude. With naive arrogance, the Sephardim looked down on other Jews; a word always charged with scorn was *Todesco*, meaning a German or Ashkenazi Jew. It would have been unthinkable to marry a *Todesca*, a Jewish woman of that background, and among the many families that I heard about or knew as a child in Ruschuk, I cannot recall a single case of such a mixed marriage. I wasn't even six years old when my grandfather warned me against such a misalliance in the future. But this general discrimination wasn't all. Among the Sephardim themselves, there were the "good families," which meant the ones that had been rich since way back. The proudest words one could hear about a person were: "*Es de buena famiglia*—he's from a good family." How often and *ad nauseam* did I hear that from my mother. When she enthused about the Viennese *Burgtheater* and read Shakespeare with me, even later on, when she spoke about Strindberg, who became her favorite author, she had no scruples whatsoever about telling that she came from a good family, there was no better family around. Although the literatures of the civilized languages she knew became the true substance of her life, she never felt any contradiction between this passionate universality and the haughty family pride that she never stopped nourishing.

## 26. "A LIFE FULL OF DRAMA AND DANGER": MEMORIES OF AN OTTOMAN JEWISH POLICEMAN (1911)

*This source is drawn from the second chapter of the memoirs of an Ottoman Jewish police chief who served his state during the era of the Ottoman sultan Abdülhamid II (r. 1876–1909). Publishing his account in a Ladino newspaper of Izmir just two years after a constitutional regime removed Abdülhamid II from power, the author speaks of his mistreatment and arrest at the hands of former government officials. By the time of his writing, it had become fashionable to criticize the autocratic policies of the old regime. However, the appearance of Raphael Chikurel's story was occasioned not only by the trends of his day but also by a personal tale of tragedy; of unsubstantiated accusations of conspiracy against the government, of midnight arrest, economic deprivation, and social isolation. In the following passage he promises to spare no one of any religion or rank in his quest to expose his one-time accusers and persecutors.*

All the false rumors made me suffer morally, but I never lost my courage at any point. I always maintained my sangfroid, as I was convinced that sooner or later my innocence would come to light. Little by little the rumors subsided and the question was closed, as I was unjustly suspended from my position. This was the generous payment that the government saw fit to give me in exchange for my many services rendered to the Ottoman state. For a certain time I let things pass quietly, but six months after my dismissal I officially demanded a certificate of good service, which was given to me with the best marks on July 1, 1907.

During the 4,596 days of my service with the police I only slept 697 at my home. The rest I spent in different police stations. It is hardly necessary to add that throughout my career those colleagues who were jealous of my advancements made me suffer morally and without reason to the extent that, while everyone believed I was the most fortunate among them, I was without any doubt the one who suffered every agony, although without showing it.

On the other hand, people believed that I was in good financial shape while in fact I also suffered materially and searched for a way to support my family after my dismissal. This concern preoccupied me day and night. After five months of being unemployed I began to consider associating myself with the "Francos' Press," where I had certain economic interests.[121]

Because the financial state of this press did not yield sufficient profit for three partners, we decided to enlarge the business and its capital. I did not then have the necessary funds, so I was obliged to sell a little house I owned in the mountains along with all of my family's jewelry to Mr. Shalom Core of the French Quarter, all of which yielded 250 liras. In this manner we came up with some 2,000 liras, 460 of which were mine. On July 1, 1907, under the title "Chikurel, Franco, and Company," we founded our new business, with Hezekiah Franco as the head associate.

In this world everything, or almost everything, is illusion and dreams. In the moment when everything appears bright and clear, in the moment when the entire path in front of you seems smooth and without obstacles, in the moment when only smiling faces appear from all directions, suddenly a negligible thing, a silly little thing, a simple suspicion surfaces to throw trouble into the soul and pain into the heart.

Such was my situation when I suddenly found that I was lucky to be free and independent. It was precisely at that moment that I began dedicating all of my energy and influence toward the advancement of our press.

One day (it was a Thursday, 4 Heshvan 5668 [September 29, 1907]) as I stood in front of the barracks waiting for the tram to arrive, Mr. Jacques Hazan, a real estate agent, approached me and said, "Mr. Daniel Shaul has charged me with communicating to you that a certain bey[122] at the imperial palace has opened a case against you. If you want to avoid the confusion and peril that awaits you, you should find him and make the appropriate arrangements." I thanked Mr. Hazan for the trouble he had taken, and with a clear conscience I attributed little importance to the matter.

At midnight on 8 Heshvan, in other words four days after my encounter with Mr. Hazan, at a time when my wife was quite pregnant, my house was surrounded and blockaded by a group of deputies and agents of police. Among them was a certain hunchback by the name of Hacı Kadri who had once been the bootblack and waiter in a local café

---

121. At the time the partners in the press were Hezekiah and Gad Franco.
122. An honorific referring here to someone in the employ of the Ottoman government.

and was now the furniture maker and spy of the imperial palace as well as one of Mr. Daniel Shaul's henchmen.

After a thousand hesitations and many whispers among themselves they knocked on the door. I opened it. I was surprised to see so many police agents at first, but soon the words of Mr. Hazan seemed to have been written in letters of fire before my eyes. I quickly decided to invite the police in. As soon as they entered the house my wife and children were struck with terror. All at once I attempted to calm my family and ask these good people why they had decided to pay me a visit.

The police agents began combing the house, overturning the furniture, drawers, mattresses, and carpets. They took everything that they thought might compromise me. This job completed, they arrested me and brought me to the printing press. There too they helped themselves to many papers.

I was placed under surveillance without being able to communicate with anyone. I remained completely in the dark about the reasons behind my mistreatment and arrest. Nonetheless I had strong suspicions concerning the identity of the person who had worked to bring my downfall. In fact the same day I was arrested, I saw Hacı Kadri pass by in a carriage with Mr. Daniel Shaul. This small incident as well as the warning Mr. Hazan had given me began to shed some light on this mysterious drama in which I was soon to become the principal actor. But for the time being I will limit myself to relating the facts. Later on everything that needs to be revealed will be revealed and without mercy.

Among the documents that were confiscated at the office of the printing press were letters sent to me by Gad Franco[123] during his time in the capital. They contained certain passages in which he discussed the injustices and indecent acts that the government functionaries of that time committed. As a result Mr. Franco, fearful of remaining in Izmir, departed for Egypt.

All of these documents and letters were translated at the palace by Mr. Solomon Crispin, the former accountant of the [Jewish] community of Izmir. During this period he was visiting the capital together with Mr. Bekhor Arosas on community business. I learned all of this

---

123. Gad Franco (1880–1952), relative and business partner of Hezekiah Franco, was a journalist and lawyer in Izmir. (For more on Gad Franco see source 68; for more on Hezekiah Franco see source 133.)

directly from Mr. Crispin himself; when he ran into me some time later
he informed me that in order to do me a favor he had not translated
the documents word-for-word and had attenuated their harsh tone.
He continued by telling me that this mission had been assigned to him
by none other than the brother of Mr. Bekhor Arosas, who spent a
great deal of time at the palace in those days.

Seven days after my arrest I learned that I stood accused of having facilitated the escape of Ali Haydar Bey, son of the late Midhat
Pasha,[124] during my time working at the passport office. Ali Haydar
Bey was then living in Europe, and I was also accused of maintaining a
correspondence with him.

Raphael Chikurel, "Una vida yena de drama i perikulos: mis memorias," *La Boz del Puevlo* 18
(March 3, 1911), 1. Translated from Ladino by Julia Phillips Cohen.

## 27. ABUSES IN THE REGULATION OF KOSHER MEAT
## IN BELGRADE [1913]

*The place of Jews in the fledgling nation-state of Serbia remained precarious for much
of the nineteenth century. It was not until 1888, almost sixty years after Serbia gained
autonomy and a full decade after the Treaty of Berlin required its Balkan signatories
to give equality to all subjects, regardless of religion, that the Jews of the country were
granted full civic and political rights. The decades following their emancipation witnessed the emergence of a generation of Serbian Sephardim who were well integrated
into society, fully proficient in Serbian, and who began to consider themselves Serbs of
"the Mosaic faith." Yet the Serbian Jewish community remained small, with no more
than a few thousand persons residing in the entire kingdom, the majority of whom
lived in Belgrade. The following report, which decries the organized corruption of the
trade and distribution of kosher meat in early twentieth-century Belgrade, illustrates
well the challenges facing a small and marginalized community, and the compro-
mises it sought between the rigors of religious observance and realities on the ground.*

To the Administration of the Jewish Community, Belgrade,

I am honored to inform the esteemed administration that in response to the memorandum I received from Moša Avramović, a local
butcher, in which he accuses the innkeeper David Adanja of buying

---

124. Midhat Pasha (1822–1883) was an Ottoman reformer, provincial governor, and two-time
grand vizier who died under suspicious circumstances while in exile in Ta'if (present-day Saudi
Arabia).

*treyf* [non-kosher] meat, I called the said Adanja and asked him about his conduct. Mr. Adanja denies everything. The issue requires further investigation in order to ascertain whether the accusation has merit. Only then should we pursue the measures at our disposal.

Likewise I am informing the esteemed administration that I called upon all Jewish innkeepers and grocers, and warned them that they should strictly obey all regulations of our holy faith when selling meat products and fat to the Jewish public or else their grocery stores will be proclaimed *treyf*.

In this connection I am honored to inform the esteemed administration that all Jewish innkeepers have subsequently issued a collective complaint to the rabbinate, suggesting that on the day in question (the 19th of this month), they did not receive meat for their stores from our [kosher] butcheries; some received barely a third of what they requested and many received nothing at all. As the survival of their stores depends on the regular provision of meat . . . they are addressing the rabbinate with an urgent plea that the current state of our butcheries be improved lest all Jews be forced to eat *treyf* meat.

In response to these and other pleas that our citizens address to the rabbinate daily, the rabbinate called a session of the spiritual court in which the question of our butcheries and meat was investigated from all angles. The court determined that in our community the issue of *kashrut*[125] has been debated by experts and lay people alike. Cardinal mistakes are made by butchers, certain inspectors, and almost all innkeepers, not to mention the private Jewish public.

The court found that strict measures against guards, meat handlers, and others can be undertaken only if the contractual basis of our leases with the butchers is fundamentally changed, that is, if order can first be introduced in this realm and an opportunity provided to Jewish citizens to find and buy what they are looking for. Of the various and sundry accidents and deceptions happening every day among current lessees, the court has established the following violations based on witness statements:

1. *Treyf* is taken into butcher stores where only kosher meat is sold.
2. Butchers slaughter on Saturdays and sell the resulting meat to Jews.

---

125. Jewish dietary, or kosher, laws.

3. In the case of fat, the most amazing deceptions are perpetrated. Butchers skillfully mix kosher fat with unrefined lard and sell the mixture to our [fellow Jewish] citizens. Some were caught red-handed just last week. On Friday, the 14th of this month, there were only about eight to ten kilograms of kosher fat in both stores, and on Sunday twice as much was found there in addition to a certain amount of fat that was sent to a Jewish grocer on Saturday itself. In general the fat cannot be controlled properly as long as its sale is in the hands of butchers, who reap profit from it. At present, after the ritual slaughterers purify the fat, they leave it in the custody of the butchers as if they own it. Because of the lack of controls in place, the latter can in turn mix finely chopped impure lard into the kosher fat such that the inspector can detect this [impurity] only with great difficulty.

*crazy*

4. Two stores for the sale of kosher meat, leased by the same person, without any competition, are not enough for our population. They are unable to supply all citizens of our community with kosher meat. If the supplies of meat run out in general sales to the public, one could even forgive the lessee, but one can in no way forgive him when he does not supply the Jewish inn-keeper with the needed supplies of meat, because the latter is then stripped of his profits.

From all listed proofs and misdeeds of our butcheries, at the session held on June 19 of this year, the court made the following decision:

To draw the attention of the esteemed administration for a final time to the chaotic situation in our butcheries.

To recommend to said administration, on the basis of the above proofs, which violate the contract, that they annul the contract with the current lessee, and offer the lease to *at least three* independent lessees. Among the provisions given to new lessees, the sale of kosher fat should be completely denied them and given [instead] to the inspectors, who will sell it either for their own profit or for the benefit of the community. This will without any doubt preempt deception and fraud, because the butchers would lose any interest in the matter, while on the other hand the inspectors would pay special attention to it, as their personal interest would be involved. One butchery should inevitably be opened in the vicinity of Jalija, where the majority of our citizens, mostly poor ones, live.

On this issue the esteemed administration should be guided by pure religiosity and put religious principles at the top of their list of priorities. The issue of *kashrut* is one of the principal concerns of any Jewish community. Only then [after resolving this issue] can the community approach the possible material profit promised by the institution of a butchery lease. Religion is the goal, while the material gain of the lease is only a means toward maintaining our religion. In no way should the ends be sacrificed for the means.

Informing the esteemed administration about the decision of the court, I ask that as far as possible it work to modify and reorder the issue of kosher meat in our community following the spirit of this decision. Should the esteemed administration, for whatever reason, not be in a position to restructure this issue within one month in accordance with the abovementioned decision of the court, I am honored to inform the administration in advance that the court will be forced to proclaim all meat sold by our butcheries as *treyf*, and thus relieve itself from the heavy responsibility burdening our soul.

Hoping that the esteemed administration will resolve this question quickly, in accordance with our holy religion, and to the benefit of all members of our community, I remain with extraordinary respect,

Rabbi Isaac Alcalay

Isaac Alcalay, "Upravi Crkveno-školske jevrejske opštine," June 20, 1913. United States Holocaust Memorial Museum (Washington, D.C.) RG-31.037M, reel 15. (Original in Fond 497, opis 1, sprava 177, Central State Historical Archives of Ukraine in Lviv). Translated from Serbian and introduced by Emil Kerenji.

## 28. EYEWITNESS TO THE FIRE IN SALONICA [1917]

*On August 18, 1917, a fire destroyed two-thirds of the city of Salonica, home to the world's largest and most populous Sephardi community. The fire, which raged for more than thirty hours and covered one square kilometer, destroyed the Jewish district and the city's commercial heart, including its vital port. By different accounts over 50,000 Jews were left homeless, along with 10,000 Muslim and 10,000–15,000 Christian residents. Thirty-two synagogues were burned, as were nine rabbinical libraries, 600 Torah scrolls, the archives of Salonica's chief rabbi, eight Jewish schools, and most of*

*the city's printing presses. Afterward nearly half the city's Jewish population emi-*
*grated, and the government used the opportunity to Hellenize the city, which had*
*come under Greek rule only five years earlier. In this intimate letter between siblings,*
*a witness to and victim of the fire describes its horrific dimensions to her brother in*
*Manchester. The writer, Esther Michael, is the great-granddaughter of Sa'adi Besalel*
*a-Levi, whose voice appears in sources 21 and 33.*

Impressions of the night of August 18, 1917, begun August 23 and continued on August 28 and September 6.

My dear brother,

By this time the newspapers must have reported the great catastrophe that struck our exceptional city of Salonica, now gutted and destroyed. Before going into the exact details of this sinister night, which
marks the death of a city, and before describing the horrible visions
that remain in my mind, I will reassure you.

The Campagne [Kampanyas] Quarter was obliterated. Only our
house is still standing and, thank God, we remain under our own roof.
Although we suffered great losses after the offices burned down and
we had only very limited insurance coverage, we continue to thank
the Heavens for having spared us from mortal danger [as well as] the
nighttime exodus of the unfortunate victims who abandoned their
homes to the flames and ran, breathless, into the unknown, exhausted
beneath the weight of their burdens and not knowing whether it was
better to stop and perish rather than face tomorrow's miseries. Forget-
ting our misfortune, which appears insignificant when one thinks of
others', we tremble at the sights we see every day since that terrible
night. We are the terrified witnesses of the blackest of miseries, and
we are indeed wretched in that we could do [so little] to help. All that
we have done so far is but a drop in the ocean. We have taken in some
refugees, including Juliette Levy and her sister Lucie, Moïse (Kirbatch)
and Aunt Djentil, among those you know. We gave away a good portion of our things in order to clothe our relatives; we began with them.
Yet those unfortunates who came were only yesterday no doubt richer
than we. One sees clearly that these people do not know how to beg.
Though we have grown accustomed to these miseries, tears come
often to our eyes and it is almost more than we can bear, but we muffle

our sobs so that we do not further distress those unfortunates who come knocking on our door. Nevertheless, a [Judeo-]Spanish proverb says: the house of the rich empties out and that of the poor does not fill up. How well we understand this sad truth.

Despite all our goodwill . . . our modest contribution scarcely reduces the misery, and God knows how great such misery is at this moment. Salonica, the opulent city whose riches I described to you, . . . Salonica, the silver city, the pearl of the Aegean is now nothing but a mound of ruins and rubble, a vast tomb whose treasures are forever buried and on which we must engrave in black letters "Misery City." Thus history offers us a new lesson; all that reaches an apogee [also] falls fatally into decadence. But here we find not the persistent decadence of a city that consumes itself slowly then perishes. It is a fall, a frightful fall, the wind of destiny and the finger of God. "For dust you are, and to dust you will return,"[126] [God] said to man. The city has become nothingness, chaos; and man, that fragile toy and insignificant atom, has had to flee before the fury of the elements. Like the great man of history, everyone proclaims his pride: "The future is mine."

The future is no one's, Sir, the future is God's.
Every time the clock strikes the hour, all that is says goodbye to us.[127]

The poet was right. All that is says goodbye to us, and each time the hour strikes, Salonica, in an apotheosis of light, bids us farewell!

It was a Saturday. We were taking our siesta, and we were expecting visitors at five. All of a sudden Papa, who had been at the shore, called out to us, "Come see, a great fire, bring the twins; it's already been going for a while!" We went to see and indeed it appeared to be quite a vast fire. We watched for a few minutes and then . . . went back inside, for the burning sun and the forceful wind drove us crazy. At about six, Papa, who had not stopped going to the shore, exclaimed, "Oh! The fire is gaining ground; half the city is in flames!" I told myself he was exaggerating, for I hardly anticipated the fire's progress. I went to look, and indeed a large part of the city appeared to have fallen prey to the flames. After this we couldn't stop watching the fire. We

---

126. Genesis 3:19.
127. A quote from Victor Hugo, *Les Chants du crepuscule* (Paris: Hetzel, 1835).

wanted to pull ourselves away, but as if magnetized, we were drawn to
that small corner of the terrace on the water, where we saw the whole
city. We asked Papa if he wouldn't go find out what had happened, for
we had an approximate understanding of the location of the fire and
some of our relatives lived nearby. But Papa asked what good it would
do, getting so close to the fire. He wasn't curious. Assuming the role
of savior? He isn't capable of that. And so we continued to look on
anxiously in the direction of the flames, which the wind was pushing
to the south.

A sudden explosion gave us a start. We went to ask for information
by the roadside. No one could answer us at that moment. Later we
learned that they had exploded several homes with dynamite in order
to create a barricade against the fire. At half past seven, Karsa arrived,
crying like a child, which was not normal for him for he is a withdrawn
and stoic person. "Papa! Dear Papa! We've been ruined! What will become of us? Finished! Salonica is finished. . . . Our store is threatened!
. . . the fire has come to Venizelos Street (formerly Sabri Pasha Street).
What misfortune! What misfortune! We are lost! . . . It's heartbreaking to see the city. Quick, give me some water, I'm going to faint. I'm
afraid! I'm so afraid! Oh, the images I've seen! . . . Children, women
fleeing, and despite the horror, the city is calm; the exodus is happening in a mournful, dreary silence. A woman gave birth on the pave-
ment! Many people surrounded her as she cried out! . . . You don't
know, you couldn't understand. Oh, how I am broken! Papa, go and
see what must be done!"

Karsa's excitement scared me; he spoke incessantly, he sobbed and
his body was shaking all over. He was feverish but it was impossible to
get him to lie down on such a night. No one stayed still. We all walked
about nervously and were dismayed. Papa went out without warning
and Karsa ran after him. "You're not going alone! I want to come with
you." "Stay calm and go back quickly," [Papa replied]. Karsa returned
crestfallen. "What to do? What to do? My God!" We stayed by the
door near the street, leaning against the bars, watching with anxiety
for our relatives and friends to arrive, to give us some news from the
city. Solomon, Papa's brother, arrived. He wanted to go see the office
but Papa had the key. Papa had taken the keys with him. He had probably gone there [to the office]. Karsa hastily grabbed Solomon and

pulled him along [saying:] "Let's go see!" And the two of them disappeared into the shadows, for it was night and all streetlights were out.

And now our wait began in all its anguish. It had to have been about half past eight. There was a lot of movement in the street. The English trucks and Red Cross cars came and went . . . continually. Without a doubt they were evacuating the military hospitals of the city, for we only saw soldiers and sick people in these vehicles. Then on the sidewalks we saw the parade of ghosts that the fire, with its burning breath, had chased to the countryside. Minute by minute the sky took on a reddish tint; the sparks were like shooting stars crisscrossing the sky, which we followed with our eyes until they disappeared behind the houses.

Upon spotting a family of refugees, Michel suddenly said to me, "Look at the poor little one . . . and her mother. . . . " Can you imagine the pang we felt when we recognized the approaching group in the light of a passing tram, poor Eléonore with her husband and children: "It's you, Aunt Fortunée, we nearly went too far; how lucky that you were by the door!"

For strong people this was neither a moment to cry nor to lament. Quickly I grabbed some [of their] bundles. They contained jewelry they had managed to save. How we lose our heads in such situations; they hadn't brought any underclothes either for themselves or for their children! We immediately began caring for our unfortunate relatives. We offered them a bit of lemon balm tea to relax them and they told us that when they left their house the quarter had been intact. Uncle Daut, Aunt Vida, and Emmanuel stayed behind to see what they could grab. But Eléonore was immediately sent away on account of the children. We arranged beds so they could rest. We helped get the children to sleep. At about ten Karsa returned. Papa's office was still standing. If he could have he would have waited to take the merchandise with him.

Hours passed and each moment we heard explosions that became more and more frequent. The shimmering fire of the inferno became more intense as if driven by a gigantic wind. The fugitives were pressing up against one another in tight lines, and now the English trucks began relocating [entire] households. Children passed by: "Where are you going all by yourselves?" "We don't know. We lost our parents, so we travel on, abandoned." An old woman paused exhausted against the door: "What's wrong good woman? Where have you come from and where are you going?" "I came from . . . the Romanian school and I'm going to Kara Ağaç to seek refuge with my daughter." Farther away another woman with about twelve children: "And your husband?" "He stayed in the house to save a few rags and told us to flee."

It was nearly midnight. What had become of Papa? I was waiting in the hallway, shaking: "Esther! Karsa!" It was him! . . . But his voice was unrecognizable and I ran to him by myself for Karsa was sick; he had hurt his foot and I advised him to stay in bed. Papa was carrying a package of books on his head and I took them from him quickly. He walked forward, stumbling, and fell half-asphyxiated on the couch. Mama arrived and we unbuttoned his shirt and removed his collar. His eyes were swollen and very red, his face was pale as candlewax. We helped him breathe. We had him drink a glass of water with some lemon balm. At once he felt relieved, and he told us how he waited in vain at the office, hoping to save something. But upon seeing that the fire was still gaining ground and that he risked being trapped, he randomly took some of the books and fled with Uncle Daut, Emmanuel, Solomon, Jacques, Frances, and Aunt Vida. All of them had gathered at the office, with these packages, these books. But seeing that it was dangerous, each one picked up a bundle and continued home. Thus the group stayed together for some time. On their way, they lost sight of one another. The smoke was blinding. [Papa] wanted to go on anyway, struggling to breathe but fearing that everyone at the house would be worried. He continued through the thick smoke, which explained the state he was in when he came home. As for the others, he didn't know what had happened to them. I will stop here for today and continue next time.

I embrace you, your sister, Esther.


September 6, 1917
My dear brother,

Without further preamble I continue with the story of the night of August 18, which I could not finish in my last letter. . . .

Another truck came and dropped off a new batch of refugees. A woman called out to Papa by name: "Mr. Salem, I beg of you, give me shelter in your courtyard." We didn't know her, but Papa, upon seeing her with her children, brought her in and we gave them some space under the stairs. Now they too had lodging. . . .

While we were chatting, Papa returned to the door. A truck came and stopped in front and he heard a woman's voice cry out [in Ladino]: "Man, young man, are there no Jews here?" This voice called out for pity, for help. Papa approached and asked what was going on. "I want to get off [the truck] here," said the young woman, "I have my old, ailing mother with me, she is dying. I don't want to go any further; do not abandon us if you are a Jew." Papa could not conquer his emotion, and told the driver in English to let the young woman and her mother off the truck, and to carry the mother into the house. "It's been six years now that she's been paralyzed," said the young woman. "Why does God still leave her to live? Wouldn't it be better for her to die?" We prepared a makeshift bed on the balcony for the sick woman; the daughter watched over her until the break of dawn. Little by little, the courtyard filled up. One could have easily believed that we were in a camp or a hospital. . . .

At a certain moment I saw a glimmer, more intense than before, through an open door that looked towards the sea. I ran to the balcony and what did I see? Now, looking over the city, one could have believed oneself transported to the time of Nero, for it was the burning of Rome in miniature. At present it was the sea that was on fire. It was an episode from the Punic Wars, when Archimedes set fire to the Phoenician fleet. One . . . two . . . three sailboats caught fire one after the other and drifted away. My word, it was an unforgettable sight to see. I hallucinated about it for two hours. In vain did I close my eyes in the dark, for my imprinted retina still had me seeing the flaming ships on the trembling sea. . . .

Nevertheless to the east a vague light informed us that dawn was breaking. The crests of the mountains became crisp against a pink and azure sky. Above our heads was a single star, the evening star, resembling a great diamond lost in a sapphire sky, appearing to defy the day. The wind, which started to weaken, changed into a fresh breeze. Everything came together in the splendor of this sunrise. One would say that it was the prelude to a calm and blessed day, and one was tempted to forget the distress and unhappiness that threatened this awakening. But the trucks full of victims made one think of the following verses of the poet, which under the circumstances beg a slight modification:

> When everything changes around you, nature is the same
> And the same sun rises over the days.[128]

Day has now broken. Far away, over there on the sea, we see only clouds of black smoke that indicate that the fire has been contained. The fire is contained and diminishes in intensity. Too late! Salonica has forever perished! I will stop again for the day. But I will continue my reflections on this event, for what to do in our home but reflect!

Save these pages, because they will be a great memento for me.

I embrace you dearly and hope to go and join you, for life is becoming impossible here.

Your sister, Esther

Letters written by Esther Michael (née Salem) in Salonica to her brother Jacques Salem in Manchester. August 23 and 28 and September 6, 1917, Collection of the Manchester Jewish Museum, 1998.5/1a–b. Translated from French by Alma Heckman.

## 29. MEMORIES OF THE *MELDAR*: AN OTTOMAN JEW'S EARLY EDUCATION (1920)

*Alexander Benghiat (ca. 1863–1923) was a Sephardi journalist, editor, and translator active in late Ottoman Izmir. He adapted dozens of European classics for serialization in the Ottoman Ladino press, including works by Jonathan Swift, Harriet Beecher Stowe, Victor Hugo, and Alexandre Dumas, père. Benghiat was also the founding editor of Izmir's Ladino periodical* El Meseret. *The following excerpt, drawn from Benghiat's memoir, details his childhood years spent in the meldar, the traditional Jewish primary school for Sephardi boys in the empire. In its derision of his former teachers and their lessons, Benghiat's account echoes those of Eastern European* maskilim,[129] *for whom traditional Jewish schools were a favored target of reformist critique. (For the political platform of Benghiat's newspaper see source 65; for his wife's views on feminism see source 76.)*

Did you go to a *meldar* as a child? Have any of you been so lucky and blessed? I am sure that, seeing these two questions, you will all object that you had no idea what a *meldar* was and that you went to

---

128. This is a quote from the poem "Le vallon" by Alphonse de Lamartine (1790–1869).
129. Jewish enlighteners, or proponents of the Haskalah (Jewish Enlightenment).

a [modern] school. But I will forgive you this lie or truth and will tell you what a *meldar* is and what happened there.

A *meldar* was a room with a couch in a neighbor's courtyard. On the couch, some benches, and the floor, sixty or seventy children sat and crouched, one dirtier than the other, scratching their heads all day, putting their fingers in their noses and taking them out, pushing, pulling, pinching, or biting each other, until the teacher would see them and yell, "Scoundrels! Bastards! Rascals!"

In winter every child had to bring a couple of coals, because the teacher's wife would put a stove without fire in the middle of the *meldar*. And while the students were supposed to get warm by looking at the empty stove, the teacher, who was sitting in front of the burning stove, was busy heating his bread and roasting his cheese. Then he would scratch his chin, comb his beard, pick the hairs that had fallen out, and put them between the pages of a book. Having taken care of his face, he would begin teaching the alphabet to the youngest students by chanting the letters. . . . But all of this started very slowly with the young students, and since the others also enjoyed it, big and small children began chanting in unison and shouting at the top of their lungs. The Turks who passed by on the street, hearing this shouting and not knowing what was going on, asked each other, "Is this a mental asylum?" If it was winter and the teacher was cold, he would put his hands close to the fire and warm them. If it was summer and he was tired, he would recline and fall asleep. Sometimes when he was sleepy the teacher would leave us with his aide and go to a coffee house to have a coffee. . . . The *meldar* had a low window that faced the street. The teacher always kept an eye on it, and when he saw a Turk passing by with some chickens, he would call him, buy the chickens, and keep them tied up in the middle of the *meldar*. Once, Obadiayico Veisí's father, who came to scold his son, saw the chickens and asked the teacher about them. The aide, who was a real devil, immediately responded, "A Turk brought them and left them here as students so that they would learn to read."

"Shut up, you rascal! Don't you say another word!" yelled the teacher.

And the aide who, despite his impudence, was afraid of the teacher, immediately shut up, while the teacher went to wash his handkerchief at the well and then placed it to dry on the windowsill. A Turk passing by stole it, and we students cried over it.

On Thursdays the teacher's wife made dough, and we students put the pita on the stove. On Fridays older students mopped the floor and helped with other things, and Jamila, the teacher's elder daughter, would slip in her galoshes, fall down, and roll her eyes. On Shabbat there were no classes. On Sundays the teacher would be tired and irritated from not sleeping the night before, and we would not study much. . . .

A note: All the things you have just read about and many more happened in the *meldar*s of Izmir, the interior [of the Ottoman Empire], Constantinople [Istanbul], Edirne, Angora [Ankara], Bursa, and everywhere in Bulgaria before the establishment of the Alliance Israélite Universelle schools. (Since Salonica had contacts with Vienna, that is to say with Europe, long before 1870, we cannot say how things were there.)[130] The Alliance schools in our city saved us from this plague, may their unforgettable first directors, the late [David] Cazes and [Shemtov] Pariente, rest in peace. And may the venerable [Gabriel] Arié, who was the director before the present one[131] and who adeptly headed his institution, leading it to great achievements, be blessed. But now with the current director the old plague has returned. To see what happens with [the students'] instruction, it is enough to test a student from the highest grade. And as proof of their level of education it is enough to stop in front of the door of the Alliance school at midday or in the afternoon while classes are in session . . . and you will find chaos and turmoil.

Alexander Benghiat, *Suvenires del meldar: Estudio verdadero de lo ke se pasava en un tiempo* (Izmir, 1920). Translated from Ladino by Olga Borovaya.

## 30. CAN AN ASHKENAZI MAN JOIN THE SEPHARDI COMMUNITY OF BELGRADE? [1923–1924]

*Because Sephardim constituted the majority of Jews in nineteenth-century Serbia, in 1866 the government officially recognized the Sephardi community as the sole Jewish communal organization in that country. For some time Ashkenazi Jews who lived in the kingdom and wished to follow their own rites found that they had to do so*

---

130. A reference to the fact that after 1870 Alliance schools opened in all the major centers of Sephardi life in the Ottoman Empire, including Izmir.
131. Israel Benaroya.

*outside the confines of communal institutions. After decades of lobbying, and despite Sephardi representatives' vociferous protests, the Ashkenazi community finally succeeded in gaining the state's formal recognition as a separate community in 1892. Tensions lingered between the two groups for many decades, however, as can be seen in the following source, dating from the interwar period. Here we learn of a conflict between the Sephardi and Ashkenazi communities of Belgrade that revolved around one man and the question of which community he belonged to. As this source demonstrates, Sephardi identity was a flexible category that could be both claimed and contested by various parties.*

[Letter from Moric Štajner to the Administration of the Jewish Community, Belgrade, June 28, 1923]

As I have been part of this community through marriage since 1900 and because my two children are members of this community, I ask that I likewise be entered into community books as a member [of the Sephardi community], and that a school tax be assessed for me.

[Letter from the Jewish Community of Sephardi Rite to the Jewish Community of the Ashkenazi Rite, Belgrade, July 5, 1923]

Moric Štajner, a local resident, who has not been taxed by this community for reasons of poverty, appealed to this community on the 28th of the past month to ask that the school tax be assessed for him as for all other members, since he is now able to pay the sum and considers himself a member of this community, not only because he was married in our synagogue in 1900, but also because the children born of this marriage are listed as community members in our books.

As per that appeal and in addition to the reasons listed by the appellant, because it is well known that the appellant and his family belong to the Sephardi rite and were brought up in that rite and should by language be considered Sephardim, the administration of this community decided to accept the appeal of the aforementioned petition, to inform your community about this, and to introduce your community to the logic that guided us in this matter, in order that your community, either out of ignorance of the matter or because the appellant is called "Štajner," should not conclude that our community tried to win over a member of your community.

At the same time we are honored to ask your administration for the answer to the question of whether the aforenamed Štajner is listed as a member of your community.

Please accept at this occasion expressions of my extraordinary respect.

[Letter from Secretary of the Administration Pavle Vinterštajn and President of the Jewish Community of the Ashkenazi Rite Dr. Fr[idrih] Pops, Belgrade, October 31, 1923]

Mr. Moric Štajner, a local salesman, is a Jew of Ashkenazi rite, like his brother Gotlib Štajner, so according to article no. 1 of the bylaws of this community, they are both members of the Ashkenazi Jewish community.

We can only reiterate that in all cases concerning individual Sephardi Jews, we remain committed to the only proper solution to this question, that Sephardim should remain in the Sephardi community, leaving Ashkenazim to their community. Only in this way can discord between the two communities be averted.

[Letter from the secretary and president of the Jewish Community of the Sephardi Rite to the Administration of the Jewish Community of the Ashkenazi Rite, Belgrade, November 20, 1923]

The Administration of this community at its session of the 13th of this month and adhering to its response of October 31, 1923, no. 153, resolved to suggest that in accordance with its earlier suggestion to the administration [of the Jewish Community of the Ashkenazi Rite] the latter appoint delegates who will, together with the delegates of this community, seek to reach an agreement on questions contentious to the two communities. The appointed delegates for this community, in addition to the undersigned, include Dr. Hugo Horovic.

Convinced as we are that your community will perceive this suggestion to be helpful to both communities, we beg you to accept this expression of our extraordinary respect.

[Letter to the Administration of the Serbian Jewish Community of the Ashkenazi Rite, Belgrade, December 16, 1923]

In association with your act no. 164 of November 20 of this year, the administration of this community at its session of December 13 of this year received a suggestion from [the Jewish community of the Ashkenazi Rite] about the continuation of ongoing talks designed to reach an agreement about the issues affecting the two communities, and we appointed as delegates the president of the administration, Mr. Rafailo Finc, the vice president, Mr. Sol. J. Alkalaj, and Mr. Mihailo Levi, a member of the administration of this community. . . .

Please accept in the meantime expressions of my extraordinary respect.

[Letter from Elijas Levi to the Serbian Jewish Community of the Ashkenazi Rite, Belgrade, June 11, 1924]

The administration of this community, at its session of May 29 of this year, considered the application of Mr. Moric Štajner, a stoker at the Danube Elementary School, to be accepted as a member of this community.

The Administration has resolved that said Moric Štajner the stoker is not the same person as Moric Štajner the salesman and that he is not at all related to the brothers Štajner (Moric and Gotlib), mentioned in your act no. 152 from October 31, 1923. Moric Štajner the stoker was married in this community in 1900, and the children born to this marriage have been entered into the record books of this community. The entire family has been brought up purely in the Sephardi rite, attends our synagogues, and speaks our mother tongue [Ladino].

In light of all these circumstances, which Moric Štajner the stoker proved with documents and certificates, the administration of this community has decided to accept him as a member of this community, of which you are hereby informed.

[Letter from Elijas Levi to Mr. Moric Štajner, the stoker, Belgrade, May 11, 1924]

We are honored to inform you that, according to the decision of this community on May 29 this year, you have been accepted as a member of the [Sephardi] Jewish community in Belgrade, and that the administration of this community has assessed that you owe the amount of thirty dinars as a school tax, of which you are hereby informed.

"Upravi Crkv.-škol. jevr. opštine," RG-31.037M, reel 8, United States Holocaust Memorial Museum (Washington, D.C.). (Original in Fond 497, opis 1, sprava 83, Central State Historical Archives of Ukraine, Lviv.) Translated from Serbian by Emil Kerenji.

## 31. BECOMING ALBERTO: A SERBIAN ORTHODOX MAN CONVERTS TO JUDAISM [1925]

*The following source details the conversion to Judaism of a Serbian Orthodox man living in Greece during the interwar period. Strikingly, the man in question chose to convert from Christianity, the majority religion—albeit from a different branch of Orthodox Christianity than that practiced by most Greeks—to the religion of a minority group that faced political scrutiny from Greek authorities and increasing pressure to Hellenize since Salonica became Greek in 1912. Because he would have had little to gain socially or at the state level from this decision, his apostasy was likely personally motivated, whether by religious conviction or out of love for a Jewish woman we do not know. Perhaps more striking still, we see that this man, who began his life with the name Lazar and was assigned the Hebrew name Abraham after his conversion, made a special request to be registered as Alberto once he had become Jewish. In so doing he made clear that he intended not only to convert to Judaism but also to align himself with local Sephardi cultural norms, according to which the name Alberto, adopted from Europe, was considered "Jewish."*

During the meeting of the Religious Court of Justice [*Bet Din Ha-Tsedek*], which took place on the 23rd day of the month of Tamuz 5685 [July 15, 1925], there stood before us Mr. Lazar Tinčević, son of Nesto Tinčević and his wife Zlata, residents of Mirović, and presented us with a letter of request having the following contents:

"I, the undersigned, Lazar Tinčević, son of Nesto Tinčević, thirty-four years of age, of the Serbian Orthodox faith, a resident of Salonica, hereby express my will and desire to convert to the religion of Israel, after full and thorough consideration, without any coercion, temptation, or petition. I am now prepared to accept and to observe with all my heart all of the laws and strictures of the Torah of Israel."

After we received the response of a Serbian Orthodox priest dated August 7, 1925, in response to our letter of July 27, 1925, in which he acceded to his [Lazar Tinčević's] request to convert to the religion of Israel, we apprised him of some of the "lighter" commandments and some of the "heavier" commandments, as is written in the *Shulḥan Arukh* (Yoreh De'ah 268:2), and he was circumcised (September 2, 1925 in the registry) for the sake of his conversion before the Religious Court of Law in the Hirsch Hospital of our community, and before the circumcision we saw to it that the mohel[132] pronounced the bene-

---

132. Ritual circumciser.

diction of circumcision without mentioning the Holy Name and His kingship, and after the circumcision we recited the blessing over a cup of wine and included the Holy Name and His kingship, and the blessing "Who sanctified us, etc., to circumcise converts and to draw a drop of covenantal blood from them, etc." as written in the *Shulhan Arukh* (Yoreh De'ah 268:5).

On the 9th day of the month of Tishre in the year 5686 [September 27, 1925] the ritual immersion for the sake of conversion was enacted before the Religious Court of Law and his name was called among Israel "Abraham, the son of Abraham our forefather." After the name Abraham was bestowed upon him, he requested of us that he be called by everyone "Alberto" instead of Abraham, and we agreed to abide by his wish, and this was on the 24th day of the month of Heshvan 5686 [November 11, 1925].

On the 15th day of the month of Shevat 5688 [February 6, 1928] he was given a certificate bearing his name, "Alberto, son of our forefather Abraham" (by the secretary, Alfonso [Levi]),

Hakham Rabbi Pinhas Barzelai and Hakham Rabbi Isaac Hassid.[133]

Records of the Jewish Community of Salonica, Greece, RG 207, folder 12, entry 253, YIVO Institute for Jewish Research (New York City). Translated from Hebrew by David M. Bunis, Devin E. Naar, and Rivka Schiller.

---

133. These names appear in abbreviated form in the original.

## II. VIOLENCE, WAR, AND REGIONAL TRANSFORMATION

## 32. EUROPEAN JEWS IN SALONICA ATTEMPT TO EVADE THE JERUSALEM TAX [1749]

*During much of the eighteenth century, the Jewish leadership of Istanbul imposed a special tax on Jews throughout the Ottoman Empire in support of the Jewish community in Jerusalem, many of whose members lived off charity in order to dedicate their days to the study of holy books. In order to collect this tax, Istanbul's Jewish leaders dispatched emissaries to ensure delivery of all contributions pledged for the Holy Land. In the following document we learn of European Jewish merchants in Salonica who sought to avoid paying the Jerusalem tax on account of their foreign status. These individuals, known locally as* francos *("Europeans"), enjoyed special protection and exemption from Ottoman government taxes under the capitulations[1] regime, which granted extraterritorial rights to holders of foreign papers living within the empire. As this document suggests, the* francos *also believed themselves to be exempt from Ottoman rabbinic authority, a stance that prompted bitter protests by local Jewish authorities.*

We have received a letter from our emissary . . . Jacob Ashkenazi . . . in which he informs us that he has appointed you to the divine service of collecting the para [tax] contributions that the residents of your city have pledged . . . and to oversee with compassion all the matters concerning the Holy City of Jerusalem, whether in regard to the payment of your city or that of its environs and to procure to collect each one and send it forward in its time, as was the practice in the days of the great rabbi . . . Moses Amariglio.

We saw that our emissary, the abovementioned *hakham*[2] [Jacob Ashkenazi], complained and protested about the issue of the *beratlıs*,[3] because they worked against him by not committing to make the para payment. . . . You should speak with those people, so that they do not withdraw from the community, for we are all the sons of one man and we, like they, are all obligated to fulfill this commandment. If they refuse to listen to our words, God forbid, know that we will speak with the ambassadors [in Istanbul] and insist that they write to the [relevant] consuls [to clarify] that the exemption of the *beratlıs* only applies to the taxes owed to the sultan and the gov-

---

1. Dating to the sixteenth century, the capitulations were commercial agreements between the Ottoman Empire and European states that granted European subjects who resided in the empire special benefits, including tax privileges and the legal protection of their respective consuls.

2. Sephardi sage or rabbi.

3. Individuals under foreign consular protection.

ernors, such as the poll tax and the like, but not to matters related to the Jewish religion.

Letter from the Officials for the Holy Land in Constantinople to Aaron Amariglio, Benveniste Gattegno, and Samuel Amariglio in Salonica, 17 Elul 5509 (September 12, 1749), ms. 4008, p. 38b, Pinkas Kushta, Courtesy of the Library of The Jewish Theological Seminary (New York City). Translated from Ladino and introduced by Matthias Lehmann.

## 33.  A JEWISH WOMAN IN SALONICA SEWS UNIFORMS FOR OTTOMAN SOLDIERS {1820s}

*For many centuries Jews in the Ottoman port city of Salonica earned their liveli- hood by producing woolen cloth for the Ottoman palace and for the uniforms of the elite infantry troops of the sultan known as the Janissary corps. Although the general Salonican Jewish textile trade began to decline starting in the late sixteenth century, the city's Jews continued to be the principal manufacturers of uniforms for the Janissaries until 1826. In that year Sultan Mahmud II (r. 1789–1839) abolished the corps after repeated rebellions, massacring its members by the thousands and building a modern army in its place. While many Jews who had depended on their economic partnership with the Janissaries suffered great losses, others stood to benefit from the new arrangement. Among the beneficiaries of Mahmud II's reforms were the textile merchants and tailors specializing in the new style of military uniforms Mahmud II had chosen, a group that included the family of the Salonican Jewish publisher Sa'adi Besalel a-Levi (1820–1903). His memoir describes how soldiers came to his home so that his mother could fit them for shirts in the European style that was her specialty. It is tempting to speculate that Sa'adi's lionization of Mahmud II was influenced by the benefits his own family accrued during Mahmud II's reign. As Sa'adi himself makes clear however, there existed a tradition of Ottoman writers who praised Mahmud II as a great reforming monarch, even if many others judged his policies to have been ruthless and destructive.*

After the massacre of the Janissaries at the Hippodrome [in Istanbul], Sultan Mahmud the Second proved to be a wise and courageous man. He was lion-hearted, as is often mentioned in royal chronicles. He suc- ceeded in gaining to his side the *ağa pasha*, who was head of the Janis- saries, thanks to the promises the sultan made to him. He convened and addressed at the Hippodrome the entire Janissary corps, who numbered forty thousand souls from the Istanbul barracks, to convince them to give a satisfactory response to the sultan. The *ağa pasha* returned to the sultan. In the meantime he had twenty thousand souls dressed in vests and pants, arming them with rifles, while he also prepared two artillery batteries, one on one end at the entrance of the street leading to the Hippodrome, and the other one at the other end, with ten thousand souls behind each battery. On the other side, by the sea, he armed all the battleships to open fire from their guns at the first sign. Upon his return from the sultan, he went up to an elevated spot and said to them, "The Sultan doesn't need to give an accounting to anyone. As head of the nation, he knows best how to rule over his empire."

When the Janissaries heard this answer, all in unison shouted a call to vengeance, unaware that the entrances to the Hippodrome were blocked with special soldiers. The Janissaries were headed toward their barracks to pick up their weapons but encountered artillery fire and bullets from the guns. When they turned toward the sea for their escape, they met with artillery coming from the navy. In the space of a couple of hours, forty thousand souls perished, and the Hippodrome became a carpet of bodies. At the conclusion of this incident the sultan ordered the demolition of all the Janissary barracks where the Janissaries held their meetings.

After an interval of cease-fire, the sultan sent out criers carrying the holy flag and companies of armed soldiers prompting the people to open their stores and their shops and run their businesses with peace of mind. He also dispatched to all the major cities soldiers dressed European style to get rid of any remaining Janissaries in many localities.

He sent to Salonica eight to ten battalions of soldiers who rounded up anyone who belonged to the Janissaries, incarcerating them in the White Tower. Every night, they killed from ten to fifteen of them, according to how many they arrested that day. For each one killed, they fired a bullet; this informed the population about how many had been killed that night.

This is why this tower was formerly called "Bloody Tower" until our sovereign, Sultan Hamit II [Abdülhamid II, r. 1876–1909], ascended the throne and ordered that henceforth it should be called the "White Tower."[4] Immediately, they brought a number of whitewashers, and they whitewashed it, transforming it into a "white dove" as seen today.

When these soldiers came to Salonica with their military brass, con-

---

4. Known in Ladino as the *Torre Blanka*.

sisting of a lieutenant colonel, a colonel, a regiment paymaster, an army major, and a captain, they were all wearing gold filigreed uniforms. Each one of these high officials occupied a mansion for his private use. This also was the beginning of calm for all the religious communities.

These high officials were not accustomed to wearing European-style shirts. When they decided to dress in the European style, they asked a certain *ham*,[5] Daniel Andjel, whose shop at the Women's Market was their meeting place, to help them get such shirts. He inquired about who sold such shirts, but he didn't find any, simply because sewing machines were not available. And those worn by *frankos* had been hand-sewn by my *sinyora* mother, who inherited this craft from her mother and her grandmother.[6] Then, *ham* Daniel needed to call on my *sinyora* mother to sew a dozen shirts for each one of them, and he tried to take my *sinyora* mother to see these gentlemen. My *sinyora* mother replied that she was unwilling to go to a Turkish home, but anyone who wished was welcome to her house to be measured for her to sew the shirts. The *sinyor* Daniel asked how much she charged for sewing a shirt. She answered that she charges all consuls and businessmen one *altılık* to sew a shirt.[7] *Ham* Daniel replied that he would charge a 100 percent commission on the total amount of her sale to these gentlemen.

My *sinyora* mother replied, "Fine, if they pay me two *altılıks*, you will get the second one." This *sinyor* said to her, "I'll bring here three people for you to sew a dozen for each one." My *sinyora* mother thought that only three people would be coming; yet by the time she heard the sound of the twenty armed horsemen who accompanied each one of them, the streets were filled to capacity with all these people. To be precise, streets around our home were alleys rather than streets, varying between three and two *pikos* in width.[8] As soon as mother looked through the window and caught a glimpse of the gold-embroidered uniforms and the hanging swords, she immediately hid my three maiden sisters in one of the rooms. In came the three top military officers, accompanied by four to five majors. She didn't

---

5. Shortened form of *hakham*, used for ordinary Jews who are not rabbis.
6. *Frankos*, or "Franks," meaning Europeans.
7. An Ottoman unit of currency, one *altılık* equaled six kuruş, or piasters.
8. One *piko* is approximately thirty inches.

even have enough chairs for sitting! She had to borrow extra chairs to seat them all—tall, hefty, and covered in gold embroidery. *Sinyor* Daniel was no less impressive: He was quite fat and tall, wore a silk turban around his head, and his body was wrapped in a loose robe of red damascene fabric, an alpaca robe with a sash from Tripoli. He sent his employees to the market to bring bolts of embroidered fabric. They brought in about forty to fifty bolts of this fabric to make about a dozen shirts each. When my *sinyora* mother took a look at this fabric, she reacted by saying that her original price was inadequate because this is a thicker fabric, hard to sew. *Ham* Daniel agreed on three *altılıks* to get half of it for himself. As for the customers, they had no interest in these price changes, beyond what he told them, especially because *Chilibi* Menahem's coffers paid any bill that came.[9] My *sinyora* mother took the measurements of every one of them for the fabrics they chose, making sure to set aside one-tenth of the fabric from each dozen shirts, [all of which equaled a] sum total [of] two robes, five half-shirts, and five jackets for my wedding. As soon as they left, my *sinyora* mother with her three daughters and three helpers started the work, and within a month they finished eight dozen shirts.

Aron Rodrigue and Sarah Abrevaya Stein, eds., *A Jewish Voice from Ottoman Salonica: The Ladino Memoir of Sa'adi Besalel a-Levi*. Translation, transliteration, and Glossary by Isaac Jerusalmi (Stanford, CA: Stanford University Press, 2012), 44–47.

## 34.  A BLOOD LIBEL IN RHODES (1840)

*The year 1840 saw not one but two major blood libels, the first in Damascus and a few weeks later a second on the island of Rhodes. In Damascus the torture and killing of Jews who were accused of the ritual murder of a Capuchin friar and his servant attracted international attention. The lesser-known incident in Rhodes was no less devastating however. The following testimony of four Jewish witnesses from Rhodes depicts the persecution of their coreligionists as a heinous scheme by the island's Christian consuls to eliminate a commercial rival. The second source presented here, a letter sent by the Ottoman chief rabbi to the empire's foreign ministry, refutes the ritual murder accusations against the Jews while praising the Ottoman government on whose protection these Jews relied.*

---

9. *Chilibi*, or *Çelebi*, a title of respect for men.

The [three] men who, on the day of the alleged kidnapping, had walked through Trianda on their way to the city of Rhodes were summoned by the pasha and the consuls, who asked what they had done with the boy whom they had met on the way from the village to the city. The poor men were greatly astonished and insisted that they had not met any boy. Upon providing this negative response, they were flogged and thrown unconscious into the prison, where the unfortunates were tortured through the night.

After these three Jews had been questioned and tortured, the rabbi, Jacob Israel, who was an Austrian subject,[10] as well as four representatives of the community were brought in. The interrogation began as follows: "Tell us finally, where did you leave the Christian child whose blood was used for your Passover bread?" The main investigators were the English and Swedish consuls. "We know nothing at all about this child," was the answer, "but none of our laws or religious books require the horrible and unnatural sacrifice of which we are accused, and we are incapable of such a crime. We would be unworthy of being God's children if now, after the Hatt-ı Şerif of Gülhane,[11] which has bestowed upon us its benefits, we would cause the government the smallest unpleasantness by our behavior. Yusuf Pasha, strict master, let us explain to you why all of this has been said against us. Your own reason will tell you which of those present here is to blame." When the rabbi wanted to continue, Wilkinson [the English consul] interrupted him: "Shut up! We did not summon you to listen to your false justifications or long-winded explanations, but to hear a short answer: where is the Greek boy?" After explaining that they knew nothing about the Greek child, the Jews were abused and ridiculed by the consuls and thrown out of the room with the words, "Go for now, Jewish dogs!" The pasha added, "Remember that I expect the boy from you Jews."

On Sunday night after the rabbi and the elders were released, the pasha, prompted by the consuls, had the Jewish quarter surrounded by ten *kavas*es,[12] so that nobody could enter or leave and so that the Jew-

10. Although he belonged to a rabbinic dynasty established in Rhodes since 1714, the rabbi held a *berat*, or patent conferring upon him the status of an Austrian subject, which granted him various extraterritorial benefits, including tax privileges and the protection of the Austrian consul.

11. The Hatt-ı Şerif of Gülhane (Noble Rescript of the Rose Chamber), proclaimed on November 3, 1839, guaranteed all Ottoman subjects equality and security of life and property without distinction of race or religion.

12. Gendarmes.

ish population would be locked inside. This caused great consternation and lamentation in the community, because the unfortunate besieged inhabitants, unprepared for this outrageous violence, lacked basic supplies, particularly bread. On Thursday evening the poor experienced shortage and hunger. The *subaşı*, chief of the gendarmes, who felt sorry for the hungry and beleaguered Jews, bought two baskets of bread with his own money and distributed it among them. When the Christian Protestant [sic] English consul Wilkinson learned about it, he regarded the kindness of the Muslim *subaşı* as a crime and denounced him to the pasha, who had the compassionate Turk flogged, then fired him from his job!

Exacerbating the suffering of the unfortunate inhabitants, the Jewish quarter in the city of Rhodes lacked drinking water, since the two wells located there had brackish water that could be used only for cooking or washing. The besieged suffered from thirst and begged for water in vain. In order to ease their thirst and in order not to drink pure saltwater, they made it sour with lemon juice. Yet owing to the shortage of lemons, the prices rose from two to thirty para[13] apiece. As this was unaffordable for the poor, one could see children and old people lying on the streets and at the gates [of the Jewish quarter], burning from the thirst caused by the salty water.

*terrible scene*

On the fourth day of this stringent blockade, the *naib*[14] and the Muslim religious leaders met at the pasha's palace, in the consuls' presence, to pronounce a verdict on this sad matter. They summoned the rabbi, the four Jewish elders, and the plaintiffs (two Greek women and a priest), and no other defendants. The pasha demanded that the claimants once again announce what they knew about the kidnapping. They responded that they had seen the boy entering the city with a basket of eggs and a turkey but had not seen him since, which is why they assumed that he had been murdered by Jews. Upon hearing this statement, the *naib* requested that the city's gatekeepers and customs officials be brought in and questioned in the plaintiffs' presence. After the claimants had described the boy and indicated the day and the hour when he had entered the city carrying a basket of eggs and a turkey and never returned, the gatekeepers and the customs officials

---

13. A small Ottoman coin.
14. A Muslim judge of a rank lower than a *qadi*.

declared that such a boy had not entered the city through any gate. Having heard these contradictory statements, the *naib* and the Muslim religious leaders declared that under such circumstances, in the absence of any grounds for suspicion, it could not be proven that the case merited further investigation; they also concluded that the Jews deserved to be freed and their persecution halted immediately. Yet despite this decision, the blockade of the Jewish quarter continued, and during that time Wilkinson met with some Jews to whom he said hypocritically, "Ask God to create that child in heaven again and send him to you or else this is the end of you, because only such a miracle can save you, since you did murder the boy."

Coincidentally, after the beleaguered Jews had suffered for twelve days from fear, hunger, thirst, and other afflictions, a *muhassıl*[15] came from Constantinople to Rhodes to gather the collected taxes. As he passed by the besieged Jewish quarter he inquired about [the situation]. Upon learning what had happened he told the pasha that it was wrong to punish the whole community for an alleged crime of two people. Since the pasha did not listen to him, the *muhassıl* wrote to him saying that if he did not immediately lift the blockade, he would inform the authorities in Constantinople. For this reason, the *kavas*es were removed, and the starving and half-dead inhabitants of the quarter rushed to the wells and bakeries to enjoy a piece of bread and a sip of water after twelve days of deprivation. But on their way out [of their quarter], the Jews were met by the Christians—namely the Greeks—who threw rotten lemons at them.

Everybody thought the matter would be forgotten, and the Jews thanked God for delivering them from the danger, shame, and misery. But two weeks after the siege was lifted the Austrian consul, Giulianich, and the English consul, Wilkinson, visited some Jewish shops, saying they were tired of waiting and if the boy was not found by the following morning, they would hang the rabbi on the synagogue gate. These words caused renewed alarm among the unfortunate people. Indeed the next morning, which was a Jewish holiday [Passover], a few *kavas*es took the rabbi and four elders and brought them to the pasha's palace, where the consuls were already waiting. A new interrogation began, and the

---

15. The official in charge of taxes and finances in an Ottoman administrative region known as a *sanjak* (or *sancak*, in Turkish).

pasha announced that it was time to put an end to leniency and that the Jews must finally confess what had happened to the missing child. The rabbi once again stated that both he and his community were innocent and cited the *naib*'s verdict. The English consul retorted, "What? You are still denying it? What do we care about the *naib*'s verdict after the same thing has happened in Damascus and it has been proven that the Talmud requires that you use Christian blood for your Easter bread?" The rabbi answered, "It is the same libel as in Damascus. But if you, Wilkinson, say that the Talmud requires that we use Christian blood for our Passover bread, tell me: Where did we get [such blood] when Christianity did not yet exist?" They were unprepared for this retort, and in response the Jews were flogged and thrown into separate prison cells.

good question

The English consul pressed the pasha to use torture again for without it they would never get a confession. Yusuf Pasha promised to do so, and in the evening, when the consuls were gone, he went to the courtyard of his palace (where the prison was located) and ordered the rabbi to be suspended from the ceiling of one of the halls in the following way. A rope was tightly fastened under his arms, chest, and stomach. Afterwards they put two copper pans with smoldering coals under his feet. He swung this way all night. The next day, the cruel consuls amused themselves with this savage sight. When the rabbi realized this, he cried, "Giulianich! Austrian consul, have pity on me, I am an Austrian subject after all!" Giulianich's response was blood-curdling: "Rabbi: What are you complaining about? You are not yet dead!" After the martyr had swung this way for forty-six hours, with the horrible burning coals under his feet and without food or water, his arms and legs started bleeding heavily. This infamy did not provoke him to confess anything, but he was reduced to the point of death. When the pasha learned of this, he ordered him removed from the hook, taken to prison, and thrown on straw. After the rabbi, they tortured and suspended from the ceiling the unfortunate Danish dragoman[16] David Mizrahi. . . . Being weaker than the rabbi, Mizrahi reached the same condition within six hours but without confessing anything either. There was just enough time to inform the pasha about his imminent death. Already unconscious, Mizrahi was removed from the hook and

16. Interpreter.

taken back to his cell. Four days later the rabbi and the four elders were released. The rabbi's tormented appearance must have moved the pasha because as the former was leaving the prison the pasha said, "I am sorry for you. It was Giulianich who demanded that I torture you." The other accused men remained in prison.

Meanwhile, the chief rabbi of Constantinople was informed about the accusations against the Jews of Rhodes and their gruesome treatment. About a month later, after the chief rabbi had appealed to the Sublime Porte and made reference to the Hatt-ı Şerif of Gülhane, the pasha of Rhodes received an order from the government requesting that he send to Constantinople the child's mother, the three Greek claimants, and four delegates chosen by the Jews from their community. These four delegates were the abovementioned Abraham Amato, Barukh Benatta, Isaac Capeluto, and Yakim Mizrahi. Before their departure Yusuf Pasha called them to his palace and strictly forbade them to say anything bad about him at the Sublime Porte because, he said, all of his regrettable actions had been prompted by the consuls. Two weeks after the delegation's departure, on the order of Reşid Pasha[17] the other Jewish prisoners were released. Since that time the community has been living in peace, though if the Jews do not want to be abused by the Christians, they should stay inside their quarter. . . .

[Letter sent by the Ottoman chief rabbi to the Ottoman Foreign Ministry]*

It is believed among the nations that we need human blood for the unleavened bread that we bake and eat as required by our laws. The use of blood that they speak of is absolutely forbidden by our religion. We had hoped to be acquitted of this libel and have been searching for ways to clarify our views on this matter.

We praise and glorify the Lord for this administration, which spreads wisdom and kindness.

Thanks to the infinite mercy and compassion of the Benefactor of

---

17. Mustafa Reşid Pasha (1800–1858), an influential Ottoman diplomat and statesman who served as grand vizier six times during the reign of the Ottoman Sultan Abdülmecid (r. 1839–1861)

* Letter sent by the chief rabbi to the Ottoman Foreign Ministry, 25 Ramazan 1256 (November 20, 1840), İ. HR. (İrade Hariciye), 349, Başbakanlık Osmanlı Arşivi (Prime Minister's Ottoman Archive). Translated from Ottoman Turkish by Kürşad Akpınar and prepared for publication by Olga Borovaya.

the World and the Protector of all Peoples, our Emperor, Emperor of the World, our Benefactor, our Lord, thanks to His Excellency's abundant benevolence, and in accordance with the new and exalted laws, this case was investigated in the Supreme Council of Judicial Ordinances and the aforementioned allegations were declared to be falsehoods and libel. Once the magnificent imperial order . . . was unfurled publicly and read aloud in the presence of the rabbis and the heads of the [Jewish] *millet*, its contents proclaimed and the good news announced as is required of us by the *dhimma*,[18] it was received with prayers for the prolongation of His Sovereign Majesty's prosperous and glorious days. . . .

A continuation of the auspicious prayers for His Imperial Majesty shall be announced to his servants of the Jewish *millet* in his imperial and protected domains for the imperial assistance and mercy that has been bestowed upon [us] . . . unworthy beings.

Your servant Mishon [Haim Moses Fresco], current chief rabbi

"Licht und Schattenbilder aus der jüdischen Geschichte der Gegenwart: Die Juden in Rhodos," *Der Orient* 32 (August 8, 1840): 245–48. Translated from German and introduced by Olga Borovaya.

## 35. OTTOMAN AND BRITISH OFFICIALS SPAR OVER PROTECTION OF THE JEWS [ca. 1840]

*Over the course of the nineteenth century British interest in the Jewish communities of the Middle East was shaped both by imperialist ambition and the ascendancy of a millenarian evangelical movement whose adherents sought the restoration of the Jews to their historic homeland in Palestine. These currents motivated Lord Palmerston (1784–1865), British secretary of state for foreign affairs, to advocate European Jewish settlement in Palestine under British protection, which he suggested would allow Jews to escape persecution in their home countries while also advancing British foreign policy in the region. In the summer of 1840, Palmerston asked Lord Ponsonby, British ambassador in Istanbul, to present his cause to the Ottoman authorities. The Ottoman grand vizier's note to the sultan summarizes their failed negotiations.*

---

18. A pact of protection between Islamic rulers and their non-Muslim subjects.

Grand benefactor endowed with noble and magnanimous qualities and inclinations, Your Illustrious, Gracious, Munificent, and Glorious Excellency, my Sire. . . .

My recent detailed and humble note regarding the request to allow English Jews to settle in the Damascus region states that Lord Ponsonby requested mediation of the English consuls and the ambassador in presenting and petitioning the cases of the aforementioned Jews. Later, Pisani, the chief dragoman, visited the Ministry of Foreign Affairs numerous times asking for a response to this request. With the purpose of ensuring the safety of the Jewish *millet* in the future, and in view of the persecution and torture of the Jews in Damascus and Rhodes, he stated that this mediation in cases of potential grievances was intended for all Jews now living in the domains of the Great State. The following is the answer given to him by the Ministry of Foreign Affairs:

> Although it is clear that [Jews'] settlement in the imperial domains will be beneficial for the Great State, as those who will immigrate there are useful and wealthy people, they will [only] be allowed to settle in the Protected Domains and purchase land on the condition that they pay the *cizye*[19] and in all matters obey the laws binding the Great State's subjects together.
>
> However, their refusal to pay the *cizye* will prevent the Great State from granting them this permission.
>
> If they agree to accept the status of His Imperial Excellency's subjects [by contrast], the Great State will consider them full subjects on a par with the rest. Thus, if they have any complaints, they will have to address them directly to the Great State rather than resorting to English consuls or officials as intermediaries. . . . [After all], justice, fairness, and rights are all presently mandated and executed by His Excellency in all parts of the Exalted Monarchy's domains.
>
> Even though these Jews will certainly not be mistreated, because they are accustomed to different procedures and another manner of governance in England, it is necessary to remind those who cite this fact as the reason for demanding mediation that two modes of governing cannot coexist in one sovereign state. In view of this it has been deemed [most] appropriate to put aside the question of Jewish immigration for the moment.

---

19. Turkish version of the Arabic *jizya*, or poll tax imposed on non-Muslim subjects.

The following was [subsequently] communicated to the dragoman:

It should be evident that . . . official mediation on behalf of the Jews who are already subjects of the Great State shall not be permitted. Is it not known to all that the Exalted Monarchy immediately took every measure to stop the terrible events in Rhodes? Although the Great State was unable to do anything during the abominable events in Damascus, due to the . . . situation in the region, there can be no doubt that it is making every effort to prevent any further incidents.

The aforementioned dragoman replied that he would inform the ambassador about [what was discussed in] this interview. When he returned the next day he did not ask for the settlement of English Jews again but [instead] stated that the request for mediation concerned all Jewish subjects of the Great State. [He then explained that] there was absolutely no doubt that the Great State highly desired and wished for the safety and welfare of its subjects . . . but that these requests had [simply] been made because the provincial officials could not be trusted. Having explained this, the dragoman asked if there was any harm in consenting to those requests.

He was given the following answer:

While it is possible that inappropriate actions might be taken by provincial officials, such things shall not be ignored, and they shall be amended in accordance with the new state procedures, thus serving as a lesson to others. . . . It is clear that if, contrary to the [sultan's] lofty wishes, persecution occurs in the provinces, the local representatives of the friendly states can unofficially express to the Great State [their concern regarding] the situation, not only on behalf of the Jewish and Christian communities but also on behalf of the Muslim *millet*. However, if, as you suggest, all grievances of the Jewish *millet* are presented for mediation to English officials, His Imperial Majesty's exalted administration will be divided into two parts, and a sizable portion will be given to the aforementioned state [of England]. This can in turn lead to further harm. No doubt, as soon as the ambassador hears this he will give up his demand; if he had considered it before, he would not have even permitted himself to raise this issue . . . as is well known, they [the Russians, French, and Austrians] have obtained certain privileges from earlier capitulations. Claiming that [the Orthodox Christians and Roman Catholics] are their coreligionists, they would make the protection [of said Christians] the central issue of their foreign policies. In particular they would use the matter [of British mediation] as a precedent and the Russians would take the Greeks under their official protection, while the French and the Austrians would do the same with regard to the Catholics. This would mean the complete ruin of the Great State's sovereignty. As the state of England more than any other has been striving to protect the exalted monarchy's independence, it certainly would not want to open the door to such a harmful policy.

The dragoman seemed to accept these words, but he expressed regret that [England's] suggestion had been rejected outright. He was then told the following:

This cannot be considered a complete rejection, because if oppression or hardship inflicted by [Ottoman] officials on a group of the Exalted Monarchy's subjects in any location of the Imperial and Protected Domains is reported to the Great State by any party, the necessary investigation shall be immediately and readily initiated, and the execution of the required actions shall be authorized. . . .

It was recommended to the dragoman that he . . . inform the [British] ambassador in writing about the anticipated harm [the policy he proposed would have]. . . .

İrade Mesail-i Mühimme 1007, Başbakanlık Osmanlı Arşivi (Istanbul). Translated from Ottoman Turkish by Kürşad Akpınar and prepared for publication by Olga Borovaya.

## 36.  A KOSHER KITCHEN IN THE OTTOMAN IMPERIAL
##      MEDICAL SCHOOL [1847]

*By the mid-nineteenth century the Ottoman government began to endorse a new project of state patriotism known as Ottomanism, which sought to ensure the loyalty of Ottomans of different faiths by fostering a sense of shared investment in the empire. In the process the government began to admit Christian and Jewish pupils into the new state schools, including the medical school, which opened its doors in 1827. In an attempt to accommodate Jewish students and assure them that service to the state would not force them to abandon their traditions, the government created within the medical school a special place of prayer and a kitchen equipped to prepare food for Jewish students according to their dietary, or kosher, laws. They also allowed Jewish students to visit their families on the Sabbath. Although Muslims continued to constitute the overwhelming majority of state employees, as a result of this and other related efforts Jewish and Christian graduates of the new imperial schools came to serve in various branches of the Ottoman government, including the ministries of justice, education, finance, police, and foreign affairs.*

13 Şaban 1263 [July 27, 1847], Office of the Grand Vizier
Your Majesty,

May God increase your lifespan. On the basis of the imperial decision that allowed Jewish children to be accepted into the imperial medical school, an imperial decree was promulgated. Some community leaders and the chief imperial physician gathered to consider how to implement this decision. At that meeting it became clear that Jewish children will need to be offered kosher food and drink and that they should also be free to follow their religious obligations [while in attendance]. This decision will raise our *millet* out of a state of ignorance. You demonstrate your great magnanimity by providing [our children] instruction and knowledge, which are the sine qua non of humanity. Thanks to your beneficence our *millet* will regain honor and vitality. We have been subjects of the Ottoman sultans for a very long time and no one protects us as the Sultan does. We do not know how to acknowledge [properly] this decision or express our gratitude. May God increase the power of our ruler, the Sultan, and secure his reign over us forever, amen. Those children who will attend the medical school will be chosen by your humble servant and will be sent to the chief imperial physician [for examination]. The ultimate decision belongs to Our Sultan.

Chief Rabbi of Istanbul and surrounding areas

18 Zilkade 1263 [October 28, 1847], Office of the Grand Vizier
Your Majesty,

In order to support and cook for the twenty-nine Jewish children who were accepted into the imperial medical school thanks to your decree, [a man by the name of] Raphael was appointed supervisor and another man as cook. Because they have not yet been assigned an official salary however, we thought we might use the amount that we [now] have at our disposal as a result of Doctor Emin Efendi and Salih Efendi's removal from office, some 250 kuruş for Raphael and 150 kuruş for the cook. Moreover, a Jewish butcher will [need to] be found in order to deal with buying and selling the necessary amounts of meat and oil for the Jewish children. The memorandum to this effect was composed by the officer in charge of expenditures. These allocations have similarly been approved by the military council. I present these documents to you here. If you order an imperial decree to be promulgated regarding this issue, the abovementioned officer will be notified.

Istanbul chief rabbi to the Office of the Grand Vizier, 13 Şaban 1263 (July 27, 1847), İ. HR. 41/1935 and note to the Office of the Grand Vizier, 18 Zilkade 1263 (October 28, 1847), İ. DH. 159/8269, Başbakanlık Osmanlı Arşivi (Istanbul). Translated from Ottoman Turkish by Onur Şar.

## 37.  A MUSLIM INTELLECTUAL ON THE EMANCIPATION OF OTTOMAN NON-MUSLIMS {1856}

*Between 1839 and 1876 the Ottoman government initiated a series of reforms known collectively as the* Tanzimat *(literally, "Reorganization"). Intended to instill fiscal and administrative order while also securing the loyalty of different communities within the empire, these reforms included an 1856 decree, known variously as the Hatt-ı Hümayun and the Islahat Fermanı, that declared all Ottoman subjects equal. For many, the edict went too far. From a diplomatic standpoint certain Ottoman observers were unhappy with the role Britain and France had played in forcing the sultan's hand in the matter of "emancipating" the empire's non-Muslims from their subordinate status. Others objected to the overturning of a centuries-old arrangement that had placed Muslims above Christians and Jews in the social hierarchy of the empire. In this source, the Ottoman Muslim jurist, historian, and statesman Abdullah Cevdet Pasha (1822–1895) describes the conflicted emotions the 1856 decree elicited among various parties. As his account makes clear, the opinions Ottoman subjects formed on the decree did not divide neatly along Muslim/non-Muslim lines.*

In accordance with this firman,[20] Muslim and non-Muslim subjects were to be made equal in all rights. This had a very adverse effect on the Muslims. Previously one of the four points adopted as the basis for peace agreements had been that certain privileges were accorded to Christians on condition that these did not infringe on the sovereign authority of the government. Now the question of specific privileges lost its significance; in the whole range of government the non-Muslims were forthwith to be deemed the equals of the Muslims. Many Muslims

20. A reference to the Hatt-ı Hümayün, or Islahat Fermanı of 1856.

began to grumble: "Today we have lost our sacred national rights won by the blood of our fathers and forefathers. At a time when the Islamic *millet* was the ruling *millet*, it was deprived of this sacred right. This is a day of weeping and mourning for the people of Islam."

As for the non-Muslims, this day, when they left the status of *ra'aya*[21] and gained equality with the ruling *millet*, was a day of rejoicing. But the patriarchs and other spiritual leaders were displeased because their appointments were incorporated in the firman. Another point was that whereas in the Ottoman state in former times the communities were ranked with the Muslims first, then the Greeks, then the Armenians, then the Jews, now all of them were put on the same level. Some Greeks objected to this, saying, "The government has put us together with the Jews. We were content with the supremacy of Islam."

As a result of all this, just as the weather was overcast when the firman was read in the audience chamber, so the faces of most of those present were grim. Only on the faces of a few of our Frenchified gentry dressed in the garb of Islam could expressions of joy be seen. Some notorious characters of this type were seen and heard to say, "If the non-Muslims are spread among the Muslims, neighborhoods will become mixed, the price of our properties will rise, and civilized amenities will expand." On this account they expressed satisfaction.

Reprinted from *Jews of Arab Lands: A History and Source Book* by Norman Stillman. Copyright 1979 by the Jewish Publication Society of America.

## 38. THE OTTOMAN CHIEF RABBI'S AMBIVALENT RESPONSE TO THE PROCLAMATION OF JEWISH EQUALITY {1856}

*In 1856 the Jewish philanthropist, reformer, and German-language author Ludwig August Frankl (1810–1894) set out from Vienna for Jerusalem, where he hoped to establish a school that would offer a combination of religious and secular schooling for Jewish boys. Because the school he planned represented an innovation for the Jewish community of Jerusalem, Frankl came equipped with a suitcase filled with letters of recommendation from Habsburg government officials and European rabbis.*

---

21. From the Arabic for "grazing cattle," the term originally referred to the general population without the privileges of the military class within the Ottoman Empire. By the nineteenth century it was commonly used in reference to non-Muslims in particular.

*En route he also stopped in Istanbul, where he sought the blessing of the chief rabbi of the Ottoman Empire. During their meeting Frankl asked the rabbi how Ottoman Jews felt about the recently announced Hatt-ı Hümayun decree, which had declared all subjects of the empire equal. Although the rabbi initially responded that the reform had "removed a stigma" from the Jews of the empire and offered reason for rejoicing, his ambivalence soon became apparent. As he explained to his Austrian interlocutor, the Ottoman chief rabbi feared that both the new freedoms and the new obligations citizenship entailed threatened to weaken the hold of Judaism on his community.*

Finally, the ceremony of reception was concluded, and the rabbi addressed me.

"You come from the capital of the German Sultan,[22] may God and His hosts protect him."

"I come to pay my respects to you and to beseech you to support my undertaking at Jerusalem, if such is your pleasure."

"It is my duty to do so. You have heard what our powerful Sultan, may God and His hosts protect him, has done for us Jews! We are no longer the oppressed and despised ones of the earth. But it is his desire that we should be civilized; he has ordered schools to be established, and we will prove our gratitude by obedience. It is a proof of God's love that He has given you grace to proceed to the Holy City and to establish a school [there]. I and my pious colleague will use our influence on your behalf and on behalf of the object which you are about to accomplish in the name of a great lady.[23] My secretary will have the honor of delivering the letters to you."

"Your Grace, what effect did the proclamation of the Hatt-ı Hümayun produce upon the Jewish population of the Turkish empire? We, in the West, have twice experienced the same favor; in the year 1782, and at Purim, the feast of deliverance, in the year 1849."

"I have learned that you, in the West, understand better what is meant by exemption from slavery and the equality of all men, without distinction of religion. The Jews of the East must first learn this and then begin to extend their knowledge. When the great law was passed, believers rejoiced that the stigma was removed from the servants of

---

22. Apparently a reference to the Habsburg Emperor.
23. A reference to Elise Herz Lämel, who sent Frankl to Jerusalem in 1856 to establish the Jewish boys' school in her father's name.

the true and only God, and unbelievers rejoiced, because all restraint was withdrawn and they were left to the freedom of their own wills. But there are many who believe that the holy ordinances of religion are endangered by it and fear that it may sink into decay and lose its luster, as among the Franks.[24] But the chief ground of their apprehension arises from the Jews being now obliged to serve in the army. The descendants of the heroes of God, and of the Maccabees, are not afraid to meet death in the battlefield, but they know that as soldiers they must violate many of the precepts of our holy faith."

"Mr. Brunswig observed that the Turkish government is extremely humane, as it has appointed a butcher for the special use of the sixteen Jewish students who have been admitted into the medical school, so that none of the regulations regarding different kinds of food may be violated. A rabbi resides with the young men and directs their religious services. The son of the rabbi Haim has already completed his studies at this school and has recently received the appointment of hospital surgeon at Aleppo with an annual salary of 24,000 piasters."[25]

The chief rabbi replied:

"May God bless the Sultan, our all-powerful Lord. May the Lord preserve the crown for his descendants forever. All kinds of golden fruit are ripening under his mild reign. And now the luster of our religion will be conspicuous for the first time, because every man will do willingly what the world has hitherto compelled him to do."

Ludwig August Frankl, *The Jews of the East*, trans. Rev. P. Beaton, vol. 1 (London: First and Blackett Publishers, 1859), 170–72.

## 39. A RABBI OF ISTANBUL CONDEMNS THE TEACHING OF EUROPEAN LANGUAGES {1858}

*A self-declared traditionalist, rabbi, and judge active in mid-nineteenth-century Istanbul, Rabbi Isaac Akrish (d. 1888?), campaigned actively against those who sought to reform Jewish education in the empire. Just two years after a new-style school teaching secular subjects and non-Jewish languages opened in the imperial capital in 1856, Akrish and various other rabbis led an initiative to close the school, arguing that*

---

24. Europeans.

25. Presumably a reference to Samuel Haim, who held the position of Ottoman chief rabbi between 1839 and 1841.

*the teaching of French and other "foreign" subjects was endangering the Jewish obser-*
*vance of its pupils and provoking immoral behavior. In the following source, Akrish*
*rails against the efforts of Jewish reformers and counsels against innovations. Despite*
*his commitment to keeping Jews from studying foreign knowledge, however, it appears*
*that Akrish was primarily concerned with preventing his coreligionists from being*
*exposed to what he considered the corrupting influences of European culture. In ad-*
*dition to studying Hebrew in order to read their "holy Torah," he reasoned, Jews were*
*permitted to learn "the language of Ishmael"—that is, of the Jews' Muslim neigh-*
*bors—since this was an "established practice" among Jewish communities. Despite the*
*opposition of rabbinic authorities such as Akrish to the introduction of new forms of*
*secular learning into Ottoman Jewish schools, the contingent of Jewish reformers who*
*supported this platform grew more numerous, and influential, with the passing of the*
*years. (On these reformist elements, and Akrish's opposition to them, see also source 14.)*

There is a matter well known and widely publicized among all those
who have come through the gates of our city, Constantinople [Istan-
bul], may God preserve it. . . . [I]t occurred about two years after the
establishment of the school among us here in Constantinople, may
God preserve it, that was to teach Jewish children, the little students
of the rabbi's house, the languages of the gentiles with their books.

A plague broke out among most of the children who studied there
at that time; they went off into an evil way of life. They threw off the
yoke of heavenly rule from themselves—from reciting the *Shema'* declaration and from worshipping God (worship meaning [the *'Amidah*]
prayer). They mock the ritual washing of the hands and other things of
this type. They say things to their mothers which we would not want
to hear, all of which they have learned from their teacher there. [The
teacher] was brought in from a distant land, a land of strange language, just as [the school was founded], in order to teach the children
the languages of the gentiles. He would teach them from the books of
religions of the nations of the world, the belief in that certain man and
his mother,[26] may our ears be spared from hearing of it. Woe to the
generation in which such things occur!

For this reason a committee of householders of our city, may God
preserve it, has arisen to protest and complain to the Torah scholars
(may God preserve them), saying that they are in the right in raising the flag of Torah and that such things may not be done among

---

26. A euphemism for Jesus and Mary.

[the people of] Israel—to teach Jewish youngsters the languages of the gentiles while they still lack discernment, Torah knowledge, and fear of God because they are so young. This brings them to read books about the religions of the nations of the world, and [about] natural philosophy, which is forbidden because it contradicts knowledge of the Divine, God forbid, as well as [the doctrine of] the creation of the world, and similar things. These are the sorts of matters written in the books of the nations in their languages and according to their peoples, as is known. The fathers and mothers [of the students] understand nothing of this because they themselves are unfamiliar with the writings of those languages. This is how [students] end up throwing off the yoke and coming to heresies or the types of actions that occurred with some of the children, as was mentioned.

When a group of Torah scholars, may God preserve them, heard about all this they were deeply saddened. They asked themselves, "What can we do? The matter can only be solved by the greatest scholars of the generation, those rabbis, may God preserve them, upon whom the entire House of Israel rests!" The issue was very painful. Faith was almost lost entirely from the mouths of babies and infants, the little students of the rabbi's house from whose mouths we derive life, as the sages say in various places.

For this purpose the Torah scholars, may God preserve them, acted with zeal and gathered together. There were about eighty rabbis, may God preserve them, and they determined together with God[27] not to allow any Israelite to send his son or his daughter to the school where they learn any one of the languages of the gentiles; rather [they must study] only our holy Torah and the language of Ishmael specifically and nothing else.[28] The reason for this permission for the language of Ishmael is a secret, as is known. They announced this agreement in synagogue on the holy Sabbath, in all the synagogues in the city. Happy is Israel! Almost everyone accepted it gladly.[29]

Isaac Akrish, *Sefer Kiryat Arba'* (Jerusalem, 1876), Question 13: 185v–193r. Translated from Hebrew by Matt Goldish.

---

27. I.e., in a legal decree.

28. Likely a reference to Ottoman Turkish in this case, although elsewhere the expression "Language of Ishmael" is employed by Jewish authors to refer to Arabic.

29. Although Akrish leaves off on a positive note here, later in the text he acknowledges that divisions on this issue continued to plague the Jewish community of Istanbul.

## 40.  A CHOLERA EPIDEMIC LEADS TO CONSULAR
## LITIGATION IN RUSÇUK [1865–1866]

*Throughout much of the nineteenth century, various national and imperial au-
thorities vied with Ottoman representatives for influence in Southeastern Europe
and across the Levant. A preferred means of competing for influence was the granting of protection to Ottoman subjects. Those who became protégés of foreign states
were relieved of certain tariffs and came under the jurisdiction of consular authorities within the empire. This political contest plays a prominent role in the following
document, drawn from the unpublished memoir of the Jewish intellectual and reformer Abraham ben Israel Rosanes (1838–1879). Rosanes writes of how a devastating outbreak of cholera in his native town of Rusçuk (present-day Ruse, Bulgaria)
led to a dispute within his family and, in turn, between the Prussian representatives
who protected them and the Ottoman authorities to whom they turned for help. A
Prussian subject when the strife in his family began, Rosanes hoped to enlist the aid
of Midhat Pasha (1822–1883), then governor of the Ottoman Danube province, in
order to procure Ottoman nationality for himself and his family, and thus to extri-
cate himself from the Prussian consular court case his relatives had brought against
him. Although Rosanes ultimately failed in his bid to change his citizenship, his
close relationship with Midhat Pasha, one of the most influential Ottoman reformers of the nineteenth century, nonetheless offers a striking example of the ties that
were often forged between Ottoman reformers of different faiths.*

In the abovementioned year (5625 [1865]) in the month of mercy [Elul;
early fall], a major event befell our city (long may it live), a cholera epidemic. Two or three Jews were dying every day. . . . Our entire family,
with the exception of my oldest brother who was in Vienna, secluded
ourselves in the house of my brother Isaac, may his lamp shine, and remained there for about four days. We were forced to escape from there
to some place that offered respite and salvation, so when some other
people with their women and children joined us shortly afterward, we
agreed to go to Bucharest. We needed first to go to the examination
station at Giurgiu[30] to pass through an inspection (quarantine) for
three days. We were afraid that we would all die, God forbid.

During the days of our quarantine, I was informed that back home
my brother-in-law, Abraham Shevah, may his lamp shine, had fallen
deathly ill. I ran like a deer to his house and rushed to bring him a
physician and medicines as well as a servant to guard and serve him.
This occurred on Friday late in the afternoon. On that holy Sabbath

---

30.  City in present-day Romania across the Danube from Rusçuk, present-day Bulgarian Ruse.

evening and the next day we prayed in my home with a quorum. In the morning, immediately after services, I went to see how my brother-in-law was doing, and, thank God, the danger to him had passed. I was nevertheless terribly upset to learn that on that day there were three dead waiting to be buried upon the departure of the Sabbath.

Following afternoon prayers, I returned to visit my brother-in-law again, and I gave thanks to God. The moment I arrived, however, I saw that his eldest daughter, a young girl of about six years, was struck with full force by the horrible plague. There was nothing I could do but to speak comfortingly to my sister [so] that she should not worry or be distressed—God would have mercy on her [the daughter] as He had on her husband.

I returned home to find that two of my neighbors—Moreno and Moses, may their lamps shine, had become ill. We rushed to make medicines for them, and it was close to the fourth hour of the night when all the members of the household were able to lie down and rest a bit from our efforts. Indeed the physician had ordered us to be very careful in our eating and resting. After about a quarter of an hour had passed, I was lying on my bed with eyes open in prayer to God and thinking my thoughts in my heart: Tonight I am on my bed but who knows if I will not be lying in the grave in the morning, God forbid?

Just then a man began to knock violently at the door of my brother's house. "What do you want?" asked the servant woman. "Tell *Hakham* Abraham [the author] to hurry to the home of his sister for her eldest daughter is at death's door and his sister has spread out her hands filled with despair." "What can I do there?" I asked. I discussed with other members of my household the fact that my arrival there would not be helpful or useful, and I would furthermore put myself in danger by disobeying the physician's orders. I ultimately put the man [who had knocked] under oath that he would go to my aunt, the wife of my Uncle Haim of blessed memory and would ask her in my name and the name of my whole household that she remember the kindness of my honored father and mother and go to the home of my sister. She should speak to her heart and comfort her from her sorrows, for her soul was bitter about her daughter who had died and her ill husband who stood at death's door. This man did as I instructed, and shortly afterward he returned to report that he had already brought my aunt with him to my sister's house.

In the morning I arose from my bed and went to the door of my house to find out what news there was in the city and whether anyone had undertaken the burial of my sister's daughter. I was informed that the plague had increased in the city. My brother-in-law's brother, whose name was Meir, had taken care of the abovementioned burial, and I therefore chose not to visit my sister for the time being until her distress had passed. In the meantime we were pressed to leave the city and go to Wallachia as was mentioned above. I very much wanted to visit my sister for a little while to comfort her and speak to her heart in order that she gather strength as well as to tell her that we were leaving. But everyone in my household would not allow me to do as I planned, both because of the contagion of the disease and because it might deepen [my sister's] sorrow. Despite her anguish over her daughter, who had died in front of her, she could not flee the city as well, because her husband was sick and terribly weak.

I therefore relied on our servant, Shabbetay ben Abraham, may his lamp shine, with whom we left everything, that he should go each day to my sister to comfort her in our name. He took a solemn oath to do this. It is impossible to explain the great turmoil in which we left the city, for we could find no wagon or porter to carry our things to the Danube. We were all tired to the point of utter exhaustion and we were unable to take even a change of clothing with us. Our departure looked to me like the exodus of our ancestors from Jerusalem into the Babylonian exile. All that befell us until we arrived in Bucharest is impossible to describe, for they would in no way allow us into the quarantine at Giurgiu. Money takes care of everything however. We paid a large bribe to the physician and officials until they accepted us. We stayed in Bucharest for seventeen days. . . .

When we returned, I rushed to the home of my brother-in-law and sister, though I had been told that they were furious with me and everyone in my family. When I arrived there, not only did they fail to welcome me as usual, they showed me the face of anger and tremendous wrath. I tried to justify my actions to them but to no avail, for hatred had engulfed their hearts. They had secretly begun to plot a lawsuit against us concerning an inheritance for my sister out of the property of my father of blessed memory, who had passed on about eight years earlier. According to them there was a good reason for doing this evil thing, the fact that we had gone to Bucharest and abandoned them in such a condition, as I described. We knew nothing of this plot.

In that year 5626 [1865–1866] we first passed the days of [the holi-day of] Sukkot. The enmity of our brother-in-law and sister did not diminish from their hearts, and the secret of their plotting the day of vengeance could be seen in their eyes. We did not know what to do or how to reconcile. Then during Hanukah a trusted friend of ours revealed the secret to my older brother. He had found out for certain that our brother-in-law, with the support of his wife, was planning to take us to court at the house of the Prussian royal consul (under whose flag we are all protected) to claim an inheritance in the property of our father. We did not for a moment give credence to this report, for a suit for the inheritance of a daughter in a situation where there were sons was unknown among the Jews of these regions.

The next day, the eve of the holy Sabbath of Hanukah—at 9:00, the consul's envoy suddenly appeared at our shop carrying a summons to adjudication at such-and-such an hour the following Wednesday at the consul's house, for that is where he held court. We would respond to our brother-in-law in his suit demanding a portion of the inheritance, including usufruct and all its proceeds from which we had profited, etc., etc. He had accused us of not informing him or showing him ac-counts of our father's property until that day and behaving with our father's property as one would with one's own, as if our sister had no portion in it, etc. We were unable at that point to do anything else; we all simply agreed that we would not speak at all—neither positively nor negatively—with our brother-in-law and sister.

The day of the holy Sabbath passed and the situation became known around the city. All the members of our community joined together to investigate and consider what to do in this matter, but in the end not a single one among them could find any fortitude in his soul [to help]—or at least to speak with my brother-in-law and sister [to con-vince them] that they should abandon their suit, because they knew from the outset that the whole enterprise would come to naught. Thus they agreed to leave us to whatever fate would befall us. We would tell the court that there was no law of inheritance like this in the laws of

Israel. We knew from the beginning, however, that this would do us no good.

However it would go, Wednesday arrived and we went to the consul. His first act was by way of deceit to have us sign that we would return at a time appointed for us on a Thursday after the days of their festivals and holidays [Easter] had passed, about three weeks hence. We signed it without understanding that this was the snare that would entrap us. During those three weeks my older brother went day and night without respite to consult with numerous officials about what to do and how to respond when the appointed day arrived. One said one thing and the next said another. One of them, the most high-ranking, was the [senior] Austrian consul, who said that there was no way to avoid this crooked court case and the fury of the [local] consul who was wholeheartedly on the side of my brother-in-law. Who knew what our end would be? All we could do was take shelter under the Turkish government and shake off the control of the Prussian flag [i.e. renounce Prussian citizenship and return to Ottoman citizenship.]

After investigating and examining the matter among the brothers (may God preserve them), the following solution seemed the best in our eyes. We talked it over and wrote a letter of request to the honored Midhat Pasha requesting that he accept us under his flag and government. The letter patent [citizenship papers] with Prussia contained the signature of our father (peace upon him), written and signed by us three brothers, as well as the two sons of my brother, Israel and Moses, may their lamps shine. We all went together before the Pasha, may his glory rise, and he received us kindly as is his way. In the morning the [Prussian] consul was informed about this.

That was when we truly went out to find the greatest hand of suffering we ever endured. During those days we knew neither food nor sleep. The consul was furious about the matter and the humiliation it caused him. The issue of the legal case and the events that had occurred were revealed to the envoy of the King of Prussia in Constantinople [Istanbul], may God protect it, who attempted to intercede with the Ottoman Empire's top official [the grand vizier]. On three occasions—in Nisan, Tamuz, and *Rahamim*[31] [from spring until fall] of the

---

31. The Hebrew month of Elul.

above-mentioned year [5626 (1866)], one time after the other, he sent word to [Midhat] Pasha that he should force us to go to the [Prussian] consul. We must perforce see our case through there in front of him [the consul], since we had signed and committed to appear within three weeks as was explained above. One who begins something must see it through to the end.

Each time this happened we put forth great efforts to justify our position to the pasha, and he, out of his great love for us, declined to take us by force to the consul. Each time he would make excuses to the government in Constantinople saying that he did not understand [or that it was not so], but in the end he did not succeed. On the third round the vizier upbraided him harshly and demanded that he bring us by force to the consul no matter what. . . .

During the Ten Days of Penitence [between Rosh Hashanah and Yom Kippur, during the fall of 1866] . . . the matter of that lawsuit came to press upon us; it reared up to destroy us. [Midhat] Pasha sent for my brother and said to him, "You know how much I struggled on your behalf. Three times I managed to deflect the orders I received from my superiors. Now however there is nothing I can do for you beyond advising you to come to some compromise with your sister. If not, you can choose to go for adjudication to the consul at my command, or I can send you off with letters of support to Constantinople, may God preserve it, where the great pashas are—perhaps that would help you." Meanwhile however, the consul had been informed by his representative in Constantinople that we no longer had any alternative except to go to him [the consul] for adjudication of the case.

On the eve of the holy Sabbath of Repentance [between Rosh Hashanah and Yom Kippur] he sent one of his servants a summons for us to appear at court on the eve of the Day of Awe [Yom Kippur] shortly before the dividing meal [just before the Yom Kippur fast begins] in order to infuriate us and add to our distress. My brother did not want to accept the letter, but the consul had ordered that it be affixed to the door of his house. We left it alone as it was and did not remove this document from the door the entire holy Sabbath day. This just added to the joy of our brother-in-law and sister, who said "Look! I was victorious and will now destroy you at my will! Know and see that I will now exact my vengeance on you as I wish." To all the abuse and malice he heaped on us in a great torrent we did not respond at all, may God look upon us and judge, for we have none else on whom to rely, may God forgive them and never remember their sins in this world.

Thus passed that Sabbath day upon us as if we were mourners with downcast heads because of our fear of the consul. Who knew what the outcome would be for all our property and the honor of our merchant house as a result of this fraudulent judgment?

But on that very day a different mood overcame the pasha. He called two of the most respected men of our community and charged them, using words of kindness and supplication, to do something for him: try with every effort to work out a compromise between us and our sister. In our tremendous distress we had almost sworn not to give up even a penny in this matter, despite having seen the evil end it would bring upon us. The pleading of these sincere men, however, and the Days of Awe in whose midst we then stood, turned us around with a new attitude so that ultimately, after that Sabbath had ended, and after colossal efforts, the matter was brought to a good end. A compromise was reached between us for 200 Turkish liras, which we were required to give to our sister with the stipulation that this money would remain with us as an investment, which we would pay at 12 percent annual return, according to the desire of my sister. All this occurred before the consul and his household and was agreed with witnesses. It was confirmed with the consul's seal.

We were nevertheless unable at that time to overcome within ourselves our anger and the altercations with our brother-in-law. It was not about the 200 liras, thank God, for what did that matter to us? Everyone in the city knew that we would even have given our brother-in-law 500 liras if it had been done through good relations and not like this! It was rather because of all his insults and curses, which he uttered unceasingly for a long time after these events, in which his goal was to anger us, may God repay him.

Excerpts from an unpublished memoir of Abraham Rosanes of Rusçuk, Private Collection of Sivan Toledo. Transcribed from *soletreo* by Zvi Keren and translated from Hebrew by Matt Goldish.

## 41. WHEN A JEW CAN WORK DURING THE SABBATH: A SALONICAN RABBI ON WAR AND LABOR
(1890/1891)

*As Jews began to acquire new rights during the modern era, they invariably faced the question of whether they could bend the rules of their religious tradition to fit the new requirements of citizenship. In many places Jewish representatives announced their willingness to put their country first under exceptional circumstances that required them to work on the Sabbath or break their dietary laws. This source offers an unusually candid discussion of the dilemmas such circumstances posed to those who were dedicated to upholding Jewish law. As its author explains, the decision to allow fellow Jews to perform duties for the government on the Sabbath was not always an entirely voluntary one. Fearing that government representatives might force his coreligionists to work on their day of rest or imprison them for not doing so, the Salonican chief rabbi Samuel Raphael Arditti explains how he was "forced to step beyond" his bounds to announce that the Jews of his city were permitted to load a steamship that had docked at port on a Saturday because their country required it of them.*

I have been considering for a long while responding with my opinion on the law and the truth concerning occasional improper events that occur thus. For years wars have raged between kings, as is well known and perceived by all. Those wars are fought between the Turkish kings and the Christians. During these events various weapons and Turkish soldiers would arrive by sea on steamships. These [steamships] would transport them by sea from one place to another. They need long-shoremen as well as experts who have lighters that are called *kayıks* and *mavunas*[32] in order to take them these weapons and soldiers from the steamboats to dry land. They also need to transport supplies and various foodstuffs from the land [to the ships]. [For this] they need men who are porters to load their animals with various foods and the like—all the known types of things they would need.

Now it once happened that the steamships arrived on the Sabbath. Representatives of the ruler of our city of Salonica, may God protect it, as well as representatives of the army came and requested that we give the Jews sufficient permission that they be allowed to perform their work on the Sabbath. Their claim was that this was deemed urgent by the king, and that the situation requires it. They pressed us about it, saying, "Is it not enough that we go to war while you, the House of

---

32. Rowboats and barges.

Israel, sit in security?" Were we not to give sufficient permission it was possible that they would go out into the streets and markets and grab them. It was also possible that they would imprison them for refusing to obey an order of the king. It was a common saying of the rabbis that "the law of the land is law." This situation arose several times in the periods of our great rabbis . . . and they of blessed memory, gave the Jews who practiced those professions sufficient permission to perform their work as if it were a weekday.

*precedent for obeying secular law*

So it is now in my time that an event like this occurred. This year 5642 [1881/1882] two steamships arrived [on the Sabbath] loaded with soldiers and weapons. The matter was imperative because they wanted them transported from here to another location the very same day. I tried very hard to have the job done by non-Jews if at all possible so that the Sabbath would not be violated, but I was not successful, for they were in a rush [and were] moving very quickly in order that the operation not be delayed. I was forced to step beyond my bounds and command the nation [Jews] to perform their work in order to fulfill the demands of the officials and their assistants (none of whom are Jews) and to do as they wish. I told myself that when I would have an opportunity I would study this topic. This is how I come now to take pen in hand, with the intention of pulling together and arranging [rabbinic opinions on these matters].

Raphael Samuel ben Jacob Arditi, *Sefer Divre Shemuel* (Salonica: Ets ha-hayim, 1890/1891), Question 9: 50v–51v. Translated from Hebrew by Matt Goldish.

## 42. EYEWITNESS TO MASSACRES OF ARMENIANS IN ISTANBUL {1896}

*Following the seizure of the Ottoman Bank in Istanbul by members of the Armenian Revolutionary Federation, in the summer of 1896 Muslim rioters in the imperial capital took to the streets, massacring thousands of Armenian civilians and pillaging their property. Much of this violence occurred in neighborhoods densely populated by Jews, who became involved in the events as witnesses, participants, and protectors of their Armenian neighbors. The following source consists of interviews conducted by Albert Adatto (1911–1996) in Seattle in the 1930s with a number of Jewish witnesses to the 1896 massacres, including his parents, Sam Adatto and Anna Perahia Adatto. (The Istanbul-born Adatto is pictured as a child on the cover of this book with his sister, Emma Adatto Schlesinger [1910–1997]). These rare testimonies reveal former Ottoman Jews' ambivalent attitudes towards the violence and the various parties involved, exposing a range of responses by Jews in Istanbul both during and after the massacres. (On Emma Adatto see source 145.)*

## [Account of] Mr. Sam Adatto

I was bringing a suit from Galata to Stanbol [sic] at 10 o'clock in the morning to an Armenian shop. The owner, an Armenian, told me that Armenians were being killed in Galata and that an attempt had been made to threaten officials in the Ottoman bank. The dynamiting of the banks was used as a threat to secure Armenian independence. This Armenian was a tailor for the Turkish officials.

After he explained the situation to me he said he was going into hiding in a nearby building because his life was not secure. (Later on I will tell you what became of him.)

About noon I went to Galata. I saw Turks killing Armenians with huge sticks. No guns were used by the Turks. These Turks were a very low class type. There were no signs of Turkish officialdom on the streets. I didn't see a Turkish uniform. Just men—civilians. It appeared as if the lower class Turks were killing the harmless Armenians of the working class. I never heard of a rich Armenian being killed; it was just the common Armenians, the lower class.

I was frightened and walked hurriedly on my way to Galata. I never stopped once, even to ask questions. I did not run but walked rapidly. The streets were rapidly cleared of all people. It seemed as if all the Armenian "hamals" (porters) were being killed. It was a terrible sight.

When I arrived home in the afternoon, I never went out again for twenty-four hours. It was a horrifying experience.

During this fighting, to my knowledge, there was only one Jew killed and it was an accident. He was the son of the local *shamas* [sexton]. While passing by the Ottoman bank he was killed by a stray bullet fired by the Armenians. The Armenians were the only ones who had guns and they used them to no great advantage. The Armenians who possessed guns seemed to have lost all their wits and were frightened out of their senses. The Turks only used big sticks. It seems that of all the people that were killed that day only one per cent were Turks, the rest were Armenians.

Next day all was calm. I saw wagons hauling the dead bodies off the streets. My shop was in Galata and I went to my work as usual. The excitement of the massacre caused a business slump for two weeks.

The richer Armenians seemed to have left town as soon as the rioting started. Only the poor Armenians were killed.

Three days after the riots the Armenian tailor to whose shop I brought a suit on the day of the riots told me what happened to him. This Armenian's name was Onik Alem Schaihean [sic]. He told me that as soon as I left he closed his shop and went into hiding in a nearby building. He stayed there until evening. Then he put on a Turkish fez that indicated he was a Turkish official and had his Armenian servant men trail behind him in Turkish fashion. He passed as a Turk and when he arrived in Galata he was safe. From there he went to his home to Pera Taxim [sic] and it was very calm.

This Armenian tailor was an excellent craftsman and was liked by the Turks. In fact, most of his customers were Turkish. After the rioting was over he went back to his shop and it was business as usual with his regular Turkish customers. A few months later he moved to Galata because he was disgusted with the past riots in Stambol. If the common Turks had known he was an Armenian in all probability they would have killed him. As it was, Onik associated with the better class Turks and they treated him with respect.

These riots were aimed only at the Armenians. The Armenians were at fault and the Turks had just cause. The Turks were forced to defend themselves because the Armenians threatened the destruction of the government. I don't care what the history books say. The Turks were in the right. The riots were directed only by the low class Turks. Many fine Turks saved their Armenian friends. Even among these low class Turks, I saw no children or women being killed. Just men. It seems no matter what happens the lower class people pay for it.

I knew of a few Jewish families in Galata who hid their Armenian friends until the excitement was over. It was very difficult to explain the Armenian riots to Americans. If someone attempted to overthrow this government I would be against the idea. Those who attempt to overthrow the government are not good. The same with the Armenians. I liked many Armenians, but I do not like the idea of forcing a revolution on any government.

[Account of] Mrs. Anna Adatto

When the fighting took place between the Armenians and Turks, I was at my home in Peri Pasha. I was up in the morning and noticed two girls who usually were at work during the day returning home. They told me that their place of work had been closed temporarily. I asked them what the cause was? They said the Armenians are being killed. Immediately I took two girl friends and began to walk toward the place of the trouble.

I heard a neighbor yell to the top of her voice, warning us girls to return home at once because of the grave danger. Just as we approached our home we looked up at a nearby wall and saw a Turk with a huge stick knock down an Armenian. It appeared as if the Armenian was killed instantly. We then ran into the house and soon there were many rumors about the danger and fights between the Armenians and Turks.

A few minutes later I saw a neighbor carrying household goods on his back. Upon asking him what he was doing, he replied, "The Armenians have left all their household goods and fled and we are helping ourselves. My father rushed out to the neighbor and scolded him very bitterly for committing such a despicable act. My father told [him] he was committing a sin and told him to return the goods. This neighbor did return the goods because he respected my father and was afraid of incurring his enmity. But I know that some of the lower class people in our district were guilty of looting. There were also two lower class Jews who participated in looting and they were ostracized by the neighbors. No good ever came to them because they were cursed by the stolen goods. Their lives were full of evil happenings.

I and my family remained in the house all day and saw no other fighting except the one scene on the high wall. That midnight, the *shamas* came to our home and told us the fighting was over.

I knew of many Jews who hid their Armenian friends in their homes. There were also many Armenians who were saved by their Turkish friends.

In Bademlik, the Armenian quarter, as well as in Yeşildirek, the heaviest toll of lives took place. I saw no Turkish officials or policeman participate in the fighting. The Turks who killed the Armenians were civilians and they used no guns. The Turks had for weapons huge sticks. . . . The Turks who engaged in this fighting were Kurds and the lowest class of Turks.

The Turks, prior to the fighting, called the Armenians "rats" and, after the fighting it seems as if the Armenians disappeared like rats because there was not a sign of them anywhere.

Some of my playmates were Armenians and were good friends of mine. We often would sing Armenian songs and have nice chats together. There was no ill feeling between the Jews and the Armenians. Most of the Armenians we knew fled to Paris.

The Armenians that my family used to know were very refined and well educated in French. My father had a large number of Armenian friends and our family did everything we could to aid the distressed Armenians. I am very happy to say that Jews in many instances took extraordinary risks in saving the lives of their Christian friends. Though we liked our Armenian friends, the fault of the fighting it seems, rested on their leaders. The Armenians attempted to overthrow the Turkish government and the Turks believed that retaliation was necessary. As individuals, the Armenians were excellent citizens. As a group they wanted to do things too fast. My sympathies were with the suffering Armenians but the Turkish government was not to blame. . . .

[Account of] Mr. Shemuel Brudo

The Armenian massacre in Constantinople is a very delicate question and to pass judgment will be almost impossible. Personally I sympathized with the Armenians and felt they should be granted political autonomy.

I wish to point out that many Turks saved their Armenian friends and even hid them in their homes. Many Jews saved the lives of Armenians because they supplied them with phylacteries and prayer books. When the Turks would enter the homes of these Armenians they would not disturb them because they were shown the phylacteries and Hebrew books. Also the Armenians would say "*Yahudi, Yahudi*" (I am a Jew, I am a Jew) and the Turks would leave immediately.

It was ironical that the Armenian Christians very effectively used Jewish symbols to save their lives. I am quite sure many Christians were glad that Judaism had not become extinct prior to the Armenian massacres.

[Account of] Mrs. Dorah Cohen

I was a very young girl when the Armenian massacres took place in Constantinople. Many Armenians were killed but we Jews saved many

from death because we loaned them religious garments and phylacteries in order that they would pass as Jews.

I knew an Armenian who had his shop in a community surrounded
by Turks. He was well liked and when the fighting took place, his
Turkish friends hid him until conditions were calm.

The Turks had warned the Jews to identify themselves in order to
prevent them from being mistaken for Armenians. Every nationality
was told to identify itself in order that the Armenians might be spotted.

My father was an Italian subject and on the eve of the rioting we
quickly improvised an Italian flag and hung it outside of our door. No
Turk ever entered our home during the rioting.

Albert Adatto, "Sephardim and the Seattle Sephardic Community" (M.A. thesis, University of
Washington, 1939): 258–62. Courtesy University of Washington Press. Original in English.


## 43. A CONTROVERSY OVER THE CHIEF RABBINATE
   OF JERUSALEM (1909)

*The Young Turk Revolution of July 1908 unseated the veteran Ottoman Chief Rabbi
Moshe Halevi (1827–1910). Spiritual head of Ottoman Jewry since 1872—thanks
largely to his collaboration with the government of Abdülhamid II—Halevi appeared to supporters of the new constitutional government as too close an ally both of
the old regime and conservative forces within the Jewish community to survive the
revolutionary era. Within a year of Halevi's deposition, a self-proclaimed liberal and
ally of the Franco-Jewish Alliance Israélite Universelle (AIU) assumed the post of
Ottoman chief rabbi. The new chief rabbi, Haim Nahum (1872–1960), soon received
correspondence from Jewish communities across the empire, including Damascus,
Jerusalem, and Saida, requesting the dismissal of their own spiritual leaders, whom
they charged with corruption. New elections resulted in the swift removal of former
chief rabbis from office in many communities. A comparable transition of power
did not prove possible in Jerusalem. Rifts between progressives and conservatives,
Ashkenazim and Sephardim, and Zionist and pro-AIU camps foiled numerous
elections. In the midst of the ongoing struggle over the chief rabbinate of Jerusalem,
Nahum and his allies unseated Elijah Moses Panijel (1850–1919), who served as acting Sephardi chief rabbi of Palestine from 1907 to the year of his forcible removal from
power in 1909. What follows are the words of Panijel's supporters, who considered their
Gallicized Jewish opponents to be antireligious fanatics who were willing to sacrifice
the future of Judaism on the altar of the AIU's modernizing mission.*

Suddenly there was a great revolution that occurred in the government of our sacred country. The voice of the generations and liberty

and freedom were heard all across the land. The revolution also brought about a transformation in the seat of the rabbinate.

The righteous rabbi Moshe Halevi, head of the rabbis of Turkey, quit his position, which was inherited by a young man, a teacher in the schools of the AIU, Mr. Haim Nahum. That teacher, who is the product of the methods of the AIU and has imbibed them with all his being, saw fit to replace all those rabbis who did not share his thoughts and vision. Instead he brought to power those people who were suitable to him and who would help him increase the prestige of the AIU and of French among our people. The victims on this altar were the Torah in its entirety and all of the hopes of the people of Israel, all of which are insignificant [to Nahum and his allies] compared to their goal of expanding the AIU and its schools in all the lands of Turkey.

Afterwards they added libel upon libel, and without taking into account the opinions of the believers of Israel, [Nahum] turned to his friend Mr. Antebi. Together they made a pact to bring down the rabbi of Jerusalem, the righteous man and scholar E.M.P. [Eliyahu Moshe Panijel] because, in addition to being a hated soul, Antebi[33] . . . [concluded that] there is a great "fault" in the rabbi because he is pious before the Lord and Antebi and his camp could not forgive him this "fault."

'Al Homotayikh Yerushalayim (Jerusalem: n.p., 1909). Translated from Hebrew by Michelle Campos.

## 44. A COUP IN THE CAPITAL: THE OTTOMAN CHIEF RABBI WATCHES IN FEAR [1909]

*In July 1908, members of the opposition to Ottoman sultan Abdülhamid II's autocratic rule successfully orchestrated a bloodless coup that forced him to reinstate the Ottoman Constitution of 1876 and reintroduce parliamentary government in the empire. Although Abdülhamid II managed to retain the sultanate, a new group, known as the Committee of Union and Progress (CUP), became the de facto force behind the government. While various parties initially rejoiced at the unprecedented freedoms they believed the Young Turk era promised, others were disgruntled with the new arrangement. Among them were soldiers loyal to the sultan as well as Muslims who believed the new regime favored its non-Muslim members and threatened to under-*

33. A descendant of prominent rabbinical lines in Aleppo and Damascus, Albert Antebi (1873–1919) became principal of the Alliance Israélite Universelle's vocational school in Jerusalem in 1897.

*mine the Islamic nature of the state. By the spring of 1909 these forces came together and briefly took the imperial capital by force. In the midst of their counter-revolution Ottoman Chief Rabbi Haim Nahum wrote to the president of the Alliance Israélite Universelle in Paris to describe the state of chaos reigning in the city. In a second letter written after the CUP regime had returned to power, Nahum explained that Jews had been singled out as targets during the violence. He also hinted at disturbing news from the Anatolian interior, likely a reference to the situation in Adana, which witnessed two large-scale massacres of Armenians during this period of instability.*

Constantinople, 14 April 1909

Dear Monsieur Bigart,

You must have heard by telegraph of what has been happening here since yesterday. For more than twenty-four hours we have been living in real anarchy. All the troops have mutinied. After tying up their officers, the soldiers besieged Parliament and the Sublime Porte. They are demanding the literal enforcement of the Law of the *sheri*[34] (religious law) and the removal of the Young Turks. Even at this very minute, they are still roaming the streets, shooting into the air. We are anxiously waiting for it to end. Will there be a reaction? For the moment, there is no sign of it. If things become serious, there is danger of revolution. In that case, I will seek refuge in the French embassy.

Constantinople, 17 May 1909

Dear Monsieur Bigart,

You must have learned from the newspapers of the difficult times that the whole population of the capital has been living through. We have escaped a terrible massacre. The reactionary movement was going to "attack the Israelites" first. The population did not repudiate it. We are still not completely out of danger despite the state of siege and the harsh measures the present government is taking to repress any reactionary initiative. But in spite of this severity, confidence has not yet completely returned; there is general malaise, particularly in diplomatic circles. The news from the interior, although very exaggerated, is far from reassuring. . . .

Esther Benbassa, ed., *Haim Nahum: A Sephardic Chief Rabbi in Politics, 1892–1923*, translated by Miriam Kochan (Tuscaloosa: University of Alabama Press, 1995), 158–59.

---

34. Turkish version of the Arabic *shari'a*, or Islamic law.

## 45.  LETTERS FROM JEWISH CONSCRIPTS TO
## THE OTTOMAN ARMY (1910)

*In the wake of the Young Turk Revolution, the fledging regime fixed its attention on implementing universal conscription. The Ottoman parliament voted in favor of this reform in May 1909, extending mandatory military service to Ottoman Christian and Jewish men for the first time. Many non-Muslim youth initially expressed enthusiasm for this reform, announcing their eagerness to serve their empire. The following source, culled from the newspaper* Journal de Salonique, *presents the enthusiastic testimonies of two young Ottoman Jewish soldiers, accounts that the paper's editor no doubt hoped would inspire readers to embrace their new duties as Ottoman citizen-soldiers. The new measure was not without its critics however. Opposition soon emerged within the Jewish community as reports suggested that enlisted Jewish men were being forced to forgo their religious duties while in the army. In the face of these challenges, as well as a period of successive wars including the Italo-Ottoman (Italo-Turkish) War (1911), the Balkan Wars (1912 and 1913), and the First World War (1914–1918), Jewish emigration from the empire soared.*

I was on leave last Saturday so I took a boat ride. Seeing a vendor on the bridge, I bought the *Osmanischer Lloyd* from him and began to read.

At the same time a group of travelers circled around me. They found it strange that a simple khaki[35] would know how to read, and a Western language at that.

The Constantinopolitans [Istanbulites] didn't take long to understand that they were in the presence of a recruit from the new regime, and they overwhelmed me with questions. The word Salonica has the power to fascinate all these good people, who believe our city to be akin to Paris or New York. . . .

My superior officer had me go every day to the workshops of the Oriental Railroad. All the khakis that know a trade are put to work and receive a daily salary of three to five piastres.

Military life, such as we live it, is a dream. If it goes on this way, we will return home big and fat, healthy in body and spirit, and bearing fond memories of the barracks. . . .

Isaac Montequio

We could not be more satisfied with our lives as soldiers in the Azap Kapı barracks. Last Saturday I received permission to stroll through

---

35. Soldier.

the neighborhood, which is densely populated by Jews. Upon recognizing me my coreligionists welcomed me warmly and insisted that I join them in their homes.

In the one dormitory we are seven Greeks, two Bulgarians, two Jews and thirty-seven Muslims. We live together like true brothers. But there is a downside: during meals the tables are set with [non-kosher] bowls of soup, including vegetables and rice. Our companions from the countryside delight in it. For us [Jews], it is still very difficult to [bring ourselves to] eat it. . . .

If the government could find a solution to the question of food, I am convinced that many Jews would not only perform their service joyfully but that others would ask to register as volunteers.

At night in the dormitory a sergeant stands guard, and every time he sees a soldier who is not well covered, he tucks him in with care. The minister has ordered beds and new blankets.

I must also take advantage of this opportunity to ask you to thank the valiant members of the Club des Intimes[36] through the pages of *La Epoka*.[37] We are indebted to them for having undertaken their work armed with superhuman courage. The beautiful and unforgettable celebrations that the Club des Intimes organized on our behalf remain engraved in our hearts and will never be erased. . . .

Abram Aruh

"Lettres des conscrits," *Journal de Salonique*, March 24, 1910, 1. Translated from French by Alma Rachel Heckman.

# 46. RESPONSES TO THE ITALIAN OCCUPATION OF RHODES [1912]

*In the fall of 1911 the Ottoman Empire became embroiled in a war with Italy over the territories of Tripoli and Cyrenaica in Libya. Although the conflict began in North Africa, Italy soon set its sights on other Ottoman territories. By early 1912, Italian forces wrested the Dodecanese Islands from Ottoman control. In the process the island of Rhodes, which had been Ottoman since the sixteenth century, came under Italian occupation. At the time the island's Jewish community numbered around 4,500. This*

36. A Jewish philanthropic and social club active in late-Ottoman Salonica.
37. A Ladino newspaper published from 1875 to 1911 by the a-Levi (Levy) family of Salonica.

*account, written by an Alliance Israélite Universelle teacher to his superiors in Paris,*
*describes the moment of occupation, offering detailed information about this chaotic*
*period as well as philosophical meditations on how Jews, as a vulnerable minority,*
*experience transitions of state authority.*

Ever since the Italians arrived in Rhodes our school is visited daily by lieutenants and captains of the Italian army. For the most part their knowledge of the French language is as extensive as that of the French. They ask me for information about our students, what they know, their level of instruction, and how long they study at the school. I plan their class visits carefully and allow them to walk around the school grounds.

The Italian governor responsible for civilian affairs on the island of Rhodes goes by the title of General Commander of the Italian Naval Forces. He was once the Italian consul-general to Salonica. After he was installed his first task was to carefully investigate all Young Turks who were members of the Committee for Union and Progress and the foreigners who sought exile in Italy.

To date we count four hundred people exiled in Italy, among whom there are many Greeks.

Four of our coreligionists, among them the most notable members of our community, have been accused of being Young Turks and have been asked to present themselves before the governor.

They might soon have shared the fate of their Turkish compatriots. [However], thanks to the intervention of the chief rabbi and to the overtures that the French and Austrian consuls made to the governor, our coreligionists were released, on the condition that they would not involve themselves in any political activities that would compromise them in the eyes of the governor of Rhodes.

How embarrassing this situation was for our coreligionists in Rhodes!

The Oriental Jew, having been subject to hundreds of years of suffering, considers himself to be the weakest among all of his compatriots of other religions. He appears to double over with gratitude to . . . the people that surround him. Self-interested, he lavishes praise and flattery on those in his city who enjoy influence. Above all he never fails to demonstrate to the government under whose rule he lives his highest respect and his great devotion.

Now the Jews of Rhodes, whose sentiments of devotion toward

the government are universally appreciated (more proof: recently they gave money on the occasion of the legislative elections), see themselves obliged to modify their conduct, for they no longer depend on the Turkish government but rather the Italian government. Yet this does not deter them. Why should this change of master matter to them? Are not all Jews condemned to pass constantly from one government to another? Their history is rich in such examples; they have been used to it for a long time! Provided that the power that governs them does not bother them too much, they attach themselves to it. Yet it is just this condition that makes the Jews of Rhodes ashamed. They wish with the greatest desire to be judged honestly and fairly by the Italians who are today their masters; but if the Turks gain back possession of the island, the Jews will pay (at that time) dearly for their expressions of friendship toward the Italians.

This is why our coreligionists in Rhodes, after deep reflection, have determined to observe the greatest caution whenever they must pronounce themselves in favor of one of the two hostile governments. In the presence of Turks the Jews affect a servile and somber air as if they were mourning their fall from grace with them [the Ottomans]; in the presence of Italians the Jews display a joyful and happy air.

Because the Jew is accommodating, he knows [how] to have good relations with everyone, and if today the chief rabbi and the leaders of the Jewish Community of Rhodes were to go visit the Italian governor of the city to pay their respects and to wish him a good arrival, tomorrow when Rhodes might again become Turkish they would do the same for the Ottoman governor. "Long live the King! Long live the League!" says the proverb.

Letter by Léon Mehrez to the central office of the Alliance Israélite Universelle (Paris), May 15, 1912, Archives of the Alliance Israélite Universelle, Paris, I. C. 38. Translated from French by Alma Rachel Heckman.

## 47.  A ZIONIST'S PROPOSAL TO MAKE SALONICA AN INTERNATIONAL CITY [1912–1913]

*In the course of the Balkan Wars of 1912–1913, Bulgaria, Montenegro, Greece, Serbia, and the Ottoman Empire battled for control of Macedonia. Although Greece occupied the Aegean port city of Salonica in October 1912, fighting continued in the region for another year while various powers vied to define the city's legal status. Austrian representatives, intent on preserving their own access to the Aegean Sea, proposed that Salonica be established as a free and neutral Jewish city under international auspices. The Austro-Hungarian Foreign Ministry, in tandem with the Jewish community of Vienna, argued that Salonica had been majority Jewish for generations, with Jews essentially controlling its commerce and port. In a series of letters addressed to the Zionist Organization in Berlin, two of which are presented here, the Salonican Zionist activist and journalist David Isaac Florentin (1874– 1941) embraced the Austrian position, arguing that "internationalizing" Salonica would ensure the economic interests of the city and protect Jews from the Greek impulse to Hellenization. Florentin's plan to internationalize Salonica found favor with Jews and non-Jews in the region. It was ultimately rejected however, both by international Jewish groups and Greece itself, which annexed the city and its hinterlands in August 1913. (For Florentin's thoughts on Zionism see source 72.)*

Salonica, December 15, 1912

To the Committee of the Zionist Organization in Berlin, c/o the president,

Dark days approach; misery and grief are coming and as inevitable as death they strike the Jews of Salonica.

This is the fear; this is the nightmare that haunts our minds here.

However exaggerated this may seem, there is much truth to this picture. The happy times of Turkish rule are long gone. Jews have ceased to be the indisputable masters of the place. Fierce competitors challenge their position with a previously unheard of degree of bitterness; it will never again be possible to gather around a city this collection of provinces, which earned their livelihood from Salonica and were held together by Turkish might. The prosperity of Jewish Salonicans is greatly compromised. Greek control strangles the city. Under Greek domination, the port of Salonica appears eternally blocked.

An entirely different situation would be preferable. Bulgarian Salonica would be able to keep a significant part of its current hinterland (Macedonia and Thrace) and to attract some of the commerce of eastern Rumelia and western Bulgaria. It would be the great western port of a greater Bulgaria.

As the capital of an autonomous Macedonia, Salonica would preserve at least some of its current trade.

An internationalized Salonica, like Tangier or Dalny in Manchuria, would cease to be the theater of ethnic struggles, while benefiting from the many countries interested in its prosperity. It could continue to be used as an entrepôt by a large number of Balkan countries. This appears to be one of the solutions that best suits our population.

But what good are the wishes of a population with neither defenders nor officials in the face of persistent forces? All hope is in vain. . . .

It is for this reason that we come to you, Sir, to say:

"However modest is the influence of one association amidst a concert of international voices, it can always make its presence known through the press or with the aid of certain powerful individuals. If all Jewish societies banded together, uniting their efforts, such concerted and enlightened collaboration might alleviate the cruel fate that appears to await the single most important [Jewish] community in all the Orient, one which comprises nearly one-fifth of Turkish Jewry.

"Time is of the essence. Your action, together with that of other Jewish societies, can save 70,000 of your coreligionists from ruin. Your society is powerful and respected among the people of Israel. It is to you that the Jews of Salonica turn in anguish, and they say to you: Brothers, in the name of martyred Israel have pity and act!

"This is the respectful prayer that I transmit to you, Mr. President. Strong is your ardent love for Judaism and your unshakable faith in leading the hesitant and convincing the skeptics."

D. Florentin

To the Committee of the Zionist Organization in Berlin
Salonica, January 3, 1913
Mr. President,

The question of Macedonia was addressed in London and will soon be resolved. What will be done with Salonica? What will be the fate of the Jewish population of the city?

In a prior communication we made the apprehensions of the community clear to you. We explained to you why we dread Greek rule and how this rule would irreparably lead to the economic ruin of the city, which, deprived of its hinterlands, would be turned into a naval port and fortress while being constantly exposed to the bold enterprises of the Bulgarians. Indeed the rich Salonican community would swiftly disaggregate, and those members who are energetic or have some money will go elsewhere to find a land that is more welcoming of their activities and more favorable for their business.

The horizon remains full of uncertainty as we write you this communiqué. There is clear evidence to show us that which will *not* benefit the Jewish community. We seek to bring this to your benevolent and vigilant attention. We still do not know, however, what will best ensure the wellbeing and unhindered growth of our community.

Today the situation is becoming clearer: we understand the advantages and disadvantages of each of the proposed solutions to the Macedonian Question. Trusting that you will not fail to take notice of the most important Jewish community in the Balkans, we communicate to you the results of the deliberations of the community's active members. What we present to you here is an ideal, almost a dream. Yet who can say that this dream is impossible if strong wills work to transport it to solid ground?

The preferred political regime of the Salonican Jews is the internationalization and neutralization of the city as well as a very small zone of surrounding land. The city and its environs (comprising the current townships of Salonica as well as Yenice-i Vardar, a total of 400 to 600 square kilometers of land with a population of 260,000 inhabitants) would constitute a small state that would enjoy some kind of mitigated autonomy, ruled by a statute elaborated by the Powers—the Allies and Turkey. It would be placed under the protection of the Great Powers. Locals would assume the role of administrators and police, headed by Swiss or Belgian managers and instructors. The consuls would have permanent control and would maintain strict observance of the international statute. The port would be free. The restricted zones of the township of Yenice-i Vardar and of Lower Vardar, which would contain a highly fertile region of Lake Yenice on the Thermaic Gulf, would assure the independence of these places, allowing for future urban development, and at the same time furnishing the city with provisions and offering the secure placement of water for factories and workshops that would no doubt flourish under a regime of security and calm in this corner of the Balkans. Thanks to the prudent and intelligent activities of our merchants, the capital they possess, and their profound knowledge of the Orient, its resources, and its tastes, Salonica, situated as it is in the middle of the Balkans, would soon become the emporium of the wealthy countries that surround it. Its attractive radius would extend much further than it currently does. The port would tap the agricultural wealth from the Vardar valley and provide access to manufactured products brought in by western European steamships.

The states most interested in the economic prosperity of Salonica— Austria, Germany, England, and France—would be able to assure this gateway to the Levant the status of a most-favored nation in their commercial agreements with all neighboring states while simultaneously ensuring that preferential tariffs enacted by these states would not obstruct or compromise rail traffic.

In this way the merchants of Salonica, agents of the city's current prosperity, would not see themselves stripped of the fruits of centuries of labor.

This solution will have the advantage of suppressing forever the hatreds that exist in these lands. Depending on the region, Macedonia is Bulgarian, Serbian, or Greek. If it is made an autonomous state, the impassioned and murderous fighting between nationalities will break out once again. If on the other hand Macedonia is shared between the allies of Macedonia's populations, stability will reign in the Balkans. But Salonica is neither Greek, nor Bulgarian, nor Turkish; it is Jewish. Whichever state possesses it will view it as a problem, as a heterogeneous region with a population that, due to its demographic importance and its advanced intellectual milieu, resists all attempts to assimilate it into an ethnically delineated and yet still poorly unified mass. Millions of peasants, bent by . . . long centuries of servitude and oppression cannot pretend to absorb an urban elite of 70,000 souls, proud of its independence and accustomed to complete freedom. The introduction of this inassimilable population into a tiny nation can only cause trouble and discontent.

Perhaps these reflections can be published in the press; perhaps you can use them with powerful men, friends of peace and justice, who are in some way interested in the fate of the Jews.

It is in this hope that we transmit them.

D. Florentin

Letters from David Florentin to the Zionist Committee, Berlin, December 15, 1912 and January 3, 1913, Central Zionist Archives (Jerusalem), Z3/2. Translated from French by Alma Rachel Heckman.

## 48. A MUSLIM-JEWISH-VLACH COMMITTEE FOR INTERNATIONALIZING SALONICA [1913]

*For nearly two years after the city of Salonica came under Greek oversight in the course of the Balkan Wars of 1912 and 1913, the city's legal status remained undetermined. Its fate prompted heated local and international debate. While Habsburg officials, Viennese Jews, and local Jewish groups advocated for the transformation of Salonica into an international Jewish city, this memorandum proposed an alternative plan. The work of a committee composed of Muslims, Jews, and Vlachs (speakers of a Romance language indigenous to Southeastern Europe), the memorandum proposed that Salonica become an autonomous territory under the control of European forces. The authors of this document allied, it seems, because all were minorities whose interests were unlikely to be represented by any of the nation-states that vied for control over the city.*

Memorandum:

Your Excellency,

On February 16, 1913, the Committee for the Defense of the Interests of the Muslim, Jewish, and Vlach Populations of Macedonia had the honor of submitting a memorandum to Their Excellencies the esteemed Great Powers' ambassadors to the government of His Majesty the Sultan of Turkey, in which the committee made known its goals and requested said ambassadors' intervention on behalf of their respective governments, in accordance with the principles of humanity and justice, to halt all massacres and any other attacks of a religious or ethical nature perpetrated by armies or any other groups.

We have no doubt that the ambassadors living in Constantinople [Istanbul] have transmitted this memorandum to their respective governments and have received their kind attention.

The goal of the Turkish-Jewish-Vlach Macedonian Committee is based on the same historical and ethnic considerations as those underlying the allied governments' declarations of war against Turkey. This same goal draws an ineluctable strength from the results of the war, whose strangeness strikes even the most biased observer.

In effect the contradictory aspirations of the populations living in each of the occupied areas toward the occupying state results in divisions so inappropriate that giving Macedonia to the Macedonians is the only natural and inevitable solution to the problem.

This is why the Macedonian Committee, in its meeting of March 5,

1913, decided to dispatch a delegation formed by the signatories to advocate in favor of this cause before the chancelleries of the Great Powers.

It is by this mandate that we permit ourselves, Your Excellency, to draw your exalted attention to the following:

First we must clarify one point. Concerning our mission, we have no ties to the Ottoman government nor to any other political organization apart from that which has appointed us.

We come from Macedonia and the nature of our mandate is clearly defined in the document we have the honor of attaching here.

We seek through this preliminary declaration to remove from Your Excellency's mind any false reports about our mandate that may have come to you from any of the parties interested in the matter.

Having stated this point, we have the honor, your excellency, to summarize the arguments on which our case is based.

In their struggle against Turkey the Balkan allies have employed historical principles in order to justify their acquisition of the territories of Rumelia.[38]

We do not currently seek to criticize this right.

All the same can we not also invoke the same principle for the Turks, Jews, and Vlachs?

Indeed we can.

Is it not time that confers this historic right on the populations of each land?

Many centuries of residence have conferred it.

Is not the bond established by the happy or sad events experienced communally by populations of the same territory basis enough that one might go out and proclaim it?

The Turk above all has fought for the conquest of this country and worked toward its development, even under the worst of governmental regimes! He would certainly have fared better than anyone had the tyrannizing regime that dominated the country for centuries not gotten in his way. Yet at the very moment in which he glimpsed a bit of happiness, he found himself under another regime marked by continual and internecine struggles. . . .

---

38. A term for the Ottoman territories of Southeastern Europe.

Sentiments of justice and humanity will not accept this.

The same argument can easily be made for the Jews and the Vlachs.

When it comes to the number of each nationality found among the Macedonians, this represents the strength of our argument.

According to the most precise statistics, what is the respective proportion of each element?

We will be strict in our calculations as is evidenced in the example below:

| Sancak (prefecture) | Bulgarians | Greeks | Turks | Jews | Vlachs |
|---|---|---|---|---|---|
| Salonica | 92,805 | 194,739 | 228,989 | 110,000 | |
| Serres | 118,027 | 36,244 | 114,386 | 20,000 | |
| Drama | 5,194 | 43,093 | 124,968 | 5,000 | |
| | | | | | 50,000 |
| Total | 216,026 | 274,076 | 468,343 | 135,000 | 50,000 |

How can one commit such a flagrant injustice, to preach the principle of nation-states, to give away territories whose majority populations include Turks, like the Drama sancak, or Jews, who indeed ought to have a special regime in the city of Salonica?

How can one give Serres to the Bulgarians, or Köprülü to the Serbs? These are political impossibilities.

With this artificial and forced partition the conflicts that have bloodied Macedonia since 1902 will rise again with an even more savage force, now that the Ottoman government, which served as a buffer and equilibrating force, has disappeared.

It is Macedonia that must now constitute the buffer state. It is impossible to partition it under foreign domination, except provisionally, by fire and blood.

By accepting the results of the war Europe had hoped to put an end to all these conflicts. But it will soon find itself obliged to intervene once again. The pacification it desired will not occur without an autonomous territory under the control of the Great Powers, with Salonica as its capital.

We therefore have the honor to summarize our requests in the following proposals:

1. Creation of an autonomous territory in Macedonia with Salonica as capital;

2. Guarantee of this autonomy by the Great Powers;

3. European control.

In our view this is the only possible solution to the problem that Macedonia will pose for Europe. . . .

Trusting in the future and the justice of Europe, we request of Your Excellency to take up our cause, the cause of those populations who no misfortune has spared until now.

It is with the firm hope of a favorable action from Your Excellency that we remain respectfully yours,

| President of the Delegation, | Delegate, | Delegate, |
|---|---|---|
| Halim Sami | Nissim Rousso | Nehmed Gelib |

"Mémoire," The Gaster Papers, Albanian Committee, File 3, Document 115/286, University College London Library Services, Special Collections (London). Translated from French by Alma Rachel Heckman.

## 49. A SEPHARDI JEW IN MARSEILLE CLAIMS SALONICAN NATIONALITY DURING THE FIRST WORLD WAR {1914–1918}

*from the height of European nationalism,*

*Ottoman empire*

*With the retraction of the Ottoman Empire and the creation of myriad nation-states in Southeastern Europe, many Ottoman Jews who had emigrated or were in the process of emigrating found themselves with ambiguous legal status or insufficient documentation to prove their nationality. This became ever more crucial during the* Crumbling *First World War, when Jewish men were conscripted by both the Allied and Central* by this point *Powers and when subjects of the Ottoman Empire living abroad risked being labeled or interned as enemy aliens of France or Britain. Perhaps to avoid these pitfalls, the subjects of the following account sought to have themselves formally registered as "Salonicans" living in France, that is, citizens of nowhere but the city of their birth.*

After speaking to their mother, Vidal and Henri sent a telegram to their father asking him to intervene to rid them of their Italian nationality. The telegram was intercepted by the censors, and the two brothers were summoned by Borelli, the special inspector who, after a fit of anger, agreed to let the telegram go but asked them to state their nationality immediately. They answered in chorus, "Salonicans." "What?" They had thought it out thoroughly. To declare themselves

Italian meant being sent to the Italian army; to declare themselves Greek, to be sent to Salonica; to declare themselves Turkish, to be arrested as enemies; to declare themselves Belgian meant to be incorporated into the army of the Soldier-King.[39] They did not have the choice of another nationality, and moreover all were at war. Hence the logical necessity of declaring themselves nationals of what was in fact their little homeland, the city of Salonica.

But Salonica was not a nation-state, and the inspector exclaimed, "You are making fun of me, my dear fellows. I demand [that you state] a nationality immediately or else I will throw you into jail." The two fellows resisted and remained in the police station. But their telegram reached their father, who notified his nephew Paul, who notified Longuet, who notified Briand, and again, David Nahum pleaded for the cause of his sons: "They are not Turkish, although born in the Ottoman Empire. They are not Greek, although Salonica is Greek. They are not Italian, although they have been Italian subjects. Thus they are Salonicans." "What a Macedonian salad," repeated the president of the French Council, who was temporarily distracted from the torments of war by this bizarre incident. Then, convinced by David Nahum's logic, he immediately sent a telegram to Marseille for the brothers to be freed on the spot as Salonicans. They must have gone to prison on May 11, but they left for good on the 16th.

The whole affair had turned out well thanks to David Nahum's skill and intelligence, Paul Nahum's crucial help, the generosity of . . . Salomon Beressi, the intervention of a great French socialist leader, and finally, to the miraculous decision of the supreme head of the French government. . . . All of this thoroughly confirmed Vidal's oriental conception of power.

[The document they submitted read:]

> Name: Nahum.
> Forename: Vidal.
> Age: 22
> Nationality: Salonican.
> Residence: Aubagne Street.

---

39. A reference to King Albert I (r. 1909–1934) of Belgium.

Mr. Nahum is authorized to reside in Marseille during the war with his family. He is informed that he will only be able to move during the hostilities on condition that he carries a laissez-passer delivered by the police inspector or the mayor of his place of residence.

He will have to obey strictly the orders to be given to all the inhabitants in the commune either by the military authorities or by the civil authorities. He is warned that in case of breaking with the above prescriptions, he will be arrested immediately on grounds of espionage.

Marseille, May 18, 1916
Special Inspector Borelli

The document in our possession is not the residence permit itself but an unofficial copy written by Vidal. However on this copy Vidal crossed out "Salonican" and later wrote "Levantine Jew." In a postscript to this document he wrote, "I say Levantine Jew [signed] Borelli." In his own hand he also copied the partial copy of his identity card no. 762003, which was delivered to him in Marseille on December 18, 1917, by the very same Borelli under orders of the prefect under the name Nahoum (no longer Nahum) and stating the nationality as that of "Levantine Jew."

The formula "Levantine Jew" was found after the residence permit of May 18, 1916 was established. Salonican nationality could only be a temporary lifeline. Nevertheless, the status of an émigré community provided all the advantages of French national protection without the military inconveniences that came with nationality. It was the flow into France of the Sephardi Jews after the great fire that struck Salonica on August 5, 1917 that prompted the search for a special status appropriate for all the Francophones who were neither Greek nor Turkish, such as Vidal. This is why it is possible that in December 1917, owing to the necessity of making an identity card on the basis of the officially delivered residence permit, Inspector Borelli had retrospectively, but illegally, crossed out the word "Salonican" from the permit, as if it were an error corrected in 1916 when it was originally written, and not in 1917 when Vidal's identity card was issued. . . .

In any case Vidal evaded the nation-state thanks to his urban Salonican nationality as much as to his vague Levantine Jewishness; this meant that he avoided the army, war, and death. After being Salonican for a period that lasted perhaps more than a year, Vidal would remain a Levantine Jew for a few years, until he found the, albeit provisional, Greek solution in 1925, before becoming permanently French in 1931.

Edgar Morin, "Vidal and His People," *Journal of Mediterranean Studies* 4:2 (1994): 332–34.

## 50. ENEMY ALIENS? CHALLENGING A WARTIME CLASSIFICATION IN BRITAIN [1915]

*During the First World War (1914–1918), when the Ottomans aligned with the Central Powers, Jews born in the empire but living in Great Britain or France found that they were under threat of becoming "enemy aliens" in the eyes of their adopted states. Some Jews responded by seeking the novel, state-approved legal designations "citizen of the Levantine nation" (in France) or "Ottoman subjects of Jewish nationality" (in Great Britain). In the British context, the Board of Deputies of British Jews, the main representative body of Anglo-Jewry, negotiated with the Home Office to spare Jewish subjects of the Ottoman Empire the label "enemy alien" on the basis that they were Turkish "by accident of birth." This did not prevent individual Jews from being interned, because British officials and Sephardi Jews alike continued to be confused by the ambiguous legal status of the émigré Ottoman Jew.*

February 8, 1915
Sir,

In reply to your letter of the 20th ultimo with regard to the recent Aliens Restriction (Armenians, etc.) Order in Council, I am directed by the Secretary of State to inform you that the Order was intentionally limited to Christian subjects of the Ottoman Empire. There are special reasons in history why the Armenian, Greek, and Syrian Christian subjects of the Ottoman Empire should be recognized as hostile to the Turks and treated accordingly. These reasons have not arisen in the case of Jewish subjects of the Ottoman Empire, and the Secretary of State is unable to advise that the Order in Council should be extended to include them.

I am, Sir,
Your obedient Servant,
John Pedder [Home Office]

11 May 1915
Sir [Home Office],

Your letter of the 8th February last headed 270431/87 has been communicated to the Committee of Turkish Jews at Manchester. They appreciate the historical difference between themselves and the Armenians, Greek, and Syrian subjects of the Turkish Empire, but assure this Board that though Turkish subjects by accident of birth in Syria, Mesopotamia, or other Turkish territory, they are separated from the normal Turk by difference in religion, language, and race, and moreover, that they have by virtue of residences and commercial interests in this Country long since ceased to have affinity or sympathy with Turkey, if they ever had any. They further assure the Board that they have no community of interest with the Ottoman Turks in political or national affairs, and that their interests as dealers in and exporters of Lancashire cotton goods to the markets of the world are intimately bound up in the prosperity of this country and its ultimate success against Germany and her Allies in the present struggle.

They therefore beg that an appeal be made for some relaxation of the existing regulations against alien enemies, if not in favor of all Turkish Jews, at least in favor of selected persons of that class who may be able to furnish substantial and satisfactory sureties.

With this in view they have provided the Board with a first list of 13 persons who, they assure the Board, are all of well-known and established commercial position in Manchester, and each of whom has obtained two written guarantees.

I am instructed to enclose [for] you a copy of the list, in which you will find full particulars of each of the applicants. I further enclose the originals of the guarantees and a letter from the Secretary of the Manchester Chamber of Commerce expressing the support of that Body to the Appeal.

I learn that the prohibition against travelling outside the five mile radius is the restriction from which these people chiefly suffer, as it very largely affects their business, and should you therefore feel that their circumstances merit consideration, and yet be unable to accord to them so full an exemption as has been accorded to Turkish Christians, it would be a welcome concession if you could see your way to free approved cases of Turkish Jews and their respective wives and children from that particular restriction, subject always to the proviso that they should not journey into a prohibited area.

Commending this application to your favorable consideration,

I am, Sir,

Your obedient Servant,

Charles H. L. Emanuel

Memo to Reginald McKenna, Board of Deputies of British Jews, ACC/3121/C/11/012/047, Folder 1. London Metropolitan Archive (London). Original in English.

## 51. A REPORT ON THE DEPORTATION OF ARMENIANS FROM BURSA [1915]

*At the time of the Ottoman Empire's entry into the First World War on the side of the Axis Powers, between 1.3 and 2.1 million Armenians lived within the boundaries of the empire. Considering the Armenians as a fifth column with ties to the Russian enemy and seizing upon the dynamics of war, various Ottoman statesmen in the leading Committee of Union and Progress party began a systematic assault on the empire's Armenian population. Mass arrests and executions of Armenian intellectuals and political figures were followed by the widespread confiscation of Armenian-owned property, the abduction and forced conversion of Armenian women and children, and massive, forced marches of men, women, and children to the deserts of Syria and Iraq. During this process as many as a million Armenians died of exposure, starvation, and massacre. The following report provides a rare Ottoman Jewish perspective on the Armenian genocide. Its author, Leon Sémach (b. 1869), was an Alliance Israélite Universelle school director who served in Bursa during the war.*

Armenians: this community is destined for complete destruction if the war lasts a few months longer. In Bursa during the month of August [the authorities] gave the Armenians three days to sell their houses and all of their possessions. Refusing to believe that there would be a mass expulsion (there were 1,700 families in Bursa), they thought they would be able to attenuate this measure through protest or by converting to Islam. After these attempts failed, they came to terms with reality. They asked for another three days, which they were granted.

Each family had a wagon pulled by two cows with space enough to carry their bedding and food. The women and children rode in the wagons while the men followed on foot. Those who were willing to pay for the privilege were permitted to go by carriage. Yet they were authorized to take only one carriage per family, no matter how large. All this served as a means of forcing the Armenians to sell off their belongings at very low prices.

Only Turks had access to these auctions. Greeks and Jews did not dare, for the simple reason that they received threats from Muslims. They alone made their purchases under the benevolent and encouraging eye of the police, while the poor Armenians got rid of their goods in crises of desperation. In a village near Bilicik, the Armenians preferred to burn down their homes along with all of their possessions rather than let them fall into Turkish hands.

It was a horrible spectacle, seeing so many families crowded into wagons and carriages all in a line on their way to the interior of Anatolia, not knowing their precise destination, fearing what fate awaited them.

Sometime after this indescribable exodus we learned that a great number of people died of hunger and thirst. The bread they had with them had gone bad. Others succumbed to disease, while the women who gave birth along the way were unable to survive their deliveries. I should add that paid assassins were stationed along the road to rob certain wealthy Armenians who had managed to take a bit of money with them.

There have been rumors that the majority of these families have been sent to Baghdad. The route is so long and taxing that few among them will arrive at their destination.

Those spared by the assassin's knife yield to fatigue and privation along the way. The Gregorian Armenians of Bursa, Ada Bazar, Bazar Köy, Panderma and all of the towns of Anatolia have shared the same fate. The Catholic Armenians have been spared. I should add that the expulsion order was given after making the enemy suffer every possible torture imaginable, including beatings with sticks, tying their hands and feet, and tearing out their nails in order to make them say where they had hidden their weapons, because bombs had been found in the Gregorian church.

A few hundred Armenians were sentenced to hanging. And that is not all. There was still the matter of getting rid of the Armenian soldiers who had been conscripted. They had to be exterminated as well. This was accomplished in the following manner: all Armenian soldiers were given leave. Without understanding this order issued in the middle of war, they were sent on their way and told to return home.

Turkish regiments that had been warned in advance positioned themselves along the road and killed each and every one, despite their protests, on the pretext that they had deserted. The scenes we have witnessed were dreadful and indescribable.

If the exodus from the provinces was sudden and frightening, this was not the case in Constantinople [Istanbul]. Every night 300–400 Armenians were sent from the capital to the interior of Anatolia to a certain fate, either being murdered en route or left in such a state so as to be reduced to begging.

At present the town is under military guard day and night. The authorities are suspicious of everyone. Above all they fear that people have weapons, even though they confiscated everything they could find this past June and July.

I mentioned above that the Armenians were authorized to sell off their possessions, but they were rarely able to sell their homes. Who will occupy them? The rumor is that the best homes will be given to state officials and that the others will go to the *muhacir*s.[40] As for stores and merchandise, they have been seized. This should give you an idea of the financial chaos that has ensued.

If one asks Muslims why such extreme measures have been taken against Armenians, they cite the part Armenians played in ensuring the Russian occupation of Van. However, before the Turkish government decided to finish off the Armenians, it consulted with the German and Austrian ambassadors. It was with the consent of these parties that the abovementioned horrors took place.

Letter from Léon Sémach in Bursa to the central office of the Alliance Israélite Universelle, October 11, 1915, Archives of the Alliance Israélite Universelle (Paris), Turquie I. C. 4.3. Partially reproduced in Aron Rodrigue, "L'Etat impérial ottoman et le politiques de déportation," in Bertrand Badie and Yves Déloye, eds., *Le temps de l'Etat: Mélanges en l'honneur de Pierre Birnbaum* (Paris: Fayard, 2007), 185–86. Translated from French by Julia Phillips Cohen.

---

40. Turkish for immigrants or refugees; here the term refers to Muslims who had been displaced during the war.

## 52. TRAVELING FOR WAR RELIEF:
## A SERBIAN RABBI'S JOURNEY [1919]

*As densely settled areas of Southeastern Europe became front lines in the First World War, Sephardim, like all residents of the region, faced trauma, displacement, and impoverishment. In Serbia by some estimates three quarters of a million people—approximately a fifth of the total population—succumbed to disease, famine, or military operations. Responding to the dire situation of wartime, the Jewish community of Serbia called upon the chief rabbi, Dr. Isaac Alcalay (1882–1978), to travel across the country and survey the state of its Jewish communities before embarking on a major European and American tour to represent their cause abroad. Between 1915 and 1918, Alcalay traveled to France, Britain, and the United States, where he appealed to Jewish representatives for aid and also lobbied on behalf of his government. In the following account Alacalay describes his journey.*

Belgrade, December 31, 1919
To the Administration of the Jewish Community,

When Austria declared war on Serbia the majority of our people left Belgrade to avoid the bombardment. Having moved to various places in southern Serbia, especially to Niš, these folks wandered around without a home or homestead, lacking basic provisions. Representatives of Serbian Jews, headed by the president of the Jewish community in Belgrade, took on the responsibility of caring for the poor refugees and finding ways to help them; they decided that the undersigned, a rabbi, should travel to Europe to interest the wealthy and influential Jews in our cause and our predicament.

I left the country immediately, spent several months abroad, and did everything in my power as much as was possible. I returned to Niš in July 1915. No sooner had I prepared a full report of my trip, work, and success, intending to submit it to the president of our community, than our political situation took a dramatic turn for the worse. Not only were there suddenly many more urgent matters to attend to, but everyone grew concerned about their very survival. People started leaving the country, and I myself, following the signal of the higher-ups, left Serbia. In my great haste I left behind most of the data I had collected during my trip. Believing, however, that the community should have in its archive a document recording the efforts I had undertaken, I decided to put together this report and give an account of everything retrospectively. I ask the administration not to seek precision or details in this report as not only has much time passed since that trip, we have also lived through a lifetime's worth of events since then.

The itinerary of my trip was Sofia–Bucharest–Constantinople [Istanbul]–Egypt. I also traveled to the countries of Western Europe. Turkey's entrance into the war during this time hindered my ability to travel from Bucharest, so I returned to Niš and from there via Salonica went to Western Europe. Sofia was the first stop on my trip. All promises notwithstanding and despite the fact that an aid committee and other humanitarian organizations had been created, I did not collect a penny for our people. In Bucharest the Sephardi community received us warmly; it immediately volunteered 1,000 lei[41] and organized a collection of contributions that brought in about 2,000 lei. Apart from this my intervention at the B'nai B'rith lodge in Bucharest, resulted in the sum of 10,000 francs being donated towards the same goal by the American headquarters of that organization. In order not to lose time I did not wait for all these funds to be collected. Instead I asked for the money to be sent to Niš, which it apparently was.

I continued the fund drive in the same manner in Salonica. There too a committee for the collection of contributions was established, and I engaged several humanitarian organizations and left the address to which to send the funds. Seizing an opportunity to board a ship, I traveled from Salonica to Brindisi, from where I traveled to Paris via Milan, immediately proceeding on to London. In London I organized the largest fund drive. I had to dedicate the first days to orienting and informing myself about people and circumstances, because everything was new and unknown to me. The only acquaintance and friend I had was Mr. Elkan Adler, son and brother of the two principal rabbis of Great Britain, who had been my guest during the Balkan Wars as a member of the Committee for Aid. The mention of his name alone opened the doors of the most distinguished people, important families, and prominent organizations to me. He introduced me to journalistic circles, where, apart from the purely humanitarian goals for which I had come, I had an opportunity to say a few good words about my fatherland. In that vein a few of my articles and interviews were published, and I was received warmly and cordially. All this at-

---

41. Romanian currency.

tracted the attention of our embassy in London, and it kept me in London for a little while longer.

During my very first days [in London], Mr. Adler introduced me to the house of Lord Rothschild, with whom he had been on friendly terms since childhood. All three Rothschild brothers (all of whom later died) received me cordially, and, hard as it is to believe, in the most intimate of conversations showed a great deal of interest in our life and circumstances, the Serbian people and its characteristics, the economic and cultural conditions in our country, and the general situation in the Balkans. After I informed them of the dire state of our Jews, they contributed a certain sum, whose amount was publicized alongside all other amounts by a Jewish periodical, which published a list of contributors in two or three of its issues. The relatively small contribution made by the house of Rothschild can be explained by the circumstance of war, for that same house was called upon for help by various parties. In the first five or six weeks of my sojourn, about 10,000 francs were collected through my personal connections and published appeals. I extended my stay because I realized that such a long journey deserves to raise more than a meager sum, and because I reached the conclusion that the English need to get to know a person and his opinions well before paying him heed. The trust of English Jews needed to be earned, and that was possible only after I broadened my circle of acquaintances and friends and was able to enter their homes, which foreigners do only with great difficulty in England.

The sum that was later raised is the result of my initiatives and was collected because of who I am rather than in view of the general cause. Thus for example during a visit to an English Jewish family, I was introduced to Sir Herbert Samuel, home secretary at the time. During our conversation I drew his attention to the circumstances in the fatherland. I presented all the political, economic, and social conditions in Serbia, as well as our disposition towards the former Austro-Hungarian monarchy, all our suffering and the crises that led to the world war. He paid heed to my words and after a few days, when Great Britain organized an official reception in honor of Serbia, Sir Herbert, the first speaker, gave a brilliant speech, informed and well documented, in which I recognized my own explanations to the home secretary. (I note this in passing in order to demonstrate that when necessary I understood my mission broadly.) As to the matter of supporting Serbian Jews, I was recommended by the secretary to see his brother, Sir Stuart Samuel, who assumed a leading position in the campaign to help our poor. He directed me as to whom to contact personally, gave me names and addresses of certain prominent citizens whom I might write, which was necessary for my success, and I sent letters daily to all the addresses I received in this manner and engaged in prodigious official activities. On Sir Stuart's advice, I visited other British centers as well—Manchester, Liverpool, Glasgow, and Birmingham. As in those centers a large drive was already underway to help suffering Jews from around the world, I added Serbian Jews to the list of those who needed help. This can be seen from the enclosed newspaper articles.

In April 1915 I left England with the intention of continuing my activity in Paris. I began my work by using the letters of introduction, to the Rothschilds and other institutions in Paris, which I had received from my newly made connections in England. But my time in Paris was consumed by the work of accommodating refugees from occupied territories. I saw immediately that the outlook for my plans was quite bad. Mr. Rothschild received me very cordially and contributed a modest amount. . . . I also visited the representatives of Alliance Is-raélite Universelle and at the meeting that was organized for my visit a small loan of 3,000 francs was approved.

Seeing how it went, I thought that I should leave as soon as possible, and I intended to return to Niš via Switzerland and Italy. However, when I reached Switzerland, Italy declared war. Railways were mobilized for the military's use and it was practically impossible to travel by train. So I was forced to stay three or four weeks in Switzerland, until traffic had normalized somewhat. I used this time to interest Swiss Jews in our cause, especially those in Zurich and Basel. Although no spectacular result could have been expected, I collected a respectable sum, considering the circumstances, somewhere in the range of 3,000 francs. In Italy I did not even begin my work, since Italy had just entered the war and everything was bustling with [military] preparations. I returned to Niš after a lengthy trip through Italy, due to extremely irregular traffic and many inconveniences in travel.

I considered it my duty to submit this short but complete overview of my work to the esteemed administration for its information, as a document that recalls the awful days we have lived through.

Seizing the opportunity to assure the esteemed administration of my respect, I remain sincerely,

Dr. I. Alcalay, rabbi

Isaac Alcalay, "Upravi Crkveno-školske jevrejske opštine," December 31, 1919. United States Holocaust Memorial Museum (Washington, D.C.), RG-31.037M, reel 1. (Original in Fond 497, opis 1, sprava 29, Central State Historical Archives of Ukraine in Lviv). Translated from Serbian by Emil Kerenji.


## 53.  A TURKISH MINISTER SHUNS JEWISH COMPANY AT THE LAUSANNE TREATY NEGOTIATIONS {1923}

*In 1922–1923, Turkish nationalists headed by Gen. İsmet İnönü (1884–1974), a future prime minister and president of the Turkish Republic, engaged in peace negotiations with the Allied Powers in Lausanne. Among the Turkish representatives who arrived in Switzerland to negotiate the creation of an independent Turkish republic in Anatolia and eastern Thrace was Dr. Rıza Nur Bey (1879–1942), then minister of health for the Turkish national government based in Ankara. Although he held important political positions in late Ottoman and Turkish contexts, Rıza Nur frequently ran afoul of political authority because of his strong views and sharp tongue. One of the striking qualities of Rıza Nur's worldview is its virulent racism. Although he inveighed against members of various non-Turkish groups, his greatest hatred appears to have been reserved for Jews and Dönme (descendants of Jews who had followed the self-proclaimed messiah Shabbetay Sevi into Islam in the seventeenth century), whom Rıza Nur viewed as racially Jewish. In this selection Rıza Nur discusses his suspicions about the intentions of a man who had approached him claiming to represent the interests of Macedonian Turks against Greece as well as his unwillingness to work alongside the former Ottoman chief rabbi, Haim Nahum, who had come to Lausanne to participate in the peace negotiations on Turkey's behalf.*

The project of this man [Muslihiddin Âdil] was not what he claimed it was. He was setting up a Jewish plot with a moving and powerful lie. Freedom for Macedonia and so forth was just dust in our eyes. He was going to con us. . . . His job was simply to get Salonican Dönmes exempted from the population transfers.[42] So it seems that the Dönme paid for him to come to Lausanne for this. His claim that

---

42. A reference to the population exchange outlined during the Treaty of Lausanne negotiations. It eventually dictated the forced migration of as many as 500,000 Muslims from Greek territories to the newly established Republic of Turkey and as many as 1.5 million Greek Orthodox Christians from Turkey to Greece.

he represented the Macedonian Turks was a lie. It appears that the Dönme wanted to stay in Salonica. In fact those in Istanbul were even going to migrate back to Salonica. It was clear that they were a group in Turkey who thought differently than Turks and who had different interests. The tragedy of this was that these people looked like Turks. Greek Orthodox and Armenians were better than they because at the very least we know that they are Greeks and Armenians. This group [the Dönme] were parasites that hid in our own blood. They hid their faces and eyes with our blood. To choose somebody from this group and make him a professor at Darülfünün [University] was a horrible thing! However these people were mistaking their own interests. Were the Greeks going to leave them to go about their business? Especially since [the Dönme] were a commercial people, the Greeks would attack and destroy them before anyone else. Or they would immediately be required to convert to Christianity and speak Greek. But they would receive lowly treatment. Even the Karamanlıs had this happen to them.[43] At this point, that is, while the Turk's head and heart were filled with worry, the children of Shabbetay Sevi were plotting something.

While we were dealing with the Europeans, with the official deliberations, and with our own people, this sort of people came and bothered us with all sorts of different ambitions.

At one point Haim Nahum, the former chief rabbi of Istanbul, began to be seen around the hotel. I saw that he started meeting with İsmet. What he was doing, for whom he was acting, I don't know. He approached İsmet. Awful Jew! He wouldn't leave İsmet alone. He knew when dinnertime was and would be waiting by the elevator, immediately taking İsmet's arm or grabbing him by the waist. İsmet would do the same. He would escort him around the [conference] hall when it wasn't necessary. Later in the dining hall he would be making jokes and laughing with İsmet. It was clear that he wanted to—and did—show everybody that he was İsmet's intimate friend. In short he approached [the situation] with all the doggedness of a Jew. He wouldn't leave İsmet's side and now he wouldn't leave İsmet's room. İsmet appointed him as an adviser [and] started to pay him a stipend without telling

43. Karamanlıs were Turkish-speaking Greek Orthodox Christians resident in Ottoman Anatolia.

me. He treated the official delegation like a farm, using it anyway he pleased. I don't know how [Nahum] deceived him, but this gullible İsmet walked right into the Jewish trap. At this point the chief rabbi took to sitting at our table. I hadn't spoken up until that point.

I asked İsmet, "How did we end up with this Jew? You're meeting so freely with this Jew blackens your dignity and the dignity of Turks and of the official delegation. Don't show him so much respect, or at least don't do so in front of everybody." [İsmet] got angry with me.

[Nahum] exploded. He was giving orders to everybody in the delegation. He cut in front to walk ahead of me. Most likely İsmet had told him what I had said. But was I going to stop? In any case I can't stand Jews. When the chief rabbi cut in front of me, I dealt with him rudely and pulled him by the arm so that he was behind me. I said, "From now on walk here!" I did this in the lobby of the hotel and everybody saw. The guy was finished. He not only stopped cutting in front of me, he didn't even come near İsmet when I was around. This was really something that İsmet needed to do though. Alright, he doesn't like me and uses a Jew to insult me, but he doesn't see that it isn't only me personally but also my position. I am a Turkish minister and delegate. If this dirty Jew sullies that position . . . does [İsmet] even care? Who knows what dealings he had with the Jew?

I said to İsmet again, "This [man] is a Jew [and] Jews are very lowly creatures. Who knows what sort of vile business he is up to?! Don't expect anything beneficial to come from him! The circle of people he knows is the world of Jewish gold-sellers. His goal is some plot to make money through a concession or some such thing. Don't debase yourself! I don't want this guy at dinner. In fact, I'll move to a different table." He didn't listen. I moved to a different table and only then did he send the Jew away. The Jew was hoping to eat companionably with our delegation and when we let slip something [of value] immediately go to our enemies. Demonstrating to everyone that he was with us, he was going to make some profitable intrigue.

Rıza Nur, *Hayat ve Hatıratım*, vol. 3 (Istanbul: Altındağ, 1967), 1080–82. Translated from Turkish and introduced by Howard Eissenstat.

## 54. A SALONICAN JEWISH SCHOOL REMAINS IN RUINS SIX YEARS AFTER THE 1917 FIRE [1923]

*After the Balkan Wars (1912–1913) ended nearly five hundred years of Ottoman control in Salonica, the local Jewish community found itself under the rule of the expanding Greek nation-state. Efforts to educate Jewish children in communal schools, to instruct them in the Greek language, and to develop a sense of Greek consciousness achieved mixed results over the course of the subsequent two decades. The catastrophic fire of 1917 destroyed the center of the city and obliterated the majority of Jewish communal schools, libraries, and synagogues. After the fire, the task of turning the children of the last generation of Ottoman Jews into the first generation of Greek Jews proved challenging. The indefatigable schoolteacher and Jewish community advocate, Yomtov Saltiel, wrote numerous letters to the directors of Salonica's Jewish communal schools over the course of twenty-five years, detailing the difficulties (and less frequently, the successes) he experienced in the classroom. Here, in an excerpt from a 1923 letter Saltiel describes the trials he faced while attempting to teach his lessons in an ill-equipped synagogue. Six years after the fire of 1917, the school where he was employed remained in ruins.*

[Letter to the Superior Commission of Communal Schools, Salonica, August 27, 1923]

Honorable sirs,

Having worked the past year in the Beth-El Synagogue, permit me to describe in a few lines how the last school year went in this locale.

In the synagogue we had four classes with more than 230 students, including one class of elementary and secondary school children mixed together. The classes were separated with curtains two meters apart in a manner such that there was widespread commotion. The teacher was obliged to stand next to each student in order to hear what he was saying. The students had to experience all the difficulties in the world just to hear the teacher. It was impossible for them to concentrate because they could not hear what was being said in the class. Add to this the fact that the Greek teacher, as a mother of a large family, was not able to arrive at the fixed time. . . . All of this contributed to the general perturbation, such that at certain moments the classroom felt like a real mental institution.

The locale is not suited for pedagogy and is unhygeniec . . . . Because the roof tiles are missing in many places, and we lack an actual roof, we have held many classes with rain and snow falling on our faces. . . .

Most of all we have suffered from darkness. Many days the darkness was such that a student could not see enough to read the book he had in front of his face. I am convinced that the eyesight of many students degenerated because of this. . . .

Because I was the only teacher in the synagogue, I was obliged to occupy myself with the smooth operation of the locale while teaching my Hebrew classes the entire day. All this overworked me to such an extent that many days I finished class literally on my back. . . .

As you can see, gentlemen, next year I will not be able to continue my work in these conditions without seriously jeopardizing my health. I beg you therefore to order my transfer to another locale, possibly to one of the three schools in the Kampanyas [Quarter].[44]

Letter from Yomtov Samuel Saltiel to the Superior Commission of the Communal Schools, YIVO Institute for Jewish Research (New York City), RG 207, file 135. Translated from Ladino and introduced by Devin E. Naar.

## 55. A MUSLIM JOURNALIST CALLS UPON TURKEY'S JEWS TO FORGO MINORITY RIGHTS (1925)

*In the years following the First World War the Allied Powers negotiated a series of agreements known as the Minorities Treaties with fourteen newly formed or expanded states in Europe and the Middle East. Designed to ensure the collective rights of linguistic, religious, or ethnic minorities in the countries in question, these treaties included provisions legalizing the use of minority languages in public and requiring state support of minority communal institutions. To many observers these measures appeared as a form of uninvited foreign interference in their domestic politics and thus an infringement upon their country's sovereign rights. Here the Turkish politician, editor, and journalist Yunus Nadi (1879–1945) asks the religious minorities of the newly established Turkish Republic to embrace the homogenizing logic of the nation-state and to forgo the minority rights the Treaty of Lausanne (1923) granted them.*

The minority question is, as we all know, among those issues championed by the peace treaties. The Great War compelled nations to pit themselves against one another with such violence . . . that we now find ourselves facing a complete upheaval [in the realm] of ideas and

44. A neighborhood on the outskirts of Salonica.

sentiments. With an eye to preventing the unrest and disruptions that have ensued, or could ensue, as a result of the current state of things, the [Great] Powers have judged it necessary to offer certain assurances to minorities with regard to their [communal or national] aspirations. The situation of minorities in Turkey in particular both during and since the war has given rise to disorders and troubles that surpass all imagination. I am therefore convinced that it is both useful and necessary to shed light upon the situation that has resulted from the various events that have unfurled around us.

First it should be noted that there were initially no questions concerning minorities and their rights in Turkey, since the Turkish state granted these rights to non-Muslims spontaneously. There was thus no need to confirm them with promises or official documents. What created a minority question for us, as well as the tragedies that have resulted from it, was the continual intervention of European states, which have stopped at nothing in the pursuit of their political aims. Those who served knowingly as instruments of foreign political interests are equally guilty. This tragic situation has a long history. Its promoters are well known, but their mindset appears to have remained the same. They should examine the question with all the depth and gravity that it requires; it is in their own best interest to do so.

Do our partners from Lausanne who signed the peace treaty really understand the rights they have agreed to uphold, [including] communal freedoms to private schools and to religious practice?

All of this has already been granted for centuries to minorities, who have never encountered any obstacles in obtaining these rights. The tolerance granted them has always been such that their national and religious assemblies functioned as veritable parliaments.

Despite all this the foreign powers have not failed to seize upon diplomatic pretexts such as finding a solution for Christians and assuring them of their protection in order to intervene continually on their behalf.

Yet this is only a facade. In reality these powers are pursuing their own political aims. Perhaps I will be better understood if I cite some examples. Everyone knows of the Armenian designs against Turkey, plans that were encouraged by Tsarist Russia and England alike. On two different occasions these designs culminated in bloodshed, for which Constantinople [Istanbul] served as the stage. As they lay dying those

[Armenians] who had been misled [by the Great Powers] cast a last look toward the Sea of Marmara in order to see whether the English fleet had [finally] appeared on the horizon.

Those who led the revolt knew very well that their actions could not end otherwise, and still, how many Turks and Armenians lost their lives in this senseless adventure! During the reign of Abdülhamid, finding myself in prison, it was sufficient for me to meet with some *komitadjis*[45] in order to understand the extent to which they had been deceived.

Until that time the Turks had great trust in the Armenians, some of whom had occupied the highest administrative positions in the country. It cannot be denied that the greatest benevolence was shown them and other communities following the proclamation of the Constitution. Despite this, during the war they allowed themselves to be seduced by promises as false as they were self-interested while also permitting themselves to commit acts whose consequences have been disastrous for both sides.

The real question is as follows: whatever the motives that drove Tsarist Russia and England to action, could their intervention on behalf of the Armenians ever have benefited the latter? There is no doubt [that the answer is] no, for just as Russia sought to reach the Persian Gulf and the Mediterranean, England tried to reach the Caspian Sea by way of our *vilayets* in the East.[46] It is clear that between these two rival powers there could be no place for an independent Armenia. As for Turkey, she must defend herself in order to destroy this senseless dream and in order to safeguard her very existence.

Another example: Is the tragedy that [Greek Prime Minister Eleftherios] Venizelos's Megali Idea unleashed upon Turkey with the support of the Europeans truly the lesser of two evils? Without taking into account Greece's position in the Balkans, Venizelos attacked Turkish soil in an action that bears a remarkable resemblance to an [ill-advised] adventure.[47] The result was heartbreaking: ruin that cannot be calculated in the millions, nor even in the billions.

---

45. Members of guerilla bands.

46. Ottoman provinces.

47. The Megali Idea was a form of Greek irredentism that sought a Greek state including all areas inhabited by ethnic Greeks. The reference here is to the support lent the platform by Greek Prime Minister Eleftherios Venizelos (1864–1936).

*hut*    In the two cases I have just cited is it possible to discern any antagonism between the rights of the majority population and those of
minorities? . . .

The instigators of the events that left a trail of destruction in their
wake have withdrawn their chess pieces quietly, as though nothing at
all has happened. When I heard Lloyd George say to the London Conference, "We accept the current state of events such as, for example,
the non-existence of Armenia," I was stupefied by the cynicism of the
Great Powers.

Thus ends my report and brief analysis. From the aforementioned
discussion, we can conclude that since there was once no minority
question in Turkey, nor even anything that resembled a [minority]
question, it was the European powers themselves that created a minority problem that has taken on a most bloody character.

The lesson to be drawn from this short survey is that henceforth interested parties should not allow themselves to be taken in by agitators
from abroad. They will thus avoid going down the wrong path. On
the contrary they will understand that the greatest happiness and the
only path to follow is to attach themselves to their home and country.

The Turkish Republic recognizes the importance and the necessity
of adopting a line of conduct that bestows equal rights and responsibilities upon all of its citizens in compliance with the conditions established by the [Turkish] Constitution [of 1924]. However, we have
not yet finished dressing our wounds or neutralizing the effects of so
recent a tragedy that its bloody reflections remain before us still. Those
Muslims who have remained in the country must also work to erase
the vestiges of this drama.

For their part, the Jews, who had little to do with these past events,
must form the vanguard of this appeasement process. We are convinced that there will be no need to create a special chapter of republican laws dealing with minority rights as long as all of our fellow
citizens remain loyally and sincerely attached to the fatherland.

Yusuf Nadi

Yunus Nadi, "Majorité et minorité," *La République*, July 9, 1925. Translated from French by Alma
Rachel Heckman.

## 56. DANCE HALLS AND DECADENCE IN ISTANBUL: THE TURKISH PRESS AIRS CONCERNS ABOUT NON-MUSLIMS (1926)

*The Ottoman entrance into the First World War on the side of the Central Powers spelled not only the defeat but also the collapse of the centuries-old empire. Following the Armistice of Mudros (October 30, 1918), Istanbul came under an Allied occupation that lasted from 1918 to 1923, until nationalist resistance forces in Asia Minor successfully repelled Allied troops from Anatolia and declared the establishment of a Turkish Republic in eastern Thrace and Asia Minor with a new capital, Ankara, based in the Anatolian heartland. Istanbul, the Ottoman capital since 1453 and once a thriving, cosmopolitan city, soon entered a period of neglect. To many the city offered a painful reminder of an Ottoman legacy they would have rather forgotten. Its foreign occupation following the war, its cosmopolitan culture, and the significant historic presence of non-Muslims in the city gave many Turkish nationalists the impression that the city was at once decadent and un-Turkish. Press reports from the period demonstrate the xenophobia that often accompanied these positions. The following editorial, written by a Turkish Muslim journalist in Istanbul, portrays local Armenians, Greeks, and Jews alike as a corrupting source in the city and warns against their influence.*

In the painful and dark years of the armistice, a group of Armenians along with some Ottoman Greeks opened dance halls in Beyoğlu.[48] These places, only some of which succeeded, unjustly acquired the reputation of dance schools, despite the fact that their purportedly esteemed clientele had no interest in decency or morality.

Although the proprietors quickly convinced the simpleminded that these halls were schools, their lies soon became apparent. The owners of these places exaggerated their status by giving themselves the title of "dance professor."

It is true that in Europe there are teachers and dance halls that offer legitimate lessons in dance; however, they require the approval of dance academies, a semiofficial committee, or officially recognized dance teachers. . . .

Here Greek, Armenian, and Jewish dance instructors receive the title of "professor," but what delegation verified their credentials to teach dance? . . .

Why does our government take no action against these dance hall

---

48. During this period Beyoğlu was a predominantly non-Muslim district of Istanbul.

owners, even though they contravene the ban on admitting students and girls who are eighteen years old or younger? . . .

Unfortunately some of our youth continue to frequent these places, where there is an unaesthetic and degenerate atmosphere of cigarette smoke, the smell of alcohol, and people dancing inappropriately. . . .

Many law-abiding citizens, be they students or directors, want to open a school. Either the Ministry of Education or the Directorate of Police is responsible for giving licenses to schools. Should dance hall owners who are primarily Greek, Armenian, and Jewish be granted such licenses?

Our response to this calamity: No!

The ministries' decision to allow such places to remain open is inappropriate.

Who patronizes these dance halls? In our investigation we found that the clients of these places are many [including]: (1) common women, (2) working men and women, (3) schoolchildren, and (4) men who roam around with vile intentions. We report with pleasure that at present girls from Turkish families are seldom among those found in such places. However, as they say, "a grape darkens by watching other grapes." In the future, it is likely that some of our daughters will frequent these places. It is our collective responsibility to prevent this eventuality.

Akil Cem, "Danslar, Dansingler, Barlar: İstanbul dans mektepleri nedir?," *Büyük Gazete* 1:6 (2 Kanunuevvel/December 1926): 6 and 1:7 (9 Kanunuevvel/December 1926): 6. Translated from Ottoman Turkish by G. Carole Woodall.

## 57. "WE CONSIDER THE CEMETERY TO BE A TEMPLE": OBJECTIONS TO PLANS TO DEMOLISH A SACRED SITE [1929]

*This letter offers a response to the plans of Salonica's municipality to seize a portion of the Jewish cemetery of that city during the interwar era, then arguably the largest in Europe. Chief Rabbi Haim Raphael Habib (1882–1943) explains that Jewish law regards the cemetery as sacred ground and does not allow for the disturbance of the graves of those buried there. This struggle, which continued for decades, ended with the complete destruction of the Jewish cemetery of Salonica under Nazi occupation.*

*The cemetery's ruins are today buried under the city's Aristotle University, where*
*they remain invisible to the public.*

Salonica, 7 Heshvan 5690 [November 10, 1929]
To the honorable communal council
*En ville*
Honorable gentlemen,

Our spiritual council together with the rabbinic courts, meeting
together in an extraordinary session under our supervision, were profoundly pained by the alarming news published in the local press regarding a proposal to transform our cemetery into a park, and, above
all, of an already proclaimed decree of expropriation of part of our
cemetery in favor of refugees from Adrianople [Edirne].

We do not want to give credence to this information, which deeply
wounds us and constitutes a great profanation according to our religion. In effect our religion categorically obliges our people to have
the greatest veneration for the resting place of the dead. This place is
considered sacred, and our religion commands us to have the greatest
respect for it, as specified in the Talmud[49] and in the *Shulhan Arukh*.[50]

This respect has remained alive and strong at all times to such an extent that we consider the cemetery to be a temple. Effectively, during
critical moments, in hours of great individual, national, or general danger, we fulfill our supreme duty to visit the tombs of our loved ones,
our forefathers, and our rabbis and sages to implore divine assistance,
[and] to pray with all of the introspection necessary to bring comfort,
consolation, and salvation.

The utilization of these holy sites for other purposes therefore constitutes according to our law a true sacrilege. The transfer of mortal
remains no matter how old is rigorously prohibited, as specified in the
Jerusalem Talmud[51] and the code of the *Shulhan Arukh*.[52]

It is permitted neither to transport the deceased nor his bones from
an honorable tomb to another honorable tomb, nor from a profaned
tomb to another profaned tomb, nor from a profaned tomb to an

---

49. Megillah 29.
50. Yoreh De'ah 386:1.
51. Mo'ed Katan 3.
52. Yoreh De'ah 363:1.

honorable tomb, not to mention [the impossibility of transfer] from an honorable one to a dishonorable one.

We therefore consider it to be an imperative duty to turn your full attention to the above matter by imploring you to take the necessary steps urgently and energetically to forestall the abovementioned danger.

We do not doubt that the liberal government of our country, faithful to its noble traditions, informed about our religious prescriptions and our frame of mind on this subject, will desire to respect them in annulling the measures [directed] against our cemetery.

We implore the help of the All-Powerful for the complete success of your actions.

May God assist you. Amen.

Please accept, honorable gentlemen, the assurance of our high esteem and consideration.

Acting Chief Rabbi Haim Raphael Habib

Archive of the Jewish Community of Salonica, file 56, Jewish Museum of Thessaloniki. Translated from Ladino by Devin E. Naar.

## 58. LETTERS TO THE EDITOR CONCERNING THE ANTI-JEWISH RIOTS IN SALONICA (1931)

*In the summer of 1931 anti-Jewish riots broke out in various neighborhoods of Salonica, sparked by tensions between local Greek groups and the Zionist Maccabi Movement, which its detractors accused of exhibiting antipatriotic tendencies. As tensions came to a head, as many as two thousand armed men rampaged through a poor Jewish district of town. Armed with knives and oil canisters, they burned down the entire neighborhood, known as the Campbell Quarter, with little intervention from local authorities or police. Some reports indicate that members of the Greek Air Force participated in the riots and were even prepared to attack any local police who might come to defend the neighborhood. These tragic events reflect the rise of antisemitism in the Balkans, where outward hostility to Jews became increasingly frequent—and enshrined in larger political movements—during the interwar era.*

July 2, 1931
Dear Editor,

I have the honor of transmitting the following telegram, which expresses the sentiment of the Jewish reservists of the Greek army [and] which I have forwarded to the Union of Reservists and NCOs [Hellenic Air Force representatives] of Salonica.

"Having served the Greek fatherland seven times and having fought for the liberation of Greek Macedonian lands, I appeal to those of my comrades-in-arms and fellow fighters who share my convictions that they may demonstrate reason and calm and cease actions contrary to the proven [tradition of] Greek religious toleration. Any attempt at antinational actions that challenge the integrity of our nation's lands, which have been liberated by . . . Jews and Christians alike, from wherever they emerge, will provoke the indignation of every Greek, whether Christian or Jew, whether of New or Old Greece. It would, however, be unjust to launch this serious accusation against law-abiding citizens who are not guilty of the actions attributed to them. My long-term, repeated service in the army, together with my fellow reservists to whom I am related by shared actions and common experiences forged on the battlefield, teaches me that I am appealing to colleagues who share with me the Greek tradition of religious toleration and devout tolerance of every law-abiding person who does not profess the Orthodox faith.

With respect,

Samuel M. Cohen
30 Evangelistrias Street [Athens]

July 11, 1931
Dear Editor,

I recently learned of the article entitled "To Salonica's Jews" that appeared in your honorable newspaper of the 3rd ultimo. . . .[53]

I believe it is appropriate to direct this letter to you in order to correct certain impressions that appear in your newspaper in relation to the Zionists of Salonica [as they] do not correspond with reality. I am

---

53. This letter, published as "Pros Thessalonikeis Israelitas," *Eleutheron Vema*, July 3, 1931, had charged the Jews with antipatriotic tendencies stemming in part from their Zionist commitments and suggested that they shared responsibility for the recent attacks against them.

confident that your concern for the truth will prompt you to correct these false impressions.

In my double capacity as senator and president of the Zionist Federation of Greece, I wish to assure you that it is neither just nor correct to assert that the Zionists are a foreign element in the country [nor that they] place Zionism above Hellenism. Despite opinions to the contrary, all the Jews of Salonica, or at least a majority of them, are Zionists. I see no crime in this. There is nothing incompatible about Zionism and well-intentioned patriotism. The Greek Zionist, like the French, the American, or the English Zionist, is as patriotic as his fellow citizen, be he Orthodox, Catholic, or Protestant. I take this opportunity to remind you of the honorable death . . . of approximately 10,000 Zionists [who fought in] the Battle of Carency during the European War in the service of the French Foreign Legion. Many other examples exist to validate my claims.

The young Zionists of our city are becoming the best soldiers. The officers under whom they serve are in a position to confirm this. That which distinguishes the Zionist from [his] fellow [Greek] Orthodox citizen is that [he wishes] to see the national [Jewish] home reconstructed in Palestine. [This is] a noble ideal that has the undivided support of civilized countries [as well as many] among the government and people of Greece. Repeatedly Misters Venizelos, Politis, Michalopoulos, and Argyropoulos as well as numerous professors at Greek universities have expressed their admiration and sympathy for Zionism, a movement that should be appreciated by the Greek people more than any other because Hellenism and Judaism have had similar fortunes, have suffered [similar] disasters, and have fought [similar] battles. One of the leaders of Zionism, Max Nordau [1849–1923], was a tireless defender of the rights of Greece at a time when for political reasons the support of small countries by persons of Nordau's stature was rare.

Throughout the world Zionism counts amongst its representatives people who are the glory of their countries and whose patriotism nobody dares to doubt. I confine myself to noting the names of Sir Herbert Samuel, deputy leader of the Liberal Party [in Britain]; the deceased Lord Melchett [Alfred Mond], former minister; Dr. [Chaim] Weizmann, president of the Zionist Organization in England; Léon Blum, leader of the Socialist Party in France; Edmund Rothschild of

Germany; [Albert] Einstein, the professor of world renown; Dr. Wassermann, president of Deutsche Bank; Louis Brandeis, high judicial functionary in America, etc. . . .

Mr. Editor, I believe I have shown that Zionism and dedication to one's country can most certainly coexist and that these ideologies constitute a harmonious whole, [just] as Mr. Papadopoulos, the distinguished professor at the University of Salonica, has stated. The Jews of Salonica, as well as those of New Greece and above all the Zionists, are all imbued with the desire of fuller understanding and a greater rapprochement with all the classes of the Greek people with whom we have shared the same fortunes for twenty years. . . . All of us—and especially the Zionists—recognize the need for and provide the greater part of our lessons [to our children] in the Greek language. We all appreciate the [progress] that comes about with the transformation of former Turkish subjects into new Greek citizens. . . .

Please, Mr. Editor, forgive the scope of this letter, the purpose of which was to enlighten Greek public opinion, by way of *Eleutheron Vema*, on the tendencies of the Zionist movement, [which is] worthy of the support and sympathy of every person in whose heart the sentiment of justice and humanism has not been extinguished.

Respectfully,

Asher Mallah
Senator for Salonica

"Oi Ephedroi Israelitai," *Eleutheron Vema*, July 2, 1931 and "Oi Israelitai kai e Ellas," *Eleutheron Vema*, July 11, 1931. Translated from Greek by Dimitrios Varvaritis.

## 59. ASSIMILATION FEARS IN GIRESUN, TURKEY [1941]

*Under the leadership of Mustafa Kemal Atatürk, the Turkish Republic vigorously promoted Turkification. While many Jewish and Muslim citizens of the new state tended to support these measures with rhetorical zeal, the promise of lessening the distinctions between religious groups in favor of their shared national identity nonetheless raised anxieties on all sides. By the 1930s, the spread of antisemitic propaganda combined with the Turkish state's desire to "Turkify" the economy by privileging Muslim businesses put new pressures on Jews. In 1934, virtually all of the Jews living in Eastern Thrace (European Turkey) fled their homes following boycotts and physi-*

*cal assaults. Many moved to Istanbul; over 1,500 emigrated to Palestine. Still others, it would seem, ended up in the Anatolian city of Giresun. In this source a Muslim state representative expresses concern over the assimilation of recently arrived Jews in Giresun, a process he worried would pose a fundamental danger to Turkish society.*

R.P.P.,[54] Regional Administration Committee Chairman, Giresun
Ankara, June 2, 1941
To the R.P.P. High General Secretariat

Because of the voluntary evacuation that is being undertaken in some regions, several Jewish families have arrived here from Thrace and Istanbul. It is understood that they came as guests of some relatives who work for a foreign company here.

There is shock in the region to see that this group of ten to fifteen people, be they women or men, carry Turkish and Muslim names. A man of military age from among these [newcomers] presented an altered document in an attempt to resettle him and his entire family here from Thrace. This insolent man attempted to dupe the state so as to save himself from military service. Thanks to the watchfulness of government officials, this fraud was detected and the necessary steps were immediately taken.

Nonetheless, this incident brought our attention to the fact that the identity cards of these [Jewish newcomers] indicate that their names had been changed to Turkish and Muslim names through a court order.

Stranger still, while their local [relatives] are [named] . . . Esther, Jacob, and Moses, their newly arrived siblings and relatives carry names like Münevver, Aykut, Sevim, and so on. In this fashion honored Turkish names are being used for who knows what sort of vile purposes. It has been observed with sorrow that this has been the cause of base speculation and gossip.

How are we to regard these people who somehow found a legal means to change their names? It is obvious what the reasons and goals of these people were in changing their names in this fashion. If we allow this to happen it will [undermine] our social structure, and in particular it will in time create individuals, who, having taken Turkish names, will become mothers and fathers and will look like real Turks

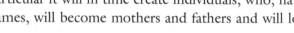

---

54. Republican People's Party, or, in Turkish, *Cumhuriyet Halk Partisi* (CHP).

in the official registers. When one considers this [sort of] future, it augurs, from my perspective, a perilous and disturbing condition.

It is true that if they demonstrate a good reason in court they [have the right] to change their names. Perhaps they were able to receive a decision in this fashion. However, taking into consideration the possible dangers posed in the application of this legal provision, and with consideration of the sensitivity of the issue, I present [this information] to you with the highest esteem and respect.

R.P.P., Chairman of the Provincial Administration Committee
Dr. Nuri Özkaya

Letter of Dr. Nuri Özkaya in Giresun to the Turkish Republican People's Party High General Secretariat in Ankara, June 2, 1941, Başbakanlık Cumhuriyet Arşivi (BBA-CA) (Ankara) 490.01.611.120.06. Translated from Turkish and introduced by Howard Eissenstat.

# III. POLITICAL MOVEMENTS
AND IDEOLOGIES

## 60. THE OTTOMAN CHIEF RABBI URGES HIS CORELIGIONISTS TO LEARN TURKISH (1840)

*During a tour of the Ottoman capital in 1840, the renowned British Jewish philanthropist Moses Montefiore (1784–1885) rebuked local Jews for their inattention to the language of their country. Montefiore's visit took place just a year after the promulgation by Sultan Abdülmecid (r. 1839–1861) of a reform decree (the Hatt-ı Şerif) that established new rights and equality for all Ottoman subjects. He and his supporters were convinced that their Ottoman coreligionists had to adapt to the changing times and prove themselves worthy of their new status. Responding to these appeals, Ottoman Chief Rabbi Haim Moshe Fresco issued the following circular in Ottoman Turkish, Hebrew, and Ladino, urging the Jews of the empire to learn Turkish. Although Fresco's appeal went largely unheeded, in the decades that followed Jewish schools in the empire began to integrate Ottoman lessons into their curricula, while various Jewish societies appeared with the aim of promoting the language. Despite these efforts, only a small portion of Ottoman Jews became proficient in the official language of their state. It was not until the modern Turkish Republic emerged from the ashes of the empire that Jews—responding to the new homogenizing pressures of the nation-state and to a relentless "Citizen Speak Turkish!" campaign—finally began to take up the study of Turkish en masse.*

A year has now passed since our great and exalted Sultan Abdülmecid promulgated the Hatt-ı Şerif, may he be blessed and his kingdom live forever. [He promulgated this decree] as one of various beneficial laws because the only desire of the almighty state is that men should have the chance to better themselves and to acquire skills of all types. This is the will of our lord, the almighty king, that all people living under his rule find fulfillment in every respect. Thus every learned man who knows how to speak fluently and, more important, to write in Turkish, is held in high regard. This is the will of our almighty king. It is for this reason that I urge all of our brothers among the people of Israel, wherever they find themselves in the dominions of our lord the almighty king, to teach their children how to write in Turkish and in every place and city to hire instructors who can teach their sons to speak fluently and to write in Turkish, which is a great skill. With such a great skill one can achieve many things and earn respect from the government. This is the desire and wish of the almighty state, for the only dream of our lord the almighty king is that [his] people seek to better themselves.

Circular of Haim Moshe Fresco, October 18, 1840, Damascus affair collection, 1840–1841, 1896, American Jewish Historical Society (Newton Centre, Mass., and New York, N.Y.). Translated from Ladino by Julia Phillips Cohen.

## 61. IN PRAISE OF INTERCOMMUNAL COOPERATION: A "ROTHSCHILD OF THE EAST" ON PROGRESS AND TOLERANCE (1874)

*The Camondos were an influential family of Sephardi financiers, landholders, and philanthropists active in the Ottoman Empire and Europe throughout the nineteenth and twentieth centuries. They earned the nickname "Rothschilds of the East" due to the enormous fortunes they amassed as well as their sustained involvement in Jewish communal affairs in Ottoman lands. Resident in Istanbul since the eighteenth century, the family hailed from a line of Sephardi Jews that had settled in Venice following their expulsion from Spain. Their Venetian connections earned the Camondos the privileged status of foreigners protected by extraterritorial rights in Ottoman realms. Enjoying the preferential trade tariffs and consular protection of Austrian and, later, Italian citizenship, the patriarch of the family, Count Abraham Salomon de Camondo (1781–1873), founded his own banking and real estate empire and exercised influence at the courts of the Ottoman sultans Abdülmecid and Abdülaziz (r. 1861–1876). Camondo's son Raphaël Salomon de Camondo (1810–1866) and his grandsons Abraham Behor de Camondo (1829–1889) and Nissim de Camondo (1830–1889) followed in his footsteps, working as bankers, administering their many properties in the Ottoman capital, and serving their Ottoman coreligionists through various philanthropic efforts. In 1863, just three years after the Alliance Israélite Universelle was founded to protect Jewish interests around the globe, the Camondos helped establish a regional committee of the organization in Istanbul, with Abraham Behor de Camondo at its head. Here he addresses Ottoman Jews in French, calling upon them to embrace the "moral and material progress" wrought by Western civilization and to learn to regard their neighbors as brothers.*

Those who are invested in the fate of Judaism will have noticed with great satisfaction how the Jews of Turkey have been emerging slowly from the slumber in which they have been submerged for centuries. This awakening, slow at first, has accelerated considerably in recent years.

It cannot be denied that this felicitous development is due in great part to the efforts of the dedicated members of the Alliance Israélite Universelle. Dear coreligionists, you all know of the noble aims this society has set for itself, which have already earned our recognition at so many junctures. Everywhere a Jew suffers because of his beliefs, it is there to protect him; everywhere our coreligionists suffer from persecution, it is there to stop it. Its beneficial influence can be felt even in the most remote countries. Yet there is also another mission of even greater import to which it dedicates itself, given that the best means of hastening the emancipation of the Jews and working to ensure both their moral and material progress is to combat their ignorance and to encourage and propagate instruction among the youth. With this goal in mind it has founded numerous schools, which have succeeded beyond all expectations despite obstacles of all kinds that the indifference of some and the prejudice of others have put in its way. It has been able to procure the plentiful resources that such a project demands thanks to the largesse of various notables, including our generous coreligionist the Baron de Hirsch, who recently established a fund of a million francs in support of the education of the Jews of Turkey, and to whom we owe our eternal gratitude.

The moment has come to prove to those men with a generous heart that you are worthy of their good deeds and the sympathy they have shown you, to prove that you desire passionately to elevate yourself to the level of the civilized nations. Because this is a question that touches you so closely and concerns the future of your children, can you alone remain quiet spectators of these noble efforts that have been undertaken for your own moral and intellectual regeneration without searching for a means to ensure [your] success, without taking an active part in the sacrifices the situation requires? No, dear brothers, doing so will appear as base egoism! On the contrary we believe that you will dedicate yourself to such a sacred project with all of your being. Your honor and your duty require this of you; your interest counsels it. You must understand that social betterment cannot be achieved without moral betterment. Schools above all are what is required, that is, instruction and education and the diffusion of the brilliance of Western civilization among the Jews of the Ottoman Empire. Without instruction man remains a strange plaything of prejudices and routine, without knowing how to elevate himself . . . above ignorance and superstition. It is due to their instruction and enlightenment that our brothers of the Occident distinguish themselves in every profession and arrive at the highest positions. Let us endeavor to follow the path of progress they have traced. Let us get to work! The task is great, but we can see it to the end. . . .

Dear coreligionists: we will soon celebrate Passover, the holiday marking the liberation of our ancestors. The All-Powerful delivered them, slaves in Egypt, from moral and material servitude and brought

them out of the darkness into the light of Sinai, where their immortal
principles, which have become the fundamental code of all civilized nations, were promulgated. This glorious past imposes upon us a number
of obligations and sacred duties. Let us hasten the complete emancipation of our brothers by giving all of our energy to their intellectual
development. Let the column of fire, that eternal symbol of progress,
continue [burning] endlessly before us, while its brightness, which has
so often been veiled by our suffering and the vicissitudes of centuries
passed, guides us henceforth, as it once did for our ancestors in the des-
ert. Let us awaken, brothers, and let us awaken before the eyes of the
entire world. Thanks to civilization and progress, the unjust hindrances
Jews once encountered diminish day by day, while under the paternal
scepter of His Majesty the Sultan, who concerns himself equally with all
of his subjects without distinction of nationality, the Jews of the Ottoman Empire enjoy the same rights and favors as all the other nations
of the Ottoman Empire. Show yourselves worthy in all respects of this
benevolent and powerful protection. Carry out the duties and obligations you have to fulfill. Know how to merit through your conduct the
esteem and affection of the different nations amongst whom you live;
prove to them through your virtues that the hostile sentiments they
have nourished against us for centuries of oppression are unjustified.

We cannot recommend enough, dear friends, that you live harmoni-
ously with your brothers of all faiths and to avoid with great care everything that might offend, even indirectly, their religious sentiments. As
Easter approaches we cannot help but feel great anxiety while imagining the scenes of disorder that have so often troubled this holiday and
during which Jews are almost always the victims. Thanks to the wise
measures taken by His Holiness the Ecumenical Patriarch, we had no
excesses to decry last year, thank God.[1] We remain firmly hopeful that
we will be able to say the same this year as well. The lofty sentiments of
His Holiness Monsignor Joachim II, as well as the honorable members
of the Holy Synod, have been made clear to us.[2] The great benevolence
they have shown us in every circumstance, and the promises they have
given us assure us that they will use their influence in order to uproot

---

1. The implication being that the patriarch had taken measures to prevent intercommunal violence during the Easter season.
2. Joachim II was ecumenical patriarch in Istanbul in 1860–1863 and 1873–1878.

completely all the prejudices that we have experienced until today. Let us do our part to contribute to ensuring this result as soon as possible. . . . Let us banish any rancor and any regrettable memories from the past. Tolerance, charity, fraternity should be our course.

Count A. Camondo, "L'Alliance Israélite Universelle," *Levant Times*, March 27, 1874, 2. Translated from French by Julia Phillips Cohen.

## 62. A PAEAN TO THE SULTAN BY THE JEWS OF THE DANUBE PROVINCE (1876)

*In addition to reciting a traditional prayer for the ruler as part of the Sabbath morning service, Ottoman Jews frequently composed prayers, songs, and poems in honor of Ottoman sultans on other occasions, including anniversaries of their rule, their tours of various provinces, wars, and numerous other important events. Here we find a prayer that Jews in the Danube province composed for the newly instated Sultan Murad V (r. 1876) and published in the bilingual Ottoman Turkish/ Bulgarian newspaper* Tuna/Dunav, *which appeared in the provincial capital Rusçuk between 1865 and 1877. Noting the coincidence of Murad V's accession to the throne with the Jewish holiday of Shavu'ot, the author(s) who introduced and translated the prayer for the newspaper suggested that the secular event also had a particular, religious resonance for the sultan's Jewish subjects.*

Your Highness:

May the All-Holy God extend the life and glory of H.I.M.[3] the Sultan, our tsar and master. Since the accession of our Most Dignified, Most Serene, and Most August tsar H.I.M. Sultan Murad V on Tuesday, May 18 of the present year 1292 [May 30, 1876] coincided with the day on which the prophet Moses received the ten Holy Commandments from God at Sinai[4] . . . and gave them to the Jewish people, who observe them through their religion, we deemed ourselves happy. [Filled] with perfect joy and pleasure, we gathered in our house of prayer, where we pronounced the following prayer:

"Dear God, Master of all! On such a holy day, You placed on the imperial throne such a virtuous tsar, Sultan Murad Han, who is so well disposed towards all of his subjects. Bestow upon H.I.M. those of your

---

3. His Imperial Majesty.

4. The passage references the Jewish holiday of Shavu'ot, the Festival of Weeks, which marks the giving of the Torah and the Ten Commandments at Mount Sinai on 6–7 Sivan on the Hebrew calendar.

divine gifts that you also bestowed upon our holy ancestors Abraham, Isaac, Jacob, Moses, Aaron, David, and Solomon; strengthen Him on His most resplendent throne for all of time; protect Him from all misfortunes and sorrows; and endow all of his subjects who live in his justice-loving shadow with complete justice."

After reciting this prayer, we cried out in one voice: "Long live our most resplendent tsar and master." With these words, which we are obliged to utter at all times, we concluded our religious ceremony.

"Chiastni Raboti," *Dunav*, 12:1074 (May 30, 1876): 1. Translated from Bulgarian by Darin Stephanov.

*Possible response paper: overlapping roles of sexism and antisemitism*

*relates to the essay we read*

## 63.  TEACHING "THE LANGUAGE OF OUR GLORIOUS EMPIRE TO JEWISH GIRLS": A PETITION TO OPEN A SCHOOL IN ISTANBUL [1895]

*The following letter was written by Victoria Danon, a graduate of an Alliance Israélite Universelle school and teacher of Ottoman Turkish to Jewish girls in the Hasköy district of Istanbul. Here Danon attempts to appeal to Ottoman authorities for permission to open her own girls' school in the Sirkeci district. Employing the language of imperial patriotism, Danon suggests that the proposed school teach the language of the empire to Jewish girls while serving to combat the influences of foreign and missionary schools in Ottoman realms. Her attempts were thwarted however after various residents of the neighborhood complained that the space she had rented to this end was located near a mosque. In this instance, religious and social concerns triumphed over state patriotism. Unable to pursue her original plan, Danon instead settled on establishing a "house for needlework" (dikişhane), a project for which she received official approval in 1896.*

Today in every district of Istanbul and neighboring areas we can see Muslim, community, and foreign schools that disseminate instruction and enlighten the people. [For my part] I work as a teacher at a school in Hasköy and teach the language of the empire to many Jewish girls.

The petition I presented to open a school at Sirkeci was delivered to the police commissioner. Despite the letter of the residents of the district who approved the existence of my school in their neighborhood, my application for a certificate was refused by the inspector of community and foreign schools due to a second petition signed by residents of a neighboring district who opposed the opening of the school. They claimed that it is improper to establish a school so close to a mosque.

The school I plan to establish shall be a place that teaches the language of our glorious empire to Jewish girls. The government spends a great deal of money to teach Ottoman Turkish to children. My initiative may seem modest in comparison with the efforts of those foreign societies that have been established on Ottoman soil and which offer lessons in the German and French languages. However, considering that women are the source of the education [of future generations], and that girls will be the targets of my instruction, the value of my initiative should be obvious.

We know that our sultan, the shadow of God on earth, appreciates schooling tremendously. If a house of enlightenment aimed at enlightening minds is banned on the pretext that it is close to a mosque, it would contradict the [sultan's] aforementioned [ambitions]. There is no legal clause banning the establishment of a school near a mosque. Furthermore, the doors of my school and the existing mosque would be located on different streets. The petition that opposes the establishment of my school was purportedly signed by residents of our district such as the imam and *muhtar*.[5] However, it was written and signed by residents of a neighboring district. Such tricks should not be allowed in a time of progress and justice.

It is legally prohibited to open a beer hall and similar establishments near mosques and other religious places. What I am trying to open is neither a beer hall nor a place meant for amusement, God forbid. I humbly request that the deceptive petition written by residents of the other district not be given preference over the petition of our trustworthy local residents. If the Ministry of Education conducts an investigation as is the usual practice, it will become known that our district is composed of Christians and Jews: there are only four Muslim houses, and they gave their written consent to the establishment of my school. I humbly ask in the name of justice and the compassion of the sultan that the necessary measures be taken so that a certificate can be granted, and so that the other petition is not taken into consideration.

Letter of Victoria Danon to the Ottoman Ministry of Education, July 29, 1895, Başbakanlık Osmanlı Arşivi (Istanbul), Maarif Nezareti Mektubi Kalemi, 271/6. Translated from Ottoman Turkish by Onur Şar.

---

5. The Islamic religious leader and the elected leader of the neighborhood, respectively.

## 64. THE FATE OF A BULGARIAN JEWISH SETTLEMENT IN PALESTINE (1895–1896)

*While a small Sephardi community had lived in Palestine for centuries, by the late nineteenth century, large waves of settlers committed to creating a Jewish home in the biblical Land of Israel began to arrive in the region. Although these new immigrants were primarily Ashkenazi Jews from Eastern Europe, small groups of Sephardi and Mizrahi Jews joined the ranks of those who began to immigrate for ideological reasons. Among them were ten Jewish families from Bulgaria, where the Zionist movement made inroads throughout the 1890s. These families founded a settlement in the Palestinian Arab village of 'Artuf, roughly thirty kilometers west of Jerusalem. As the following sources demonstrate, the Bulgarian settlement was unique in a number of respects. From the vantage point of the Hebrew-language Zionist press, the appearance of a Sephardi farming colony was a novelty worthy of celebration. For Ottoman representatives, in contrast, the new settlement posed a distinct challenge: its members, arriving from a country still nominally under Ottoman control, carried Ottoman papers. The question of whether to treat them as foreign Jewish immigrants or citizens of the Ottoman Empire bedeviled the authorities, who were divided on the issue.*

August 30, 1895*

At a time when some of our Jews are selling land to others, with God's help there are other Jews to whom people sell land. We mentioned last week that the land of 'Artuf is about to be purchased by a Bulgarian society. Today we can announce to all devoted lovers of Zion that it has been bought for 87,500 francs and ownership transferred from the mission to the guardians of Israel. The people who bought it are true farmers, that is to say simple people, with strong arms, who have loved work since they were young. Their pockets are full of money and not the hollow advice and failed hopes that have plagued our Russian brothers. We are talking about real dinars. Before they bought this land, Mr. Niego, the head of Mikve Israel, was kind enough to send his representative to inspect it.[6] Because he declared the place suitable and since he is a great expert in this field, there is no need to doubt his word. . . .

We are lucky to have a Sephardi colony, because these Bulgarians are all Sephardim. We hope that the colony will blossom in the hands

---

6. Mikveh Israel was an agricultural school founded by the Alliance Israélite Universelle in Palestine with the aim of teaching its pupils how to become farmers.

* "Yerushalayim," *Habatselet* 25:47 (August 30, 1895): 391. Translated from Hebrew by Yuval Ben-Bassat.

of its owners, [transforming] it into a paradise. Our Sephardi brothers are not idealists who dream dreams. They are people who know
the meaning of labor. Even though they might be following in the
footsteps of those who paved the way for them, by doing so they will
follow in their tracks and not fail. Therefore we say to them: God be
with you and you will succeed!

Jaffa, August 28, 1896*
The authorities in Jerusalem want to expel the Ottoman Jewish farmers (Sephardim) who settled in the village of 'Artuf. We ask for [your]
rapid intervention and beg for mercy to stop the expulsion and to prevent these poor families from suffering terrible hardships.
Eliashar, Chief Rabbi.[7]

October 30, 1896**
The colonists of 'Artuf are a great concern to those busy with the task
of settling our country. It is known that the colony of 'Artuf (located
halfway between Jerusalem and Jaffa—according to the tradition of the
local people "between Zorah and Eshtaol"[8]) was purchased twelve years
ago by the missionary society[9] for the purposes of converting Jews. But
all their efforts have failed to lure any Jews [to the area]. A year ago,
when the missionaries realized that their efforts were unproductive, they
sold the colony to a society for the colonization of the Land of Israel
[established] by Bulgarian Sephardi Jews made up of fifty upright families from Sofia, Plevna, and Tatar-Pazarjik: strong, vibrant people who
funded [the transaction]. Ten families have already settled there, with
the understanding that the rest will soon follow.

[These families] assumed that because they were Ottoman citizens
they would not be prevented from settling in the colonies of the Land
of Israel, as stipulated by [Ottoman] law. None of them believed that
the [existing] restrictions and confinement decrees would be applied to

---

7. Ya'akov Shaul Eliashar, the *Rishon le-Zion*, or Sephardi chief rabbi in Palestine.
8. Judges 13:25.
9. Likely a reference to the London Society for Promoting Christianity Among the Jews.

* Telegram from Rabbi Eliashar to the office of the acting chief rabbi of the Ottoman Empire,
August 28, 1896, Başbakanlık Osmanlı Arşivi (Istanbul), Bab-ı Ali Evrak Odası (BEO), 62126/3.
Translated from French by Yuval Ben-Bassat.
** S. Z. "Mikhtave Sofrenu," *Hatsfira*, 23:227 (October 30, 1896): 1109. Translated from He-
brew by Yuval Ben-Bassat.

them. They were therefore astonished when the local government in no uncertain terms ordered them to leave the locality within eight days. All their supplications, requests, and pleas to state officials failed to bear fruit, and the officials refused to postpone the order by even one day. Then the chief rabbi of Jerusalem sent a telegram to Constantinople [Istanbul], and to our delight, they were saved [from banishment] when an order came from the grand vizier, an order in the form of a question to the officials in the Land of Israel: "Why do you expel Ottoman subjects from their land?" When the colonists in 'Artuf heard the news their spirits were revived, and the other colonists were happy too, as it was a sign that in the higher echelons there was now an openness towards colonists who are subjects of the Ottoman government. . . . "

## 65. THE FEZ AS A SIGN OF PATRIOTISM: AN APPEAL FOR IMPERIAL ALLEGIANCE DURING THE GRECO-OTTOMAN WAR (1897)

*The month-long Greco-Ottoman War (Greco-Turkish War) of 1897 was fought over the status of the island of Crete after irredentists from the Greek mainland joined Orthodox Christian residents of the island in an insurrection against Ottoman rule. This was not the first time that revolt flared on the island, but at this moment calls for war reached a fever pitch in the Kingdom of Greece, which dispatched warships to the island to support the rebellion. After various unsuccessful attempts at diplomatic resolution, the Ottoman Empire declared war on Greece, prompting the flight of Jewish, Muslim, and Christian islanders alike. In this appeal a journalist writing for the Ladino periodical* El Meseret *of Izmir urges his coreligionists in that city to take up the cause of the Ottoman Empire during its time of need: donating to the imperial army, volunteering as soldiers, and donning the fez as a clear indication of their loyalty to their state.*

The religious ideal that forms the basis of Judaism and that should remain ever present in our Jewish hearts creates no conflict with the requirements of citizenship.

It is true that in the past we Jews formed a distinct national and political community, but it is also true that this situation ceased to exist some twenty centuries ago and that on account of our mission the descendants of Israel are destined to live dispersed throughout the world. As the Prophet Micah said, "The remnant of Jacob shall be in the midst of many peoples, like dew from the Lord."[10] As a result the fatherland of the Jew is the country in which he is born, where his ancestors lie buried, and where he lives under the protection of the law.

Each Jew must love his fatherland, contribute to its material and moral prosperity, and subordinate his own interests to those of the general interests of his country—in short, defend it at every occasion. The Prophet Jeremiah says the following on the subject: At the risk of our own lives, "seek the peace of the city whither I have caused you to be carried away captive, and pray unto the Lord for it; for in the peace thereof shall ye have peace."[11] The later sages also tell us, "You should pray for the stability of the government because its authority safeguards society."[12]

Pray! Pray! This is the first and most important duty of every Oriental Jew. Our brothers, the Ottomans, leave their homes, their families, and their little ones in order to go defend our country, which has been attacked and offended. They leave everything and go before fire and sword and bullet in order to safeguard our peace and our interests. We should pray at all times to our Father in Heaven that the heroism Turkish soldiers and officers display before the enemy be rewarded with success. . . .

Women, men, old women, old men, young girls, young boys—all of us should try to find every possible item that might prove necessary or useful to our brothers the soldiers, who bear the harshness of war so admirably. Money, flour, mattresses, tents, clothes, shoes, fezzes, and other such things—all is good; all of it can be offered by any patriotic heart that beats among us.

After prayers and donations our conduct must remain moderate. If possible we should all wear the fez as an unmistakable sign of patriotism. It is not enough simply to have one's heart full of patriotism. We are also obligated to show with our actions and our clothing that we are proud to be loyal subjects of the great and powerful Ottoman Empire.

"La gera: patriotismo i relidjion," *El Meseret*, April 30, 1897, 1. Translated from Ladino by Julia Phillips Cohen.

---

10. Micah 5:6.
11. Jeremiah 29:7.
12. Possibly a reference to Pirkei Avot 3:2.

## 66.  AN OTTOMAN JEW VOLUNTEERS FOR THE
GREEK ARMY (1897)

*Joseph Marco Baruch (1872–1899) led a colorful if short life. Born in Istanbul,
Baruch was reared in France and later spent a year teaching as an Alliance Israélite Universelle instructor in Algiers, where he ran the short-lived French-language
journal* Le Juge. *A committed Jewish nationalist, he left Algiers to travel through
various European capitals, where he preached his own idiosyncratic form of Zionism,
calling for the "immediate and systematic" settlement of Jews in Palestine and the
dismemberment of the Ottoman Empire into which he had been born. After speaking
before Zionist organizations in Berlin, Vienna, and Prague, Baruch made his way
to Sofia by foot, without a penny to his name. Everywhere he went Baruch met with
opposition and skepticism, yet in Bulgaria he managed to find a following and to
gain support for a French-language periodical he published for a short while under
the title* Carmel. *Convinced that the Jews should raise an army and seize Palestine
from the Ottomans by force, Baruch joined an Italian volunteer regiment to fight on
the side of Greece during the 1897 Greco-Ottoman (Greco-Turkish) War. What follows is his account of that particular adventure. Only two years after its publication,
the peripatetic teacher, journalist, activist, and volunteer soldier took his own life in
Florence after a failed love affair.*

Let me be frank: I was there, but as a Zionist. I thought Judaism and
Zionism in particular needed to be represented in some way. It was a
grand idea, a matter of defending a supreme liberty. Jews fully understand what liberty means to others and have tried to gain it for themselves in every age and in each diaspora. Yet unfortunately they do not
know exactly what they want their own liberty to mean. Therefore I
should take a moment to define Zionism, which I have known for
some time is not entirely clear to Italian Jews, a reality that has become
more evident now that I am here [in Italy]. Zionism is that eternal
Jewish idea, the reason we followed Moses out of Egypt and left its
fleshpots, why we fought with the Maccabees and the Hasmoneans. It
was for Zionism that under Bar Kokhba we sacrificed one and a half
million heroes on the battlefields of ancient Rome. And it is for Zionism that we now repeat the famous song: "By the rivers of Babylon."[13]
. . . And why for so many centuries we have continued to say, "If I
forget you, O Jerusalem, let my right hand wither."[14] In sum Zionism
is the true, complete, and definitive emancipation of the Jewish people

---

13. Psalm 137:1.
14. Psalm 137:5.

from the barbarians who have denied them a homeland. Now that we have established this definition, we can move on.

And so I went to Greece as a Jewish patriot. . . .

But, for those who love to examine things under a microscope and have difficulty understanding how a French Jew could risk his life fighting for the Greek cause, I must repeat these verses that I wrote in response to the initial qualms I encountered regarding this matter:

> Yes, I part for Greece though I am not Greek,
> I seek neither glory nor adventure
> I know how to make use of blood that is not yet dry
> And I know how to find my burial place abroad
> I part for Greece where nothing is Jewish, and all is Greek
> Yet since my soul is Jewish through and through
> I will learn how one spills blood that is not yet dry
> As a tiny ewe faces a tiger[15]

Later I found myself in Cairo, where I conducted courses at the Ashkenazi Jewish school. After a farewell to my students and to the members of the Bar Kokhba Society I established there, I was ready. I left the banks of the Nile for the Mediterranean coast. I set off for Alexandria on Thursday, April 23. The evening before, I organized my affairs and drafted my will. . . .

The trip from Cairo to Alexandria was only four hours, so by eleven in the morning I was already in one of the most beautiful and grand cafés in Alexandria, the Caffè del Louvre. What first struck me about this city was the great fervor animating its streets—a liveliness to which neither Cairo nor the first port of Egypt were accustomed, considering the time of year and the recent cholera epidemic. A great throng of Greeks crowded the streets in every direction, either in dense masses or small isolated groups. Most of all, those filling the sidewalks outside the Caffè del Louvre were particularly restless. They shouted, they talked, they sang, they gesticulated, they argued, they deliberated, they ripped newspapers and reports from each other's hands. The spectacle was grand, the enthusiasm indescribable.

There truly was a protector for all those on their way to die—a boat

---

15. Although *Il Vessillo Israelitico* published Baruch's text in Italian, these verses appeared in French.

was leaving the next day! There was a rush to leave with the other four hundred, everyone a Greek, no one a foreigner. Was a distinction necessary? Were we not already brothers? Did we not face the threat of death together, especially since the reports from Préveza spoke of the many casualties on both sides? So let's go, wherever we are needed, the cause is great and worthy of a Jew. I was overcome with happiness and a verse from Victor Hugo's *Hernani*, "To fight like a Roman and die like a Jew," came to mind although slightly varied, "Fight like a Hebrew and die like a Jew." Throughout the campaign this constantly resonated in my ears.

Yet a Jew cannot die on the battlefield without letting go of his Judaism, the other *armada*, perpetually at arms, which has desperately fought for the last two thousand years for its rights, for its freedom. This was where I differ from my coreligionists. The first person I went to see was the honorable Mr. Mizrahi, former editor of the Judeo-Arabic newspaper *al-Haqiqa*. I spent Thursday and Friday with him, but did not reveal my plans. He would have never believed that I was capable of going to defend the Ionian cause, that of the *Yavanim*,[16] who after *Amalek*[17] are the most entrenched enemies of the Jews.

From his point of view to die for Greece would be the greatest crime Cain's progeny could ever commit.

The young dignitary of Alexandria, Mr. Jacques Haghion, was quite another story. He insisted that one should defend a cause when it is worthy, even if it is an enemy's. Above all though, one must be practical. He foresaw the defeat of Greece and found any effort to save her pointless. He was, or so it seemed, better informed on the issue than King George and the entire Hellenic government. If this "simple Jew," as the antisemites say, had served as the Greek Prince's council, many disasters would have been averted and so much generous blood would not have been spilled in vain.

I said goodbye to Mr. Haghion, but he continued to object.

Moved now by sentiments that made him feel honorable, those innate in all Jews, he began to pity those who made the mistake of going to die for Greece, myself included.

"You are all so young!" he told me. "You're sacrificing your best

---

16. Hebrew for Greeks.
17. A biblical enemy of the Jews.

years for the Jewish cause. Isn't it time for you to start thinking about a career, a brilliant career?"

I responded: "I *have* a career, that of a Jewish soldier."

"That's beautiful! Stupendous! But even the fiercest soldier needs a rest."

"In battle a change in action is already a rest," I replied.

"So you continue to fight for the Jewish people," he stated, changing his tactics.

"Continue? . . . I've always been fighting."

"You told me that you went to Greece."

"Indeed."

"And so?"

"So listen. It's not only a matter of Greece but a matter of principle, that of *liberating the populations of the Orient*. If I were to die in Greece it would be for a free Orient, which would include Judaism. When bandits attack a house all neighbors, even enemies, must come to the aid of the attacked. If not everyone will die. . . .

"Ionia is certainly an unfriendly neighbor to Armenia as it is to Judea. Don't you think that all the tiny nations who rise up and reclaim their rights will be divided in the same way that Europe has divided Greece? To us the Jewish nation is not yet dead, and sooner or later we too will have disputes with Europe."

"You might say these efforts are fruitless. At the moment, yes. But look ahead. Good ideas always triumph in the end."

With that I left my generous interlocutor and headed to the Caffè del Louvre to hear the latest news. I found the same Greek I had seen earlier that morning, and he told me that the volunteers for the Greek campaign were invited to go to the Greek consulate, so I went. The offices were crammed. The consul and the vice consul were there, enlisting the men and giving them tickets for Piero along with a note of voluntary participation. My turn arrived, the consul noticed my name was Jewish, and I vehemently confirmed it. He seemed surprised and exchanged a few quick words in Greek with the vice consul, expressing their belief that there were still some good Jews left in the world. And I told them that Jews have always fought for freedom and now we fight for freedom in Greece. "There are many volunteers willing to die for you, not to mention the Greek Jews, even though we know you are our enemies." *"Zito evréos!"* ("Long live the Jews!"), everyone exclaimed as they rushed toward me to shake my hand. But I wanted to avoid such displays of sympathy and returned to my post.

"Gli israeliti nella campagna di Grecia: Appunti d'un garibaldino," *Il Vessillo Israelitico* 45 (July 1897): 217–20. Translated from Italian by Jessica Strom and from French by Julia Phillips Cohen.

## 67. SALONICAN JEWISH STUDENTS IN PARIS RESPOND TO THE DREYFUS AFFAIR {1890s}

*In November 1894, Captain Alfred Dreyfus, a young French officer of Alsatian Jewish descent, was falsely accused of passing secrets to the German Embassy in Paris. The following month he was sentenced to life imprisonment and in February 1895 sent to a penal colony in French Guiana. The case prompted an affair that divided France for more than a decade, with "Dreyfusards" insisting the officer had been framed and "anti-Dreyfusards" fanning the flames of antisemitic agitation. In 1906 Dreyfus was exonerated and reinstated as a major in the French army, but the impact of the affair lingered, exposing deep rifts in French society. In this source we learn of the manner in which two young Salonican Jewish men residing in France at the height of the affair became implicated and politicized, providing an Ottoman Jewish view of this crucial event of modern European history.*

[As] I disembarked from a Messageries [Maritimes] ship in Marseille with my head spinning from the noise, I cast a fearful glance at the crowd in the enormous port. Suddenly I heard a stentorian and drawling voice.

"Meir . . ."

It was the voice of Shemuel Levi [Sam Lévy]. He had come to Marseille to welcome me.

And thus I began my second life as a student. But because you're curious to learn whether I'd begun selling newspapers in the streets of Paris, I'll tell you that such a need did not arise, thank God. My parents took the bread from their mouths, as the saying goes, and continued unfailingly to send me a few dozen francs every month, an amount with which a modest student could support himself in Paris before the war. . . .

I was studying medicine, Shemuel Levi, law. We got a room together at the Saint Marcel Hotel, which was located on the street of the same name. As if it was yesterday I recall the maternal smile of the landlady as she went to show us the room. A room, that is, in a manner of speaking. It was actually a storage closet that barely held two beds. The space between the beds was so narrow that we had to decide who would get up first so as not to collide. You get what you pay for. This quasi-room, which seemed like paradise to us because we were independent and didn't have to listen to the advice and shouting of our fathers—this miserable room cost us twelve francs a month.

We ate modestly as well. Thank God, in Salonica we'd gotten used to filling ourselves up on bread alone, "which makes the mouth sweet and the broth golden." A nice portion of *frites* (fried potatoes that are sold ready-made on the street corners of Paris the way roasted chestnuts are sold in our city) for ten centimes, followed by some water to wet our whistles, and all was well!

The only luxury we allowed ourselves was clothing. You should have seen Shemuel and me with our *bonjours* reaching to the knee, top hats shining, with our collars starched high, and with moustaches that, as the *romansa* goes, "had just begun to sprout"![18]

Naturally we were inseparable. Wherever Hanna went Plata followed, and for that reason it's impossible for me to separate my memories from those of the son of Han Sa'adi.[19]

Now don't go thinking that all we thought about was food and clothing. We were greatly concerned about moral issues and both of us thirsted for an ideal. At that time, however, there was no talk of Zionism. And as for socialism, it held no appeal for us. In Salonica there was no workers' misery, or proletariat, or class struggles, or any of the other great inventions of modern cililization that have turned the world topsy-turvy in half a century's time. So there we were, searching leisurely for a purpose, when the Dreyfus affair erupted like lightning across a clear blue sky.

We entered the fray head-on, especially Shemuel. He couldn't sleep at night if he hadn't come to blows that day with some anti-Dreyfusard. There were many times when we returned to our twelve-francs-a-month storeroom with blackened eyes, bloody noses, and impressive bumps on our foreheads.

Obviously at the time I was not yet on the staff of the Rothschild

---

18. A *romansa* is the Ladino term for a song or ballad.
19. Sa'adi Besalel a-Levi (1820–1903), a Salonican Jewish publisher, composer, and reformer.

Hospital. Otherwise I'd have been hired by the hospital solely because of the Dreyfus affair. After the Jewish army officer was sentenced, a period of quiet prevailed in France. Suddenly one morning, however, [Emile] Zola's famous open letter, *J'accuse*, went off like a bomb. Paris erupted into flames. The capital—what am I saying? all of France!— was divided into two camps: the Dreyfusards [who wanted the case reopened] and the anti-Dreyfusards [who assumed Dreyfus's guilt]. By evening everything was in turmoil. The nationalists had begun demonstrating with shouts of "Death to the Jews." The democrats were organizing counterdemonstrations. . . .

At that time I was already an assistant of the famous professor Gautier in the medical school hospital. I'd been chosen among many after a competition. Professor Gautier was very fond of me. He called me "the Turk," or simply, Yoel, and entrusted me with the most difficult tasks. In short I occupied a privileged position. But once the Dreyfus affair surfaced it upset everything. Professor Gautier was an anti-Dreyfusard, and the students informed him of my activities in support of the innocent officer.

If my friends at *La Aksion* wish to ask God for something, it shouldn't be a sack of liras. It would be better to ask God to make them journalists in Paris. That's where newspapers make buckets of money. That's certainly not going to happen in Salonica, where every newspaper is read by five people. In Paris if there are five members in a family they buy five different newspapers. The head of the household has his, his wife has hers, and the kids theirs, and the husband doesn't even deign to glance at his wife's. Naturally, depending on the paper, everyone has his or her own views. Consequently one could find papers of all stripes in a single family.

What does all this have to do with the Dreyfus affair? A lot if you want to understand the extent to which passions were enflamed in France when, following the conviction of the Jewish officer, Zola detonated a bomb with his famous letter, "*J'accuse.*"

The newspapers were divided into warring factions, those insisting on a retrial, convinced that the military counsel had been deceived, and those who viewed the defenders of Dreyfus's innocence as traitors.

The people were torn apart too. What am I saying? Bitter conflicts and fierce fights erupted even within families. And given the Parisians' hot tempers, these often ended in scrapes and blows.

I myself was witness to an unbelievable scene. Our landlady was an anti-Dreyfusard, whereas her husband was pro-Dreyfus. One day the two of them got into a fight, and the missus, not knowing how to respond to her husband's arguments, shouted "Get lost you dirty Jew!" Needless to say, the poor guy didn't have a drop of Jewish blood in his veins and unfailingly attended church every Sunday.

Let's return to our own story. Sam Lévy and I had discovered a sure trick to guess the position of those we met. We'd glance at the newspaper they were carrying. If it was Clemenceau's *L'Aurore* (the paper that published Zola's notorious letter) or *Le Figaro* or *Justice*, etc., we were okay. But if by contrast it was Drumont's *La Libre Parole*, *Gaulois*, or *Gil Blas*, we'd give each other a look, saying "Watch out! That guy's Haman."[20]

This technique of guessing had its advantages and disadvantages because it also meant that we disclosed ourselves. Our carrying *L'Aurore*, as well as our names, which in no way sounded Catholic—especially Lévy, which people instantly recognize as Jewish—not to mention our bad habit of always speaking [Judeo-]Spanish, betrayed us immediately as suspect to the antisemites.

And don't think that it was any small thing to be recognized as a Jew in those difficult times in that large capital that was boiling like a cauldron. In the evening as soon as it got dark mobs of people would rise up and go out in the courtyards shouting "Death to the Jews" or "Throw the Jews into the Seine!"

In the climate that prevailed it would have been nothing for one of us to fall into the hands of these fanatics and for them to toss us into the sea just to pass the time. If by chance some anti-Dreyfus group showed up, another would form against it a moment later. And, voilà, the fights, shouts, curses, threats, and kicks would ensue, but only to a point, because then the mounted police would appear with their swords brandished and clear out the most jammed square in seconds.

---

20. The implication is that readers of such anti-Dreyfusard papers were libelers like the biblical Haman, chief minister of King Ahasuerus (Xerxes I), who falsely claimed that the Jews under Persia were rebellious and deserved death.

You'll understand why, under these circumstances, I hadn't revealed myself as a Jew either to the landlady or at the university, where I appeared as a Turk. And in truth my last name, Yoel, seemed to be of Turkish origin. The landlady, meanwhile, didn't particularly like us.

"What a funny Turk you are," she'd say. "You're always speaking Italian."

For this Catholic woman Judaism seemed to have an Italian provenance. Her husband defended us however: "Leave them alone already," he'd say. "Turkish or Italian, they always pay their rent on time."

That was enough for the couple to come to blows. Naturally we who'd caused the fight would run off for fear of catching some of the landlady's slaps.

At the university, however, things worsened. The students were divided into warring factions. Most were in favor of the officer. Others were fanatical anti-Dreyfusards because they couldn't fathom how so many judges could have been deceived. Professor Gautier was among the latter. One day, annoyed by a discussion about the Dreyfus affair, he maliciously reprimanded a French student, a Jew named Shlomo. Shlomo responded and the professor became even more enraged, demanding that he leave the class. Shlomo immediately took his case to the student association, which had 40,000 members. A demonstration was organized posthaste; measures . . . were taken, and Shlomo finally received redress from the professor after two days of suspended classes. But this had repercussions for me, because as soon as we returned to class the professor summoned me, having been informed that I was among the most fervent protestors during the action.

"Yoel," he said, "What are you?"

"I'm a Turk, sir," I responded.

"Okay, a Turk, but what's your religion?"

My Jewish pride got the best of me and I no longer wished to conceal the facts.

"Professor," I told him, "I am a Jew, that's what I am."

"You are free to be a Jew, but I am also free not to support them [the Jews] after all the upheaval they've caused France over the Dreyfus affair." And he turned his back to me.

Upon leaving the university I ran into Sam Lévy and told him what happened to me. Well, Shemuelico got busy!

"Tonight," Sam Lévy told me, "there's a meeting of the Alliance [Israélite Universelle] committee. We're going."

The truth is I didn't want to. I was reluctant to go and bother so many important people with my personal matter. Especially then, with the Dreyfus affair and the wave of antisemitism that existed in France, there should be more serious issues for them to deal with. But my friend insisted.

"Whatever is happening to the Jews concerns the Alliance," he told me. "We're going."

"I don't know. Me in front of all those bigshots?"

To make a long story short, he dragged me to the Alliance offices. The committee was in full session. We submitted a summary of the events. A few minutes later Shevalsid himself came out—he was president at the time—and listened with great interest to what we had to say. He was particularly interested in my case.[21]

"We'll discuss your matter," he told me, "and we'll see what measures we'll take to restore the respect due a Jewish student. Despite everything I don't think that Professor Gautier meant what you understood him to mean. He's an upstanding intellectual, a bit impassioned over the events, but deep down he doesn't dislike Jews. At any rate you will not suffer at all as a result of this matter. It's likely that after this incident you'll lose your post as assistant at the university, but don't worry. I'll personally see to it that you secure a comparable position or an even better one at the Rothschild Hospital."

And while I didn't know how to thank him for his kindness, the good Shevalsid added:

"It's the least we can do for Salonican Judaism, which is awakening and becoming civilized. When you return to your city, please tell the Jews that we are all brothers, and that the strong will take care of the weak and the rich, the poor. The Alliance wants to help you in every way."

The president of the Alliance spoke to me in a voice so sincere and heartfelt that it brought tears to my eyes, and as I was leaving I grabbed his hand and kissed it.

---

21. The reference to "Shevalsid" is unclear. At this time S. H. Goldschmidt was president of the Alliance Israélite Universelle.

"Whatever I'm doing," he said, "it's not for you. It's for Jewish solidarity."

I left the Alliance truly moved, and from that day on I was converted and remained a fervent supporter of that organization on behalf of Jewish solidarity throughout the world.

"Los suvenires del Dr. Yoel," *Aksion*, March 28–April 3, 1938. Translatated from Ladino in Rena Molho, ed., *The Memoirs of Doctor Meir Yoel* (Istanbul: Isis, 2011), 40–47, with adaptations by the editors.

## 68. SHOULD SEPHARDI JEWS RECONCILE WITH SPAIN? A JEWISH LAWYER FROM IZMIR REFLECTS [1904]

*Beginning in the last decades of the nineteenth century, Sephardi authors sparked a language debate in the pages of the Judeo-Spanish press. In this medium journalists and contributors argued over which language Ottoman Jews should speak, teach their children, write in, or defend. For the majority of those who weighed in on the subject, their "jargon" (that is, Ladino) symbolized a past they hoped to leave behind. The general disregard that many Sephardi authors expressed towards their native tongue in these years had its parallel in the attitudes of various European Jewish thinkers who had grown up in Yiddish-speaking environments, only to reject that language and all it represented to them. The influence of the extensive school network of the Alliance Israélite Universelle on Jewish communities across the Ottoman Balkans and Levant beginning in the 1860s accelerated the assault on Ladino, as increasing numbers of Sephardi schoolchildren began receiving lessons in French rather than their mother tongue. The language debate was revived in 1904, when a Spanish senator by the name of Ángel Pulido initiated a campaign of Spanish-Sephardi reconciliation. The letter that follows is the response of Gad Franco (1880–1952), a Sephardi lawyer, journalist, and publisher in Izmir, to Pulido's call for rapprochement between the Spanish state and the descendants of those Jews expelled from Iberia in 1492.*

I am hostile to the Spanish language option. I believe that a people like the Jews, which has not known a political existence as a nation, should divide its languages into two categories. . . . Their languages can be split, if you will, into sentimental and practical languages. I would put Hebrew and Turkish in the first category, because despite their lack of intrinsic value, each is preserved and defended [by us] for reasons of pure and simple sentimentalism, the first out of a national feeling and the second out of a feeling of patriotic duty. To be sure, Spanish cannot be classified among the sentimental languages. Rather it fits into the category of material languages, which are adopted due to the profit that can be gained from them commercially. Falling under this category (since it can be in no other), Spanish has no chance of success among us, as it is up against the living languages of industrialized nations such as England, France, and Germany. Since Spanish has no qualities that could make it preferable to other languages in this category, I can only recommend that the Jews adopt the language that can offer them the greatest number of possibilities. . . . I can assure you that the Jews of the Orient have no special sympathy for your country. They have conserved the Spanish language only because they knew no other. We see convincing proof of this fact in the students of the new generation who have benefited from a French education and now reject the language they learned in their infancy in order to speak the new language.

Ángel Pulido, *Españoles sin patria y la raza sefardí* (Madrid: Librería de Fernando Fe, 1905), 110–111. Translated from Spanish by Julia Phillips Cohen.

## 69. "YOUNG TURKS": MUSLIM, JEWISH, AND CHRISTIAN "BROTHERS" SHAPE A REVOLUTIONARY MOVEMENT {ca. 1900s}

*Leon Sciaky (1893–1958) was reared in Salonica and immigrated to the United States as a teenager. Here he speaks of his father's involvement in the revolutionary movement that operated secretly in the private homes, cafés, and Masonic lodges of Ottoman Salonica and across the empire. In 1908, not long after the period described in this account, the revolution successfully compelled Sultan Abdülhamid II to restore the constitution of 1876 and to reopen the Ottoman parliament, which had remained closed since 1878. Sciaky later recalled his family rejoicing as they heard the news of the successful revolution. Having inherited his father's commitment to political reform, Sciaky remained active in internationalist causes throughout his life. His memoir, written in English long after his emigration, is a nostalgic account of the Sephardi heartland and multicultural Salonica, both of which were eviscerated by the time of his writing.*

I was not a little surprised at first to find that the women in Shukri's household, his mother and his two older sisters admitted me into their apartment. But I was still more amazed to find myself in their midst without their making a pretense of covering their faces. They acted as if there was nothing untoward in their behavior, greeting me in excellent French and making me feel at home by resuming their sewing and embroidery work.

This, to me, unprecedented freedom in a Turkish home impressed me so much that I spoke to Father about it.

"Osman Bey, your friend's father, is a cultured man with modern ideas," he said. "Yes, I know him."

"Is he perchance," I asked, half in earnest, half teasingly, "is he one of your 'brothers'?"

As far back as I can remember, Father's bedtime had been punctual as clock work. No matter whether neighbors came to spend the evening hours with us or whether we were alone he retired early. Only on rare occasions, when a French stock company was playing at the Eden Theater, could he be induced to go out after supper and to stay up late. For days after these momentous occasions he would claim with a twinkle in his eyes that he was behind on his sleep and that he really should retire earlier. "What!" he would exclaim when urged to stay up a while. "After my late hours of last week?"

Then, suddenly, two years before, he had taken to excusing himself directly after the evening meal on a few nights a week and to leaving for mysterious meetings from which he would not return until long after I was in bed.

It was quite accidentally—he inadvertently left a book on his dresser—that I discovered the reason for such a radical change in his routine. He had become a Freemason. Of course, no one outside the immediate family knew about it, for Freemasonry was strictly forbidden in Turkey, and to have been found guilty of belonging to the fraternity might, especially in the capital, have spelled disaster. In spite of the ban, however, in Salonica, where one enjoyed a measure of freedom unparalleled anywhere else in the empire, four lodges, French, Spanish, Italian, and the Grand Orient, met in the greatest of secrecy.

For the first time, influential and forward-looking Turks, Greeks, Bulgarians, and Jews were closely bound together by bonds of brotherhood, which could not be strengthened by the conspiratorial flavor of the organization and by the common danger of the members. For many years these lodges, with no fixed habitation of their own, meeting in lonely houses and out-of-the-way spots, had been quietly recruiting the liberal elements of the population and rallying to whatever progressive thought they could find in the city.

The belief, current a few years later, that the Freemasons had established some sort of understanding with the Bektashi dervishes is not at all improbable, considering the philosophy of this order. I remember accompanying my father on several visits to the sheik, the abbot of their monastery just outside the northwestern gate of the city.

These dervishes, often celibate, formed a monastic order dedicated to a religious life of good deeds and charity. Anyone, it was said, irrespective of race or creed, could seek hospitality in their *tekkye* and be provided, for as long as they wished, with food, shelter, and whatever other assistance he might need.

A profound distrust and often ill-concealed antagonism existed between the orthodox Moslem cleric and the Bektashi, for while outwardly presenting no heretical beliefs, the dervishes were more mystical and more daringly speculative in their doctrines than the Path deemed good for the faithful.[22] Secretly, however, they denied the sole authority of Mohammed, and some Moslems even professed to think them downright atheists.

Theirs was a pantheistic philosophy conceiving of a universal substance with which the soul of man must merge and become identified before attaining a union with God. It therefore was impatient with formalism, and hated any and all man-made barriers which divided one soul from another, and hence from God. Evil, all the evil of the world, they contended, was to be found in these four phrases:

"I eat; you are hungry. I am good; you are evil."

While the Masonic lodges took no official cognizance of it, a group of Moslem and Jewish members were cautiously but steadily building up a revolutionary movement whose ultimate goal was the overthrow of the despotic Hamidian regime, and the adoption of a constitutional form of government.

The headquarters of the revolutionary society to which these lodge members belonged, established in Salonica but a year before, had found the organization of Freemasons a readymade and ideal instrument with which to operate. Having adopted the "cell" system of

---

22. *Shari'a*, or Islamic law.

recruiting, whereby each member of the committee knew only three or four others, one of whom served as a liaison with another cell, the work was being carried out in such deep secrecy that even the elaborate and all pervading espionage of the palace could not discover it.

The committee had grown to such an extent, especially within the ranks of officers and men of the army corps garrisoned in the city, that it had now instituted a powerful counterespionage of its own. Members held important positions in all departments of the administration, in the offices of the ministers, in the foreign post offices and embassies abroad and even within the walls of the palace itself. They were thus eminently placed to intercept secret messages, to know of plans and orders of the sultan, and to forewarn the committee of any contemplated threatening step.

The casual visitor to Salonica in that year would have found a calm, pleasant city whose lighthearted inhabitants attended to their business with gay unconcern. Leisurely crowds walked on Sabri Pasha, stopping before the windows of the well-stocked stores to appraise the merchandise on display. Carriages drove by, officers rode on beautiful chargers, the streetcar trumpet blew loud and often, street vendors shouted their wares, and importunate beggars followed one with outstretched hands and loudly recounted their ills.

Toward evening he would probably have had to look long for an unoccupied table in front of the cafés, where the noisy throng overflowed the sidewalks to the street. But he could be seated at last and, quaffing his beer and munching the *mezelik*, the hors d'oeuvre brought him by the busy waiter, he could not but wonder at the serenity of the people, who seemed without a care in the world.

The conflicting nationalistic aspirations, the distrusts and the hatreds, the spying and the counter-spying, the growing dissatisfaction of the troops whose long overdue pay was still being held up, the growing worry of the businessman whose trade had come to a standstill, the utter misery of the peasants in faraway villages, harassed by warring bands, the virtual anarchy in the mountains, these the casual visitor would not become aware of. For nothing betrayed the temper of the people and no outward sign indicated the approaching of the storm.

## 70.  AN OTTOMAN JEWISH ACTIVIST IN CAIRO
## PROPOSES SETTLING JEWS IN THE SUDAN (1906)

*In the early twentieth century a number of Jewish activists advocated for a new
vision for the Jewish future known as Territorialism. Its supporters diverged from
those Zionists who believed that Jews should pursue settlement in Palestine alone.
Territorialists argued that while a homeland was necessary for Jews around the
world, any land could potentially serve this purpose. At a time when thinkers of
various political persuasions continued to search for new solutions to the "Jewish Question," supporters of this approach gave serious consideration to the idea of
settling the Jews in Uganda, Argentina, and Mesopotamia (Iraq), among other
areas. The text that follows discusses a little-known proposal issued in the Ladino
periodical* La Vara *of Cairo by the Ottoman Jewish journalist and scholar Abraham
Galante (1873–1961). Galante proposed that the Sudan, jointly ruled by Egypt and
Great Britain since 1899, presented Jews with an ideal environment for settlement.
Although Jewish leaders in Europe and the United States appear to have given little
thought to Galante's proposal, his plan made waves in the Arabic press of Egypt,
where he had settled to escape the reach of the autocratic Ottoman Sultan Abdülhamid II's regime. Ever the Ottoman patriot, even from his Egyptian exile, Galante
believed that finding an alternative home for Jews outside of Ottoman domains
could solve the Jewish Question without endangering the status of his coreligionists
in the empire.*

Mr. Abraham Galante, editor of *La Vara*, has recently developed a
plan for Jewish colonization in the Sudan. Although he treats the old
proposal to settle Jews in Uganda as a point of departure, Galante offers extensive geographical, climatic, and statistical proof of the superiority of the Sudan over Uganda, while also demonstrating how easily
his plan can be put into practice.

Below we have summarized the principal points of his proposal, the
full version of which is nearly twenty pages long.

The Sudan has been open to civilization since 1898. Justice reigns and
electricity has begun to take over. The country is three-fourths the size
of Europe, with a population of nearly two million indigenous residents
and a few thousand Europeans.

The greatest work accomplished thus far has been the opening up of
the Red Sea coast and the construction of a new port called Port Sudan
on January 27 of the current year. This port, which can accommodate
as many as seventy commercial ships at a time, has a direct line of communication with England, India, and various other important locations.

The land is rich and fertile. Nearly two hundred million feddans[23] are ripe for cultivation, whereas in Egypt the number is no more than a few million. Certain parts of the country allow for as many as three separate harvests a year, while the rest of the land permits at least one. The climate of the country is healthy and superior to that of Egypt. The Nile, that great and life-giving river, also runs through the Sudan, a fact that makes Egypt dependent upon the country.

At present great attention is being given to irrigation projects and to the building of rail lines, both of which require a sum of hundreds of thousands of liras each year. A small example will suffice: before Port Sudan was opened, Khartoum, Sudan's capital, was connected to the coast and to Alexandria through an extensive and meandering railroad line. Today this road has been shortened to merely 900 English miles.

Mr. Galante concludes that the Sudan can thus serve as a site of:

1. large-scale settlement
2. agricultural colonies
3. private enterprise

He additionally asks that a scientific mission make plans to visit the country.

P.S.: A draft of this proposal was sent via telegraph to the following addresses: in London to Lord Rothschild, president of the commission formed to search for a land for Jewish settlement, and to the offices of *The Jewish Chronicle*; in Paris to Baron Edmond de Rothschild, administrator of the Jewish Colonization Association, and to the offices of *Les Archives Israélites*; in Berlin to the Hilfsverein der Deutschen Juden, and to *Die Jüdische Presse*; in Washington to Oscar Straus, Secretary of Commerce of the United States (a Jew); in New York to the important banker Jacob Schiff, and to *The American Hebrew*.

Abraham Galante, "Un nuevo projeto de kolonizasion judia en el Sudan," *La Vara*, December 21, 1906, 1. Translated from Ladino by Julia Phillips Cohen.

---

23. Units of area used to designate landholdings. According to the present source, at the time of Galante's proposal a feddan was equal to approximately 1,400 square meters.

# 71. AN ANTI-ZIONIST APPEAL FROM ISTANBUL (1909)

*The modern Ladino press was founded and run by a small coterie of Ottoman Jewish journalists known for their passionate polemics. David Fresco was among the most influential. Fresco ran various periodicals during his lifetime, including* El Tiempo, *the longest-lived Ladino newspaper ever published, which appeared in Istanbul from 1872 to 1930. The following is an excerpt from a 1909 French collection and translation (from Ladino) of Fresco's fiery writings on the rise of the Zionist movement since the 1890s, when the first Zionist congresses began to convene in Europe. An avid critic of Zionism, Fresco not only considered the new Jewish nationalist movement utopian, but also argued that it threatened the place of Jews in Ottoman society. Here he addresses an ideal Ottoman Jewish reader, cautioning him against the dangers of this new movement.*

Nearly fifteen years ago, following frequent persecutions against our coreligionists in Russia and Romania, a few European Jews conceived of the project of establishing a Jewish state in Palestine and transporting our unfortunate brothers persecuted in other countries [to that land]. Honest people of good faith who believe in the possibility of achieving such a project worked for the propagation of this idea, to which they gave the name Zionism. But a few dishonest individuals who understood that they could exploit this idea for personal profit joined the movement and worked to exalt spirits, excite imaginations, and awaken religious passions.

This movement, which to date has not achieved any results and will lead to no good, is extremely dangerous to the interests of Jews all over the world and, above all, of the Jews of Turkey. It nurtures crazy hopes among the Jewish masses, inspires in Jews a great distrust for progress, causes an estrangement from other peoples, and awakens religious and racial fanaticism.

Ottoman Jew, honest people as well as interested parties who support this movement [will] try to draw you in to this dangerous tide as well.

Ottoman Jew, listen to me closely: that which Zionism demands of you is in no way compatible with what your religion or your conscience asks of you. I speak to you in the language of reason—the language of logic. Don't let yourself be led astray by a few wretches who have let themselves be taken in or by imposters who seek to deceive you.

Neither I nor those who share my opinion have ever said that you must close your heart or deny compassion to your coreligionists who suffer. Those who have claimed as much are slanderers and people of bad faith who have used such perfidy with the intention of leading you astray and turning you against the anti-Zionists. We sympathize with all those who suffer misfortunes and even more so with those coreligionists [who suffer]; what we cannot tolerate, what appalls us, is when people of bad faith, or even those who are themselves misled, come to deter you from your duty on the pretext of coming to the aid of your coreligionists abroad. What is worse, in deterring you from your duty not only do they fail to help your coreligionists, they in fact do them great harm while bringing an immense disaster upon Ottoman Jews. . . .

Ottoman Jew . . . you have not yet stepped forward, and already Zionism troubles your mind, poisons your spirit, deters you from your duty, inspires in you absurd and absolutely unachievable hopes, and makes you neglect your efforts to uplift yourself. It seeks to make you like an astrologer who, walking with his eyes fixed on the stars, falls into an open chasm beneath his feet.

It is always the youth, the sap, the young blood of peoples full of life that works with vigor and intelligence for the good of society. If the Jewish youth of our country works in earnest to uplift Ottoman Jewry, there is no doubt that it will make great and rapid progress. But Zionism works precisely to mobilize this great and vital force of the country's Jewry and thus brings upon it the greatest of catastrophes.

Ottoman Jew, can you gauge the immensity of the disaster that will befall the Jews in this country if our compatriots and particularly our Muslim compatriots, who constitute the majority, become convinced that the Ottoman Jew is not attached to his country, that he runs toward another ideal, that he dreams of the creation of a Jewish state to the detriment of Ottoman national unity?

I am convinced that the Ottoman Jew maintains an unwavering loyalty to his fatherland. I am convinced that nothing in the world would undermine this loyalty—that the Ottoman Jew prefers Turkey to the most civilized countries. Ottoman Jew, I know that you do not need my lessons of moral honesty and patriotism, but even so I believe it my duty to warn you so that you do not let yourself be deceived by the appearance of an idea presented to you in the best light, an idea [Zionists] would have you believe is generous and representative of the true ideals of Israel but which will be, all the same, the cause of your undoing should you adhere to it.

David Fresco, *Le Sionisme* (Istanbul: Impr. "Fresco," 1909), 69–72. Translated from French by Alma Rachel Heckman.

## 72. "OUR DUTIES AS JEWS AND AS OTTOMANS": AN OTTOMAN ZIONIST VISION FOR THE FUTURE (1909)

*Following the 1908 revolution in the Ottoman Empire, new political parties, social clubs, and publications multiplied in a climate of lifted censorship. It was in this context that Zionism emerged as a powerful political option among Ottoman Jews. Like Zionists elsewhere, Ottoman Zionists envisioned a Jewish home in Palestine, yet they remained adamant that their position was patriotic, designed to bring new, loyal Jewish inhabitants into the region and to stimulate growth in the lands they settled, thus creating a vibrant and autonomous Jewish center without threatening the territorial integrity of the empire. The source that follows, penned by the Salonican journalist and activist David Isaac Florentin (1874–1941), details the author's plan to foster greater Ottoman representation within the international Zionist movement, and to turn foreign Jewish settlers arriving in Palestine into Ottoman citizens. It was through these means, Florentin reasoned, that Zionists could contribute to the cause of their country while also remaining true to their people. In his view Zionism was a movement that promised to revitalize Ottoman Jewry and the Ottoman state in equal measure.*

In nearly all regions of the empire we are confronted with a persistent apathy—an unshakable indifference toward everything that does not concern us directly and a deplorable disinterest in our communal and national affairs. Judging by this general state of affairs, we can conclude that the change of regime has merely inspired people to let out a few cries of "Long Live Liberty!" and to speak about everything while remaining passionate about nothing. Only the form has changed; the content remains the same.

Our first duty as Jews and as Ottomans is to conduct a frontal attack on the inertia and indifference that impedes all progress. If we hope to be worthy of our race and our fatherland—of Judaism and of Turkey—this is how we must begin.

In order to awaken from our centuries-long slumber, and to rees-tablish our sense of national obligation, we must continuously remind ourselves that it is completely impossible to free ourselves from those bonds that tie us to our racial and religious forefathers. Whether we like it or not and whatever our situation, the wealth or misery, the honor or opprobrium of each Jewish group or individual inevitably weighs upon us. Whatever we do, others force us to remain in solidar-ity. They will always do so, above all in order to attack us. If our indif-ference is the result of our selfishness, let us use this sentiment, which is a powerful force, in order to interest the young and the wealthy in our communal regeneration. It is to this end that we expose our col-lective situation, following the sage advice of the Greek philosopher who said "know thyself."

Of all the ethnic and religious groups that make up the empire, we are quite possibly the least numerous and consequently the least influ-ential. There are only 500,000 of us, while other groups count their members in the millions. And this is not all. We are dispersed across all parts of the empire, from the north to the south and the east to the west, from Constantinople [Istanbul] to Sana'a, and from Basra to Tripoli in Africa. This dispersion across regions so far from one another has ominous consequences, ones I would even venture to call deadly. To our great misfortune we lack the linguistic connection indispensable to any well-organized community. We speak a dozen languages and jar-gons: Judeo-Spanish, Arabic, Hebrew, Judeo-German, Turkish, Greek, Armenian, Persian, Chaldean, and who knows what other languages.

This language diversity has ensured that the Jew of Damascus or Baghdad is a near stranger to the Jew of Constantinople or Salonica, and vice versa. There is no regular contact between the Jewish com-munities of the empire. Whether a Jewish woman works or does not work, she does so without concerning herself with the situation of her sisters. Every man serves only himself: individualism is causing a situ-ation of near anarchy. Such is the current state of Ottoman Judaism.

Conditions in the large Jewish centers of the empire leave much to be desired. This is not simply due to the lack of relations between communities or their unsatisfactory organization, all of which are ul-timately of secondary importance. Above all [our situation is unsatis-factory] from an economic, intellectual, and moral point of view. It is a pity to admit that both the small isolated towns and the large communities of Constantinople, Salonica, Smyrna [Izmir], Adrianople [Edirne], Damascus, and Baghdad consistently rely upon the charity of European Jews in order to support their schools, while they still lack all of the charitable institutions they require. This fact serves as clear proof, should such proof be required, that we are very much behind our Greek and Armenian compatriots in a number of respects. . . .

All told we may be considered the least advanced group of Jews on earth after the Jews of Persia and Morocco. We are certainly very far from the political influence wielded by American or Austro-Hungarian Jews, the financial power of our coreligionists in France and England, or the labor force of the Jews of Russia and Romania, who nonetheless remain oppressed. Without a doubt we are well respected and well treated. Our loyalty is appreciated, while we are invited to enjoy the benefits of the constitutional regime and of true equality. Yet we are ill prepared. We are not adapting ourselves sufficiently to profit from the new situation. We remain at a distance from general developments, without worrying at all about our future. While everyone in our midst is working feverishly to occupy ever-higher positions, we merely remain in our old positions. . . .

The status quo, when it does not represent a veritable decline, is present everywhere and in all things. Many important communities in the administrative centers of the *vilayet*s, such as Monastir [Bitola], Üsküb [Skopje], and Angora [Ankara], for example, have no spiritual leader and thus remain without moral guidance. In numerous other communities communal administrations remain stagnant, without steady resources, a balanced budget, or sufficient reserves for future crises. No Jewish school has opened since the reestablishment of the constitution, with the exception of the Gan Yeladim of the Hilfsverein in Salonica. I am unable to judge whether the poor receive more help today than they did yesterday, while it pains me to admit that I do not anticipate a literary renaissance among Ottoman Jews.

Such a literary renaissance, which could help further a general awakening, reactivate our institutions, and encourage the establishment of new societies, remains a very difficult task for the moment: (1) because of the lack of a linguistic connection about which I have already spoken, and (2) because of our ignorance of Hebrew or any other literary

Jewish language. French, which we learn thanks to the Alliance Israélite [Universelle], is without a doubt an excellent language for commerce and general knowledge, but provides an inadequate means of teaching us about Judaism and the Jews. Jewish books in the French language are relatively few and they cost a great deal. The Jewish journals of Paris are of little interest to us as their reading public is limited. *L'Univers Israélite* and *Les Archives Israélites* cannot provide the material found in the major Hebrew papers, in *The Jewish Chronicle* of London, the *Jewish Comment* of Baltimore, the *Allgemeine Zeitung des Judentums* in Berlin, the *Wochenschrift* of Dr. Bloch in Vienna, or *Rassvet* in Petersburg. As for our own Judeo-Spanish papers, they are not without value, yet they cannot play a major role for a number of reasons, principally because they occupy themselves with a little bit of everything while lending relatively limited space to Jewish topics. The material we provide to the avid reader will hardly satisfy him, yet it is impossible for us to give him anything more or better for the simple reason that we support ourselves only with great difficulty, not to mention the fact that we address merely a third, or perhaps half, of Ottoman Jews.

Well, you will say to me, shall we lose all hope? Is there nothing to be done? Shall we give up and remain passive observers of the collapse of Ottoman Judaism?

Absolutely not. We have reached a fork in the road. Our youth, conscious of its duties and its power, does not lack zeal but rather desires to work toward a noble ideal. And which ideal is more noble than the rapprochement of 500,000 brothers who were once isolated from one another? What is more beautiful than coming together to work for the common good? The goodwill exists. Dedicated men are not as rare as has been claimed. The only serious difficulty is the task of bringing together isolated forces. By organizing, the youth should give—and already do give—the first sign of life. . . .

So that all of our youth can be ready to work and busy themselves with communal and national affairs, we must create literary societies in each community of importance. Libraries and lectures halls should be built everywhere as a complement to synagogues for some and as their replacement for others. . . . Questions of the utmost import for the future of Ottoman Judaism and for the prestige of Jews the world over are now discussed among us. Under the circumstances we are called upon to fulfill multiple duties to ourselves, to Turkey, which has always treated us with kindness, and to global Judaism, which continues to do so much for us. The old regime prepared us poorly for public life. We must undertake the preparation we lack without delay. . . .

Today as yesterday our Hebrew language is greatly neglected in boys' schools and figures in the programs of girls' schools merely in symbolic form for barely one or two hours a week. The same is true of Turkish. All of this is simply inconceivable under the new regime. Hebrew and Turkish are equally indispensable to us, and we should learn both with equal care in order to fill our duties as Jews and Ottomans. If we can learn them well the Alliance [Israélite Universelle] will have no choice but to help us.

Once all of our schools, both those of the Alliance and the *talmude torah*, teach Turkish according to the official program, government high schools across the empire will open their doors to hundreds and thousands of Jewish children who currently languish in misery and whose futures promise little more than a precarious position of low social standing. Untold numbers of gifted young people will be able to pursue their studies in institutions of higher education, while an army of doctors, lawyers, engineers, architects, agronomists, naval and army officers, professors, high-ranking functionaries, diplomats, and writers will have the chance to enhance the reputation of [the people of] Israel in the near future.

Perfect knowledge of Turkish is indispensable for us if we want to earn our place in the sun and to fulfill our duties to ourselves and to our community while also fulfilling the duties and enjoying the rights accorded by Ottoman nationality. Because Turkish is the official language of the empire, a citizen who does not know Turkish is little more than a deaf-mute. However educated, intelligent, or active he may be, he nonetheless remains mute. . . .

What is Zionism and what does it ask of us? According to the program it set during the First Zionist Congress in 1897, "Zionism seeks to establish a home for the Jewish people in Palestine, secured under public law."

Under the old administration, Zionism sought to earn certain privileges from members of the local administration in order to concentrate the Jewish people's efforts on the colonization of Palestine. The

arbitrary administration of our country, which has impeded all progress, made it impossible to turn this poor and forsaken province into
a flourishing, dynamic, and prosperous center through the work and
capital of Jewish colonists—farmers, merchants, and industrialists. One
concession, a constitution in miniature, was indispensable for the Jewish repopulation of Palestine.

The legal regime Zionism demanded for Palestine is today a reality
across all of Turkey. Since the constitution was implemented in our
country Zionism has entered a new phase, as all of the leaders of the
great Jewish national movement do not fail to remind us. Special privileges are no longer necessary. From this point on, applying the existing
laws justly is enough, for Palestine and the entire empire. . . .

It must be repeated, Zionism simply seeks to stimulate and favor
through practical means the creation of new agricultural and industrial Jewish centers in Palestine. It seeks the material, intellectual, and
moral regeneration of the Holy Land, which is doubly dear to us as the
country of the Bible and the cradle of our race. It is in no sense antipatriotic, either in foreign countries, where it remains a purely humanitarian movement that addresses only those coreligionists who have
already decided to leave their native lands, nor in Turkey, since loyalty
to the Ottomans is the first and most essential part of its program. . . .

We must study our national movement very carefully. For my part
I am convinced that once we understand Zionism well we will not fail
to support it. Our economic situation need not be an obstacle. For-
tunately we are quite far from the precarious state of the Jews of Russia and Romania, where there are nonetheless hundreds of powerful
Zionist societies and organizations. From a demographic perspective
alone, counting twelve million Jews in the world and half a million in
Turkey, we should be able to supply at least five thousand Zionists and
send some twenty to twenty-five delegates to the next congress. . . . I
consider the number of five thousand Zionists and twenty delegates as
the minimum since, as Ottoman Jews, we are called upon and should
aspire to play an important role in the Zionist Organization. This is
vital for our own interests and to the future of Zionism as a whole.
The more numerous and influential we are, the more the importance
of maintaining loyalty to Turkey will be emphasized. Our participation
in the movement and our contributions to its projects will serve as the

best proof and guarantee, should they be needed, that Zionism merely seeks to strengthen Ottoman Judaism and to increase the power of a singular and indivisible Turkey by encouraging Jewish immigrants to occupy immense stretches of unpopulated land in Palestine and neighboring areas while becoming Ottomans. . . .

Indeed, which population could be more loyal to Turkey than those immigrants who, chased from their countries by oppressive restrictions, now enjoy complete religious liberty under the protection of the caliphs and the constitution?

If all this reflects the Ottoman perspective, what of the Jewish perspective? As I mentioned earlier, we are few in number and we lack influence. The Jews of Russia, Romania, and some in Austria, who have done so much to reinforce English Judaism, revive French Judaism, and spur an incredible expansion within American Judaism, will no doubt rejuvenate us and give us a new life as well through their labor and their example. Zionism's projects in Palestine deserve our complete practical encouragement, for they increase the influence and reputation of Ottoman Jews in that land.

Such practical encouragement can be divided into three parts:

1. Direct and involved participation in agricultural, commercial, and industrial enterprises
2. Consumption of Palestinian products
3. Contributions to general and professional educational projects. . . .

As should be clear from this brief discussion of the general situation of Ottoman Judaism and of our duties to ourselves, to Turkey, and to the movement pursuing Jewish immigration to Palestine known as Zionism, there is nothing contradictory in these duties; each one completes the other. We remain small in number and without great influence. Let us uplift ourselves through work. We are dispersed. Let us join our efforts together. Thousands of our persecuted brothers search for a safe haven and are drawn to settlement in Palestine. Let us do all we can to help them settle in the Holy Land under the protective wings of the Ottomans. By doing so we will undertake a great work of Jewish solidarity while also becoming more numerous, more influential, and thus more capable of demonstrating our gratitude to the noble Ottoman nation, which has always been tolerant and hospitable. By fulfilling our duties as Jews to ourselves and to Zionism, we will become more capable of fulfilling our duties as Ottoman patriots and of working, in greater numbers and with more force, toward the economic emancipation and general development of the New Turkey, always one and indivisible.

David Florentin, *Nos devoirs comme Juifs et Ottomans* (Istanbul: M. Gorodichze, 1909), 1–16. Translated from French by Julia Phillips Cohen.

## 73.  A DEBATE ON ZIONISM IN THE OTTOMAN PARLIAMENT [1911]

*In the spring of 1911 a series of debates about Zionism enlivened the Ottoman parliament. Among those who spoke out against the movement were the Palestinian Muslim deputies from Jerusalem, Sa'id al-Husayni (1878–1945) and Ruhi al-Khalidi (1864–1913), whose voices are represented below. Both men argued that Palestine could not support further Jewish immigration. While al-Husayni praised the Jews as a fundamentally useful and intelligent nation, al-Khalidi offered a more sinister picture, suggesting that their very religion commanded them to conquer the land promised to them in the Hebrew Bible, or Torah. In response Nissim Matzliah (1877–1931), a Jewish deputy from Izmir, counseled caution, arguing that many of the claims being hurled against the Zionists were inaccurate and that the matter deserved the dispassionate investigation of government authorities. More ominous were the words of Vartkes (Serengulian) Bey (1871–1915), an Armenian deputy from Erzurum, who expressed his concerns that the debates about Zionism might soon translate into violence against Jews and other non-Muslims in the empire. Just four years later, following the large-scale arrests and deportations of Armenian intellectual and political leaders from the Ottoman capital on April 24, 1915, Vartkes Bey was arrested and deported to eastern Anatolia. He was murdered on July 19, 1915, on the road between Urfa and Diyarbakır. (For a Jewish eyewitness account of the Armenian genocide see source 51.)*

[Sa'id al-Husayni]

The Jews are a hard-working, intelligent, and productive nation. Above all they are progressive in agriculture and in crafts. It is undeniable that in the Jerusalem district both they and the local population have benefited from the scientific, agricultural, and industrial offices [Jews] have created and established. For this reason the Jews who want to immigrate from other countries to Ottoman territory should be allowed to do so, but on the condition that they accept Ottoman citizenship and that they go to districts outside of Palestine. As I noted earlier, those in Palestine have reached a sufficient number. There is no danger in accepting and registering various [Jewish] immigrants respective of the limit a district is able to receive. On the contrary I call the attention of the minister of interior to the abovementioned, positive effects [of Jewish migration].

[Ruhi al-Khalidi]
Zionism means increasing and multiplying the foreign Jewish community in Palestine, Syria, and Iraq, and establishing a Jewish state with its center in Jerusalem. The idea of establishing a Jewish state has existed among Jews since time immemorial. . . . There are many chapters and verses about this in the holy Torah. Reading the holy Torah, it is impossible not to encounter [references] to Zion, and to the whole Land of Palestine . . . . . . . In fact, nowhere in the holy Torah does it speak of Heaven or Hell—it is possible that all of the encouragements and assurances [it offers] relate solely to the Promised Land and to Zion. I will read one or two chapters and a few verses to demonstrate this fact. Just as [Haris] Vamvaka Efendi discussed the holy New Testament, I will discuss the holy Torah. . . .[24]

[Nissim Matzliah]
I will not say much. As a matter of fact I do not want to take part in a discussion of Zionism because whatever I say might be seen as biased. My humble members of parliament, I only wish to highlight the matter in a serious and truthful way, so that the country will understand what Zionism is, whether or not it is dangerous, and the extent to which Zionist ideas are spreading throughout the country. My aim is to set the record straight so that no negative thoughts or misunderstandings remain.

My dear fellow members of parliament, sadly what I hear when I discuss this [issue] among friends is far from accurate. Even today in Monastir there are those who falsely claim that the newspapers . . . *Silah* and *Süngü*, are funded by Zionists. Things have reached such

24. Haris Vamvaka Efendi, a Greek Orthodox deputy in the Ottoman parliament.

a state! Consequently, my dear members of parliament, I ask that the government investigate this matter thoroughly. . . . If Zionism is indeed harmful to the state, then without question my loyalty lies with the state. This country belongs not only to the Turks and the *Rum*,[25] but also to Ottoman Jews. In other words it belongs to all Ottomans. Furthermore, no matter how invested others are in our country, Ottoman Jews' allegiance and patriotism equal that of their peers. Finally, I do not approve of what Ruhi al-Khalidi has said here.

For example he read a few passages from the noble Torah. However, I ask how things written in the Torah can be the fault of today's generation of . . . Jews? If he likes, let him burn the Torah! Let us have the state burn it! I suppose Ruhi Bey is a Muslim—a believer. I am also a believer. In order to be a believer one must believe that the Torah's legal provisions were superseded following the dignified and honorable revealing of the glorious Qur'an. This is my belief. What is more they have no judicial value. Ruhi Bey, I appeal to your conscience and reason. Are you confident you understand the essence of Zionism? In other words are you absolutely certain that the aim of Zionism is to establish a Jewish state in this country? I believe that this way of thinking will lead to great calamity. . . .

As Ruhi Bey has stated, the Jews of Europe have suffered cruelty and oppression. . . . It is my conviction that this wise people, who live here in happiness, will not betray this land. Indeed in this land you will not be able to find a better friend or a people who serve their country more than the Jews.

[Vartkes Bey]
Gentlemen, why is Russia driving the Jews out? Perhaps over there they want to establish a kingdom as well? Why in Austria, Germany, and England are they rising up against the Jews? Perhaps over there there is another Palestine over which they want to establish a kingdom? The Ottoman state has never attacked the Jews. Why should it begin now? (Calls of "This is wrong!") Please, this is not wrong! When we say such things [about Jews] here, the primitive people outside who come across a Jew will call him a traitor! How is this so? They said this

---

25. Ottoman term for Greek Orthodox Christians.

first about the Armenians! I would not want to see people be swayed by these words and find an excuse to act against them [the Jews]. Once upon a time when people complained to the government about the activities of the Armenian nationalists the Armenians would say in response, "What can we do? This nationalist idea has been spread as propaganda throughout the Armenian population. We cannot stop it. It circulates by itself." Now, aren't we faced with precisely the same situation? (Calls of "This is different!") It is the same! Gentlemen, I am speaking as an Armenian. I am afraid that what has happened to me will happen to the Jews (Calls of "That is the problem!"). And I say this from an Ottoman perspective, not an Armenian one nor a Jewish one. The Jews are in the Land of Palestine and the Armenians in the mountains of Anatolia. They are so far apart from one another that I have no reason to do them any special favors.

*powerful statement of solidarity*

Ottoman parliamentary session minutes, 3 Mayıs 1327 (1911), in *Meclis-i Mebusan Cerideleri* 1:3 (Ankara: TBMM Basımevi, 1982), C: 2. Translated from Ottoman Turkish by Louis Fishman.

# 74.  A SOCIALIST MANIFESTO IN LADINO (1911)

*The workers' holiday of May First was celebrated with great fanfare in the Ottoman port city of Salonica in the years immediately following the Young Turk Revolution of 1908, which brought constitutional government to Ottoman realms and allowed the first open expressions of socialism to appear in the empire. A Sephardi Jew of Bulgarian origin by the name of Abraham Benaroya (1887–1979) was at the helm of Salonica's socialist movement at this time. Here Benaroya lays out the demands of his movement in the Ladino socialist organ* La Solidaridad Ovradera, *emphasizing the importance of the eight-hour workday and the right to form associations, strike, gather, vote, and enjoy freedom of speech. Benaroya suffered repeatedly for his political views, first at the hands of Ottoman authorities and later, under Greek rule, upon the orders of the Salonican municipality, which brought him to trial in June 1914 for promoting anarchist and anti-Greek sentiments among his coreligionists.*

What are the demands of the organized proletariat on this day [May 1]?

Above all the eight-hour workday. With eight-hour days we would gain work for thousands of unemployed men; we would gain time to relax, to educate ourselves, to enjoy ourselves, and to spend time with our families. With eight-hour workdays, we would maintain our strength and our health. In short we would realize the principal of working to live and not living to work.

Today we also reclaim our political rights: the right to form societies, the right to demonstrate, the right to assemble, the right to vote, the right to be voted for, the right to free speech, thought, and writing, the freedom of press and conscience, in short, rights, equality, and broad freedoms for all. With these rights and liberties we will be able to organize ourselves, arm ourselves, and fight against the all-powerful capitalist system in order to establish laws that favor the proletariat, thus through the force of law thwarting the quest of the capitalists who seek to grow rich from our sweat and blood.

We should arm ourselves with these rights and liberties in order to combat injustice and unmask hypocrisy; to demand protection for women and children, the old and the ill, the weak and the unemployed; and to promote the education of the masses. These arms will allow us to stop the insanity of war and exorbitant military expenditures. Finally these same arms will serve us so that someday we can take public power into our own hands, to realize our collective ambitions.

Yet in order to take these arms in hand it is not enough simply to demand; we also need a social force that can hold people accountable. This force is collective action. The more organized we are the better off we will be. Long live the workers' organization! Long live socialism!

Abraham Benaroya, "Muestras demandas," *La Solidaridad Ovradera*, May 1, 1911, 1. Translated from Ladino by Julia Phillips Cohen.

## 75. A EUROPEAN JEWISH FEMINIST DECRIES THE WHITE SLAVE TRADE IN THE OTTOMAN EMPIRE [1911]

*Bertha Pappenheim (1859–1936), an Austrian Jewish feminist and social activist, was a founder and the first president of the League of Jewish Women, an organization that aimed to advance women's rights. She devoted herself to philanthropy and feminist causes, including the rehabilitation of girls and women endangered by prostitution and the traffic in women. Pappenheim wrote the following reflections while traveling through Southeastern Europe to investigate and document the state of the white slave trade, which forced many poor Jewish women into prostitution*

*in the early decades of the twentieth century. Pappenheim's own views on sex and*
*sexuality were sophisticated for her time, in part because of her early exposure to psy-*
*choanalytic circles in Vienna. As a young woman Pappenheim was a patient of Josef*
*Breuer, whose notes on Pappenheim (whom he called "Anna O") informed his friend*
*Sigmund Freud's early analysis of the origins of hysteria. In addition to dedicating*
*her life to social activism, Pappenheim was the author of novellas and plays that*
*she published both under her own name and under a male pseudonym. Despite her*
*sensitivity to questions of gender and sexuality, Pappenheim employed Orientalist*
*stereotypes when writing about her travels through the "East," as the present excerpt*
*makes clear.*

Salonica, March 1, 1911
Dear Mrs. N.,

It's absolutely spring here and the trees are blooming as brightly as I have ever seen. It's curious how the Jewish men and women here still wear the picturesque traditional costume and walk around in their thick furs. The attire is very bright, beautiful, and becoming; it's a shame that only grandmothers still wear it. Young women don't want to wear it anymore. They want to wear European clothes. The men very much regret this development since European apparel is subject to fashion and therefore much more expensive.

Naturally, I can't differentiate between Jews, Turks, Greeks, and Armenians. Only today the Jews were recognizable in their Sabbath clothes. The whole city celebrates Saturday here, because more than three-quarters of the inhabitants are Jewish. . . .

The dock at the Salonica harbor, the quay, the location of the hotel, everything somehow reminds me of Trieste, although this city certainly shouldn't be compared to Trieste. The sea here doesn't give me the grand impression that I usually get from the sea, although I can't explain why . . . . The Jewish women of Salonica are supposed to be especially beautiful. The most beautiful one that I saw here, maybe one of the most beautiful Jewish women I have ever seen or perhaps that ever was, I found today in a brothel. It's a crying shame that such a proud little human flower was born into that kind of environment and for that purpose in life. I can understand how a man would want to commit every folly around such a woman, but I don't understand this twenty-year-old person who offers up the most beautiful and best that she has—her body—for sale. Doesn't she have a soul? Certainly she can neither read nor write. Also I have also heard from authoritative sources here that the Alliance schools leave something to be desired in every regard. First and foremost they do not have scientific oversight and inspections. About a year and a half ago, the Alliance sent three men from Paris to conduct an inspection throughout the Orient, and they visited twenty-eight schools in forty-two days! It seems that the system of the Baron Hirsch Schools in Galicia is indeed the right one. What the Hilfsverein der Deutschen Juden is doing here is useless in cultural terms, since it only teaches Hebrew. That doesn't help the children in any way and it places their lives at the mercy of their exploiters.

There are more than 100 houses of ill repute here and they are all concentrated in one quarter. I went through the quarter today with Ibrahim Ihsan Efendi, the dragoman of the Austrian consul general in Pera. There are hundreds of Jewish girls there, many Russians, [but also] many from this city, which indicates a certain level of depravity, since most [prostitutes] usually go to another city where people don't know them to practice their trade.

Ihsan Efendi differentiates between "female artists who have a regular job and live in boarding houses while earning something on the side, those who work exclusively as prostitutes but live in boarding houses, and, with all due respect, girls who live in those whorehouses."

It's 10 P.M. I am interrupting my report for today in order to go to bed. Perhaps I will dream of beautiful Jolanthe, who won't leave my thoughts since I saw her today. If she wore a golden crown on her head in addition to the golden crown in her mouth, I would have not found it unbefitting.

Sunday, April 2
I just read through my letter and found it a bit unscientific. No notes that I will need later to remember things. I want to catch up by listing the people I've met.

Mr I., a wholesaler, was surely amazed to see me here. He devoted some time to me since I had an introduction through the B.S. company. He doesn't have a clue about general matters and I could only convey to him the value of my efforts by speaking his language.

I explained the parallel between a country's credit in the business world and the value, or estimation, of women in that country. The fortunes of the stock exchange correspond to the fortunes of women, just as the appraisal of Jews in a country grows at the same rate at which they develop themselves.

When a community like Salonica, where sixty- to eighty-thousand Jews live in great freedom and even dominate commerce doesn't produce enough brainpower to realize the value of cultural resources for the community, then those are short-sighted traders! Leaving aside the few thousand Jewish prostitutes here, the fact that the Jewish community concedes that thousands of children from the age of ten years old work in factories that ruin boys and girls—it is not sentimentality to want to prevent that!

The secretary of a consulate here—I forgot his name—told me, "What do you expect from the Jews? They sell their children like hens!" but this kind of amorality is not limited to the very lowest classes. Today I spoke with a woman, Mrs. Ch. H.-L., born Baroness v. St., who told me that great improprieties occurred in the Alliance schools a while ago. A newspaper article that appeared here during the scandal apparently began with the words, "Mothers, keep an eye on your children." The affair was covered up, and about fifty children were removed from the school. What happened to those children? Who is at fault when they become "bad"? I think it is the Jewish community of Salonica and the Alliance, which didn't look after them. Of course, Mrs. H.-L. couldn't tell me very much. She is interested in her Greek community. But I'll still try to get to the bottom of this matter. I also talked to the editor of the *Journal de Salonique*;[26] he didn't have many good things to say about the Alliance schools either, but at least they are better than nothing. I will also ask him about the "improprieties." . . .

Constantinople [Istanbul], April 8, 1911
Dear Mrs. N.,

I hear unanimously and consistently that the market in Constantinople is ninety percent Jewish women, that almost all traffickers are Jews, and that it has increased considerably in the last three years since the constitution! In addition Jews here completely lack the ability even to recognize human trafficking as something dishonorable, a moral

---

26. A French-language newspaper founded in Salonica in 1895 by the Jewish publisher Sa'adi Besalel a-Levi (1820–1903).

defect that either resulted from living together with the Turks or, more likely to my mind, is an inherited opinion of the Oriental Jews themselves. . . .

Saturday morning I went to the Austrian consul who told me all about his endeavors regarding the trafficking of women, but I now realize that the large majority of Jewish women don't come to him. Apparently "they don't want to." I understand that they do not want to be repatriated, since what should a girl do back in Dukla or Suyatin when she was already on the path of prostitution?[27] In any case she would only be taken back to Trieste. This "they want to" or "they don't want to" drives me crazy in its unfairness. What does a fourteen- or fifteen-year-old girl know about what she wants when she is sent to the red-light district or is ruined as a factory worker for the Régie?[28]

Mr P. was kind but he didn't care at all about the issue—just like the others. But he did direct me to his clerk A. L., who has given this matter his full attention and [yet] accomplished little or nothing. He is Catholic and explained to me what a *ketubah* is, since "thousands of Jewish girls are ruined every year by this nonsensical law from the Jewish religion". . . .

I used Shabbos[29] afternoon to call on the Hakham Bashi, the rabbi whom the Salonican constitution elevated to the throne, so to speak. As you know he is interested in opposing the trafficking of women as a result of the London Conference. I was warmly received (Mr S. L. in Salonica gave me a letter of introduction) and we quickly entered into conversation with each other. He knows a lot but surely not enough, and I don't think he has the necessary power to do anything. He knows for example that there is a synagogue of white slavers in Constantinople where girls buy *'aliyot*, the honor and dignity of [public] Torah readings, for their pimps on the holidays. He must have the power to restrict this "House of God" and he doesn't do it! There's no real reason for this, otherwise I would also be afraid.

His Eminence H. N. is otherwise very likeable.[30] I asked him to recommend me to a Sephardi family for a seder and he invited me

---

27. A reference to the fact that the white slave trade targeted Jewish women in Eastern Europe.
28. Short for la Société de la régie co-intéressée des tabacs de l'empire Ottoman. The Régie had a monopoly over Ottoman tobacco production.
29. Yiddish for Shabbat, the Jewish Sabbath.
30. Haim Nahum, who served as Ottoman chief rabbi from 1909 to 1920.

himself! You know this courteousness also had an awkward side, but I couldn't decline. Indeed I'm looking forward to hearing a real Sephardi seder. The chief rabbi also has a *rabbineuse*, a pretty young woman who is modern and forward-thinking but she doesn't have a role model. There is only one orphanage for twenty children and one infirmary for all of Constantinople. The Alliance schools are on vacation, so I can't see them, but I believe that they are insufficient in terms of quality and quantity, especially for the girls. . . .

Bertha Pappenheim, *Sisyphus-Arbeit: Reisebriefe aus den Jahren 1911 und 1912* (Leipzig: P. E. Linder, 1924), 39–43, 51–54. Translated from German by Lela Gibson.

## 76. A SEPHARDI SUFFRAGETTE? A JEWISH WOMAN OF IZMIR LECTURES ON FEMINISM (1913)

*Graziella Benghiat, a French-language journalist from Izmir, was the daughter of an Ottoman Jewish lawyer named Pertev Levy, and married the Ladino-language journalist, poet, and author Alexander Benghiat (ca. 1863–1923). She is known to have edited a short-lived French-language periodical entitled* Les Annales *during the First World War and subsequently lived with her son in Paris, where she studied to become a dentist. The following text is drawn from a speech she delivered before a gathering of Alliance alumni in Izmir on the topic of feminism, about which she expressed ambivalence.*

Ladies and Gentlemen:

The word "feminism" is interpreted in different ways. Some would grant [women] exaggerated rights. Others limit their demands to their simplest form without arriving at a proper understanding of the issues or a definition that does not rely on ambiguous and equivocal phrases. It often happens that many of those men who have a say in such matters and whose positions could have a major impact speak about feminism with a note of fantasy and with a tone that could invariably be taken to be either negative or affirmative. [They read] like the letters that one is accustomed to writing to those begging for work: "Yes, in a while. We'll see . . . ", etc.

Generally even those who are truly feminists hesitate to speak up. In any case they are rare, because [most men] often offer merely lip service by repeating theses and ideas that they tout in order to prove how emancipated they are. Those who do adopt this position arrive at it only by a circuitous route. There are those who will say that women, being neither alcoholics nor as criminally inclined as men, are more adept at creating laws and thus deserve our trust. Others will say that feminism is an excellent thing in principle but perfectly impossible in reality. This is only partially true. It is at this point that one must clarify that which can, at first glance, appear ridiculous among the claims of the suffragettes, and to extract those claims that are truly feasible and cannot raise any objection.

Nature has certainly gifted men and women the same dose of intelligence, but one different in quality. Because a woman is naturally weaker, and consequently more tender, her intelligence tends towards sentiments at times incompatible with the strong nature of men, just as certain masculine sentiments are incompatible with our nature. From this we must . . . say that there is only a difference of nuance, for men and women have the same dose of intelligence. What remains then is for us to know how to share work and give to each one the task that best suits each of us in life. In the theater do we not give each actor the role that best suits him? Would we ever think to give a clown the job of wild beast tamer and vice versa? No, we wouldn't.

Now let us turn briefly to the reasons for the suffragettes' various complaints. They demand the right to enter all the professions available to men. This is a bit much to demand. A woman will never occupy the positions of magistrate, doctor, explorer, or—if we can even conceive of calling her this—conqueror, for the practical requirements of these positions would prevent her from being a good wife and mother. She would thus be reneging on her primary duties, those essential duties that nature inculcated within her. I search in vain to understand the spiritual state and the mental state of a female lawyer, rushing to defend the cause of a widow or an orphan, all while having her own baby sick at home suffering from a servant's poor and ignorant care, crying and begging for his mother's attention—a woman whom the emancipation movement pushes to declare the equal of man through such devices. These are the types of actions that, on the contrary, will rob her of her dignity and strip her of the respect to which she has a right as a woman and from the role that she is meant to play in the evolution of the world. . . .

It is even harder for me to imagine that a women would search for some second South Pole as an explorer. It takes all the pains in the world to envision such a woman on an ice sheet, harnessed to a sleigh of provisions, her view to one side being a boat stuck in ice and to the other the white and frozen expanse, an infinite plain. I also have great difficulties imagining a woman who, confronted with such an uncomfortable situation, could maintain a light-hearted and determined attitude.

When it comes to the noble tasks of the doctor, I do not see how it would be fitting for a woman. The profession demands a rigidity of sentiment and a sangfroid that is perfectly impossible to come by in a woman. With her heart being usually more tender and more easily impressionable, there would inevitably be moments in which she would feel repugnance. What would you say about a female doctor stricken with a nervous breakdown in the middle of caring for a sick patient? You see the effect that would have!

Moreover, because the role of a man is to protect his wife, is it possible to imagine a man cuddled cozily under the blankets while his wife is rushing off somewhere or at the house of some client in agony? No, this is too much. And you will add that, despite his cavalier attitude, he would have to be a model husband not to make a terrible scene of jealousy upon her return. Oh yes, horrible, atrocious jealousy! . . .

Doesn't a husband have the right to know all that his wife says, that which she writes or thinks? How to reconcile this with the confidentiality that lawyers and doctors must keep concerning their clients? . . .

Yet there are very strong and just claims among those formulated by the suffragettes that should be ardently discussed. What good is a female deputy if she is not first permitted to edit the law? The equality between men and women—how could it exist when we search for it in a code formulated by men only? Let us begin by searching for the basis of this equality. Just as the law forms the basis of all institutions and states, it is only fair that it [the law] be consulted, annotated, and revised by the two sexes equally. Legislation must be discussed by all parties, and they must agree on its formulation. Then the equality we demand would not cause so many difficulties. . . .

There are still female authors and poets! "Female poet"—these two words go well together, much better than "male poet." Further, why don't women devote themselves to scientific work? Mixing substances in a crucible heated to three thousand degrees, as one does to create an artificial diamond, is a thousand times preferable to an expedition to Africa. "Female painters"—that combination also works very well. Being first a little timid girl, sketching in some corner of the Louvre, chaperoned by a kindly great-aunt; later on, one sees her name in the salons. That is a pretty little success, gaining her the glory that until now only men have achieved.

Why make sacrifices to our delicate temperament when nature created stronger beings to make up for our weakness? Why not, I repeat, give each person the occupation that suits him, whose material obligations (rather than moral ones, since from the point of view of intelligence, equality cannot be contested) are in accord with his physical aptitudes? This is what the suffragettes do not appear to understand. It is what causes misunderstandings of their excessive demands. . . .

I ask myself who will rear the future generations of babies? Everyone will be out on the street. Men and women—since they must be equal—will only have a few minutes for meals. . . . We will turn babies into sacrifices to the state, which will raise them at great expense with artificial wet nurses [and] incubators, and the world will fare no worse. At least we will be equal. This is more or less the reasoning of our suffragettes, who are rendered extravagant at times by their excitement. There are those among the suffragettes who consider marriage to be a weakness. They say that we must know how to control those sentiments toward family and maternity that weaken us, and they shout to all who will listen to them that we must know how to control our feelings and impose our presence everywhere. But you will say such [women] are bad patriots. What case will they make for the future of a country without children? . . .

No, such women are reckless and misunderstood, more so by themselves than by others, for they do not know how to analyze the state of their own hearts. A woman has within her an invincible need to attach herself to something; she has an overabundance of affection to lavish, an overabundance of devotion to spread around her. . . .

Now that I have already usurped the attention that you have so kindly given me, I believe that it is my duty to say a word on the role of the Jewish woman in this movement that has agitated so many and excited them with a Spanish *furia*. The sensible attitude of the Jewish woman cannot be denied for an instant. She proves herself to be a good diplomat, because, being perfectly aware of the actions and gestures of her companions and also being able to display her diverse and serious knowledge, she commands an admirable reserve. . . . This is strong and wise.

All that is left for us now is to study ourselves. We must show solidarity and create a united whole so that we are not vulnerable to attacks from the outside. I believe that this is the most difficult aspect to overcome. . . .

Graziella Benghiat, "Le Féminisme," *Le Trait-d'Union* 3:4 (April 1913): 4–6 and 3:6 (June 1913): 2–3; 6. Translated from French by Alma Rachel Heckman.

## 77. A SOCIALIST RESOLUTION ON THE JEWISH QUESTION (1917)

*The city of Salonica was the third largest port in the Ottoman Empire and home to the largest concentration of Sephardi Jews in Southeastern Europe. This Jewish population, which at its peak constituted more than half the Salonican population, was heavily working-class. Blue-collar Jews labored in Salonica's port, undergirded the city's robust tobacco and textile trades, and formed the industrial base of a variety of Jewish-owned enterprises. The vast numbers of working-class Jews in Salonica rendered the city uniquely well poised to foster Jewish socialism, which thrived in industrial hubs such as Warsaw, London, and New York, all of which had large populations of working-class Jews. This resolution, issued by the Socialist Federation of the city, displays a keenness to acknowledge the particular concerns Jewish workers might bring to their socialist activism, thereby opening the movement up to Salonica's substantial would-be membership.*

With the goal of defining and clarifying its attitude toward the Jewish Congress, which will soon be held in Salonica, and in order to preempt any ill-willed interpretations from disloyal and interested parties, the committee of the Socialist Federation finds it necessary to submit to the press the following resolution, unanimously adopted by the General Assembly:

The General Assembly of the Socialist Federation convened on June 5, 1917, in order to clarify its attitude toward the work of the Jewish Congress of Salonica by acknowledging the existence of a Jewish Question, which arises under conditions different from those of other national questions, and consequently cannot be solved in the same manner, considering:

1) That the Jewish Question is before all else a phase of the Social Question, and that it cannot be completely resolved as long as the proletariat does not free itself of the salary regime, the supreme form of human slavery, and as long as it is not liberated from the yoke of private property, a means of production and exchange that favors the existence of classes as well as oppressed and oppressor nations.

2) That Jewish claims to political, civil, cultural, and religious rights; the recognition of the Jews' national rights in the countries where these rights are accorded to other nations; freedom for the Jews to establish themselves and live where they please, claims with which we declare ourselves in solidarity, cannot be realized without strengthening the power of the international proletariat, which works for the realization of universal emancipation and which requires of the Jewish proletariat greater union as well as greater union with proletariats all over the world.

3) That there can be no hope from partisan diplomacy. The emancipation of the Jewish people, like that of all other peoples, cannot be realized except by the means of democratic and class struggle [and] through the advent of socialism, which is the most effective defender of national minorities, the most sincere combatant against privilege, and the most powerful element of civilization. [The General Assembly thus] decides:

1. To combat the nationalist tendency of the Jewish Congress, a tendency which, under the pretext of asking for justice for the Jews, furthers the mystical Zionist movement. By creating a Jewish center in Palestine this movement can only solve the Jewish question in an illusory sense and in a form that tramples, to the detriment of another nationality, the very principle of nationalities invoked by Zionism for its cause;

2. [The General Assembly similarly] invites the working class:

   a. Not to hold any Zionist demonstrations that draw it away from its class struggle or attach it to the bourgeoisie.

b. To abstain rigorously from participating in elections of the National Jewish Congress, which hides a goal that it cannot maintain.

c. [The Assembly] charges the committee to remain independent from other groups and to coordinate a struggle with the Socialist International for the triumph of the above-mentioned claims.

"Communiqué: Résolution de la Fédération Socialiste à propos du Congrès Juif," *L'Indépendant*, June 14, 1917. Translated from French by Alma Rachel Heckman.


# 78. SUPPORT FOR THE BALFOUR DECLARATION IN SALONICA (1918)

*In 1917–1918, Great Britain seized Palestine from the Ottomans. The British administration of the area, which was soon formalized by means of a League of Nations mandate, accorded with an agreement the British government had struck with the French in the midst of the First World War defining the two countries' spheres of influence in the Middle East in the event of their defeat of the Axis Powers. Already in November 1917, British Foreign Secretary Arthur James Balfour expressed his government's support for the establishment of a "Jewish national home" in Palestine in a note he addressed to Baron Walter Rothschild, a Jewish communal leader with Zionist sympathies. Although this letter, later known as the Balfour Declaration, was neither legally binding nor reflective of a fundamental commitment on the part of the British to the creation of a Jewish state, supporters of Zionism worldwide hailed the declaration as a major victory for their movement. In the text that follows, Zionist societies in Salonica react to the news with enthusiasm.*

The public meeting convened this Saturday, January 5, 1918, by the Zionist societies of Salonica in the White Tower Park on the occasion of the British government's declaration on the subject of the reconstitution of a national Jewish home in Palestine and of progress in Palestine:

1. Proclaims once more the most ardent desire of the Jewish population of Salonica to realize, at long last, its millennial national aspirations in the land of its ancestors.

2. Reiterates the expression of the keenest gratitude to His Majesty's British government for its memorable declaration of friend-

ship toward Zionist aspirations and its promise to help in their achievement.

3. Asks the Liberal Hellenic government to continue to express its good will toward our movement and to press for our just claims when possible.

4. Wishes that following the way opened by British and American Jews, the Jews of the Entente countries—those of France and Italy—work together energetically to obtain from their respective governments their intervention in favor of Zionist claims.

5. Hopes that France, Italy, and the United States of America will continue their noble and chivalrous traditions as defenders of the rights of nations and that they will respond to those sentiments of love and admiration that the Jewish world, and particularly the Oriental Jews, have always held for them by also acknowledging, without reserve, our right to a national life on the beloved soil of Palestine and by extending us their support in this work of historic reparation.

"Résolution," *Pro-Israël*, 27 Tevet 5678 (January 11, 1918), 7. Translated from French by Alma Rachel Heckman.

## 79. "WE ARE A NATIONAL MINORITY": A GREEK JEWISH MANIFESTO ISSUED AFTER THE PARIS PEACE CONFERENCE (1919)

*The five treaties hammered out at the Paris Peace Conference brought an end to the First World War, delineated Europe's postwar boundaries, asserted the sovereignty of various states, listed terms of reparations, and guaranteed the rights of minorities within many of Europe's newly formed nation-states. Here a Greek Zionist, writing just after the signing of the Polish Minority Treaty (June 28, 1919), bemoans the fact that Greece was not included on the list of countries obliged to draw up a similar treaty. It would ultimately take another year until Greece signed a minority treaty in 1920. This was the Treaty of Sèvres. In the interim, the Zionists' request for minority rights remained controversial. Indeed, the press bureau of the Greek General Government of Macedonia in Salonica heavily censored the following article due to its explicit defense of Jewish national rights.*

Among the serious questions that currently preoccupy Jews across the world is the [question of] granting national rights to those Jews who live in large concentrations in various countries of the Diaspora. In the peace treaty communicated to the Austrian delegation, a special article guaranteed the full exercise of these rights for national minorities in Austria, Poland, Czechoslovakia, Romania, and Yugoslavia. Our brothers in these countries who constitute separate ethnic groups naturally enjoy the benefits resulting from this particular clause. The article concludes as follows: "These stipulations are incorporated by Austria into its fundamental laws as a Charter of Rights, and the related arrangements will be placed under the safeguarding of the League of Nations."

One must ask why Greece is not included among the states that shelter within their boundaries their national minorities, which they must recognize as such since the large and numerous Jewish community of Salonica incontestably constitutes [a national community]. With our 70,000 souls we form here in effect a great part of the population. Thanks to the special status of communal autonomy with which we have been governed for more than 400 years, we have been able to maintain a flourishing national body with its Jewish characteristics strongly intact and with our own social, cultural, and charity organizations, our own unique school system, a spiritual leader endowed with great political powers and vibrant Jewish traditions. We lead our own particular lives using our own Judeo-Spanish language.

In our view the response to this natural question can be found in the fact that the Great Powers have thought it necessary to introduce special clauses concerning national minorities into the constitutions of nations which in general have given tangible proof of their spirit of intolerance and of their systematic persecution of the ethnic elements living in their territories, both Jews and others, and against whom sanctions must be anticipated in case they neglect their essential duties. In that event the concerned populations must call upon the League of Nations as the supreme judge.

But in Greece, which will surely hold itself to the standard of the tradition of high liberalism, the dearest privilege of the truly civilized nations to which credit can be given, we must think in precisely this manner.[31]

---

31. This section is followed by six blank lines, indicating that the text had been censored after the article had already been typeset.

The Jewish community council is currently preparing to submit to the government for ratification an expanded version of the statute of communal autonomy that we have enjoyed until now.[32] No doubt the Greek Government will turn our legitimate demands into law.[33]

"Nous sommes une minorité nationale: les droits des Juifs en Grèce," *Pro-Israël*, June 27, 1919 (July 10, 1919): 1. Translated from French by Alma Rachel Heckman.

## 80. A GREEK ORTHODOX WRITER PROMOTES RAPPROCHEMENT BETWEEN JEWS AND CHRISTIANS IN GREECE (1925)

*In the wake of the First World War (1914–1918) and Greco-Turkish War (1919–1922), the Greek state faced immense challenges, including the aftermath of population exchanges with Turkey that uprooted well over one million Greek Orthodox Christians. As the Greek leadership embarked upon an intensive campaign to Hellenize its population—erasing the Ottoman imprint on the once multi-sectarian, multilingual city of Salonica, where Jews had only recently been the plurality—antisemitic forces in the country gained ascendency. In this source an Orthodox Christian citizen of Greece calls for Jews and Christian to work to forge new political alliances, identifying Jews' acquisition of the Greek language, in which few Jews had fluency in the period in question, as a perfect means for them to demonstrate their patriotism.*

With great joy I welcome the invitation to collaborate that the esteemed management of *The Jewish Tribune* has addressed to me. Because I have such great esteem for the many virtues and the civilizing activities and mission of the Jewish people and because I consider the sincere collaboration and brotherly coexistence between the Jews living in Greece and the rest of their Greek fellow citizens necessary for the . . . interests of the Greek state, I consider every activity that contributes to this cordial collaboration and coexistence an urgent duty of every patriotic Greek citizen. In any event, addressing the proposed question is not a difficult undertaking. The Greeks, who from most ancient times were and are worshippers of Zeus Xenion [the patron

---

32. From the time this article was published until 1920, the Jewish community of Salonica had no official status in the eyes of state law—a dynamic that caused great concern to Zionists and others in Salonica.

33. This last line is followed by nearly an entire column of blank space suggesting, as above, that significant portions of the text had been censored after the article was typeset.

of hospitality], coexist as brothers with their fellow citizens of other faiths on the basis of the mutual respect of their national legacies and religious beliefs. The Jews, who have convincingly proved themselves loyal citizens of many European and American countries, know perfectly well how to balance their national identity with the duties of the good and law-abiding citizen and have all the qualities necessary to be perfect Greek citizens and valuable members of the Greek family.

You will now ask: how will the better acquaintance and collaboration between Jews and the rest of their Greek fellow-citizens be achieved? . . .

Learning perfectly the official language of the state, this instrument of common understanding for all Greek citizens and the perfect handling of the language in its written and oral forms, are the first significant means towards this end. For this, may I be permitted to suggest that what is required is intense diligence by Jewish children in the public high schools and other specialized and technical schools (including the trade, commercial, and agricultural schools) and also in the highest academic institutions of the state, the University and the Polytechnic Institute? The education of Jewish thinkers and scientists in the fields of Greek language, literature, and science will allow them to participate more intimately in the social, political, economic, artistic and literary life of the nation for their benefit and that of the entire state.

As is well known many great scientists of Jewish descent are associated with the finest European and American universities, and provide, through their erudite research, significant contributions to the progress of science and art. As is well known, world literature is indebted to the contributions of Jewish authors and intellectuals. As is [also] well known, great contributions have been made and continue to be made by Jewish businessmen and industrialists working towards the commercial, industrial, and financial progress of the countries of Europe and America: like their coreligionists living in the great and robust Jewish community of Thessaloniki, they undoubtedly hope that such progress will take place in Greece for the good of the Jews of our country and that of the country as a whole.

If I am not mistaken this process will succeed once Jews in public schools, middle schools, and schools of higher learning engage in the intense study of Greek language and literature. . . .

On this issue every effort must be exerted by the Jewish Community of Salonica, which, I am pleased to have learned, has offered necessary guidance for the education of Salonican Jews. The fruits of this action cannot come too soon. Let the Jews living in Greece be aware that their Greek fellow citizens will salute with joy their wise cooperation in all areas of financial, intellectual, and scientific activity, and that they sincerely wish for the presence in Greece of great Jewish thinkers and scientists, who will enrich the Greek university, and honor their noble race and Greek fatherland.

"E Ellas kai oi Israelitai," *Evraikon Vema tes Ellados/La Tribune Juive de Grèce* 1:6 (May 15, 1925): 1–2. Translated from Greek by Isaac Nehama.

## 81. JEWISH WOMEN JOIN THE FASCIST MOVEMENT IN SALONICA (1925)

*Shaped under the leadership of Benito Mussolini, who ruled over the Kingdom of Italy from 1922 to 1943, Italian fascism (and its leading party, the National Fascist Party, or PNF) championed modern Italy as the inheritor of ancient Rome and supported the territorial expansion of an Italian empire as in ancient days. Before the 1930s the Italian fascist movement did not assume a coherent antisemitic agenda. Indeed Mussolini was joined by a handful of prominent Jews when he created one of the earliest fascist parties, known as the Italian Fascists of Combat, in 1919. This source, published shortly after the PNF enthusiastically declared Italy a totalitarian state, describes the lure of fascism for Italian citizens in Salonica, including certain female Jewish members of the local Italian Jewish community which had long resided in the Ottoman Empire. Though fascism did not command widespread appeal among Salonica's Sephardim, there as in Italy it appealed to a small group of Jewish elites who found in the movement a means of expressing their italianità, or Italianness.*

Although recently instituted, the female division of the Fascist Party in Salonica has already exhibited proof of its magnificent and patriotic spirit of initiative. This division, created at the request of the loyal fascist, Lord Lieutenant Michele Sacco, comprises a new official committee supported by many male and female members of the colony. The members of the Directive Committee are Mrs. Dr. Pia Palumbo, Nella Modiano, Rita Rocchegiani, and the young ladies Ida Capasso, Rina

Battaglini, Corinna Modiano, Maria Arrigoni, and Irma Sallusto.[34] Dr. Pia Palumbo was elected president of the division and Mr. Amedeo Aquarone was nominated as secretary.

After the initial organizational period immediately following its institution, the committee set out quickly to begin its work. Aspiring to the purest sentiments of *italianità* and brotherhood with their countrymen, the female fascists planned a day of celebration for the native children of the colony, to be celebrated along with the New Year and Epiphany. The evening was an unparalleled success. The proceeds of the party, amounting to more than 10,000 drachmas, were used to purchase gifts and clothing that the ladies of the committee personally distributed to the children. A generous donation was also made by some twenty elderly women from the hospice maintained by the society of Women for Christian Charity.

The careful preparation of the event attests to the enthusiasm members of the colony showed in support of the female division of the Fascist Party. Mothers, fathers, teachers, and students from the Italian schools volunteered their time to make the evening a success.

The party took place on January 3 in the elegant ballroom of the Regie Scuole Italiano Alumni Society, in conjunction with nearly all of the Italian residents [in Salonica], the representatives of the Fascist Party, and a select group of foreigners. The evening was beyond reproach and was punctuated by opera selections (solos and duets), short piano studies, a dance performed by the best students from the Italian elementary school, and a scene from Goldoni's comedy, *La Locandiera* ["The Innkeeper"]. The music was exclusively Italian. Mrs. Nella Modiano, Mrs. Rita Rocchegiani, and Mrs. Ida Capasso added their melodious voices to the festivities. After the concert the dancing continued into the wee hours of the morning amidst the joyful atmosphere. The fascist hymn "Giovinezza" was sung repeatedly over the thunder of uninterrupted applause by all in attendance. As we've already mentioned the proceeds were impressive. The work of distributing the donations, which began a few days later, allowed the women

34. The Modianos were an influential *franco* family of Italian nationality long settled in Salonica. Other documents from the period contain Jewish names among the list of contributors to Italian fascist causes in the city, including Maurizio Benrubi, Alfonso Levi, Carlo Modiano, Fanny and Giorgio Morpugo, and Edgardo Saias.

of the committee to learn of the true state of the Italian families in Salonica. Following this tour the female division gained further support.

The female fascists do not intend to rest on their laurels following this first success. They aspire to constitute the strong bond between families, schools, and children, and thus to play their part in the larger project of national solidarity initiated by the older division of the fascist party. They are already preparing other great initiatives. We will be sure to report them as they occur.

The new division will also help in the sublime task of rejuvenating the fatherland. Its members in Salonica will act as modest exponents of Italian kindness in the midst of the quotidian labor of emigrants, while spearheading the cultivation of future men and soldiers of the New Italy.

"Grecia: Salonicco," *I Fasci Italiani all'Estero*, February 21, 1925, 11–12. Translated from Italian by Jessica Strom.

## 82.  IS THERE A NEED FOR A WORLD SEPHARDI FEDERATION? A DEBATE BY JEWISH DELEGATES IN VIENNA [1925]

*In August 1925, just days before the Fourteenth Zionist Congress was due to convene in Vienna, sixty-two Sephardi delegates gathered in a synagogue in that city to discuss the possible creation of a World Sephardi Federation. The delegates, who came from communities that included Jerusalem, Tel Aviv, Lisbon, Salonica, Sarajevo, Belgrade, Sofia, and Corfu, expressed a wide range of opinions in response to the plan. Proponents suggested that a World Sephardi Federation could unite Jews of Middle Eastern, North African, and Balkan origin under a Sephardi umbrella, but not all present supported this approach. Among the proposal's detractors was the Bulgarian Jewish intellectual Dr. Saul Mezan (1893–1943), who argued that labeling the various communities considered for inclusion in the federation as "Eastern" was both arbitrary and counterproductive to the aims of the Zionist movement, which sought to unite rather than divide Jews. The Yugoslav delegates Isaac Alcalay and Moritz Levy expressed their ambivalence, while the Jerusalem-born Rabbi Ben-Zion Meir Hayy Uziel (1880–1953) and Yemeni representative, H. Z. Galuska, both of whom traveled from Palestine, favored the idea, seeing in it a chance to reinvigorate Sephardi and Mizrahi communities and fight against the discrimination they experienced at the hands of the Ashkenazi Jews who dominated the Zionist movement. Moshe David Gaon (1889–1958), by this time a pioneering scholar of "Eastern Jewries," believed that Sephardi and Mizrahi Jews were in need of advocates in Palestine, although he dis-*

*agreed with those who claimed that they faced systematic discrimination. Ironically, given that the goal of the conference was to promote unity among Sephardim and Mizrahim, the Yemeni representative Galuska found that he did not share a common language with his Ladino-speaking colleagues and left the congress early.*

Rabbi Uziel:

My brothers and teachers: for some years, since I was enlightened by the luminous erudition of our pious forefathers, the rabbis in Babylon and the wise writers from Spain, my attention has turned to the present state of spiritual decline in the lands of our exile in the East. Turning my sights to our glorious past, and comparing it to our bleak present and future, two feelings stirred within me: on the one hand, a sense of national pride, and, on the other hand, a deep sense of shame and anxiety. . . .

Our exilic isolation tore us apart. It shredded us into pieces and turned us into divided entities—alienated and distant communities—disconnected and detached from the great nation-building project . . . without any organic connection to unify us under a single public national leadership, or to consolidate us into a national body. With great hope and deep anticipation I have always craved that the spirit and power of God would revive our spirits and gather [our] scattered bones into a national body.

Unsettled in my heart, I wondered who would allow me to fly like a bird, who would bestow upon my hands the prophetic power to sound the horn of revival to all these communities, uniting them, consolidating them, and amalgamating them into one living party that includes all the communities from abroad. . . .

H. Z. Galuska:

I cannot put into words the utter delight that engulfs me at this moment, as I am surrounded by my Sephardi brothers who arrived here from their exilic homelands in order to discuss how and by what means we might protect Sephardi interests in particular and those of the Jews of the East in general. I apologize for not being able to attend all the sessions of this assembly. There are two reasons for my absence: (1) I am busy arranging issues vital to the Yemeni Council of the Zionist Congress that will commune in two days, and (2) Even if I attended all the sessions of this assembly it would be of no use, because to my great dismay I find that I am not familiar with the language with which you conduct this assembly—*Espanyolit*—used here because most of the participating members are not familiar with the Hebrew language.

On behalf of the Yemeni Council of the Land of Israel and the whole world I welcome this assembly heartily and wish it success in its endeavors to unify the Mizrahi communities of which we form a part, and I hope that this assembly will succeed in pursuing its demands at the Fourteenth Zionist Congress. I think it is about time that we merge our forces in order to reclaim our rights, which continue to be violated by the Ashkenazi communities of the land [of Israel]. Be courageous and brave, act and succeed, for your success is also ours. . . .

### Dr. Saul Mezan:

The Sephardi Jew of Bulgaria has more in common with the Ashkenazi who resides in his village, as it is easier for him to unite with the Ashkenazi Jew than with the Moroccan Jew, the Jew from Manchester, or the Yemeni Jew. For this reason, there is no way to create a federation of these communities, which are only known by the [collective] label of "Eastern" Jews by accident. Judaism has been marked by various influences, such as German, Slavic, Latin, and Mizrahi traditions. A mix of all these influences can together create the new Jewish Hebrew. We thus reject the creation of the Council of Eastern Jews, due to the negative effects this council might produce.

### Isaac Alcalay:

We, the Jews of Yugoslavia, have special needs. Yugoslavia is the last sphere that runs parallel to the Middle Eastern sea. It is there that the Sephardi flow ends and the Ashkenazi one begins. In Yugoslavia, Ashkenazim and Sephardim live together with strong ties. The Sephardim are the minority, numbering around thirty-seven percent; the remainder are Ashkenazim. To this day we have two central goals: on the one hand we have tried to strengthen the Sephardi element so that our sons would not be lost to the [Ashkenazi] majority. We have been concerned with educating our sons according to our tradition while on the other hand protecting our values as a minority within the general Jewish population of Yugoslavia. Through various organizations such as the Rabbinical Committee, the Rabbinical Assembly, and the Zionist Federation, Sephardim and Ashkenazim have worked together hand in hand. Now, after the recent establishment of the World Sephardi Federation, we are not sure how to respond. If we take the initiative and cease working with the Ashkenazim, the decision might not be perceived as an act of marginalization from a nationalistic point of view, yet from a local perspective it could be considered a divisive act. We are perplexed and unsure as to how to proceed.

I ask of the delegates from the Land of Israel that they clarify their views on the particular situation of the Jews from Yugoslavia. As we understand it so far, the [World] Sephardi Federation would be concerned with revival of the spiritual state of Sephardi Jews from a religious and educational perspective, as well as our relationship to practical Zionist actions. For part of this venture we are ready to join and offer all spiritual and material support for this endeavor; when it comes to practical Zionist action however, we will be able to express our views only after listening to debates on this topic. . . .

Moritz Levy:

The aims of the federation are not clear. We do not know whether the goals are educational and cultural, or political. . . . If the aims of this nascent federation are educational, or if the goals are to raise the cultural level of Sephardi Jews, then our response would be positive (although for us there is no need for a specific council for that purpose as we can achieve these aims through the organization of speakers, publications, and the publication of articles in the press). However if the aim of the federation is political, we would not support it. In that case we would therefore agree with the Bulgarian delegates who also disagree. . . .

Still I must admit that given the neglected state of several Mizrahi communities from North Africa and Syria, among other places, we need to request that the Zionist Council strengthen its interest in these centers. Additionally we need to ask that it pay closer attention to Sephardi immigrants [in Palestine].

[Moshe David] Gaon:

We are not of the opinion that the Zionist Committee discriminates against the Sephardim, but given the fact that Zionist work in the Land of Israel is conducted by humble people, without the guidance of great leaders, Sephardi issues are neglected. . . . For example, a group of immigrants from Bulgaria bought land near Acre, after which time other newcomers offered more for the land before the Bulgarians could sign their contract, thus stealing the land out from under them. Not a single voice stood up to defend their rights. [Similarly] a group of immigrants arrived to the land from Morocco but, lacking a counselor or guide, they returned to their place of origin. Fifty families from Salonica bought land together only to suffer from hunger, with no one offering financial or moral support. These families approached various foreign newspapers, disclosing their stories and describing their conditions. When we approached the Zionist Committee to sort out these matters, they claimed never to have heard of such an agricultural settlement. These events occurred because no single individual or organization was responsible for overseeing the Sephardi immigrants as they arrived, leaving them vulnerable to hustlers and swindlers.

Sephardi Jews donate great sums to the Jewish Colonization Association and other Zionist organizations, yet they are given no land on which to settle. In the *moshava* Givat Ezekiel, which was funded by a Sephardi donor, not a single Sephardi Jew resides.

The Sephardim could have helped to foster peaceful relations between [Jews] and our Arab neighbors, but so far we have not been used [for this purpose]. . . . We will continue our work. If the Bulgarians join us we will be pleased. If not, we will be disappointed, but our work will continue nonetheless.

Protocols of the World Sephardi Federation in Vienna, 1925, The Sephardi Community Archives, Jerusalem City Hall (Jerusalem), File 1268. Translated from Hebrew by Yehuda Sharim.

## 83. THE SEPHARDIST MISSION OF A RABBI FROM YUGOSLAVIA (1926)

*A native of Plevna (Pleven), Bulgaria, Sabetai Djaen (1883–1947) was a prolific writer and Sephardi communal leader active in various countries. Author of more than twenty Ladino plays and countless poems, Djaen served as the chief rabbi of Monastir (Bitola) and of Argentina and Uruguay during the interwar period. He later returned to Europe becoming the Sephardi chief rabbi of Romania, where he lived through the Second World War before settling in Argentina in 1945. Djaen's plays were as global as his career, with performances by the Serbian National Theater in Belgrade and in Egypt, Bulgaria, Greece, and the United States. Here we find a description of his work on behalf of the World Sephardi Federation (on which see also source 82).*

To the Sephardi Jews,
Brothers!

The World Sephardi Federation in Jerusalem, whose purpose is to elevate the cultural level of Sephardim in all countries as well as to focus its efforts and energy on the work of the World Zionist Organization, calls on you and invites you to take part in and contribute to its great project. The Federation hopes that you will listen to our request and respond favorably.

His Eminence Rabbi Sabetai Djaen, current leader of one of the largest Jewish communities in Yugoslavia (Bitola) and one of the original members to fight for the creation of the Federation, has kindly accepted the weighty mission of becoming our delegate and representative in spreading the ideals of our work in the Diaspora. For this purpose he will provide you with interesting details, bring you up to date on the history of the Federation, and inform you about its regional and general conferences, its aims, and its program for the near future. Our movement is charged with bringing together the entire Sephardi world. At the same time it requires the protection and encouragement of the best children of our race who have open hearts and wish to see Sephardi Jewry elevated along with the other diverse groups that make up the Jewish nation.

Brothers and Sisters!

We hope to be able to count you among the participants. Share with us the heavy burden of this onerous task. We require your fraternal and loyal support. Let us be worthy of our glorious past, so full of fortune, praise and splendor. Aid the Federation, and help raise its flag high!

Let us pray for Zion and for the rebirth of Sephardi Judaism,

The Palestine Action Committee of the [World] Sephardi Federation.

"Confederation Universal de los Judios Spharadim" (Jerusalem, 1926), Joseph M. Papo Research Materials, 1926–1992, Manuscript Collection No. 866. Courtesy of The Jacob Rader Marcus Center of the American Jewish Archives, Cincinnati, Ohio. Americanjewisharchives.org. Translated from Ladino by Adriana Brodsky.

## 84. IN DEFENSE OF THE ARABIC ALPHABET: A JEWISH SCHOLAR'S CRITIQUE OF THE ROMANIZATION OF TURKISH (1927)

*Following the creation of the Turkish Republic in 1923, its founder, Mustafa Kemal Atatürk heralded sweeping nationalist reforms meant to modernize Turkish culture. Among these was the romanization of Turkish, which was previously written in Arabic script, and the adoption of the twenty-nine-letter Turkish alphabet. Although the ostensible purpose of this language reform was to increase literacy within Turkey, the initiative also changed the linguistic basis of the language, favoring secular words and expressions over religious ones and European root words over Arabic and Persian. In this text Abraham Galante, a leading Turkish Jewish intellectual, advocates for the preservation of the Arabic alphabet while simultaneously lending support for the Turkification of the language. His efforts were soon frustrated. Within a year the Turkish Republic officially replaced the Arabic with the Latin alphabet, ushering in an era of reform and westernization. (For more on Galante see sources 70 and 88.)*

Arabic letters are not an impediment to our progress. . . .

It is well known that a Turkology congress met recently in the city of Baku[35] and that various decisions were proposed and adopted there. One of these decisions concerned the adoption of Latin letters. I won't return again to this topic as I have explained my ideas on the issue and the related issue of spelling in a work that I published nine months ago under the title of "Arabic and Latin Letters in Turkish and the Question of Orthography."

Detailing the congress's decisions, the March 20, 1926 Number III issue of *Halk* newspaper writes the following regarding the resolution that was adopted about scientific terminology:

> The congress has taken up a resolution about scientific terminology. According to this resolution, it proposes that henceforth only European expressions, not Arabic or Persian ones, be used for scientific terminology. With this aim, it proposes the establishment of a terminology commission that would determine scientific terminology in the Turkish Republic.

This resolution, far from being concerned with science—if indeed it has not been taken up with "political" intentions—is surely an "un-

---

35. Baku, now capital of Azerbaijan, was at this time located in the Transcaucasian Soviet Federated Socialist Republic.

scientific" decision. . . . In my opinion, this group also recommended to the Congress that "European terms" be used after the use of Latin letters was accepted by the Congress, thinking that it would be more suitable for terminology to be taken from Europe, and not from Arabic or Persian, due to the difficulties that spelling these terms with Latin letters would have presented. And the Congress accepted this recommendation as a resolution. While the small group was making this decision, did they, I wonder, have any idea of, or attempt to determine the number of Turkish scientific terms that are being used in Turkish today? I don't think so. Because our current scientific terms and expressions are much more numerous than is [generally] believed. After the 1908 constitutional movement, the field of knowledge that advanced the most was that of language and, particularly vocabulary, despite the great confusion present in the language. Since then, no less than ten thousand expressions and terms have entered our language. . . .

Now a question has arisen. Let's assume for the sake of argument that we've accepted European terminology. What will we do with all of our scientific terms that already exist? Will we Europeanize them too? If perchance they are left unchanged, what will we do in the future, if it is necessary for one of them to form a compound noun with one of the newly accepted European terms? Which term will we prefer? Did the group carefully examine this question? I don't think so. Again in my opinion the group just thought, "as long as Latin letters are accepted, let 'European terms' be accepted."

The ultimate meaning of the resolution that was adopted under these terms and conditions is this: Turkish will be brought down to the level of a basic language of labor, in other words, among the common people it will be a tool useful only for work and family communication. In that case what will happen to all the effort that has been exerted by the government and the nation to develop Turkish, to bring it up to the level of a language of science?! Did the group think of this? This I don't know. In my opinion the group wanted to settle the matter solely from a political point of view. If I am mistaken in this last remark I hope that I have been mistaken on behalf of Turkishness. I have claimed and proven that the group's resolution is completely unscientific and inapplicable. . . .

Every nation is at a point at which it is trying to enrich its own language. We too must try to enrich our own language. The resolution of the Baku Congress concerning terminology, in addition to impoverishing our language, has no use whatsoever because the resolution cannot be implemented.

I am a supporter of the Turkification of our language. In its current state our Turkish is not [yet] suitable to be a language of terminology. For this reason, until that time comes, we are in need of terms constructed with Arabic and Persian. The issue of terminology is connected to the issue of etymology, and the issue of etymology is connected to the issue of orthography, while the issue of orthography is connected to the issue of letters. All of these form a complete whole. Regarding this whole, a decision should be taken if and only if thorough scientific investigations have been conducted.

The other day, while defending the Education Law before the Grand National Assembly, our esteemed Minister of Education Necati Bey Efendi clearly acknowledged that science now ought to rule superior in all matters in our country by saying that "in affairs pertaining to science and [areas of] expertise, it is necessary and obligatory that the floor be given to the experts."

Abraham Galante, *Arabî Harfleri Terakkimize Mani Değildir* (Istanbul: Hüsn-i Tabiat Matbaası, 1927), 3, 5–6, 8. Translated from Ottoman Turkish by Nir Shafir.

## 85.  A TURKISH JEW'S "TEN COMMANDMENTS" FOR TURKIFICATION (1928)

*During its first decade, the fledgling Turkish Republic initiated an ambitious campaign to transform Turkey into a secular state marked by a greater degree of cultural homogeneity than was ever before permitted or required in the expansive, multi-religious, and polyglot Ottoman Empire. By the mid-1920s, mass annihilation policies as well as forced relocations had targeted the majority of Anatolia's Christian populations. The small numbers of non-Muslims remaining in the Turkish Republic found themselves increasingly at the margins of the new, Kemalist national project. While many Jews expressed discomfort with the new "Citizen Speak Turkish!" campaigns that targeted them, among others, for their imperfect knowledge of the language of the country, the prominent Jewish intellectuals Abraham Galante (featured in sources 70, 84, and 88) and Moïse Cohen (1883–1961), later known as*

*Tekinalp, were foremost proponents of the Turkification of their community. The following list, which parrots the biblical Ten Commandments, was Cohen's blueprint for Turkish Jewish integration.*

1. Turkify your names
2. Speak Turkish
3. Read a portion of synagogue prayers in Turkish
4. Turkify your schools
5. Send your children to Turkish state schools
6. Become involved in affairs of state
7. Bind your fate to those of the Turks
8. Utterly root out the "communal" mentality⌉ *int.*
9. Perform a special role in the sphere of the national economy
10. Know your rights.

Rıfat Bali, *Model Citizens of the State* (Plymouth, U.K.: Fairleigh Dickinson University Press and Lanham, MD: Rowman & Littlefield Publishing Group, 2012), 3. Translated from Turkish by Paul F. Bessemer.

## 86. TEACHING HEBREW TO THE ARABS AND ARABIC TO THE JEWS: SOCIAL ENGINEERING IN PALESTINE [1936]

*In a climate of clashes between Arabs and Jews in Palestine following a six-month general strike, Great Britain charged a royal commission of inquiry with determining the cause of the riots and investigating whether the British Mandate for Palestine ought to be fundamentally reconsidered. This letter to the commission was written by Joseph Baran Meyuhas (1868–1942), apparently at his own initiative. Meyuhas hailed from a family of prominent rabbis and scholars in Jerusalem. A leader of the Sephardi community of Palestine, a writer, and an educator, he was author of a number of Hebrew-language works, including a popular study of biblical tales in Arab folklore. Meyuhas was also among those who in 1892 founded the Jewish National and University Library (now the National Library of Israel). In his missive to the Palestine Royal Commission, Meyuhas claims that his background in Palestine renders him an expert on Arab customs. He also proposes that Britain ought to keep a tighter rein on its Muslim subjects in Palestine while simultaneously promoting mutual understanding among Jews and Arabs through the mandatory instruction of Arabic and Hebrew to these communities.*

Jerusalem, December 23, 1936
The Palestine Royal Commission
Jerusalem
My Lord and honorable Commissioners,

At the outset permit me to greet you on behalf of our Community, the most ancient Jewish Community in Jerusalem to which several other communities of Oriental Jews are attached. I wish you success in your difficult and responsible task for the welfare of all the people of this country. May your arrival here be of good augury for the future of this land.

I would take leave to introduce this statement with a brief personal observation. I have spent most my youth among the Arabs and have grown up in their company. When I was eight, my family, which is one of the oldest in the country and can trace its origin in Palestine as far back as 250 years ago, removed its residence from the Old City, which at that time, sixty years ago, was devoid of the necessary hygienic conditions, and moved to the Silwan village, the Shiloah of the Bible, which is near Jerusalem. I was thus enabled to be almost daily a regular guest in the home of my good neighbors, and to observe their customs, practices and ways of life at close range. From my personal observation I found that the Arabs have many beautiful and attractive traits that merit appreciation. I would mention amongst these, the perfect loyalty to the neighbors, which is sometimes stretched to the point of self sacrifice, when it is necessary to come to his help and even more so when it is necessary to protect the neighbor's life, as their well known [Arabic] saying "the neighbor's right" goes to prove. . . .

Yet with time I found them fanatical, especially in the following three traits: an almost unlimited extremism in their private and social lives, an excessive imagination, and a religious sensitiveness bordering on intolerance. . . .

The above premises which are based on close personal observation will, in my submission, serve as an important background upon which the Royal Commission may bare certain deductions as to how best this country and its non-Moslem population can be saved from a sure calamity resulting from false rumors that have not a grain of truth, and as to how best peace can be maintained in this country. These measures can only be the following, in my submission: (1) *A strict control and restraint of the Arabic Press by the Government and, to an even greater extent, (2) An educational policy in the schools designed to educate the youth to ideas of moderation and peace. . . .*

If, since the British occupation, [schools] have been opened for Arabs to such an extent that they could dispense with our Jewish schools, should that rule out the gauging of a curriculum of the schools with a view to imbuing youth with moderation and peace and brotherhood between the various sections of the populations? I submit that the new conditions need not rule out such an education policy. But it is for the Government to help much more than they did hitherto, by expanding the school curricula both of Jewish and of Arabs schools, and by introducing in both of these, *as a compulsory subject*, the language of the other section, i.e. the Hebrew language in the Arabs' schools, accompanied by special brief course on Jewish life and on the benefit they bring to the development of the country, and correspondingly with that, of the study of the Arabic language in the Hebrew schools accompanied by courses on the life of the Arabs in their glorious past and in their promising future, for the benefit of the community as a whole, including of course the Jews. When I speak of their glorious past I refer to that golden era in Spain, which has left in the annals of world history a brilliant and lasting imprint, a true golden page when Jews and Arabs collaborated jointly in a useful fields of human endeavor, in the field of science and wisdom, poetry and literature, from complete harmony and mutual understanding, to the glory of the race. . . .

I remain, My Lord,

Your humble and obedient servant.

Letter from Joseph Meyuhas to the Palestine Royal Commission, December 23, 1936. The Sephardi Community Archives, Jerusalem City Hall (Jerusalem), Box 6322. Original in English.

## 87. ACCUSATIONS OF DISCRIMINATION AGAINST SEPHARDI AND MIZRAHI JEWS IN ISRAEL [1948]

*In the early decades of the twentieth century a number of Mizrahi and Sephardi Jews dwelling in Palestine sought to bond together institutionally to represent a discrete voice within the Zionist party and congress. As increasing numbers of North African and Middle Eastern Jews migrated to Palestine in the late 1940s and in even greater numbers to the newly established state of Israel in the 1950s and early 1960s, they found themselves subject to systematic discrimination by the state and Zionist institutions. Immigrant Sephardim and Mizrahim were granted scant resources and were segregated from immigrant Ashkenazim residentially and in the workforce: rhetorically these two groups were homogenized as a single community of 'edot hamizrah, or "Eastern Jews." As we see in this source, in the face of such discrimination, Ladino-, Arabic-, and Hebrew-speaking Jews in the new state of Israel found the idea of a united Sephardi-Mizrahi front ever more compelling and necessary.*

The government and the Histadrut,[36] two distinct organizations, have joined forces in order to exclude Mizrahi Jews as well as Sephardi Jews from civic leadership and from any national administrative positions.

This situation demands the unification of Mizrahi Jews and Sephardi Jews so that they can respond in a serious and courageous fashion, such that the enormous population they represent, numbering approximately half a million in Israel, will be granted its legal rights by the nation.

We will never tolerate leaders who discriminate among our nation, yet the Histadrut leadership is biased against all our Mizrahi and Sephardi brothers.

We will not support national leaders who disregard our civic rights. We have the political and ethical justification to wage a battle against governmental discrimination in the parliament. The current national leadership threatens our future and the present existence of our families and children; this national leadership inhibits our brothers in the Diaspora from immigrating to Israel, as they are taken aback by rumors about the discrimination that exists here. This national leadership confiscates hundreds of thousands of dollars earmarked for helping those in need, using this money to strengthen the very leaders that discriminate against us. This national leadership impedes wealthy immigrants from settling the land and paves the way for the same wealthy immigrants to flee the country. This national leadership discriminates against Sephardi policemen serving in the Israeli police force, who, despite their skills and efforts, are rarely promoted.

Eliezer Goundi, "Giluy Da'at le-Yehude Artsot Arav ve-le-Yehude Sefarad," The Sephardi Community Archives, Jerusalem City Hall (Jerusalem), Box 6322. Translated from Hebrew by Yehuda Sharim.

36. An organization founded in 1920 in British-Mandate Palestine to represent the interest of Jewish workers.

## 88. A LEADING TURKISH JEWISH SCHOLAR OPPOSES PLANS TO WRITE HEBREW IN THE LATIN ALPHABET (1950)

*Abraham Galante (1873–1961) was a towering figure in the world of Turkish Jewish letters. A historian, educator, professor, journalist, linguist, and activist, Galante wrote some sixty books and roughly one hundred articles based on his studies of original documents in Hebrew, Ladino, Ottoman and modern Turkish, French, and German. Following the founding of the Turkish Republic in 1923, Galante vehemently opposed the initiative of Turkish President Mustafa Kemal Atatürk to romanize the Turkish language (see source 84). Here he outlines his objections to the proposed romanization of Hebrew, an idea that emerged two decades later. Unlike the case of Ottoman Turkish, which was romanized, the Hebrew alphabet did not fall out of favor, a development Galante no doubt counted as a victory.*

From time to time voices arise in favor of adopting Latin characters for the Hebrew language. These voices appear at first glance to be well intentioned and draw the attention of the public. In effect the attraction of the subject and, shall we say, teaching facilities would have me enter the cadre of partisans of the reform of characters, as if I didn't know the subject. But this is not the case. In order to treat such a subject simple desire is not sufficient. It requires scientific study. . . .

It is well known that until . . . [1928], Turks used Arabic characters, which [constitute an] alphabet [that] is fairly complicated for beginners to learn. The reform involved the simplification of words of Turkish origin as well as Turkified Arabic and Persian words. . . .

The insufficiency of the Turkish language alone, which, as mentioned, is not Semitic and which could [therefore] easily adopt Latin characters, [ensured that it] was not then developed enough to replace the richness of the Arabic language. Scientific, literary, technical, and judicial terms were almost all Arabic, to such an extent that when students finished Turkish high schools, which had adopted the new characters, they could not continue their studies at the law school, where the older professors were accustomed to using older terms that were almost entirely Arabic in origin.

In that year a congress was held in Ankara, where the state addressed the question of scientific and technical terms, which were leaving professors and students alike in a state of confusion. It was decided to review the terms that had already been allowed and to get rid of those with no linguistic value. The same question was discussed on July 7, 1950, in the Turkish Parliament, where several members declared that they had difficulty understanding the laws containing words no longer in use.

At present the works of Turkish poets such as Fuzuli, Nef'i, Nedim, Abdülhak Hamid and others are [largely] incomprehensible to the new Turkish generation. Within a quarter of a century the process [by which the new generation is alienated from the language of a previous generation] will be complete.

Why do I broach this subject? Because there is a profound analogy between Arabic and Hebrew and because the adoption of Latin characters would mean the dislocation of the Hebrew language. . . .

In the midst of all the hubbub surrounding the project of adopting Latin characters by the Turkish government, I went to the Japanese embassy in order to learn how this question had been dealt with in Japan. Below I translate what Mr. Hitoshi Ashida, first secretary of the Japanese Embassy in Turkey, told me concerning the adoption of Latin characters in Japan.

For about forty years a movement in favor of adopting Latin characters existed in Japan, a movement fueled by the publication of a monthly journal. Though the partisans of this movement belonged to different classes, their number was too small. No scientific work—not even a primary school book—was published [using Latin characters] during this period.

A student in primary school must learn by heart the spellings of one thousand ideograms and forty-eight syllabic signs. In Japanese high schools, one learns the Chinese classics, which are very difficult. Apart from the Japanese language, we teach a foreign language (French, English, or German) in the high schools for six hours per week. In the business schools the number of hours dedicated to foreign languages is increased to sixteen. As for the press, it employs 1,500–2,000 ideograms and 48 syllabic signs. Japanese people understand these challenges very well, but they say that to accept Latin characters would be to lose the link to their nationality. In China and in Japan one finds works written two thousand years ago. How could we neglect the history of our ancestors?

One of the partisans of Latin characters was Mr. [Aikitsu] Tanaka-date, a university professor and a deputy who presented a motion on the subject to the parliament. In response, the minister of public instruction took the stand and said: "The question of writing is a national question. It concerns the heritage of our ancestors: this heritage is the soul of the nation."

The first secretary showed me a typewriter two times longer than the ordinary kind, bearing forty-eight syllabic signs and two hundred frequently used ideograms.

Explaining the machine to me, he said: "You see how difficult it is, but what can we do? We must make sacrifices for the national language by subjecting ourselves to this kind of difficulty."

During a trip he took in 1949 from Istanbul to Izmir, Mr. Abraham Elmaleh, the Israeli deputy [mayor to the Jerusalem municipal council], well-known scholar, historian, and journalist, responded to a question related to the possibility of adopting Latin characters for the Hebrew language by saying, "We cannot erase the past, which is dear to us and to which we are strongly tied by the language of our Bible, of our prophets, and by our rich literature."

We have spoken above of the reform of the Greek language, [a project] that found favor in certain circles approximately half a century ago. Recently I met my friend Monsignor Gennadios, the metropolitan of Heliopolis, author of *L'Histoire du patriarcat œcuménique* and of many other historical and philosophical works. I asked his opinion on the question of reforming the orthography of the Greek language. He responded to me verbatim, "To change the grammar of a language is to change the life of a people". . . .

The [various] declarations that we have just mentioned, all of which are in favor of preserving the speakers' respective languages despite the difficulties this presents, suffice to enlighten those who believe themselves to be facilitating linguistic education [by proposing radical reform]. The Hebrew language—that language which served as the means of an alliance between God and Abraham, the language of the Ten Commandments, the basis of global morality, the language of the *Sh'ma* of Moses in which the Unity of God is taught in six words, the language of the Psalms, a compendium of morals, poetry and music, and the language of the prophets, who sang their joys and cried for the misfortunes of Israel in verse, preserves its Semitic base and its Hebrew characters. M.A. Robert, professor at the Catholic Institute in Paris and the author of an abbreviated Hebrew grammar, has said the following about the Hebrew language: "One notes as [its] general traits harmony, vivacity, concision, and a regularity in borrowings made from foreign languages. So it was in the time of Ezekiel, in the writings of Amos, Hosea, Isaiah, and so on."

To conclude, we can cite an Arabic saying about the value of a language—which we can translate into Hebrew using the same words. . . . "The language of our forefathers is a precious treasure."

Abraham Galante, *L'adoption des caractères latins dans la langue hébraïque, signifie sa dislocation* (Istanbul: Hüner Basımevi, 1950), 5, 7-8, 17-19. Translated from French by Alma Rachel Heckman.

# IV. THE SECOND WORLD WAR
# AND ITS AFTERMATH

## 89. "ARYANS OF MOSAIC BELIEF": A DEFENSE OF THE SEPHARDI JEWS OF PARIS [1942]

*A lifelong advocate of Sephardi culture, Sam Lévy [né Shemuel Sa'adi a-Levi] (1870–1959) was editor of several important Ladino- and French-language journals during the fin-de-siècle, interwar, and postwar periods. He was well known for his fiery viewpoints, including his staunch anti-Zionism and defense of Ladino. A native of Salonica, in his forties Lévy made a permanent move to Paris, where he became a prominent activist of the French Sephardi community. In the following letter, written from German-occupied France just days before the leadership of the Nazi party decided to systematically deport Jews from Western Europe, Lévy and the Parisian Sephardi communal leader Leon Rousseau argue that Sephardim should be exempted from the Nazi regime's racist and antisemitic legislation on the basis that Sephardi Jews are "Ario-Latins of the Mosaic faith." Lévy and Rousseau's attempt to use the Nazis' racial logic to save members of their community did little to convince the staff of the German Embassy whom they addressed. Sephardi Jews, like their Ashkenazi coreligionists, were sent to the death camps.*

The Sephardi Religious Association of Paris
18 rue Saint Lazare, Paris IX

13 January 1942

The Sephardi Religious Association of Paris has been operating under this name since 10 March 1930. However, its founding dates back to 16 April 1909, on which date it was registered in the official gazette of the French government under number 153609. Originally, it bore the name "Oriental Religious Association of Paris."

The Sephardim began to settle in Paris following the World Exhibition of 1900. After the Ottoman revolution in July 1908, when it became easier to leave Turkey, a close-knit group of prominent personalities and a core [group] of distinguished scholars selected the banks of the Seine as their residence. The necessity to form a separate cultural and social body soon became apparent, and Mr. Rozanes, supported by several charitable notables, created the Oriental Religious Association of Paris.

It is important to mention here that in all the countries of the world, including Palestine, where there are Sephardim (Ario-Latins of the Mosaic faith) and Ashkenazim (from Greater Germany, Hungary, Poland and Russia), two strictly separate communities exist; the spiritual directions, family and social lives, customs and habits, etc., as well as the worship of these two elements differ, approximately in the same way as they differ between Catholic and Protestant Christians. . . .

The government authorities have always looked upon the Sephardim favorably, because they are generally peace-loving, as well as orderly and honest workers, their court records are spotless, and they are extremely dutiful and law-abiding. They adapt happily and quickly to the social conditions of a country, and become its loyal and obedient citizens.

Based on reliable and easily verifiable information, we are pleased to report a fact that confirms all of our earlier data and assumptions: The German occupation authorities in the city of Salonika, capital of Macedonia, recognize the Sephardi Jews, whose population numbers over 50,000, as Aryans of Mosaic belief. They are not subjected to any restrictive racial laws.

We are convinced that the German authorities in occupied France, with their sense of justice, will treat the Sephardim of this region in the same way. In addition, they are brothers and directly related to the [Sephardim] of Salonika.

At the end of this overly brief and incomplete historical outline, we wish to mention that during the war of 1914–1918, the Sephardim of Turkey and Bulgaria fought bravely in the South of Europe, in Asia Minor and up to Kut-El-Amara on the side of and under the command of German officers, who were always satisfied with them. Many of these veteran frontline fighters were awarded the decoration for valor, the German Iron Cross, for their achievements.

Additionally, a Sephardi colony has settled in Hamburg and Altona [Germany]. They had the honor of receiving German citizenship; they enjoy the esteem of the authorities and their fellow citizens.

Sam Lévy, general secretary, and Leon Rousseau, president

Letter from Sam Lévy and Leon Rousseau to the German Embassy in Paris, January 13, 1942, Document T12 in Irith Dublon-Knebel, *German Foreign Office Documents on the Holocaust in Greece (1937–1944)* (Tel Aviv: The Goldstein-Goren Diaspora Research Center and the Chair for the History and Culture of the Jews of Salonika and Greece, 2007), 84–87.

## 90.  A TURKISH JEW INTERNED AT DRANCY
## WRITES HOME [ca. 1941–1942]

*Located in a northeastern suburb of Paris, the Drancy camp was first established by
the German authorities in August 1941 as a site of internment for foreign Jews living in France. It later became the primary transit camp for all of French Jewry. In
this intimate letter a Sephardi man named Bension Haim Yaco Soulam (1901–1942)
tells his wife, Rebecca Soulam (née Bensasson) (1900–1974), about his days spent in
the camp, urges her to keep their family safe, and attempts to arrange a clandestine
meeting with her while he is interned. Yaco's letters to his wife during this period,
written in a combination of French and Ladino, contained elaborate coded messages
and instructions, including his suggestion that their children keep a record of their
naturalization as French citizens as a form of insurance. By contrast both husband
and wife remained stateless, although they had come to France from Turkey more
than a decade earlier; having failed to renew their papers with the Turkish authorities, they were not recognized by the Turkish consulate as Turkish nationals. Along
with countless other stateless Jews of Turkish origin, Yaco was deported from Drancy
to Auschwitz, where he perished. His wife Rebecca remained in Paris for another two
years before she too was sent to Auschwitz. Having endured the horrors of the camp
and nearly dying of typhus, after the war Rebecca Soulam was reunited with her
children, both of whom survived in hiding.*

Dear Rebecca,

I am writing you these few lines in order to inform you of my good
health. I am doing well. I want you to know that I received the laun-
dry package with everything except the toilet paper. I also received the
letter, and I was very pleased to hear the news you bring of the boy
and also that I will be seeing you and the family on Sunday. [From
what you have written], I hardly recognized the boy. My God how he
must have grown! I am also very glad that you and the girl are doing
well. I have been getting reports from those who have arrived here.
Dearest Rebecca, I pray that you will be protected from any misfortune, you and the children. I beg you, dear Rebecca, not to set foot in
a café because they have brought people here from the cafés. Because
of this, my dear Rebecca, I ask of you that you do not do anything
risky whatever happens (may it be good). Please have patience and
don't lose your head. Keep your sanity and above all else pray to God
that we will be able to be together once again as soon as possible,
amen. I beg of you, if you need money sell your clothes so you can
eat. As for Haim, take care to hide him. You understand [why this is

important]. In order to advise me that you have taken care of this you should say that Haim has gone to the countryside or even better let me know that you have done the job I commissioned you with. Given the state of things, Rebecca, I beg of you that when you come here, please do not come for much time. . . . I will explain more when you come. When you do I will show myself in the window of the fourth floor. I will dangle my *tespil*.[1] You should make a sign to me with your finger, but keep walking until you reach the café. When you reach this spot there will be a small side street. Follow it and look ahead of you. I will go to the ground floor, where we will be able to see each other better, but we must look out for the devils. If there are none around you can stay for half an hour . . . but I beg you not to come too often, just once a week. Sabbath with Eskenazi is enough, or Sunday, always at 3:00. I do not want you to think that because I ask this I don't want you to come. Quite the opposite, but I don't want you and the boy to suffer. In order to let me know that you have received this letter, please include a pencil in the next care package and I will let you know if I receive it. . . .

Dear Rebecca, we must have patience until God brings us all back together again in good health, which is most the important thing. Let the children know everything. They should write down on a piece of paper like the ones they used to have our dates of birth as well as when they became French. As for you, if God brings you neither money nor jewels do not be concerned. They take it all anyway. I am already very happy with the care packages you send me.

I kiss you and embrace you with all my heart. May God bring us together soon, amen.

Y. Soulam<br>To be dispatched to Rebecca Soulam

Letter of Yaco Soulam in Drancy to his wife Rebecca Soulam (née Bensasson) in Paris, ca. 1941–1942. In the private collection of Laurent and Florence Soulam. Translated from Ladino by Julia Phillips Cohen.

---

1. A Ladino variant of *tespih*, the Turkish word for worry beads or prayer beads. Traditionally, Muslims used these beads to count the ninety-nine names of God. Christian and Jewish men from Ottoman and former Ottoman territories also commonly carried *tespih*s and used them as worry beads.

## 91.  A JEWISH COMMUNAL LEADER FROM SARAJEVO
## ASKS FOR INTERVENTION ON BEHALF OF
## CAMP INMATES [1942]

*The Đakovo camp in the Independent State of Croatia (1941–1945), a Nazi satellite state, served as a site of transit for Sarajevan Jews during the Second World War. Here we find the correspondence of a Jewish man by the name of Jakov Maestro, who formed part of the Đakovo camp administration, to Aleksandar Klein, an official of the Jewish community of Zagreb—the only Jewish communal organization still legally functioning in Croatia at this time. In his letter Maestro asks Klein to intervene on behalf of two Jewish women who had petitioned for Aryan rights, which included the right to leave the camp temporarily. The second part of his letter treats a more personal matter, as Maestro asks about the possibility of allowing his wife, who had fallen into a deep depression, to leave as well.*

Đakovo, February 15, 1942

Dear Aleksa!

I am confirming our telephone conversation of earlier today. In all honesty I was very glad that I was able to speak to you however briefly. It would make me even happier if by chance you would pass this way sometime soon.

I spoke with the women, who are waiting for Aryan rights. They remain firm in their desire to leave and they ask you to do whatever you can to ensure that their case be resolved favorably and promptly. They feel that they would profit from even a few days spent in freedom and after that are willing to accept whatever God brings. I've explained to them that this risks everything but they will not be dissuaded. So please do what you can for them and keep me apprised.

I would also like to ask for another piece of advice. My wife is still here in the camp. I don't know if you see any possibility or prospect for me to plead on her behalf. I know that her potential release is riddled with dangers and that she could be sent to another camp. But it is difficult for me to see her lose her spirit and fall into an ever deeper depression with every passing day. What shall I do? Do you think it might be appropriate to appeal to Mr. Majer to have her approved for a special program and, in case of repeated internment, return her again to Đakovo? If you can offer any advice on this issue I would be very grateful.

Heartfelt greetings to you and all our friends.

Yours,
Jakov

P.S. I forgot to mention that in case my wife's absence is approved, she would go to Vukovar to stay with friends and not to any other city.

Letter from Jakov Maestro, Đakovo camp, Independent State of Croatia, to Aleksandar Klein, official of the Zagreb Jewish community, February 15, 1942, RG-49.007M, reel 6, United States Holocaust Memorial Museum Archive (Washington, D.C.). (Original in Jewish Historical Museum, Belgrade, K. 24–8A–1/1–103.) Translated from Croatian by Emil Kerenji.

## 92.  A REACTION TO THE "WEALTH" TAX IN TURKEY
### [1943]

*In November 1942 the Turkish parliament approved the passage of a tax on the fixed assets of all Turkish citizens, ostensibly so that the country could be made financially ready for a state of war. Though technically imposed equally upon Turkey's citizens, religious minorities were made to bear a disproportionate portion of the tax, known as the* Varlık vergisi. *Armenians, Greeks, Jews, and other non-Muslims had their properties and businesses confiscated as a form of payment. Some two thousand individuals who could not pay the tax were arrested and sent to a forced-labor camp. Those who faced bankruptcy and deportation feared not only for their assets and personal safety but also that the tax signaled the ascendancy of a racist, antisemitic era in Turkey.*

January 27, 1943, Istanbul, Turkey

My dear Albert,

I received your cable of 25/1 and I replied on the 26/1 saying that the situation remains the same.

In fact, contrary to what we expected, the Turkish government did not change the law in question, which has been enforced to the letter. In recent days, they seize personal and immovable properties from tax-payers who did not pay the entire amount of the tax: starting this past week, they have been arrested and sent by last night's train to the interior of Anatolia where they will work on the road construction 'till they payoff their debt completely. Taking into consideration that 80 to 90% of the non-Muslim tax-payers have been taxed with fabulous sums, which they will never be able to pay, you can imagine the quantity of innumerable seizures of tax-payers who must be deported.

The first list of deported persons includes [many] Jews, among whom, the first-class lawyers, Chekibe Adout and Gad Franco, both being taxed with Turkish £ 400,000, Mr. Leon Faraggi, T£ 300,000, Mr. Ruben Alaluf, T£ 400,000, M. M. Nissim and Leon Saban, T£ 300,000, and many others, among whom you find Americans and Greeks. Merchants, but not one Turk, this last being group being taxed intentionally with insignificant sums, which they all paid. Every property of these persons has been seized and sold by public auction.

They will continue doing the same thing with all tax-payers who do not pay entirely their tax and it is impossible to describe the anxiety of all of us, not knowing exactly when our turn will come.

As for the foreign subjects, we have been informed by the consulates that their steps towards the Turkish authorities did not succeed in making them change their decision and they advise us to pay as much as we can, at least 20% of the tax. They also asked us to send a request to the Chamber of Deputies in Ankara demanding the annulment or the reduction of the tax. I did not fail to send the request in question. I also paid out another T£ 1,500 making a total of T£ 2,000 as part payment of the tax imposed on me of T£ 45,000. But I am not in a position to pay more and I explained my position to the consul asking for his help and protection. Our consul follows the situation closely, with regard to all British subjects, and we hope that they will protect us against any seizure of our property.

At the moment, the consul recommended that we inform him immediately if they undertake any seizures. As for the deportation, we have been officially told that this can not be enforced against foreign subjects.

In all ways the situation is serious because, if the seizures and deportations continue to be enforced as at the present, nobody will be able to live in this country for the simple reason that trade will not exist, considering that everybody will be ruined. Already many Jews and proprietors of immovable properties from among the other minorities have been forced to sell them to the Turks at very low prices in order to get the money and pay a part of their tax, while the balance is covered by the seizure of their personal properties, their goods, jewelry etc. so that they have nothing to live on, and still less to continue their trade.

The Fratelli Haim Society[2] does not exist since last week. . . . As for the other employers, their destiny will be decided soon, because in all Turkish Companies and Banks they must not employ non-Turks.

You can imagine how worried Elise is about providing for herself and for Yvette, as she has been working with the Haims for 25 years and hardly managed with the small salary she was getting [previously].

I tell you my dear Albert that as far as I remember I have never faced such a dark and embarrassing situation as this one. Fancy that, since the 17th December, date of the promulgation of the law in question, trade has completely stopped, no transaction has taken place and many confirmed businesses have been annulled, considering that nobody is calm and able to think of any business. Everybody is just thinking [about] what he will become and how will be saved of this wretched situation.

It is true that I was telling you in my previous letter that we intended to go and live in Salisbury[3] but I see now that it will be impossible to realize this project. At first we should need a tremendous sum for the travelling expenses of a whole family, which I cannot afford. Then the travelling conditions in war time are very bad, making it almost impossible, even if one can dispose of the money to cover all the expenses. And finally there is the most essential question of all, that the Turkish authorities do not allow anybody to leave the country, without paying entirely the sum which has been imposed on him, which means that to pay the balance of T£ 43,000 and the travelling expenses to Salisbury I must dispose of a sum of T£ 80 to 100,000, a sum which makes me giddy, because with the conditions in which we work in this country, we could never manage to possess such a sum out of a commission business.

Therefore, the only hope which we have is that perhaps the English government would help us and send us at her own expense somewhere—maybe Egypt or India or even Rhodesia, if the travelling conditions are easy at the time.

I think that I have explained the situation.

I am waiting for your reply. Perhaps you will find a certain way to help us, and in praying [to] God to have pity on our children, I kiss

---

2. Fratelli Haim, a publishing house in Istanbul that printed books and journals in Turkish as well as foreign languages.

3. A city in Southern Rhodesia, today Harare, Zimbabwe.

you my dear Albert with all my heart and request you to give my regards to everybody at home, your dear wife and dear children.

S. Eskenazi

Letter from S. Eskenazi to Albert, January 27, 1943, FO 371/37403, "Tax on wealth. Code 44 file 7 (papers 3004–4838)," The National Archives of the United Kingdom (Kew). Reproduced in Rıfat Bali, *The Wealth Tax (Varlık vergisi) Affair: Documents from the British National Archives* (Libra Kitap, 2012), 435–38. Original in English.

## 93.  A BULGARIAN WOMAN STANDS TRIAL FOR COMMUNIST ACTIVITIES [1943]

*In March of 1943 Bulgarian authorities rounded up more than 11,000 Jews from Macedonia and Thrace, territories the Bulgarian state had recently annexed from Yugoslavia and Greece, sending most of them to their deaths in the Treblinka ex-termination camp. Later that year the government removed Bulgarian Jews from many avenues of public life, enlisted Jewish men into forced labor battalions, and ex-pelled 20,000 Jews from Sofia to the provinces. Only a few thousand Jews remained in the Bulgarian capital. Among them was Neti Shaya Hofman, a sixteen-year-old stu-dent of business. When brought before a Bulgarian court in 1943 and asked about her involvement in the communist opposition, Hofman spoke of the idealism of a group of Sephardi and Ashkenazi youths who dreamt of a freer and more equal society. In the midst of war-torn Sofia, these young men and women had become convinced that a Soviet-style regime offered compelling solutions to society's problems, and that lib-eration by the Red Army would give Bulgarian Jews a better life.*

My name is Neti Shaya Hofman, sixteen years of age, born in Sofia, a
student in the Minerva School of Commerce, Jewish, with a clean record. . . . Until the beginning of the year [1942], I took part in the Jewish Zionist Akiva organization, which I left before it was disbanded by
the Law for the Defense of the Nation.[4] After that I remained [in touch]
with my girlfriends from Akiva, but we soon went our separate ways. . . .
[Then, one] Sunday we found ourselves at Greti Mano[a]h's place at 20
Lomska Street. Yozhko read from a booklet entitled *Philosophical Review*
about women in Russia. This book discussed women's place in Russia.
They plow, hoe, and work in factories exactly as men do. Their children
are reared in special homes according to their age. In these homes the

---

4. A Bulgarian law promulgated on January 23, 1941, modeled on the 1935 Nuremberg Laws, which restricted Jews' rights in Germany.

children are given the chance to develop. They have toys and live in conditions that allow for the development of their minds and bodies. Their parents come to pick them up each evening. Women have no idea what it is like to tend to the home. All day long they labor alongside men, whether in the field or in the factory . . . The next Sunday we went to Greti's again. Sami read aloud from the encyclopedia. Mati Ario, Sami, Ahil, Yozhko, Moni, Ninio and I were there. Sami tested us on unfamiliar words from the encyclopedia. We danced Jewish folk dances. Sami sang "Proletarian Blood," but that day we stayed only briefly and Greti gave Yozhko butter and cheese for poor families of imprisoned communists or for the prisoners themselves. . . . I gave 100 leva[5] for the lottery and almost 100 leva for the kisses.[6] Sami always collected the money . . . for us to give to the poor families of imprisoned communists. On all matters everyone consulted Yozhko, who was obviously the head of the group. Sami spoke about the Eastern Front only once, at Greti's on a Sunday at the beginning of February, noting that a Soviet city had fallen; I don't remember which one. The summer I was with them, Moritz and Kalcho were the leaders of the group. Everyone always turned to them with questions and paid special attention to them. Eventually I realized that it was a communist group, although I learned this only gradually because they had not told me anything about communism at that point. Then they read the essay on religion in my presence, although I still didn't know what the money was for. The second time I joined the group I realized what the money was for, namely to support the families of imprisoned communists or the communists themselves.

When Moni gave me Sami's booklet, *The Dictatorship of the Proletariat*, I burned it because Moni told me the booklet was forbidden. I grew scared and burned it that same evening, although Sami and Moni severely reprimanded me for burning it before reading it. The second time I joined the group they did not give me any hint that they were communists. Then we read about the favorable position of women in Russia . . . and on Sundays, we sang Russian communist songs.

They did not trust me very much because they told me I was a

---

5. Bulgarian currency.
6. As other trial records indicate, the "game of kisses" entailed assigning a girl a boy to kiss and vice versa. Whoever refused would donate a certain sum, which, along with lottery proceeds, would go to charitable causes.

coward. They told us to be wary of the Branniks,[7] because once they had started to beat Jews on the streets; that is why at the beginning of February Yozhko made us split up into two groups so as not to be too noticeable and so that they wouldn't bother us. . . . I also realized that it was a communist group because, with every reading of an essay or book, such as *Religion*, or . . . *Philosophical Review*, they always hinted that life in Russia was beautiful. Most members talked about books, used unfamiliar words, and spoke of Yozhko and Sami and [especially] Ahil, whom they considered very intelligent and even called the Philosopher. . . . Only once, in the middle of February, Sami and Yozhko said that we must split up into groups of two rather than three or four and meet only on Saturdays and Sundays, because many communists were being caught by the Police Directorate. . . . I spoke mostly to Greti Manoah, who was constantly telling me that more money was needed for the communists . . . because if the communists came [to power], it would be better and nicer. . . .

The above testimony I wrote by my own hand,

N. Hofman

Excerpt from the trial of Neti Shaya Hofman, 1943, RG-46.011, reel 1, United States Holocaust Memorial Museum Archive (Washington, D.C.). (Original in the Papers of Virgil Dimov, fond 422, opis 2, file 64, Central State Archives of Bulgaria in Sofia.) Translated from Bulgarian by Darin Stephanov.


## 94. TENSIONS BETWEEN JEWISH AND MUSLIM IMMIGRANTS IN MARSEILLE [1943]

*Following the German occupation of France in 1940, the southern and eastern parts of the country came under the rule of the collaborationist Vichy government, which soon began to exclude Jews from positions in the civil service, the military, medicine, law, teaching, industry, and commerce. At this time as many as 15,000 Jews lived in Vichy-ruled Marseille with roughly half hailing from Turkey, North Africa, or Greece. The following documents tell the story of Moïse Maurice Farhi, who came under investigation in 1943 when some of the Muslim patrons of his business brought him to the attention of French authorities. A Jewish immigrant from Izmir who settled in Marseille, Farhi had established a near-monopoly in the couscous business in the city by the war*

---

7. A Bulgarian youth organization founded in 1940 and modeled after the German Hitler Youth.

*years. Local restaurant owners who relied upon him for their foodstuffs and who were known to complain of his unfair business practices now had the opportunity to denounce him because of his Jewishness. Yet Farhi's case remains a puzzling one, for even after the city had witnessed "Operation Tiger," a major roundup of Jews in January 1943, and as Jews across Vichy territories were excluded from public life and deprived of their livelihoods, the police elected to leave Farhi to run his business. Farhi's luck did not last however. In March 1944 he was deported and his business confiscated.*

Prefecture of the Bouches-du-Rhône, Marseille, May 17, 1943
Service of Algerian Affairs[8]
Note re: Muslim complaints

Following complaints filed by Muslims on the subject of a shopkeeper, Mr. Farhi, 60 Rue Sainte-Barbe, who furnishes them presently with various foodstuffs, it would be desirable to identify immediately the nationality of this shopkeeper, his origins, and his race.

We must also verify that he is really Jewish as these Muslims indicate, and in this case whether he is authorized to maintain a business.

Marseille, August 3, 1943
Affair: Farkhi called Fahri
    Rue Sainte-Barbe, no. 60, Marseille[9]
Origins: Administrative Police Commissioner
Reference: 22.017—Number 1956 Pol.—May 28, 1943
Transmission Prefecture of the B.d.R. [Bouches-du-Rhône], June 15, 1943

Object: Investigation concerning the shopkeeper named Farkhi in preparation for an intervention by the Commissary for Jewish Questions.

Commercial Information
Corporate name: Aux Produits d'Algérie [For Products from Algeria]
Location: 60 Rue Sainte-Barbe, Marseille
Purpose: Buying and selling of products from Algeria (retail and retail/wholesale)

---

8. The *Service des Affaires Algériennes* in Marseille provided basic services for Muslim Algerians in the city while also keeping close surveillance on the population.

9. Rue Sainte-Barbe was a principal street in the Rue des Chapeliers neighborhood where many North African Muslims first settled after immigrating to Marseille.

Creation: in 1921
Form: Business in personal name
Sales figures:    1940 . . .        about 80,000 [francs]
                  1941 . . .        "100,000 [francs]
                  1942 . . .        "200,000 [francs]

Civil Status
Farkhi called Fahri, Moïse Maurice:
   born December 25, 1892, in Izmir (Turkey)
   Jewish race
   Son of: the late Moreno Farkhi (born in Izmir, Turkish nationality,
Jewish race)
      and of: the late Judith Beraha (born in Izmir, Jewish race)
      Identity card: No. 208, series G., Marseille stamped
      Domicile: 14 Avénue du Maréchal Foch, Marseille
      Naturalized French by decree of July 26, 1933
         No. 37.232x32
Military service:
      Discharged in 1934
      Exempted April 17, 1940
      No citation or decoration
Family situation:
      Married to Rachel Sulema under the authority of the
community:
            born July 24, 1898 in Izmir
            Jewish race
            Counted [in the census] in Marseille
            French nationality by naturalization
      child: Jacqueline
            born in 1926
            Jewish race
            Counted [in the census]
            French nationality

Summary of the Investigation
   Farkhi called Fahri, is Jewish, French by naturalization, is considered legal from the standpoint of the *Statut des Personnes*, as are his
wife and daughter.

Since 1931 [sic, 1921] he has maintained a small grocery business specializing in products from Algeria. Following the cessation of all communication with North Africa, his business has come to a near standstill.

Farkhi owns an apartment with four rooms, at 14 Avénue du Maréchal Foch, where he lives with his family.

Signed: Bozonnet

Conclusions of the Regional Delegate of the Marseille S.E.C.:
From the above inquiry, it appears:
1) That Farkhi, called Fahri, Moïse Maurice, is of the Jewish race and French by naturalization.
2) That he is within the law from the point of view of the S.P. [*Statut des Personnes*], as are his wife and daughter.

I am therefore of the opinion that there is no need to pursue the present investigation.

The Interim Regional Delegate of the Marseille S.E.C.

Farkhi dossier, 76 W 163, Archives départementales des Bouches-du-Rhône (Marseille). Translated from French and introduced by Ethan Katz.

## 95. A PORTUGUESE CONSUL INTERCEDES ON BEHALF OF JEWS IN FRANCE [1943]

*In the course of the Second World War, Portugal, a neutral country, became a safe haven for thousands of Jewish refugees who arrived on temporary visas, making Lisbon one of the most important transit points for Jewish refugees fleeing Nazi-occupied Europe. Among those who sought refuge in Portugal were hundreds of Sephardi Jews who had been granted provisional Portuguese nationality in the first decades of the twentieth century due to their status as "Oriental Jews of Portuguese Origin." Many of these Jews emigrated from Southeastern to Western and Central Europe during the course of the war, only to find themselves vulnerable refugees as the boundaries of the Third Reich spread. After France fell to German forces, yet larger numbers of Jews acquired Portuguese visas from Aristides de Sousa Mendes, the Portuguese consul in Bordeaux. Despite a ban on the extension of visas in German-occupied France, Sousa Mendes issued 2,862 visas over the course of six months, from January 1 to June 22, 1940. For these extraordinary humanitarian efforts, Sousa Mendes was sentenced, dismissed from office, and viciously condemned by Portu-*

*guese President António de Oliveira Salazar. In 1966 Yad Vashem recognized Sousa Mendes as Righteous Among the Nations. In the document that follows, the Portuguese Consul in Toulouse seeks official permission to repatriate forty-three Jews from France to Portugal, including, it would seem, refugees who acquired Portuguese papers both prior to and during the war.*

Toulouse, October 11, 1943
To the Distinguished Minister of Foreign Affairs, Lisbon

Your Excellency,

    1. On the fifth day of the present month a group of forty-three Jews left this city en route to Portugal, [all] duly authorized by Your Excellency in keeping with circular forty-nine of the Portuguese Consulate in France . . . dated March 30, 1943.

    2. The interested parties attested to their Portuguese nationality in Italy and France by showing consular documents (registration papers and passports) issued by Portuguese consulates in the Levant, where they are from.

    3. The majority of these individuals presented Portuguese passports with which they entered France.

    4. It seems, nevertheless, that there are still in this zone a limited number of Jews whose [legal] status, based on their documents, is identical to that of other Jews who were allowed to enter Portugal.

    5. Given the current circumstances, said Jews are seeking refuge and protection from this consulate.

    6. Given that they could not travel to Paris to deal directly with the Consulate General of Portugal located in that city, I have the honor of requesting that Your Excellency consider bestowing upon this consulate the right to grant passports to these individuals, if you deem it appropriate.

    For the good of the nation,
    Consul Ruy Vieira Lisbôa

2PA50M40 "Repatriação de judeus portuguêses residentes no Reich a territórios ocupados, incluindo a França." Divisão de Arquivo e Biblioteca, Instituto Diplomático (Lisbon). Translated from Portuguese by Julia Phillips Cohen.

## 96. TRACKS IN THE SNOW: RECOLLECTIONS OF
## A MACEDONIAN PARTISAN {1941–1945}

*Jamila Kolonomos (1922–2013), born in Monastir (today's Bitola, Republic of Mace-
donia) to Jewish parents from Yanya (Ioannina) and Üsküb (Skopje), was one of
five children in a family that spoke Ladino, Greek, French, Serbian, and Turkish.
In her youth she was active in the socialist Zionist organization Hashomer Hatsair
("The Young Guard"). After her native city was occupied by German-allied Bulgarian forces in 1941, Kolonomos, along with most of Hashomer Hatsair's members,
joined the Yugoslav resistance movement. As she details in this gripping account,
Kolonomos first evaded capture by hiding in a tobacco kiosk in Monastir just as the
vast majority of the city's Jews were deported to their deaths. After hiding with four
other Jewish women in this manner for one month, Kolonomos joined the partisans
in the mountains, where she and her comrades moved from village to village and
battled Bulgarian troops as well as hunger, starvation-induced hallucinations, and
the elements. Until the war's end Kolonomos and various other Jewish members of
the resistance fought alongside non-Jewish partisans in a shared struggle against fascism. Yet as her memoir makes clear, after the war their experiences diverged, when
the Jews among the group found they had no one waiting to receive them upon their
return. Ninety-eight per cent of Macedonia's Jewish population had been murdered
during the war.*

The Communist Party alone had organized the Resistance against
Fascism. The Jews had no choice, and they supported the party that
led the Resistance. The majority of the Jewish youth belonged to
*Hashomer Hatsair*, which completely associated itself with the resistance. More than 600 Jews were secretly organized. Thus from 1941
we helped in any way we could.

From day to day the situation was becoming unbearable. Forced to
wear the Star of David on our coats, we could not leave the ghetto. The
Bulgarians forbade all work or running an office and closed all the Jewish
shops. We became impoverished. Solidarity amongst us grew as much
as possible. We all lived with the hope that the war would not last long.

In Macedonia in the winter of 1943 there existed only a few armed
units of the Resistance. Because of the awful terror, these fighters were
located in villages far from the cities. Contact[s] with these units were
very tenuous, and the organized youth were not able to join them. In
the cities the largest part of the underground organizations was betrayed
and many members were imprisoned and killed by the Bulgarians.

On March 9, 1943, a leader of the Resistance, Borche Milyovski, advised me not to sleep at home for a few days as he did not know what plans the police had for me. He gave me an address where I could hide and spend the night.

I spoke with my father. I told him, "It looks as though we must leave the house and go into hiding." He replied, "We cannot. I don't believe that it is necessary. I cannot leave my mother who is bedridden. The Bulgarians say that they will take only the young men who can work. Kalef and Menahem are not yet eighteen. Rachel is young; she is thirteen. You should hide." He knew that I worked for the Resistance and did not give me any difficulties on that subject.

The address I was given was that of a kiosk which sold cigarettes. It was located very near a police station. The owner was an invalid, with one leg. His name was Bogoya Silyanovski, later declared as *Tsaduke Ha-olam* (Righteous Among the Nations) by Yad Vashem.[10] He took me in and quickly closed the kiosk. The night passed calmly, and in the morning I returned home. All the Jews were anxious, not knowing what might happen to them. They lay in bed fully dressed with the lights on. My father advised me to prepare a change of clothes for all of us, for who knows?

I straightened the house, cooked *fijonis* (beans) for dinner, and bathed and fed grandmother. I prepared for all of us a small parcel of underwear, socks, and a few *biskochos* (biscuits). Thinking again that I would return the following morning, I did not say goodbye to anyone and took nothing with me.

When it became dark I took Estela Levi with me, and we went to the kiosk. The owner locked the door and left. We sat one next to the other shaking from the cold, in the black darkness, for there was no window and nothing could be seen. We couldn't sleep, wondering what the next day would bring. It was after midnight, when we heard muffled voices from the nearby police station. The hoof beats of horses and the creaking of rolling carts broke the night silence. Bulgarian soldiers and police had seemingly surrounded the city. The hours stretched and we did not know what was happening. At dawn, we heard voices coming nearer. The shouts, cries, and prayers of the women and the rending of their garments (a sign of mourning among Jews) were becoming

---

10. The Holocaust Martyrs' and Heroes' Remembrance Society, Jerusalem.

so loud we became deathly afraid and pained. We began to cry and we wanted to come out and join our loved ones.

But we were locked in. Nothing could be seen through a small hole in the door, only that snow was falling. No one came during the entire day. Like a dead city, it was silent beyond our kiosk, as no one walked the streets. In the evening, the owner came back with three Jewish women: Roza Ruso (née Kamhi), Estreya Ovadya, and Adela Faradji. They told us that the Bulgarians took everybody, and locked the houses, and the police took the keys. The Jews were taken to the rail station and searched, the Bulgarians looking for money, valuables, and anything that struck their fancy. The Jews were then taken to Skopje in cattle cars. Much later we would learn of the horrors and indignities to which they were subjected at the Tobacco Monopol in Skopje.

Thus, five Jewish women were enclosed in a kiosk of three square meters (thirty-two square feet). Only a curtain separated us from the side where cigarettes were sold. We were without food, without water, with no means for hygienic purposes, not even a blanket for cover. Seated on the planks, we couldn't move during the day or night. Every day, the policemen came to the kiosk to buy cigarettes and would stay to talk to the owner. Being so near, we could hear everything, but we couldn't talk, cough, or breathe.

We remained in these unbearable conditions for a month. Seeing the days pass, and exposed to many risky situations, we felt obliged to insist that we be taken to the mountains as soon as possible. On 7 April, our request was met. The Partisans received us cordially. The Jews who had joined the Partisans since 1942 approached us and, with great interest, inquired after our loved ones. We, of course, knew nothing.

From these first days in the mountains we were given *noms de guerre*, or aliases. I was called *Tsveta* (Flower). Because Bulgarian propaganda portrayed the Partisans as Serbs, Jews, and Communists, we pretended to be Vlachs.[11] There was a perception among the general public that Jews were weak, feeble, and not good fighters. Because of that, we, the Jewish Partisans, jointly swore to fight Fascism, which had caused us so much harm, with all our strength—we were going to be an example for all. And that is the way it went. . . .

---

11. Vlachs, also known as Macedo-Romanians, Macedo-Vlachs, Kutzo-Vlachs, and Tsintsars, are Romance-language speakers indigenous to Southeastern Europe.

A new life began for us, different than anything we had experienced before. We lost the fear that, at any moment, we would fall in[to] the hands of the Fascists who would torture us and, in the end, kill us. I don't know from where we got the strength and courage to be at the front line of combat. It was as if we wanted to avenge our loved ones without knowing what befell them. Allied against us was the Bulgarian Army, joined by the Germans and the *Ballistas* of the Albanian Fascists. They burned the villages that supported us, and many villagers were imprisoned or killed.

The winter of 1943–1944 was harsh, with a lot of snow and hardship. February was the toughest month. For fifteen days joint enemy forces surrounded us. Led by our brigade commander, we were able to fight our way out and find a route from one mountain to another one. As there were many soldiers in the villages, we could not find food. Hungry and tired from lack of rest, the Partisans began to weaken and freeze. We had to be constantly walking, otherwise one succumbed to the cold's *muerte blanka*, or "white death." We didn't lack for hallucinations—in some, one thought of falling into a fire with outstretched arms and a smiling face; in others, one imagined slicing [his] backpack as if it were bread. And there were some about lying on the snow, falling immediately asleep and never awakening. I caught the same "disease"—I saw villages in front of me, heard disagreeable voices and was eating a very tasty roast of young lamb. Even now I can feel the taste in my mouth.

A friend, whom I have dubbed *"Salvador"*—"Savior"—saved my life from certain death five times. Seeing me fall behind, he would take my hand and drag me along the path by force. There were a few Englishmen with our unit serving as liaison[s] with the Allies. They gave us a couple of pieces of sugar, which restored us. . . .

The snow did not abate. Wherever we marched we left tracks in the snow and the Fascists found us quickly. The cold air froze our garments, which became stiff like a drum skin. We received help from other brigades, though, and we positioned ourselves in more secure places, got a little rest and comforted ourselves. From my brigade, eighty fighters remained in the mountains and snow—we lost them forever.

It was not easy to move each night from place to place to fool the enemy. During the day, we hid in the depth of the forest. Many were hungry. Many gave their lives in this war.

And our young men and women fell in combat. We always remember them and we will never forget them. I will mention only a few: Estreya Ovadia—later proclaimed Yugoslav Heroine; Rafael Batino; Mordehai Nahmias; Aron Aruesti: Marsel Demayo; Samuel and Salamon Sadikario; Mois Bahar, Josif Shurna; David Navaro, and many others. All the Jews who took part in the Resistance rose to high levels of command in brigades and divisions. I ended up a *Komesaryo*—Commissar of the forty-second Yugoslav Division. We were all decorated with high medals and awards.

At the end of 1944, Macedonia was liberated. All the population, happy that the war had ended, were embracing members of their families. Only the Jews were bitter in their thoughts—we found no one, the houses were empty, and we had no reason, and no one with whom to rejoice. We cannot forget what we went through and what our loved ones went through.

Today, there is war in all places in the world and in our own neighborhood. Everything is being repeated in ever worse ways. Now we must fight to have peace. All we desire is for the coming generations to live without the pains we suffered and not go through what we endured.

Jamila Kolonomos, *Monastir Without Jews: Recollections of a Jewish Partisan in Macedonia*, ed. Robert Bedford and trans. Isaac Nehama and Brian Berman (New York: Foundation for the Advancement of Sephardic Studies and Culture, 2008), 57–62.

## 97.  GREEK AUTHORITIES COLLUDE WITH NAZI OFFICERS TO RAZE THE JEWISH CEMETERY IN SALONICA {1943}

*After Greece was occupied in April 1941, the German authorities commenced an intense assault on the Jewish community of Salonica. Within a week of the occupation, they arrested the city's Jewish leadership, confiscated hundreds of homes and properties, and plundered cultural and religious artifacts. The German leadership also created a Judenrat[12] to represent Salonica's Jewish community to Nazi officials: Chief Rabbi Zvi Koretz (a graduate of the Berlin Rabbinical Seminary who held a doctorate from the University of Vienna) was chosen as its leader. Among the sites targeted was Salonica's ancient Jewish cemetery, which was located close to the city center and, at roughly 300,000 square meters, was one of the largest Jewish burial sites in Europe.*

---

12. Jewish Council.

*Salonica's municipality had longstanding designs to raze the Jewish cemetery, given its location at the center of the city. Local officials working out of the Greek governor-general's office thus sought the cooperation of the German military to orchestrate the destruction of the Salonican Jewish cemetery. As this source reveals, however, Jewish community members condemned the actions not only of German and local Greek officials, but also those of one of their own, suggesting that their spiritual head, Chief Rabbi Koretz, had proven overly pliant in German hands. It did not take long before German troops stationed in the city began to use the desecrated Jewish tombstones to build a swimming pool and pave walkways. After the war Greek Orthodox Salonicans used Jewish tombstones as building materials in the reconstruction of their city, covering the site of the historic cemetery itself with the Aristotle University of Thessaloniki.*

A few days after the signing of the agreement with Dr. Merten (October 17) the Macedonia General Governor's office, acting on the authority of an order of the Salonika-Aegean Military Command, sent a letter to the Jewish Community instructing it to collaborate with the municipality in the transfer of the Jewish cemetery and to cooperate for the establishment of two new Jewish cemeteries, one on the eastern side of the city, at Toumba, and another on the western side, at Zeytinlik. A very brief time limit was set for the implementation of the orders under penalty of demolition of the cemetery by the municipality and removal of the monuments and their building materials. Simultaneously, burial of the dead in the old cemetery was prohibited after a short time limit. Thus, at a period when the community was tormented by two big problems, the drafting of thousands of its members to forced labor and the collection of the substantial sum of two billion drachmas for the buyout of the labor, a third problem came to be added, one of a religious nature, which affected the family traditions of all the Jews of the city and of those who had moved out of Salonika but had left their beloved relatives buried in its cemetery. As soon as this problem arose, in order to spread the responsibilities and the community work, the Central Committee decided to form a special large committee that would assume the handling of the whole subject of the cemeteries: the transfer of the bones, the salvaging of valuable materials (valuable marble stones, building materials, etc.), and the establishment of two new cemeteries. Naturally the new committee was placed under the chairmanship of the Chief Rabbi and it started its activity by the end of November. . . .

An agreement between the German Military Command and the Greek Governor General's office assigned to the latter the project of dismantling the old Jewish cemetery and the establishment of two new ones. Next came deliberations between the appropriate German military offices, the technical services of the municipality of Salonika, the Greek Governor General's office, and [the office of] the Chief Rabbi Dr. Koretz, at which the following decisions of the Germans were imposed: immediate demolition of the monuments; permission granted to interested relatives to transport the marble stones of their dead; urgent establishment of the two new cemeteries so they could be used within a short period of time, during which temporary permission was given to conduct burials in the old cemetery.

On this occasion too the leaders of the Jewish Community showed their well-known laxness in attempting to comprehend reality. . . . By procrastinating in taking decisions—which was the Chief Rabbi's notorious characteristic flaw—they gave the opportunity to the Greek technical services to bypass the community and to take over the massive demolition of the cemetery. In effect, the Greek services, showing zeal suitable for higher endeavors and using hundreds of workers, devoted themselves to the work of destroying the monuments, ancient, newer, and even the most recent ones. The hurried manner and the excessive zeal shown by the Greek authorities make it obvious that it wasn't only out of motives aimed at the city's beautification that they were moved to dismantle the Jewish monuments so quickly. For, in reaction to the Chief Rabbi's request to postpone the demolition work for a few months due to the winter, a high-ranking technical official of the Governor General's office was heard remarking in the presence of German officers that the request was only an attempt to gain some time until the British came to the aid of the Jews. And besides, it came to be known later that Christian delegations visited the German military commander to thank him on behalf of the Greek population of the city for the final settlement of this matter. Therefore it was in order to satisfy an old demand of the Christian public opinion that the Germans got involved in this non-military but clearly political matter, and that the local Greek authorities proceeded to this hurried and destructive action. The results of the misguided stance taken by the Jewish Community leadership before this important matter were the shameless destruction of valuable graves and the looting of building materials of great value by opportunists. Only a few hundreds of Jewish families, acting privately, took care to transport the bones of their beloved relatives to the new cemeteries. Thus came to a close in the most sad and unseemly manner, by its massive destruction and looting, the story of the ancient Jewish cemetery, a precursor to the imminent total destruction of the whole Jewish community of Salonika, the most populous center of Judaism in the East.

"The Memoir of Yomtov Yacoel," in Steven B. Bowman, *The Holocaust in Salonika: Eyewitness Accounts*, trans. Isaac Benmayor (New York: Sephardic House, 2002), 71–72, 75.

## 98. MESSAGE IN A BOTTLE: THE BURIED MANUSCRIPT OF A GREEK JEWISH INMATE OF AUSCHWITZ [1944]

*A native of Salonica (Thessaloniki, Greece), Marcel Nadjary (1917–1971) fled his native city once it fell to the Germans, fighting with the Greek resistance until he was wounded. While seeking medical aid, he was arrested, deported, and in 1944 sent to Auschwitz. Nadjary wrote an account of his experiences in that camp, including a description of his work as a Sonderkommando—or squad of prisoners assigned to burn the corpses of the camp's murdered victims. According to one testimonial, Nadjary was an incorrigible jokester who brought temporary respite to the camp's prisoners through his antics, provoking laughs even from an occasional German guard. Nadjary's fragmentary account of his wartime experience was found in 1980, buried between Birkenau's crematoriums I and II, and was subsequently published in Greek. Although much of his diary was lost to the ravages of time, the portions that survived bear testimony to Nadjary's dogged refusal to be cowed by the dehumanizing experience of the camp, his enduring faith in God, and his deep sense of Greek patriotism.*

Page 1

[Illegible. . . .[13] In lower right]: Stephanides Street, Number 4, Thessaloniki—Greece]

Page 2

To my loved ones, Demetrios Athan. Stephanides, Elias Cohen—Georgios Gounaris. My beloved companions. Smaro Ephremidou (of Athens)

---

13. Many long passages of Nadjary's text are illegible and are indicated here with ellipses.

and many others whom I always remember, and to conclude, my Beloved Fatherland "Hellas," [Greece] where I always was a good citizen.

We started from our [city of] Athens on April 2, 1944, after I suffered a month in the camp of Haidari, where I always received the packages of the good Smaro and her efforts on my behalf, which have remained unforgettable to me during the awful days I am experiencing. . . .

Page 3

later . . . Birk[enau] . . . where we stayed about one month and from there they sent us . . . where? . . . where? . . . he, who is ready, enters naked and, when they have finished [processing] 300 individuals, they close the doors and kill them with gas. After six to seven minutes . . . of agony they die . . .

Page 4 [illegible]

Page 5

. . . dramas they poured gasoline over them . . . shipment . . . we transported the corpses of those innocent . . . we transported in the ovens . . . one hundred . . . they put in the ovens those who still . . . combustible material . . . who have from one . . . but . . . who . . . they forced us to sift it and we passed it through a coarse sieve and then . . . in an automobile and they threw them in the river which flows near there . . . Vistula and thus . . . they obliterated every trace . . . the miseries that my eyes have seen are beyond description . . . my eyes. About 600,000 Jews from Hungary, Frenchmen, Poles . . . in this interval . . . about . . .

Page 10 [missing]

Page 11

In Birkenau . . . I don't regret that I will die, but because I will not be able to avenge myself, as I would want and as I know . . . and, if by chance you receive some letter from my relatives in foreign countries, I beg you to write them immediately that the family Nadjari was extinguished, murdered by the civilized Germans (New Europe) they call them strangely as:. . . . My Nelly's piano, Mitso, get it from the family Sionidou and give it to Ilia. This will now be with him to remember her, one whom he loved so much and she also him. Each day we wonder whether God exists, and in spite of all these things I believe that He exists and what God wills, let his will be done. I die content because I know that at this moment . . . our Greece is liberated. I will not live, but let survive . . . my last words will be:

Long Live Greece.

Marcel Na[dja]ry

Marcel Nadjary, *Chroniko 1941–1945* (Salonica: Ets Ahaim Foundation, 1991), 2–23. Translated from Greek by Isaac Nehama.

## 99. "THE ROAD WAS COVERED WITH CORPSES": MEMORIES OF A DEATH MARCH {1944–1945}

*After the Red Army liberated the first major Nazi concentration camps in the summer of 1944, Heinrich Himmler (1900-1945), head of the SS, ordered that all camp prisoners be evacuated and forced westward, toward the interior of the Third Reich. Himmler's goal was to maintain Germany's slave labor pool, to prevent the prisoners from falling into Allied hands, and to preserve the possibility of using prisoners as hostages. Some of these prisoners were evacuated by trains or ship: others were compelled to travel by foot, bereft of proper clothing, food, or shelter. SS guards were ordered to kill prisoners too weak to walk. Among those forced on the "death marches" was Marcel Nadjary, author of the buried diary presented as the previous source. Even after all the hardships of camp life, Nadjary described the forced marches as inflicting "unimaginable agony" on survivors.*

Leaving the camp of Auschwitz, we went in a westerly direction. After advancing some two to three kilometers we arrived only to see shacks and barbed wire fences no different from those in Auschwitz. We always marched like dim-witted people, observing everything around us and above all trying to discern in the faces that looked at us some acquaintance of ours, a father, a sister, but in vain. Not knowing ourselves where we were going, we didn't meet even one Greek who could offer us any encouragement. We advanced until we arrived at the so-called *sauna* . . . .

January 18, 1945, the evacuation of Auschwitz-Birkenau was coming to an end. That morning they locked all of us in Block 13. One hundred in number. Our agony was indescribable. While the others were leaving the camp, they kept us locked inside. The entire camp had emptied out. Besides some other small groups and almost all the Germans, we were the only ones left. Every once in a while we heard explosions taking place around us, particularly in the crematoria. Around sunset we saw suddenly a huge phalanx of prisoners who had left at noon and were now returning to the camp. We who had been shut inside couldn't resist, and we came out of the block and mixed with the others. Once or twice they looked for us but none of us showed up.

At night we left Birkenau for Auschwitz, where we stayed several hours. Suddenly, whistles again, they summon[ed] us again, and as we entered the kitchen one by one they gave us one loaf of bread, one can of meat, and 250 grams of margarine. During our departure we Greeks were obliged to abandon Maki Yohanan (from Arta) because he had twisted his leg and could not walk. Only twenty-five of us Greeks were left.

Upon our departure we began to throw everything along the roadside even though we were equipped with blankets. A phalanx of about six to seven thousand men and quite a few women gathered separately. We began the endless march. The more we advanced the more the road was covered with corpses of female and male prisoners. In short, those who were slow were sentenced to die. During the first days we marched continuously with only infrequent stops of one quarter of an hour. The Germans in our midst were very tough. During our march, through all the Polish villages we passed, we didn't chance to see a single demonstration either for or against [the German troops]. The cold was biting. After a few days of marching, it began to snow. My shoes were still in good shape. Our march took place only during daylight and continued for six days, during which time the cold grew stronger. During the nights they put us in some large fields surrounded by high walls, and left us there to rest, which proved to be impossible. Even though the field was large the space could not hold us, for there were many thousands of us. As best we could we shoved ourselves into a small corner when one could be found. . . .

Our march continued until we reached a railroad station, where they loaded us into open cars, about 150 individuals per car. Our joy was great that at long last we would no longer tire ourselves by marching, but then began another torture—the lack of room and the hunger and thirst. It wouldn't do to lose our strength and be lost. Those who died we threw out of the train. We went through several cities. We stayed in Brno for two to three hours. At dawn the inhabitants gave us, or rather threw to us, whatever food they had with them—extraordinary human beings. There my Polish *Vorarbeiter*[14] Melakh (Behaïacol) escaped.

After several days' trip by train, with unimaginable tortures, we arrived at Mauthausen station and traversed the city situated on the Danube, where the inhabitants looked at us with great enmity. We climbed partway up the hill, where I noticed people in the street taking large chunks of ice from the river and loading it onto their carts. Finally we arrived at the impressive camp of Mauthausen feeling quite uneasy, wondering what they were going to do with so many thousands of us. The cold was most terrible. They placed us behind the baths, at the entrance, one on top of the other, and in groups of thirty to forty individuals we entered the underground bath. We left all our clothing behind. They cut our hair, and from there we emerged into another yard. We waited naked in the cold, and one of the detainees took us to a block where, forbidden to speak one word, we sat cross-legged, one next to the other. . . . I had lost Danny Benahmias, Joseph Barouh, Saul, and others, and was alone with Leon Cohen. We were given the regular soup. For water I went to the lavatories (European style) and drank from the water that flowed into the bowl. After a few days they gave us clothing—a thin uniform with stripes. They gathered about a thousand of us and put us on a train. We arrived at Melk.[15]

In the Melk camp there were three shifts of eight hours, yet along the path from Melk to work, which was in the tunnel *Shaftbau*, the cold made us suffer, as did the work itself. The brothers Venezia, Isaac, and Dino, with whom I became good friends, were with me. Our work consisted of shoveling sand onto the conveyor belts or putting the nozzle into the pipe. After striking a friendship with two strong Russians and working in the section with the nozzle, I was given a double ration of soup.

---

14. Supervisor.
15. A labor sub-camp of the Mauthausen-Gusen Concentration Camp near Linz, Austria.

The first day I went to work there will forever remain imprinted in my mind, since, in an attempt to show my cleverness in the task of transporting a huge moving carpet (weighing about 375 kg), I showed them a way in which we could raise it all together. This pleased the German *Meister* and during the entire day I pursued this task exclusively. Several times I worked the pump for pumping water out of the gutters. The difficulty was great but there was a small reward: we stole wood from the *Schaftbau* and sold it in the camp for a liter of soup. The cold was very severe, as were the beatings with rubber hoses. We suffered. The food, or rather the soup, was meager. Then one evening I was picked up along with Leon Cohen, and, because we had declared ourselves to be electricians, they sent us back to Mauthausen. Leon Cohen as well as a few other German detainees were with me. There they gave us a different uniform and took us to *Gusen II*. It was very close to Mauthausen.

It housed a branch of the Steyer armament factory and the Messerschmitt airplane factory. There they put us in Block 6, while I worked in Halle 5 with the airplanes as an assembly electrician—although I was an electrician only in name. I had learned the trick. In spite of the cold I would go out, shut myself inside an airplane with a sponge in my hand, and pass the entire day there. In the meantime my hunger was growing. Jack Stroumsa (an engineer), who [usually] brought us good news, was with me. While there we learned of the death of [Franklin D.] Roosevelt. The truth is that it did not affect us, because we too had begun to die as a result of our suffering.

Marcel Nadjary, *Chroniko 1941–1945* (Salonica: Ets Ahaim Foundation, 1991), 42, 62–69. Translated from Greek by Isaac Nehama.

## 100. SEPHARDI SURVIVORS SETTLE IN PORTUGAL
### [1944]

*Under the dictatorship of Prime Minister António de Oliveira Salazar (1899–1970), Portugal became an exit route for certain Jewish refugees seeking to flee German-occupied Europe during the Second World War. In part because of the activism of certain of its consuls (see source 95), the regime was most accommodating of Jews who appealed for entry from Vichy France. This refugee population included French Sephardim and*

*Ottoman-born Jewish émigrés from Southeastern Europe, both of whom could claim*
*Iberian lineage. The following account describes the flight from France to Portugal of*
*167 Sephardi refugees who had managed to obtain Portuguese papers in France dur-*
*ing the war. In Portugal the refugees were partly supported by the American Jewish*
*Joint Distribution Committee, whose representative penned this report.*

We refer to the various memoranda we have sent you regarding the
immigration to Portugal from enemy-occupied territory of Sephardi
Jews who have been recognized as Portuguese nationals and who received Portuguese passports from the Portuguese Consulate in Paris.
We recently advised you that the refugee budget for Portugal had to
be increased due to the fact that part of this group has been forced to
apply for maintenance assistance from the local committee here.

These Sephardi refugees are of Portuguese derivation. Their ancestors first began to emigrate from this country in 1497, for in that year
20,000 Jews gathered in the Rossio[16] in Lisbon, in accordance with the
orders of the government at that time, to await embarkation on ships
that were to take them overseas to North Africa and the Near East.
When the group was assembled, the government reversed its decision
to permit them to leave the country and only a few of the 20,000 were
able to escape the Inquisition that was begun in the Rossio. Some of
those who escaped finally reached cities in Greece and Turkey, and
later many more reached Salonica. Some of the descendants of these
people immigrated to France at the end of the last century and the
beginning of this one and some have now returned to Portugal. It is
of interest to note that, although hardly any of the members of this
group who have now arrived here ever visited Portugal before, they
and their children all speak Portuguese fluently and have maintained
the customs and traditions of Portuguese Jews.

The group that is now in Portugal came directly from France. The
first group of thirty-two Sephardim reached Portugal on September 2,
1943 and the Portuguese authorities assigned them to residence in Curia.
These people were permitted to bring with them their personal belongings and their furniture and a small sum of money. Up to the time of this
writing a total of 167 Sephardim have arrived in Portugal from France.

The situation of these repatriates is different than that of the Sephardi

---

16. Pedro IV Square in Lisbon, commonly known as Rossio Square.

group in Spain. Although the Portuguese authorities did assign all new arrival[s] to places of assigned residences in Curia and Figueira da Foz—they did not exert any pressure on them to emigrate from this country and the repatriates were not given to understand that they were to remain here only until such time as they could obtain overseas visas. On the basis of documents in their possession in Paris (birth certificates, marriage certificates, and so on) the Portuguese Consulate there had issued Portuguese passports to them. After their arrival in Portugal, however, the authorities began to carefully examine their documents and have been passing on the claims to Portuguese nationality.

When a claim is found to be justified, the authorities issue a *Bilhete [de] Identidade* (the official identity card carried by all Portuguese citizens), which permits the holder to leave his place of residence and move freely about the country; to seek and obtain employment; to take part in the commercial activity of the country; and to enjoy most of the rights granted to native Portuguese. For obvious reasons the authorities here do not wish to release large groups at once, preferring to grant complete liberty to one or two families at a time.

It must be borne in mind, however, that despite the fact that part of the group has already received the right to leave their places of assigned residence and the right to work, and although it is expected that the rest of the group will also eventually receive their *bilhetes*, it is rather difficult at this time in Portugal to obtain employment or the necessary capital to engage in a business enterprise. Although these repatriates are Portuguese it must be understood that they have spent many years in France where they assumed the culture and living standard of France and are, in many cases, finding it rather difficult to adjust their lives to the ordinary living standard prevailing in Portugal now. The little money that they were permitted to bring with them from France has, in most cases, already been exhausted, with the result that they have been forced to apply to the local committee for maintenance assistance.

With the issuance of the official identity cards we find that members of the Sephardi group have left their places of assigned residence. At the present time the 167 who arrived in Portugal are divided as follows:

| | |
|---|---|
| Lisbon | 87 |
| Coimbra | 10 |

| Ericeira | 3 |
|---|---|
| Curia | 29 |
| Figueira da Foz | 37 |
| Spain | 1 |
| | 167 |

Of this group the following members are receiving assistance from the Transmigration Bureau:

| Lisbon | 36 |
|---|---|
| Coimbra | 4 |
| Ericeira | 3 |
| Curia | 16 |
| Figueira da Foz | 26 |
| Spain | 1 |
| | 86 |

We have advised you previously that the people receiving assistance in this group are on the rolls of the Transmigration Bureau.[17] In view of the fact that some members of the Sephardi group receiving assistance (especially those in Lisbon) do have an opportunity to obtain employment, their cases are carefully reviewed from time to time to determine whether they have need of continued maintenance aid. Although they are not transmigrants they are not, technically, stranded refugees and it is expected that they will not have to be kept on relief indefinitely. During the next few months, however, it is expected that many more of this group will be forced to apply for assistance. But it is hoped that eventually these people may become finally established here in Portugal and will be able to maintain themselves without the aid of the committee. We shall keep you advised of developments.

Robert Pilpel

Memo to AJDC New York re: Sephardic Refugees in Portugal, May 27, 1944, United States Holocaust Memorial Museum Archive, Selected records from the American Jewish Joint Distribution Committee (AJJDC) Archives (Jerusalem), 1937–1966, RG-68.066M, IS/4/2. Courtesy of the American Jewish Joint Distribution Committee. Original in English.

---

17. The American Jewish Joint Distribution Committee established the Jewish Transmigration Bureau in 1940 as a nonprofit agency responsible for dealing with the emigration of Jews from across Europe.

## 101. A TURKISH JEW IN ANKARA REFLECTS ON THE EXTERMINATION OF EUROPEAN JEWRY [1945]

*As was true elsewhere, in Turkey Jews had only vague impressions of what was happening to their coreligionists in Europe during much of the Second World War. With the liberation of the camps during the first months of 1945 the devastating dimensions of the genocide of European Jewry began to emerge. The following letter, written by a Turkish Jewish man in Ankara to a friend stationed at a military hospital in Merzifon, describes the author's dismay upon learning of the numbers of Jewish victims. The letter itself survived only because Turkish military intelligence monitored the correspondence between the two Jewish friends. Having judged its contents to contain matters of national importance and believing—erroneously—that the letter offered proof of U.S. President Franklin D. Roosevelt's personal interest in the Jews of Turkey, the Turkish minister of defense forwarded the letter to the offices of the prime minister, who filed it for posterity. In this intimate source we gain a sense of the horror that greeted Turkish Jews as they learned of the scope of wartime violence as well as some of the means they pursued to express their outrage.*

My dear brother Yasef Parlakyıldız,

I received your precious letter of February 22, 1945, with great joy. You ask how I am. Thank goodness, I am doing well and I pray to God night and day that you will be well always. . . . Now, my friend, listen to what I have to tell you. Nine thousand liras arrived from America for the Jewish poor in Ankara. This money was spent on clothing and shoes for the poor. Then a letter from Roosevelt arrived in Ankara.[18] The wording of the letter was as follows: "There will be ten days of mourning and one day of fasting for the Jews murdered in Europe. The day of fasting will occur on Wednesday, March 14, 1945. On that day everyone should go to the synagogue to read from the Psalms for the entire day and ask that God grant us redemption [and] liberation."

Later a letter from Palestine called for mourning and a day of fasting for the Jews burned in the ovens of Europe. The [date of the proposed] days of mourning was the same. From that day on we began mourning. When you see our friends, show them this letter and ask them to fast for ten days. Roosevelt has revealed that the number of murdered Jews is 5.5 million. Is it not devastating when you hear these figures? Tears well up in your eyes and you begin crying in spite of

---

18. It appears that the author erroneously attributes to Roosevelt a communiqué that was more likely issued to the Jewish community in Ankara by representatives of the American Jewish Joint Distribution Committee.

yourself. Now as I write these lines to you, alas, there is so much anger inside of me. When will we seek revenge? But the end of the war and the day of reckoning quickly approach. My letter will likely sadden you, but what can I do? I had no choice but to write these things to you. I have received a letter from my brothers. In my next correspondence I will forward it to you. For now I am busy and must stop writing here. Forgive me. Warmest greetings to our friends. I lovingly embrace you and kiss your eyes,

    Your brother, Yasef Altıner

Letter from Yasef Altıner in Ankara to the soldier Yasef Parlakyıldız in Merzifon. Başbakanlık Cumhuriyet Arşivi (Ankara), Dosya: 24891 Fon Kodu: 30.10.0.0; Yer No: 206.408.11. Translated from Turkish and introduced by Corry Guttstadt.


## 102. REFUGEE CHILDREN ARRIVE IN PALESTINE (1945)

*Thousands of Jewish children who survived the Second World War were orphans by the war's end. Along with hundreds of thousands of adult survivors, many of these children sought refuge as displaced persons in camps administered by the Western Allies. Others joined the thousands of Jewish refugees who sought to enter Palestine illegally after the British severely limited immigration in the immediate postwar period, while small numbers entered Palestine legally with the aid of the United Nations Relief and Rehabilitation Administration (UNRRA). Here we read of the desperate state of a group of young Sephardi immigrants, about half of whom had been orphaned when their parents perished in the death camps of Europe.*

Haifa, Wednesday.—In poor health, scantily clothed, and undernourished, the 239 refugees from Greece and Bulgaria who disembarked from the S.S. *Empire Patrol* this morning will have a long way to go towards physical recovery while settling down, under the Youth *'Aliyah* scheme.

There are 169 children from Greece, their ages from four months to seventeen years; nineteen trained young agricultural workers from the same country; thirty-nine from Bulgaria, three Polish refugees and nine of various origins.

The group from Bulgaria was in a somewhat better state than the children from Greece. They too were of Greek nationality but had been deported to labor camps in Bulgaria by the Germans.

Half the number of children are orphans, their parents had perished in labor and extermination camps. The children were picked up in the streets of Athens, Thessaloniki, Volos, Larissa, Patras, and Piraeus, half-starved and diseased. Four children who arrived here today were left of a family of nine. Their parents were slaughtered by the Nazis, and three brothers and sisters died of hunger. Another orphaned brother and sister aged eight and ten had lost their younger brother just before the ship left for Palestine; he succumbed to tuberculosis. Those who were not orphaned had to leave their parents in Greece in utter destitution.

The children wandered about the deck and dining hall of the ship, taking an occasional sip straight from a tin of condensed milk or munching on a piece of bread. . . .

A twenty-year-old girl from Poland who had been in the notorious Majdanek camp and the Miendijez Ghetto[19] told how she had fought in the Polish underground movement after her escape, and how she had left Poland three months ago, tramping all the way through Czechoslovakia, Hungary, Romania, and Yugoslavia to Greece in an attempt to reach Palestine: "I did it on foot, all the way—or rather, with my heart."

She also related a horror tale of Thessaloniki, where she saw the Jewish cemetery in a shameful state with many of the graves dug up, the remains of the dead scattered and all the tombstones removed. In their despair the Greeks had searched the graves for gold teeth to barter for food. One had used tombstones to make a dance floor in a café near the cemetery, where people were dancing when this girl first visited the place.

When Jewish stevedores, who had themselves come from Salonika to settle in Palestine many years ago, picked up the unhappy children, they kissed them and carried them down the gangway. The disembarkation took under an hour, and by nine o'clock the new arrivals were on their way in buses to *Athlit* Clearance Camp.

Before their departure from Piraeus last Friday, these newcomers had spent some time in a transit camp, where they were embarked under the auspices of UNRRA with insufficient equipment and provisions for the journey.

Ernst Aschner, "Children Arrive from Greece," *Palestine Post*, August 9, 1945. Original in English.

---

19. Possibly a reference to the Międzyrzec Podlaski Ghetto.

## 103.  A GREEK NEWSPAPER PRINTS THE HOLOCAUST TESTIMONY OF A SALONICAN JEWISH WOMAN (1945)

*In June 1945, just weeks after the Allied Powers proclaimed an end to the war in Europe, a Greek newspaper in Salonica published a serialized interview with a Jewish survivor by the name of Stella Sevi (1917–1993). In this searing condemnation of Nazi horrors, Sevi offers one of the first Holocaust testimonies ever recorded. Her account provides a unique depiction of a Sephardi woman's experience of the war— including her attempts to flee capture while still in Greece, time spent in Auschwitz, and work in a German military factory alongside approximately 500 Jewish women from various countries. Sevi's narration points to alliances forged between members of different communities, such as romances between Jews and non-Jews (including her own engagement to a Greek Orthodox Christian man) and the aid Sevi and other Jewish inmates and forced laborers received from Jewish and non-Jewish female supervisors in the camp and French male coworkers in the factory where they were forced to work. Despite her portrayal of such instances of solidarity, Sevi's account is also a story of the most extreme forms of brutality imaginable—of madness, attempted suicide, and senseless murder.*

That the misdeeds of the various barbarians we read about in history books and novels pale before those perpetrated by the Germans in recent years is an oft-repeated adage. Unfortunately for our civilization this adage is true, with the caveat that what the Nazis did to the various peoples they conquered was something very minor compared to what they did to the Jews. This nation [Germany], which aspired to conquer the world, undertook to eradicate calmly and scientifically an entire race in the name of an "ideal." Heads of households, innocent girls, and sinless babies passed by the thousands through the German blade, which took the modern form of a scientifically installed oven for humans. Pharaoh's persecutions and Herod's slaughter are small toys compared to the synchronized methods of extinction of Goethe's great-grandchildren, which they applied with the greatest apathy and the most refined sadism. . . . *Heil Hitler!*

The living story that we relate below possesses the burning and unadulterated sincerity and objectivity of a young woman who returned last week from the hell of Kraków[20] together with ten other girls—the

---

20. Although here and elsewhere the original Greek source refers to Kraków, it appears that Sevi was in fact interned in Auschwitz, some 30 miles to the southwest of that city.

only ones who survived among so many of our female Jewish fellow-citizens. It was recounted to us by its true heroine as she lived it just yesterday.

This woman is Miss Stella Sevi, an extraordinarily attractive and educated young woman, whom we visited in the house of a local Greek family where she is a guest. How she survived and escaped from the death camps through which she was shuffled one after another is a true miracle.

"I survived only because I was able to keep from losing my morale," she told us.

Truly one discerns in the attitude, speech, and movements of the heroic young woman all the elements of the will and the courage that she showed during the two years of her travail. All this lends to her face a severe charm and an unshakable certitude when she speaks.

"Miss [Sevi], why didn't you try to hide or escape before the Germans caught you in Thessaloniki [Salonica]?" [we asked].

"I had everything ready, even a house my fiancé had secured for me in Toumba.[21] (He is Greek and well-known in Thessalonikan society.) I was on my way to Toumba while my brother was headed to Athens, but we were betrayed and they soon caught us. From that time on our travail began."

With an admirable composure and unmistakable willpower the young woman related her life from the day when they put her on the train with her mother and her married sister along with her sister's husband and small children, on May 2, 1943, until the day of their liberation by Russian troops.

"Our journey lasted one week. Piled up like animals inside a freight car, we could neither sit nor sleep. . . . At each station they took away some of the bundles we had with us. When we arrived in Kraków, they separated men from women and sent us to the concentration camp. Old people, children below the age of sixteen, and mothers who had brought children with them were separated immediately and sent elsewhere. I will say where"—added Miss Sevi with an expression of horror and pain. "They shut the young men and young women into separate camps intended for 'Arbeit'—work."

---

21. A quarter in eastern Salonica.

"Where did they send the old people and the mothers?"

"To the ovens, the crematorium! It was there that the mass slaughter of Jews took place! As I've told you, as soon as the transports arrived they sent those unable to work there . . . in order to empty the camps for new transports—new Jewish oven loads still due to arrive. The camp in which I found myself was the newest, and we had an unobstructed view of the smokestack of the crematorium, which from time to time sent uninvited the horrible column of its smoke towards the One on High.

"The crematorium was a nightmare. Each week there was a 'selection,' that is to say a sorting among the women of our camp to transport [them] to the crematorium. As I mentioned before, room had to be made for the new Jews who arrived. When the arrivals were frequent, the transports to the oven grew more frequent. I recall that that there were times when it happened that three 'selections' took place in one day!"

"How were the 'selections' carried out?"

"We came out completely naked, even with snow, and were paraded before the doctor, who for the most absurd reason—a small pimple or a slight skin abrasion he judged as a bodily incapacity—sent women to their death."

"We have read a lot about these ovens into which those sentenced to death entered naked, were suffocated by an asphyxiating gas, and then burned. Is it true that they extracted from the cadavers soap and fertilizers, among other things?"

"Most true. We learned that they placed the cadavers in twos, a man and a woman together. This made an impression on the prisoners. It seems that this macabre pairing was necessary, technically, for the purpose intended for the cadavers. Note that the personnel of the ovens was made up of Jews, who, after occupying themselves for six months with this horrible work, were themselves burned in order to take with them the secrets of their profession, only to be replaced by others."

"In what work were you engaged?"

"The heaviest. We built roads, we dug, pulled the roots of trees, and undertook other similarly painful work for twelve hours each day. We worked almost naked, even in winter. Our ration was a watery soup with radishes for lunch, and a slice of bread at night with a little marmalade, cheese, salami, or margarine. You understand that life under these conditions, completely shut off from any hope or any ray of light, is something more than a burden, so that the prospect of death becomes a pleasure. For this reason those of us who did not go crazy—and there were daily new cases of madness—made many attempts at suicide. The worst means for doing so was to touch the electrified barbed wire that surrounded the camps and die immediately. Yet, besides the guards who surveyed the area and forbade anyone to come near it, the desperate ones were prevented from going near the wire by their fellow inmates. This is not to mention that many times the guards amused themselves with the unfortunate women and took shots at them just for the fun of it!"

"Did you ever find yourself in such a state of final despair?"

"I told you, I owe my life to the fact that I exerted all my efforts to preventing myself from losing my morale. Perhaps it was the memory of my fiancé who remained in Thessaloniki, perhaps it was the few alliances I was able to establish with the female Jewish supervisors, or perhaps it was luck. [Whatever the reason], I was able to hold onto life and to escape from the serious dangers I faced and the various illnesses that my body was able to overcome."

"What was the greatest danger you experienced?"

"When I was able to escape from the crematorium, to which they had decided to send me. Let me explain: After having worked for a year performing arduous field work, the *blokova*, that is to say a Czechoslovak Jew who was the leader of our team, sent me to the camp hospital as a nurse. There, I recovered a bit, because the Czechoslovak woman liked me and protected me a little. Still what I saw there would have driven a woman more sensitive than myself mad. Then one evening the Czechoslovak woman told me that an order had come down to send all the patients and the personnel of the hospital to the ovens. Out of my mind, I jumped from the window and ran like a crazy woman into a snowy field. From the running, anxiety, and fear I fell unconscious. When I came to, I found myself lying in a hospital bed in the company of my boss, the Czechoslovak woman. As she explained it to me, they had collected me from the snow and transported me there. In the meantime, in accordance with official orders, the hospital had been emptied into . . . the oven. I had been saved."

Miss Stella took a break from speaking for a moment, letting her gaze wander aimlessly and motioning as if she wanted to relieve herself of a weight that pressed upon her chest. I noticed her forearm, where her serial number, 44573, was written in beautiful characters.

"We worked hard," she went on, "in an atmosphere of pain and death. On the slightest pretext—slackening of work, fatigue, fainting—the stick fell down hard on one's head. Dizziness, loss of feeling, then a fall. A second hit obliged you to get up. . . . Among other means of discipline they had ferocious dogs, which they hurled at us out of punishment or fear, and which bit savagely and often tore people apart. One day they brought a young fellow-countrywoman, Brudo, who lived in the White Tower [district of Salonica] and was a pupil of Schina, to the camp. She was disemboweled by dogs and died shortly thereafter."

"A question, Miss [Sevi]. In all these examples of inhumanity that you faced, did you ever happen to see a gesture of humanity, an expression of sympathy, from a German man or a German woman?"

Her answer was terrible in its brevity:

"None!"

"Did you witness people being killed?" we asked Miss Stella Sevi.

"Many times!" she replied, "but by then we were used to everything and it no longer impressed us. The most tragic example involved a love affair that began in our camp and continued far beyond it, only to meet its tragic and bloody end back in our camp and in front of our very eyes.

"A German prisoner, an 'Aryan' who served in our camp, fell in love with a Belgian Jewish woman. They had planned things so well that they decided to escape. Disguising themselves, they succeeded. They escaped to the town of Auschwitz. There someone denounced them, and the pair was arrested. I don't know for sure what happened to the young man, but they sent his lover to our camp. One morning they brought her to us with much ceremony, and with a severe and disdainful air, the officer pointed to her and told us that, having ignored the laws of the Reich, the prisoner had dared to escape and that now she stood before us as an example and had to suffer the consequences of her act. At that very moment the young woman took a razor blade that she had hidden out of her shoe and attempted to cut the veins in her arm, preferring to shed her own blood herself rather than allow the Germans to shed it. But the officer intervened and with a blow to the face stopped her attempt and took away the razor. *Umdrehen!* ("Turn around!") he told her. And as soon as she turned around he emptied his pistol into the back of her skull, in front of our eyes. I assure you that the horrible scene did not impress us very much—we had been so hardened and dehumanized! After being served with this spectacle, we picked up our axes very quietly and carried on with our jobs, just like an employee who returns to her bank after eating her breakfast! . . ."

I perceived that in spite of her admirable coolness my interlocutor had grown tired. I asked her to relate the end of her travail.

"Six months before the Russian troops approached Kraków, we were moved from there to the German-Czech border in the Sudetenland. There they placed us into a Telefunken factory, where they built assorted military machines. We were about 150 girls from the Kraków camp, and some 500 Jewish women from different countries, most of them Hungarian. In that factory there were eighty French workers who had been conscripted by force. There, for the first time after two years of captivity, we came face-to-face with men, and we experienced the sweet feeling that we too continued to be human, despite our misery and the deplorable state we were in.

"Those conscripted French workers"—continued Miss Stella—"who worked with us in the same factory displayed a great sympathy and a truly gentlemanly behavior towards us from the first moments. Our common fate had united us. Understandably we didn't exchange a word there nor did we have any contact—we knew it was strictly forbidden! But we found other ways to correspond secretly and to exchange our thoughts and hopes. The Frenchmen consoled us as much as they could and told us to not lose courage. You cannot imagine how encouraging it was to read a few words from humans who shared our fate during our life in hell. Yet the Frenchmen's help was also more substantial. They gave us bits of bread they had saved from their rations, and occasionally, something to accompany it: marmalade, margarine, cigarettes—always in secret. This generosity on the part of our suffering comrades sometimes cost us dearly. One day I suddenly became embroiled in a terrible row with an overseer of the factory, a wild German woman of the SS, who discovered in my drawer a small slice of bread, whose provenance she guessed. Without even asking for an explanation, she took me to the toilets and began to rain blows upon my face. I returned to my post with my face fully swollen, content that I had escaped with a relatively light sentence.

"One day, we woke up and saw no Germans in the factory. Our hearts were pounding. The pleasant news of the Russians' advance somehow reached us in spite of all the measures that our guards took [to prevent us from learning of it]. 'We are free!' shouted a voice, which was then repeated like an echo inside the factory. It was the sixth of May. In fact as we soon learned on that same day the armistice was signed and the Germans left Weisswasser (as the Czech city where we were living was called). Our French comrades who stayed in Schilbert, five kilometers away, began to look after us immediately and stood guard in our factory in order to prevent the retreating Germans from harming us. In fact during this period we experienced a great danger. On the eighth of May a German truck loaded with a machine gun and charged with transporting us to Germany came to the factory. But the Frenchmen who watched sleeplessly over us took over in a timely manner and transported us to Schilbert, where we arrived on the ninth of May. There the Czech population and the leadership of the town showed us a warm welcome. The same night at midnight the Russian troops arrived.

"It is hardly necessary to describe the terror of the German families of the region. We Jewish women, the despised victims of the Germans, became suddenly their . . . ideal! They all vied for the honor of giving a Jewish woman to their sons, supposing that with such an act they would be absolved and escape the punishment they dreaded. But it was now our turn to show contempt towards our recent executioners.

"The Russians showed a touching interest in us. In contrast they behaved towards the Germans as they deserved . . . forcing German women to serve and feed us, while the Russians distributed sundry provisions to us from German homes. As a Russian infantryman told one of my fellow inmates, Rachel Negrin of Thessaloniki, pointing to the rosy cheeks of a fat German woman, 'Don't worry, my girl. You will eventually have cheeks like hers, while she will grow thin, just like you!' We stayed ten days in Schilbert. We were eleven young women from Thessaloniki, precisely those who later returned to our country.

The rest scattered. The Russians took care of ensuring a means for our repatriation together with our French comrades and the Czech town authorities. The Russians' concern for us was such that they gave us several jewels to save in order to have money during our trip. We left by train on the twentieth of May, the same day as the Frenchmen. They went to Prague, we to Budapest, where we arrived on the twenty-fourth. The damage suffered by this beautiful capital is frightful. . . . Our journey was far from pleasant, but, somehow, we were able to reach Greek terrain via Belgrade at noon on Sunday the third of June. . . . "

"A last request, Miss [Sevi]. Would you tell us as a matter of information some names of women from our city who died while interned with you?"

"I can hardly remember them all, but I can give you offhand a few names: Mrs. Tseniou, wife of the wholesale merchant, with her daughter; Mrs. Bensussan, with her daughter; Stella Cohen, Rozika Abravanel, Etti Yacoel, Lilly Santi, the three sisters Rachel, Suzanna, and Sol Santi, daughters of the postman, Allegra and Sol Santi, Frieda Hassid, Dora and Stella Cuenca."

"Omilei e Stella Seve pou sotheke apo ta nychia tou Charou," *Nea Aletheia*, June 13–16, 1945. Translated from Greek by Isaac Nehama.

## 104.  SURVIVAL IN HIDING: A CHILD'S TALE {ca. 1940s}

*At the outset of the Second World War, approximately 1.6 million Jewish children lived in territories that would be occupied by Germany or its allies. It is estimated that somewhere between 1 and 1.5 million of these children were systematically murdered in the course of the war. Among the children who survived were those who passed as "Aryan" and those who were hidden in attics, cellars, farms, churches, convents, and forests. In this account we read of an extended Sephardi family that relied upon a variety of strategies to survive the war, including flight, the dispersal of family members in a single city, the hiding of children, the bribery of non-Jews who were in a position to aid them and, ultimately, escape to Palestine.*

My father's roots were in Skopje. He managed a date factory. He bought wild dates from all the Greek islands and Crete. He sent them to Piraeus, and from there we got them, made honey, sugar, and feed for cows. We sent the pits to Germany, where they used them to make [photographic] film.

My father traveled a lot for his affairs. During the Occupation when he made it to Athens, he made the acquaintance of a military commandant from Italy. My father still had three brothers in Thessaloniki [Salonica]. Because the Italian knew what was going on, he said, "I will send my driver to Thessaloniki, and, if you have relatives in the ghetto, I can get them out and bring them to Athens." The driver went to the Hirsch quarter and found them, but they explained that they didn't want to leave and be separated from their children. The driver returned and said that they didn't want to come, as the Germans had told them to not be afraid, that nothing was going to happen to them. [My father] sent him back again, and they told him to take their children [instead], my first cousins Sarah, Shoshana, and Haim, who [soon] arrived in Athens and stayed with us, I believe it was on Aristotelous street, not far from the museum. Then Mussolini fell and the Germans entered Athens. At that moment we knew that we were in danger. The Italian warned us and advised us to escape. Father dispersed all the children, each to a different place.

I was sent to a building that the Italians had turned into a hospital—it was in Maroussi or Kifissia; it still exists. It was full of nuns. At the time I thought it was a monastery. At the hospital they called me Niko. For one whole year I remained in a small room, and only the mother superior, who brought me food, knew that I was Jewish. I didn't know Italian, she didn't know Greek, and thus I had no idea what was happening outside. Each day felt like a year.

At some point my father came and took me away. I was then eleven years old. . . . We arrived in Athens and we were all together again. I then saw my cousins from Thessaloniki for the first time as well as my brothers, whom I hadn't seen for some time. When we arrived at the house, I realized that they were getting ready to flee. One day a truck came with other Jews. We got on. There were lots of people—about thirty individuals. We went to the Plaka Lavriou and stayed there some months. One afternoon we came to a little bay. It was raining. A ship was supposed to come to get us. We waited the entire night. It was winter and the rain was torrential. At two in the morning father realized that the ship wouldn't come and that we had to travel at night. We walked to the house of a Greek man and heard dogs barking, without knowing what was happening. The man realized that we were refugees and fed us. He didn't know we were Jews. Then a car came and took us back to Athens, not to the monastery [where I had lived] but to new locations.

We dispersed again, each one in a different house in Nea Smyrni. I remember that I stayed in the house of an old woman at the end of Nea Smyrni next to a mine where the Germans had made a camp. They came with big horses . . . and we children stood by the barbed wires to observe them. One of them gave me a rubber sling. We played there often. One day father came again and took us. We went to Evia on a small boat. There were partisans there who were communists. We stayed in the house of [a woman named] Mary, who was later declared Righteous Among the Nations. There were also Greek soldiers among us who were heading from Evia to Cairo. They took Greeks [aboard] without the knowledge of the boat captains, together with Jews, who paid a lot of money.

Before departing father had collected gold coins, which were sewn onto our coats like buttons. Each button was one lira [English gold sovereign]. The partisans needed money. When we arrived, they began to search us. They took all the liras they found, telling us it was for the revolution. We remained in Evia for a month and a half. . . . One day we saw three or four trucks with Germans, and all the Jews said, "It's over. They are going to get us." Then father said, "If we are saved and I still have money, I'll give it away." Ever since, our family gives scholarships once a year through the B'nai B'rith.

There was a cave that only the locals knew, and when the Germans would come, we went and hid there. The entrance was closed and no one knew that it existed. One evening we went to a [place] where the partisans were hiding. Again they [the partisans] searched us, and we began to fight with them because there was not enough room for everyone on the ship. Fights also started among Jews who were hoping to board, because there were also many soldiers. We succeeded in getting on board.

That night as we navigated among the islands, the partisans said to us, "You Jews have a lot of money; when you get to Turkey, send us guns." They had Italian guns and a few carbines. Suddenly a searchlight turned on us and the captain told us to lie low, covering us with a sail. Perhaps he bribed the Germans. In any case we passed [unde-tected, and soon] arrived at Çeşme, near Izmir. There was a tavern there. We were all hungry. The owner came. After understanding that we hadn't seen so much food for some time [he fed us]. Afterwards many threw up. It was like a theater production.

Afterwards a bus came and picked us up. The trip lasted half an hour until we arrived in Izmir. There was a large camp, which I think the Jewish Agency had begun to organize. There were other Jews there. They told us not to say anything because journalists were coming. The first thing we did was to go to a *hamam* [Turkish bath]. We hadn't washed for a long time. I almost drowned from the steam. Someone came and started to beat me with the loofah. Father explained that it was not a beating but a massage.

We had been in Izmir two to three weeks when they put us on a train and we crossed Turkey. I was so weak that I slept where the lug-gage was stowed. They sold salep[22] in the stations. At the frontier we got on a freight train loaded with animals. English soldiers boarded the cars to guard us—in order to prevent our journey to Palestine—because we were illegals. Now I know that we were in Syria, in Aleppo. My sister Sarah was fifteen years old, my girl cousin sixteen. They were gorgeous, and we sat with our legs outside the cars; the Englishmen spoke with us and two Arabs on horses followed the train and asked father if he wanted to sell one of his daughters. It's funny but true.

We arrived in Palestine via Lebanon in Rosh ha-Nikra. It was the beginning of the spring of 1944. We could smell the oranges: it all seemed very beautiful to us. We arrived in Haifa and from there we continued on to Gaza, to a huge English camp, where refugees and soldiers were housed. We lived in a tent, the whole family together, and the English gave us food, as we hadn't eaten for some time.

We stayed a month and then a small bus came and took us to Tel Aviv. . . . There was a camp for Jewish refugees there. Henrietta Szold welcomed us on behalf of the new immigrant services. They scattered us children across various locations. I was sent to Kibbutz Ramat David. They put me in a room. Not knowing a word of Hebrew, I began to cry out in Greek that I did not have lice and asked why they

---

22. A hot beverage made from the flour of orchid tubers.

had shut me up inside the room. I was the first child to arrive there. Then other people came from Syria, Belgium, [and elsewhere]. . . . I stayed there three years.

Testimony of Haim Cohen, "E zoe ap'ten arche," in *E metanasteuse ton Ellenon Evraion sten Palaistine (1945–1948)*, ed. Ya'akov Schiby and Karina Lampsa (Athens: Alexandria Publications, 2010), 338–40. Translated from Greek by Isaac Nehama.

## 105. THE AFTERMATH OF THE WAR IN TURKEY [1945]

*Though Turkey remained neutral during the Second World War, its Jewish community faced heavy taxation, pauperization, and forced labor as its members watched the war—and the destruction of European Jewry—unfold. In this account an American observer representing the American Jewish Joint Distribution Committee tasked with aiding Jewish war refugees describes a visit to Istanbul shortly after the war's end. Through his letter Istanbul emerges as a vital way station for goods being sent inland to European Jewish communities and as a point of transfer for Jewish refugees looking to emigrate to Palestine or other locations. It also appears as a final destination for hundreds of Jews of Turkish origin who survived the war in Europe on account of their Turkish citizenship and who, after having returned to the country—often after many decades or even a lifetime spent abroad—had to learn to adjust to life in Turkey and seek out a livelihood for themselves.*

Although Turkey has not been ravaged by war, its Jewish population has nevertheless been seriously impoverished in the past two years. Communities like Istanbul and Izmir that for generations maintained their synagogues, hospitals, schools, relief, and other welfare agencies found themselves in 1943 on the verge of closing the doors of these institutions (some, including a number of schools, had already done so), when the JDC came to the rescue.

Another important phase of JDC work has been with Turkish Jewish repatriates. In the spring months of 1944, about 850 repatriates, most of them from France, some from Greece, arrived in Istanbul. By virtue of their Turkish nationality status, they had been permitted to leave German-occupied France and Greece and were accepted for repatriation by the authorities here. However, most of the group has had a difficult time obtaining work or making a living and their adjustment to the local scene from which many had been away a good part of their lives—in some instances all of their lives—has been an extremely difficult one. Today, after having been here more than a year, there are still 192 people on the relief rolls at a cost to the JDC of about 2500 dollars per month and this is half of what the costs were six months ago.

Subsidies to the local institutions in Turkey and the program for repatriates has cost the JDC about 250,000 dollars in the past two years. This figure might have been even higher, but for the good work carried on by the *Caisse de Petits Prêts*—the Jewish small loan societies, branches of which exist in Istanbul, Izmir, and Edirne. This society, as the name indicates, grants small loans to petty shop keepers, trades people, and artisans, and thus enables many of these people to provide for themselves where they might otherwise have had to apply for relief. The *Caisse de Petits Prêts* and its various branches were established with JDC loan grants in the early 1920s.

Conditions of local Jewry seem to be bettering themselves somewhat in recent months and we are hopeful that our grants here will be materially reduced in the period ahead.

A situation of special interest occurred during the second week of April 1945 when the *Drottningholm*, a Swedish diplomatic liner, docked at Istanbul.

The ship carried, among its other passengers, 146 Jewish refugees. Everyone of them—men, women, and children—had been taken directly from the unspeakably horrible German concentration camps of Auschwitz, Bergen Belsen, Buchenwald, and Ravensbruck and placed on board the *Drottningholm*. But for this fortunate circumstance, many of these people would undoubtedly have met the tragic fate that was meted out to the other inmates of the camps in the days immediately preceding Nazi capitulation.

Jacob Trobe, another JDC representative, then in Istanbul, and I boarded the ship on its arrival. The excitement and joy that swept the entire group when it learned we were "Joint" representatives is difficult to describe. They gathered round us as if we were God's chosen disciples. Seldom have I felt so humble. And seldom have I been so proud—proud to be connected with an agency the mention of whose very name instantly could produce so much happiness.

The Turkish nationality of 116 members of this group is being presently investigated by the authorities here. Pending a decision, they are not permitted free movement, but must remain in the vicinity of the hotels where they are staying. The full cost of their support, which is being paid for by the JDC is running about 500 dollars per day. Should the authorities grant permission to these people to remain in Turkey, they will of course be moved out of the hotels, and we hope that work will be obtained for many, thereby reducing considerably the present heavy costs of their maintenance.

Heretofore, a very special chapter of JDC's program in Turkey was the assistance extended to refugees *en route* from the Balkans to Palestine. Almost 9000 of them coming by rail and ship stopped at Istanbul for several days and in some cases for weeks before arrangements for the continuance of their trip could be made. Such movement has for the time being ceased, but we are, of course, on the alert and the community is thoroughly organized to again assist in any new migration that may come through Istanbul in transit to Palestine or any other country. . . .

With all good wishes,

Sincerely,

Arthur Fishzohn

Letter by Arthur Fishzohn to Henry C. Bernstein, May 24, 1945, United States Holocaust Memorial Museum Archive (Washington, D.C.), Selected records from the American Jewish Joint Distribution Committee (AJJDC) Archives (Jerusalem), 1937–1966, RG-68.066M, IS/ 7/1. Courtesy of the American Jewish Joint Distribution Committee. Original in English.

## 106.  YOUR DRESS ON ANOTHER'S BACK: WARTIME MEMORIES OF A JEWISH WOMAN IN MONASTIR {1943–1945}

*Timelines clearly track the increasingly draconian restrictions placed upon Jews living in territories occupied by or allied with the Third Reich. More difficult to measure is the dehumanization experienced by individual Jewish women, men, and children. Here Jamila Kolonomos (1922–2013), a Sephardi Jewish woman from Monastir (Bitola) who survived the war as a partisan, describes the pain she experienced before and during the Second World War as loved ones emigrated under duress, her family slipped into extreme poverty, and those closest to her were deported to the death camps. (For Kolonomos' account of her time as a partisan see source 96.)*

In 1940 in Monastir there were 737 Jewish families with 3,264 members. There were 394 families without means, and they lived on the charity of the more affluent communities of Yugoslavia. Until the end Monastir remained the poorest community. For this reason, from 1935 to 1940, many Jews emigrated to other countries. Four hundred twenty-nine Jews went to Palestine, and with them went our dressmaker and friend Madame Dudu.

In Monastir, after elementary school, many girls would go learn a vocation, which very often was learning to sew. As a result, there were many dressmakers of all levels of skill. The best was Madame Dudu. All the prominent women of the city, Jewish and Christian, were her clients. Madame Dudu was widowed while still young, and raised a daughter by herself. She worked day and night to sustain family and home. She was my mother's age. They loved each other and were like sisters. Before she married and came to Monastir from Skopje, my mother was a seamstress and sewed bed sheets and pillowcases—the "whites"—for dowries.

Madame Dudu brocaded, did needlepoint, and ironed materials for weddings. She only sewed dresses for holidays, engagements, weddings, balls, and other ceremonies. She always came to our house to sew. On such days nice meals and desserts were prepared. They chatted while sewing. Madame Dudu always came one week after *Purim* to sew for my mother, my sisters Bela and Rachela, and for me. Thus *Pesach* [Passover] was the day to show off the new dresses.

Madame Dudu worked fast and, for this reason, all wanted and loved her. But she harbored a great yearning: Her daughter was somewhat retiring, shy, very modest, didn't socialize with anyone, and was tied to her mother's skirts. She was good and decent—*Era buena komo el pan*—good like bread, as we say. But they couldn't find a husband for her, and the years passed and stretched. For this reason, poor Madame Dudu decided to go to Palestine. The word going around was that many more young men were to be found there. It is possible that that's where her luck was!

Before getting ready to leave, Madame Dudu came to see my mother and begged her to buy silk for a dress she would sew for her, a dress to remind my mother of her all the holidays. Said and done! She sewed a dress in the "Charleston" fashion, of black silk and using silken thread, *sirma* (wire), and blue silk, embroidered a peacock's tail. Truly, a work of art. All who saw it marveled. "*Es manos de oro ke lo fizyeron*" ("Hands of gold made it"), said my mother. For her it was the best present, she much appreciated it, and wore it with great joy.

The day to leave for Palestine finally arrived. Madame Dudu and her daughter came to dinner at our house. Before giving them our presents, we exchanged embraces for the last time. After a few months, we received the good news that her daughter was married, thus realizing her dream. After that we heard nothing more. Every time my mother wore the dress, it was an occasion for reminiscing.

*Pesach* of 1940 was the last time the Monastirlis celebrated this holiday before the *Shoah*. The entire family gathered in our house, including my father's sisters Rebeka and Ana. My mother prepared the table with the tray in which she had put: *boyos* (pastries, usually with a filling of spinach), *alharosa* (*haroset*—a blend of fruits and nuts), *apyo* (horseradish), *un guevo inhaminado* (a hardboiled egg), and *una pyerna di gayina* (the heel of a chicken leg). She covered it with a white napkin, embroidered with silver thread and blue flowers, and, in the center, a yellow Star of David. Who knows how many years she had this napkin to use only for *Pesach*. The Paschal wine, *las masas* (matzoth), the *boyos*, the *Pesach* utensils for eating and drinking—all were arranged around the table.

My father—*la Agada* (the Haggada) in his hands, *il tale* (the *talith*) around his shoulders—gave the sign for all to sit, to listen and take part in the ceremony (the *Seder*) of the eve of *Pesach*. My mother, wearing the dress made by Madame Dudu, beautiful and happy seeing all of us together, would flit from one person to the next, carrying the basin for hand washing, serving the *haroset*, *apyo*, wine, and, finally, the meal cooked in our oven. Afterwards, we all sang "*el kavretiko*" ("The Kid"—the folk song *Had Gadya*, sung in Ladino at the end of the meal on *Pesach*).

My mother was thin, and suffered from heart disease. She took to her bed. In March 1940, my sister Bela became engaged. My mother wanted to have a nice engagement party with all the family and friends. My father granted her wish, knowing that she would not live very much longer. She arose from bed, we put on her the dress embroidered by Madame Dudu, and sat her with all the guests. She was happy to marry off the first daughter. She greeted everyone.

A short time later, in February 1941, she died in my arms. In deep mourning, we sat in *syete* (*shiva*, the period of mourning lasting seven days). She was fortunate, dying one month before the Germans came. She didn't see what happened to us after that. On the day of her death the women came in the evening to wash her and put her inside the shroud. They left only a hand on the outside for us to kiss for the last time. All the while, the women were *indichando*—lamenting in grief and asked us for a dress to cover her. We gave them the dress made by Madame Dudu, the one she liked most of all.[23] We had made an effort, for a long time, to ease her pains and worries, and all loved her.

Thus, we parted forever from my mother, Esterina. Rabbi Peres (Isaac) Russo recited the *kadish*. He gave a great eulogy and all who attended were moved.

The Germans and Bulgarian Fascists came shortly afterwards and so began *los diyas pretos*—the black days—for the Jews of Monastir. My father collected all my mother's things and took them to the neighbor, a Vlach, a female friend of my mother.

On 11 March 1943, the rest of my family, along with all the other Jews from Monastir, Skopje, and Shtip were deported to the Treblinka death camp, from which no one survived.

In 1945, when I returned from the Resistance, alone, with nothing, hunger forced me to sell the few things my father had left. I sold mother's dresses, one by one, in the bazaar.

Finally, the time came to sell the last dress, the one that was much loved and beautifully embroidered by Madame Dudu. With a heavy heart I took it, pressing it to my bosom, and with tears in my eyes, I walked the streets. I felt my mother's breath, and I saw before my eyes the holidays and imagined how she was dressed. I wavered *"Ke lo vende, ke no lo vende!?"* ("Shall I sell it, shall I not sell it?"). Then a voice was telling me, *"Va, los chikos stan fambrentos."* ("Go ahead, the little ones are hungry.") At that moment, a young woman passed in front of me, wearing an expensive blue dress, which I recognized. I started to turn right, and she turned around, and what did I see? A dress of mine with the monogram embroidered by me. I was shaken and embittered, as if hit by lightning—I was out of my mind. Running, I went to the bazaar and sold the last dress to the first village woman I met, for a little flour, two eggs, and a scoop of butter. How much I wanted to hold the dress

---

23. According to Jewish custom, the dead are buried in a plain shroud. The dress covering Jamila's mother's corpse was therefore removed before burial and returned to the family.

against me! But worse pains and indignities that we can never forget had befallen us—our loved ones who would never return. . . .

Jamila Kolonomos, *Monastir Without Jews: Recollections of a Jewish Partisan in Macedonia*, ed. Robert Bedford and trans. by Isaac Nehama and Brian Berman (New York: Foundation for the Advancement of Sephardic Studies and Culture, 2008), 51–55.

## 107. THE TRIAL OF A NAZI COLLABORATOR [1946]

*Created and imbued with authority by the United States, the Soviet Union, and the United Kingdom, the International Military Tribunal (IMT) tried twenty-two major war criminals between October 1945 and October 1946. An additional twelve high-ranking German officials were tried by American prosecutors working under the aegis of the IMT from December 1946 to April 1949. An overwhelming proportion of the trials that resulted were of low-level officials. Only one Jewish collaborator was formally tried for his crimes at the behest of a Jewish community: Vital Hasson. A native of Salonica and a tailor by trade, Hasson had served the Nazi authorities as they targeted Salonican Jews for persecution and deportation and was known for his sadistic behavior, which included the rape of Jewish girls and women. One Jewish witness at Hasson's trial, which came before Greek courts in Athens, claimed that: "Hasson was more powerful than the Germans, [and] that the Germans stood at attention before him." Hasson, whose trial record notes that he smiled repeatedly throughout the proceedings, was found guilty of the charges against him. He was executed in Corfu in March 1948.*

Karasso (witness for the prosecution): I am a victim. I was hiding in the house of a Greek friend, Anastassios Maretis, together with my entire family. This friend informed us about the deportations of the Jews and about the situation in general. Maretis was arrested on the first Sunday in June and was accused of hiding us. At this point, we were warned to disappear. We then thought of going to some village. Unfortunately, we did not have time to escape. Hasson came by car to the house where we were hiding, accompanied by two Germans in civilian clothes. They broke down the doors and arrested all of us—that is, myself, my father, my mother, my sister, and all the others. Hasson started to beat us, as well as the owner, Maretis. Maretis had been betrayed by a member of the "Security Battalion" (Greek collaborators) under Poulos and after being severely beaten, admitted that he was hiding us in his home. When they took us away, shoving, and kicking us, they put us in two cars and took us to the Baron Hirsch camp. Hasson was driving the car. During the ride, we complained to him about what he was doing and he replied that there was one way we could save ourselves: tell him where our gold was hidden. When we arrived at the Baron Hirsch camp, we were interrogated. They started to severely beat us, using a whip. The Germans did not beat us as much as Hasson did. They beat all of us. They took the gold that we had hidden in the heel[s] of our shoes. But they were not satisfied and continued to hit us to make us tell them where we had some gold bracelets. They even searched the women's genitals for gold. They did this to all of the women, to the little girls and my elderly mother, too. After this horrible scene, the women were taken to a barrack and the men thrown into a basement cell, where they were told that they would be shot. We had no contact with anyone in this cell for a whole day. As I learned from my wife while still in jail, Hasson proposed to her a scheme to free us. She and her sister should surrender to the Germans and to Hasson.

At this time, the judge turns to Hasson's wife, who is among the defendants, and says ironically, "Behold this guy!"

Witness: I warned my wife to keep away from Hasson and not to pay any attention to what he was saying. They should die rather than submit. Hasson made these proposals daily. Such orgies took place every day, for which Hasson and his organs were responsible. They would enter the camp and get any girl they liked and do with her anything they wanted. After being detained in the cell for three weeks, they took us out and we remained in the camp.

Judge: What else did Hasson do?

Witness: He went regularly to other towns together with others and would bring back Jews who had been hiding in various villages. There were some 165 of us in the camp and we were waiting for those who had been sent to labor camps in Thives and elsewhere in Thessaly, so that there would be a sufficient number to send a convoy to Poland. These workers returned to Thessaloniki nearly naked, hungry and in terrible condition. Their families that had already been deported to Poland had left some packages for them in the hands of acquaintances. When Hasson found out about these packages, he threatened the people who were holding them. He took the packages from them and sold them. On 7 and 8 August, once the required number of men had been reached, they put us

into sealed cars and sent us to Birkenau. We were locked into the
cars and bound with chains.

Judge: Did you see whether the Germans marked the place from
where the people were sent for execution?

Witness: I had heard about that. It was done in our case. My wife had
been afraid and anxious and very sad for about two months. She
was inconsolable. I could not understand what was the matter with
her. Finally, one day, as I insisted, she told me that Hasson had
handed her over to the Germans, together with her sisters.

The witness then states that the Germans separated the men from the
women when they arrived in Poland. Those who were not fit to work
were put in cars or walked to their ultimate destiny. We had the impression that nothing bad would happen to those who were being
transported by car. Unfortunately, they were leading us, and those in
the cars, to a swift death. We men who had been led away on foot for
Birkenau were left naked one whole night and we were freezing. The
next day, we found some Greeks and asked them about our parents
who had been transported by car. They told us not to ask about them.
Just look after yourselves, they said. Don't think about them. Try to
save yourselves. Then they took us to the showers and gave us some
rags to wear. We were terrorized in Birkenau. Many criminals from
various countries and of different religions would savagely beat the inmates so as to exterminate the Jews, whom they did not allow to come
into contact with older inmates. Some Jews who were electricians told
us that the chimneys that we saw were the crematoria, where people
enter and disappear. From that moment on, we lost all hope of salvation, because the crematoria were for us.

Judge: What kind of work did you do there?

Witness: We stayed in that camp for fifteen days, and then they sent
some 500 Greek Jews to Warsaw to clean up the ghetto. In the interval between the first of September and January, my two brothers
died of hunger and suffering. Meanwhile, of course, the other members of my family who had been transported by car had been thrown
into the crematoria. Out of the nine members of my family, I was the
only one to survive. As the resistance activities of the Poles had increased, the Germans transported us to Dachau, where we stayed for
a few days in a labor camp. We had to carry enormous tree trunks,

and when we complained, we were savagely beaten. Between four
and five inmates died every evening from the torture and hard work.
Prosecutor: Who appointed Hasson to the militia? The Germans?
Witness: The Germans never made anyone enter the militia. Most of
the militia members were volunteers, because it was said that they
would get special treatment from the Germans as the privileged
ones and be deported last. Most of the members who were deported
to the camps not only came back safe and sound, but also brought
back the children born in the camps. If Greeks had been members
of the militia, surely the Jews' convoys would have been delayed and
many Jews would have been saved, because in six months, many
would have been able to join the Greek resistance in the mountains.

To a question from the judge, the witness states that Hasson did not
have a job, but lived from his black market profits.

Judge: What do you know about Albala?
Witness: Just like Hasson, he was inhumane and had no feelings. He
offered his services to the Germans like Hasson did. . . .

The defense tries hard to question the witness in order to extract some
statement favorable to its clients.

The witness gives the proper response to the defense's questions
and stresses that all the defendants harmed their fellow Jews, and that
Hasson bears the greatest responsibility.

When questioned by the defense about Hasson's father and sister,
who was married to Sarfati, the witness states that he does not know
anything specific, but wonders how Hasson's father and sister managed
to survive and returned from the camps, when so many Jews, and especially the elderly, were sent to the crematoria.

"The Hasson Trial" (July 2, 1946), Accession #2003.4, 12–14, United States Holocaust Memorial
Museum Archive (Washington, D.C.).

## 108. IN THE DP CAMPS: AN EARLY INTERVIEW WITH
## A SEPHARDI HOLOCAUST SURVIVOR [1946]

*Born in Libau (Liepāja in present-day Latvia), David Boder (né Aron Mendel
Michelson) (1886–1961) studied and taught psychology in Germany, Russia, and
Mexico before pursuing a master's degree and Ph.D. in this subject from the Uni-*

*versity of Chicago and Northwestern University, respectively. In the immediate aftermath of the war he sought to create a record of wartime suffering, explore the effects of extreme trauma on individual personalities, and communicate to American audiences the story of the Holocaust. In 1946, Boder traveled to France, Switzerland, Italy, and Germany, interviewing 130 subjects in a number of displaced persons camps. He recorded the results on wire recorder, producing the earliest known audio recordings of Holocaust survivors. Although Boder conducted most of his interviews with Jews of Eastern European origin, here we read one of the few interviews he conducted with Sephardi survivors from Greece.*

## Nino Barzilai, August 4, 1946

David Boder: [In English] Paris, August the 4th, Sunday, in the home for adult Jews. We are now going to interview a gentleman from Greece, Señor Nino Barzilai . . . who speaks Spanish.

David Boder: [In Spanish] Mr. Barzilai, can you tell me if you were born in Greece?

Nino Barzilai: Yes, Sir. I was born in Thessaloniki [Salonica], Greece.

David Boder: How old are you now?

Nino Barzilai: Fifty-four years old.

David Boder: Oh, you are fifty-four! You don't look . . . you don't seem that age! So, tell me . . . have you always lived in Greece?

Nino Barzilai: No, Sir. I lived in Spain for twenty years. When the war was declared—the Spanish Civil War—I came back to Greece where I had family.

David Boder: Are you married?

Nino Barzilai: Yes, sir. I have a fifteen-year-old son.

David Boder: What about your wife?

Nino Barzilai: My wife is also here with me.

David Boder: They are here with you. So, please tell us . . . how were you affected by the occupation of Greece by Germans?

Nino Barzilai: Well . . . you see . . . as I have told you, we came back to Greece because we had some relatives, and we were going to wait until the end of the Spanish Civil War to come back to our place. When we arrived in Greece, the Italian-Greek War started and, naturally, we had no chance of returning to Spain, either because communications had been interrupted or because the Civil War had not come to an end in Spain.

David Boder: And what did you do for a living, Mr. Barzilai?

Nino Barzilai: In Greece I sold fabrics for women's garments. I was well established. . . . I had my own office. . . .

David Boder: In Greece.

Nino Barzilai: In Greece, Athens, near [unintelligible].[24]

David Boder: And what did you do in Spain?

Nino Barzilai: In Spain I was in the jewelry business.

David Boder: So, you came back to Greece. Were the Germans already there?

Nino Barzilai: When I came back to Greece, the Germans had not invaded yet.

David Boder: OK, then . . .

Nino Barzilai: Later the Italian War started. . . . Italy and Greece, and then after some time the Germans came and occupied Greece. We left Salonica [sic] and moved to Athens, where we settled. As I told you I had a nice business there, but when the Germans came, they published an announcement in the newspapers: all Jews were summoned and they had to present themselves as Portuguese foreign subjects, so I had to do so. . . .

David Boder: Are you Portuguese?

Nino Barzilai: Yes, I am.

David Boder: Were you born in Portugal?

Nino Barzilai: No, Sir. I am . . . [unintelligible] . . . my family was from . . . [unintelligible] . . . so . . . I presented myself to the German authorities as Portuguese, with Portuguese documents. And since the chief rabbi was a relative of mine and happened to have the same name as my father, the Germans took me for the rabbi's son. They sent me to a concentration camp in Haidari, Athens, where I spent five and a half months performing forced labor.

David Boder: What kind of labor did you perform at the concentration camp?

Nino Barzilai: We had to move stones and sand during the whole day from one place to another. It was hard and we were hit and punished a lot.

David Boder: What did you do with the sand?

---

24. The notation ". . . [unintelligible] . . ." marks words or exchanges Boder and his researchers were unable to make out from the original recording.

Nino Barzilai: They "invented" this job for us to work, so as to wear us out, because we transported stones from one place to another, and the following day we would move the same stones back to their original place. We were not working on the fortification nor doing any other tasks: we just carried stones and they made us work every day. . . .

  After more than five and a half months in the Haidari concentration camp, all Jews from Athens were brought to the same camp. We were together . . . for about eight days . . . all Jews coming from Athens.

David Boder: Still in Greece?

Nino Barzilai: Yes. In Greece. And the day of our deportation came . . . we were woken up at four in the morning and we were given ten minutes to prepare for our departure.

David Boder: How many people do you think there were in that camp?

Nino Barzilai: I think there were around two thousand people.

David Boder: Two thousand Jews. Look, Mr. Barzilai, in this research we usually do not speak about the mem— . . . about papers, but since you have the memorandum about Jews in Greece and we do not know much about this, we are going to make an exception and I will ask you to read the memorandum you have here.

Nino Barzilai: Allow me to tell you that in the convoy that was sent to Poland all foreign subjects were included and we were sent in a separate convoy. This means the Argentine subjects stayed in the Haidari camp while the Spanish and Portuguese subjects were placed on a separate train and were informed that we would be sent to Spain and Portugal in a period of twelve days. After having traveled for eight days by train, we arrived in Germany. We were taken to Bergen-Belsen camp where we were held for fourteen months. . . .

  As I told you, we were there for fourteen months and we were placed on a train and we were told we were to be taken to Spain, but we arrived in Börgermoor. There, we experienced a number of bombings by Americans that lasted for a whole night. In the morning when we woke up, we noticed the Germans had left the train and we had been left on our own in the camp . . . completely abandoned. A number of us marched to some nearby German houses in order to see what was going on. We were looking for some food, because we did not cook and we had eaten all the food we had been given for the journey. We found some potatoes and we came back to the train where we boiled them to eat something. Meanwhile, there was a rumor that the Americans had arrived. And some time later we happily received the Americans who had come. . . .

David Boder: And what are you doing now, Sir?

Nino Barzilai: We are still in the center, located on [unintelligible] Street. We still have not found a house in which to settle. My son is learning a trade in the French school.

David Boder: What trade is he learning?

Nino Barzilai: Woodworking.

David Boder: Oh, woodworking.

Nino Barzilai: As I am an electrician, I have been given a job.

David Boder: So you are working.

Nino Barzilai: Well, I will soon start to work. We believe we can stay here in France, in this area.

David Boder: To settle here.

Nino Barzilai: Yes. To settle here. I have a list that will be of great interest to all Jews from Greece who are still abroad. It is a list of the few Jews that returned to Greece in each Greek province. It includes the inhabitants before the war, and the ones left or those who returned.

David Boder: Good.

Nino Barzilai: In the Province of Didymoteicho, there were 900 Jews, and thirty-three have returned to date, so 96 percent are missing. In Orestiada town [audio interruption] . . . three have returned, 98 percent are still missing. In Alexandroupoli, 140 Jews, 97 percent are missing; in Komotini, there were 819 [Jews], twenty-eight have returned, [which means that] 96 percent are missing; in Xanthi, 550, six have returned, 99 percent are missing; in Macedonia, in Kavala, there were 2,100 Jews. Forty-two have returned, 98 percent are missing; in Drama, 1,200, seventy-nine have returned, 97 percent missing; [unintelligible] 600, only three have returned, 98 percent missing; in Thessaloniki, the great Jewish community, there were 56,000, 1,950 have returned, 96 percent are missing.

David Boder: Ninety-six percent missing?

Nino Barzilai: Missing, Sir. Veroia, 460 Jews, 131 have returned. . . .

David Boder: Well, Sir. . . .

Nino Barzilai: Thirty-two percent.

David Boder: Can you give me a copy of this document or can we get it somewhere?

Nino Barzilai: I will be pleased to give it to you, Sir.

David Boder: All right.

Nino Barzilai: I will give you the copy. Let's continue . . . Kastoria, 900 Jews, thirty-five have returned, 96 percent missing; Florina, 400 Jews, seventy-four have returned, 84 percent; Thessalia, 520, 360, 31 percent.

David Boder, interview with Nino Barzilai at the Jewish Committee home for adult Jewish refugees, Paris, August 4, 1946. Interview is adapted from the Spanish translation of David Boder. Accessed from Voices of the Holocaust project, http://voices.iit.edu/interviewee?doc=barzilaiN.

## 109. A TURKISH JEWISH CHILD SURVIVOR WRITES HIS "GODMOTHER" IN THE UNITED STATES [1948]

*Formed in 1934 in New York City by Yiddish-speaking labor organizers, the Jewish Labor Committee sought to aid the fight against Nazism and support Jews who fell within its dragnet. After the war the organization turned its attention to the crisis of Jewish refugees, organizing, with the aid of the American Federation of Labor, the Child Adoption Program. The children in this program were not formally adopted but rather supported by donors in America. For $300 a year an individual or organization could contribute to the care of a designated child, thousands of whom were supported in this manner. Here a Turkish Jewish orphan in Paris writes in English to his "godmother" in the United States to thank her for sponsoring him and report to her about his daily activities.*

[Undated]

Dear Godmother,

Only a few words to give you some news about myself; these news are good, and I hope for the same for you. I am going to school but not for long now because summer vacations are approaching fast. I am glad to have a godmother in America. As it is I can consider her as a member of my family. I thank you for the packages which you sent me already and give you a hearty hug.

Your godson Edmond

Paris, July 8, 1948

Dear Godmother:

I am writing to you to give you news about myself. I am all right and hope the same for you.

I am very glad because I am going on summer vacation. I am leaving in two days for a whole month. I will write to you on my return to tell you whether I had a good time. There is nothing more to write for today, and I kiss you,

your godson Edmond

Letters from Edmond Altabef, Jewish Labor Committee Records, Tamiment Library/Robert F. Wagner Labor Archives, New York University (New York City), Record Group 67.002M, "Jewish Labor Committee, Child Adoption Files," Box 118, Folder Altabef, Edmond, accessed at the United States Holocaust Memorial Museum.

# V. DIASPORIC AND ÉMIGRÉ CIRCLES

## 110.  FOUNDING THE FEDERATION OF ORIENTAL
## JEWS IN NEW YORK CITY [1911]

*In the early twentieth century, tens of thousands of Jews from the Ottoman Empire
began arriving in New York City in search of economic betterment. Many attributed
their migration to new laws mandating the universal conscription of non-Muslim
men into the Ottoman army at a time when the empire was embroiled in three successive wars, including its conflict with Italy over Libya in 1911 and the two Balkan
Wars of 1912–1913. In New York as in other American Sephardi émigré centers new
philanthropic organizations arose to meet the needs of this new immigrant population. Certain of these institutions mirrored those that had been created for the mass
of Eastern European Jewish immigrants who settled in New York City beginning in
the 1880s. In early 1911 the Hebrew Immigrant Aid Society established the Bureau for
Sephardic Jewish Immigrants (later the Oriental Bureau); the following year, prominent Levantine Jewish activists created the Federation of Oriental Jews, with the
Istanbul-born Joseph Gedalecia as its first president. The foundation announced its
aim as the "Americanization and betterment of the condition of Oriental Jews." (For
more on Gedalecia see source 118.)*

Whereas the maxim that in union there is strength has been repeatedly
demonstrated in the annals of the history of civilization

And whereas improvement in social and economic conditions of the
Oriental Jews in the United States can only be obtained by conservative action and united endeavor

And whereas there is a crying need for improvement in the physical,
social, and economic and industrial conditions for the Jews from the
Levant

We, the undersigned delegates, in convention duly assembled, hereby adopt this Constitution.

Sec. 1. The name of this Organization shall be known as the Federation of the Oriental Jews of America; the headquarters shall be in
the City of New York.

Sec. 2. Its object shall be the improvement in economic, industrial,
educational, civic and religious conditions of the Oriental Jewish
Community in the United States of America. With these purposes in view this Federation shall charge itself with the duty of
spreading information and securing for the Oriental Jews in the
United States of America means whereby their industrial, social,
and educational conditions may be improved. It shall be the duty

of this Federation to instruct the newly arrived immigrants from the Orient in the laws and institutions of this free country; to obtain for them an opportunity for evening classes for instruction of English; and Talmud Torahs for proper religious instruction. It shall be the duty of this Federation to charge itself with the supervision of all activities which tend to be beneficial to the Oriental Jews of America. . . .

Proposed Constitution of the Federation of Oriental Jews, 1911. Courtesy of the Library at the Herbert J. Katz Center for Advanced Judaic Studies, University of Pennsylvania (Philadelphia). Original in English.

## 111. WILL THE OLD SEPHARDIM WELCOME THE NEW? A SERMON TO NEW YORK'S OLDEST JEWISH CONGREGATION (1912)

*The earliest Jewish community in North America dates to 1654, when twenty-three Sephardi refugees fleeing the Portuguese Inquisition left Recife, Brazil, for New Amsterdam (later New York City). Known as the Old Sephardim, their descendants as well as other Jews of Spanish and Portuguese origin founded the first congregations in what would later become the United States. The second immigrant wave of Sephardi Jews included those who arrived in the country from the Ottoman Empire and its successor states in the first quarter of the twentieth century. By this time the Old Sephardim were a largely acculturated, Anglophone, and affluent community, whereas the New Sephardim were mostly working-class, often reached the United States knowing little to no English, and were easily recognizable as immigrants. In the sermon excerpted here Dr. David de Sola Pool (1917–1984), the rabbi of the Spanish and Portuguese Synagogue Shearith Israel, New York City's first Sephardi synagogue, urges the Old Sephardim to welcome their Ottoman coreligionists with open arms, suggesting that the recent newcomers might infuse new life into his dwindling congregation.*

Everyone who passes among those numbered from twenty years old and upward shall give his tribute to the Lord.[1]

. . . As we number the congregation and lament that the young do not always take the place of the old trusted warriors who are taken from us, shall we not aver that no congregation can live wholly on its inherited forces? Every historic community needs accretions from

---

1. Exodus 30:14.

without if it is to endure in vigor. Throughout the two hundred and fifty years of our existence as a congregation, the requisite rejuvenation has been infused into us in every generation by the coming of a new member here, a fresh family there, and from time to time even of a small immigrating band of families. But at this moment there is presented to the congregation a more wonderful opportunity of gathering into its ranks new warriors to serve in God's cause than it has known ever before. For there have come thronging to our doors ten thousand of our nearest kin, able and willing to offer the same service to the Lord as the founders of this congregation gave. We dare no longer rest supine on the decaying merit of past achievement. We shall be culpably false to our duty if we sit inertly dreaming of our past or passing warriors, if we number our people by the nominal membership list, while ten thousand of these, our own closest brethren, have come to our doors awaiting a word of welcome. It is true that we welcome anyone and everyone who comes to us prepared to serve God with our ancient traditional forms of service. But before all we should welcome those of our brethren, be they poor as Hillel or of as lowly birth as the prophet Amos, whose ritual is our own, whose Hebrew accent is our own, whose traditions are our own, and whose ancestry and history are our own.

It is the most urgent and imperative duty of our congregation to-day not to stand passively aloof awaiting their coming to us, but to go out to them offering a friendly, helping hand of welcome. For our own future as a congregation and for their future as faithful servitors of God in this land of unknown trials, we are obligated with the sacred force of moral and religious compulsion to go out to them and bring them to us to unite together in the service of God. Some of the active members of our congregation are awakening to this unique opportunity of swelling the ranks of those who may be counted as offering our Sephardi tribute of service to the Lord; but to the shame of our men be it said that the realization of this new responsibility has been left largely to the women of the Sisterhood.

The religious organization of our Oriental kith and kin is a labor that calls immediately for the most willing and energetic service of the whole congregation, men, women and children. It is a work that demands the tact born of sympathy, the self-sacrifice born of human love, and the truest feeling of brotherhood born of love of God. If this God-given opportunity of numbering living Jewish men and women able to give service to God, and of no longer counting by a meaningless list of names, be neglected by the members of the synagogue, then woe for the congregation upon which will fall the stroke of God, as it fell upon King David and his people when they were numbered in pride without giving to God the tribute of service.

But if we as a congregation undertake this work of the religious organization of these Oriental Jews, then shall the blessing of God fall upon us as we number no longer the inert members on the list, but the living active men of twenty years old and upwards who are able to give their tribute of service unto the Lord. Then shall our community blossom forth into a new life that shall be brilliant and glorious; and, when we number the people, there will be fulfilled in us the ancient blessing: "May the Lord, God of your fathers, add to you the like of you a thousand times, and bless you as he has promised to you."[2]

Rev. Dr. D. de Sola Pool, *"The Numbering of the People: The Congregation's Paramount Duty."* *Sermon preached in the Spanish and Portuguese Synagogue Shearith Israel, Central Park West and Seventieth St., New York City, on Sabbath Ki Tissa, 20 Adar 5672, March 9, 1912* (New York: The Synagogue, 1912), 1, 3–4. Original in English.

## 112. AN OTTOMAN JEWISH IMMIGRANT IN NEW YORK CITY DISCOVERS SIGN LANGUAGE {1910s}

*Born in the Ottoman Anatolian town of Milas, Albert Amateau (1890–1996) emigrated to New York City as a young man. This selection of an oral history conducted by Rachel Amado Bortnick in 1986 describes Amateu's first encounter with deaf peers. With his wife, Rebecca Nahoum Amateau (1894–1976), Albert Amateau would go on to act as a pivotal hearing leader of the Jewish deaf, working as executive director of New York's Society for the Welfare of the Jewish Deaf (from 1913 to 1925), an editor of The Jewish Deaf, and after his ordination as rabbi by the Jewish Theological Seminary in New York serving as the first rabbi of a congregation for deaf Jews (known first as the Hebrew Congregation for the Deaf and, later, as the New York Society of the Deaf), to whom he delivered sermons in sign language. Subsequently, Amateau also served as a leader of the Sephardic Brotherhood of America. The following vignette illustrates how many forms of Jewish difference constituted the*

2. Deuteronomy 1:11.

*immigrant milieu, with an Ottoman Sephardi young man becoming entranced by a Jewish subculture he never knew existed.*

Rachel Amado Bortnick: Let's go back to your life [as a young man] here.

Albert J. Amateau: . . . You know what a settlement house is?

Rachel Amado Bortnick: I've heard about them.

Albert J. Amateau: Like a big club, like a YMCA. They were constructed in the East Side, in the quarters where there were mostly immigrant[s], to try to Americanize them. . . . because the Board of Education didn't have classes for adults. The young children could go to school, but the mothers and fathers, the elders, the adults, could not go to school unless they paid—there were private schools. These settlement houses—they had social workers who did nursing in the neighborhood to people who were sick or who were pregnant, or people who had problems, [which] the[y] discussed with them, trying to Americanize them gradually.

Rachel Amado Bortnick: Who operated them?

Albert J. Amateau: The Universities. Now that University Settlement was operated by Columbia University, downtown. They had a director, social workers, doctors, lawyers, everything. If an immigrant had some trouble with the law, he came there, they listened to him, they helped him. They tried in every way to become helpful to the immigrants in the neighborhood and gradually they established evening classes to teach English. I used to go there because they had a beautiful library. [I would] sit there and read, and sometimes I used to take a walk on the East Side. And one day, I'm coming back. . . . So I come under the elevated railroad on Allen Street and Rivington, and I see across the street three young men and a girl gesticulating [demonstrates.] I looked—I never saw anything like this. One of them got angry or annoyed at me. He put his tongue out at me, so I went near him and saw him writing. I asked for the paper, I wrote down, "I beg your pardon, I didn't mean to be nosy. I was curious. I've never seen people communicating with their hands."

He wrote back: "We are deaf and mute. We are communicating in sign language. We live in this neighborhood and we come here

under the elevated [railroad]. We socialize, when we're not working, because the noise of the elevated doesn't bother us—the hearing people cannot stand it." [laughs] . . . So, I said, "Why don't
you come to the settlement house and meet there instead of in the
street?" They don't know what a settlement house is.

All right. "Are you here every day?" Yes. All right. So I went to
the director and told him what happened. I said, "Why don't you
give them a room? Let them come and meet here. Why should
they meet in the street?" He says, "By all means, provided you become responsible for them. You attend their meeting."

I said, "All right, I'll try." So I started to attend their meeting
and I made a list of words and I asked them to teach me to say
these words. And I found out that in addition to knowing how
to make the gestures, you have to have good eyesight, and quick
eyesight to catch the gestures and interpret it in your own mind.
He said [Amateau gestures in sign language], "I . . . am . . . a very
. . . good . . . man." [Continues to show in sign language] You . . .
came . . . (that's past: [showing] come . . . came . . . You . . . came
here . . . today . . . to look . . . to interrogate . . . me . . . about . . .
(look at these gestures) about . . . Spanish . . . Jews . . . See?

Yeah, but when they go very fast it's not so easy to catch it and
translate it. When they are doing this with their fingers they're only
spelling. The language is gestures. This is [showing] A, B, C, D,
and so on. You saw that card before.

Well, a couple of times some of these fellows asked me if I'd
go with them to a prospective employer to talk for them and say,
"Look, he can't talk but he can do your work, why don't you give
him a chance?" and so on.

This eventually got to the directors of the Society for the Welfare of the Jewish Deaf. They operated the institution for deaf children in New York.

Rachel Amado Bortnick: That institution was already in existence?

Albert J. Amateau: Oh, yes. There was a Society and there was an institution for the deaf-mute. There were a number of institutions—
there was a Catholic institution, a state institution, and this was a
Jewish institution.

Rachel Amado Bortnick: Established by German Jews?

Albert J. Amateau: Established by the Rosenfeld family—German Jews.

So one day, one of the directors came to visit the group. He had been told that I had been helping them [the group of deaf Jews at the University Settlement House] and he came to see what kind of a man is this who is taking the trouble to assemble them in a meeting, [who] goes and helps them? Let's see.

He came and talked to me, he said, "Look, what are you doing now?"

"I'm collecting money for . . . [an insurance company]."

He says, "How about working for us?"

I said, "Doing what?"

"Going out to find jobs for these people. We'll pay you. How much are you making now?" So much. "We'll give you more. We'll pay you more."

All right, I'll try it. I don't know that I'll be successful, [but] I'll try it.

"One Century in the Life of Albert J. Amateau 1899– . The Americanization of a Sephardic Turk." An interview conducted by Rachel Amado Bortnick on 26 March 1986. Transcribed 1989, 64–66. American Jewish Archives, Collection 604, Box 3, Folder 1. Courtesy of The Jacob Rader Marcus Center of the American Jewish Archives, Cincinnati, Ohio. Americanjewisharchives.org. Original in English.

## 113.  A CATHOLIC CHILDHOOD IN HAVANA {ca. 1910s}

*Beginning in the early twentieth century, growing numbers of Sephardi Jews who left Ottoman Anatolia and the Balkans chose Cuba, other Caribbean islands, or South America as a final destination. The family of Elvira Levi de Cohen (b. 1907), who came to Cuba from Istanbul around 1910, was among the first of the Ottoman Jewish immigrants to make a home on the island. In the overwhelmingly Catholic environment of that country, as elsewhere in Latin America, some of the earliest émigré Sephardim experienced the drifting of the young generation away from Judaism. In this interview, conducted toward the end of her life, Cohen describes coming of age in a Catholic environment she found enticing, and from which her parents removed her during her adolescence (bringing her to live with her extended family in Turkey) in order to expose her to Judaism.*

Elvira Levi de Cohen: . . . In the beginning Jews were viewed negatively in Cuba. They had a very bad reputation and because of this my parents did not want to be seen as Jews, so they would say that they were French. They assumed my mother's last name, Abouaf, instead of my father's, which was Levi. There was discrimination. [Non-Jews in Cuba] didn't like Jews, so much so that the apartment where we lived had several pictures of Jews with horns. My mother did not want to involve us in all that. That was how I grew up. I grew up among Catholics or, better put, I inclined toward Catholicism, because my friends, my school, everything was Catholic, and thus I felt Catholic and I would absolutely not permit anyone to say I was Jewish.

Monika Unikel:[3] Did you ever mention that you were a Jew in school?

Elvira Levi de Cohen: Never. I was always Catholic with French parents and that was it. Naturally I would go to church with my friends. They were very active Catholics. But within a few years greater numbers of Jews began to arrive and a large colony was soon founded. My cousins came from Turkey. My mother brought them. I would not allow them to tell me that I was Jewish because I grew up in this environment of hatred. My mother grew very anxious, but my father would say, "Leave her. When she is older you'll see how she is going to change."

Monika Unikel: So you felt Catholic?

Elvira Levi de Cohen: I felt Catholic. Really. I enjoyed Catholicism a lot. All of my friends were Catholic Cubans, so I would go to church and everything. I felt it profoundly, so much so that when they distributed the palms on Palm Sunday, I placed my palm at the headboard of my bed. My father hardly held any Jewish beliefs, but he also wasn't Catholic at all. He was different. My mother was more attached to the religion. That is how they lived. By that point there was already a synagogue and a Jewish community in Havana. Still, when I was fifteen my father and mother thought that it would be best that I did not continue thinking this way, so they took me to Turkey for a vacation. When I arrived in Tur-

---

3. Monika Unikel, a sociologist by training, conducted this interview as part of an oral history project that produced over a hundred interviews with Jews in Mexico in the late 1980s. The interview with Cohen was included because she left Cuba as a young woman and settled in Veracruz and later in Mexico City.

key, I saw that my Jewish family was not as I had assumed they would be and I soon began to incline more toward my religion. We remained in Turkey for two years. . . . The truth was that even though I inclined slightly toward religion, I did not actually accept it. But then I arrived in Turkey and I saw my mother's family there. They were a very distinguished family, as was my father's family. I related to them exceedingly well, and my cousins made me see an alternative path. I went to synagogue there and began to find my religion. After two years we returned to Havana. Naturally my friends came looking for me, saying, "Come and stay in our house. We're going to Mass on Sunday." [I responded]: "No, not anymore. I've adopted the religion of my parents. I now follow the Jewish religion. Things aren't going to be as they were." . . . I had detached myself from Catholicism.

Monika Unikel: Were there no problems with your friends?

Elvira Levi de Cohen: No, they understood. We loved each other so much that this development did not change anything. I continued my friendships, but I never again went to a church.

Interview with Elvira Levi de Cohen, January 27, 1988. The Mexican Friends of the Hebrew University. The Oral History Project—Jews in Mexico. Alicia G. de Backal, Ph.D., coordinator. Monica Unikel, interviewer. Translated from Spanish by Devi Mays.

## 114. A SOCIOLOGICAL STUDY OF SEPHARDI IMMIGRANTS IN CINCINNATI (1913)

*This report is drawn from the sociological survey undertaken by the German-born Maurice Hexter (1891–1990) and his assistant, Maír José Benardete (1895–1989), on the Sephardi émigré community of Cincinnati in 1913. While intended by the authors to illustrate the challenges facing American Sephardi immigrant communities, the report also contains crucial information about the socioeconomic profile of Jews of Ottoman origin in the early-twentieth-century United States. Benardete, then a young émigré from Çanakkale, would go on to become an important scholar and author in Hispanic studies, a professor at Brooklyn College and cofounder of Columbia University's Sephardic Studies Section. (On this see source 146.) Later in life Hexter would receive a Ph.D. in social ethics from Harvard University and serve as a social worker within the Jewish community, directing influential organizations such as the Federation of Jewish Charities. The two men's collaboration on this endeavor formed part of a growing social scientific interest in poor and working-class Americans.*

Within the past few years there has come to the United States a new stream of Jewish immigration—the Turkish Jews—sometimes called the Spanish Jews, or *Spanuoles*. These people are a new social type. Their tendencies are unlike our other Jewish immigrants; their occupations have little or nothing in common with the occupations of our Russian and Roumanian coreligionists; their psychological forces and sociological tendencies are not at all like what we see in our Jewish brethren. For this very reason, that they are to a certain extent a social entity, they can be handled as such. Any problems that arise at present or may arise in the future must be attacked with due reference to this condition. While drawing lessons from past failures, we dare not forget that theirs is a different viewpoint. They deserve attention because we are responsible for them and because we want to steer clear of any difficulties that can be foretold in the light of experience.

Many of these immigrants go to interior communities. At least thirteen cities have colonies that are large enough to be noticed. . . . Because interior cities have [the] advantage of smallness, it is incumbent upon them to survey the situations in order to aid larger cities in the solution of the problem. With this end in view, an intensive survey was undertaken in Cincinnati; astonishing data and interesting results were obtained.

The investigation shows that the growth of the Cincinnati colony from without—that is, by immigration—has been steady and rapid [rising from 34 in 1908, to 219 in 1913]. . . . These figures do not include 27 native-born children and 3 wives of Russian extraction. The Cincinnati colony is closely interrelated. There are two groups. One group—eight families, totaling 45 individuals—is from Salonica, Turkey in Europe; the other group from Dardanelles consists of 42 heads of households, making 174 individuals. This close relationship and a strong feeling of brotherhood that exists among all of this newer element of our brethren make possible intensive removal work. The attractive force of the immigrants is of a high degree, and the Removal Office should take advantage of it. . . .

These newest immigrants are almost completely isolated from their co-religionists of other nationalities. This is due to language, ritual and other distinctions. Their language (Ladino) is spoken by none other.

They can with difficulty understand Spanish, unless they are especially educated. Their ritual is different from all others. This precludes contact with fellow Jews even in the synagogue. There has arisen out of this isolated condition a feeling of solidarity throughout the colony. . . .

Isolated by synagogue, ritual and language, it is inevitable that this latest element in Jewish immigration should settle in certain localities. This is the only way they can protect themselves from spoliation. So they have done in Cincinnati. The unfortunate feature in Cincinnati, however, is that the zone they have congregated in is within the restricted district. Of the 249 individuals (this includes native-born children), only 25 live without [outside] this district. A district of one homogeneous group can and does exercise wholesome influences upon its members, but when such a district is interspersed with the low characters of a restricted neighborhood the wholesomeness is lost, and instead, devitalizing and enervating forces act and interact. . . . [T]o counteract these forces is impossible, considering the neighborhood. The only plan remaining is to remove all of the families from such a center. Inducements should be offered to the families, which, it is hoped, will cause the families to move to a more wholesome district. This does not necessarily destroy their social entity; such a feeling of solidarity and homogeneity is protective. The Spanish society, La Hermandad, is considering purchasing a synagogue. Efforts should be made to induce them to locate this building near the Jewish settlement. By tackling this problem arising from the location of their district at this time, Cincinnati may prevent a recurrence of past evils.

[Other] than language, there is no one element which more effectually can cut off a group of people from its neighbors. In this respect, the community of our Turkish coreligionists is no exception. Special means must be devised to teach English to these people. The night schools cannot serve because the basis of instruction is Spanish instead of Ladino. There are in the Cincinnati colony 134 persons over 16 years of age who do not know how to read, write, or speak English. Of this number, but 15 attend night school; most of these attend irregularly. The correct method would be to use their own people as agents in this work. A good index of the lack of knowledge of English and the slow Americanization is the number of males who have acquired citizenship. Of 29 men over 21 years of age, and who have been in America longer than 5 years, only one is naturalized. This feature also shows lack of facilities especially adapted to their needs. It is a community need as yet unmet. . . .

Maurice Hexter, "The Dawn of a Problem," *Jewish Charities*, December 1913, 2–5.

## 115. MARRIAGE AND MIGRATION: THE TRIALS OF A JEWISH IMMIGRANT IN CUBA [1913]

*In Cuba as elsewhere, émigré Sephardim faced many travails associated with migration, including slow and unreliable communication with their erstwhile homes. In this letter a Sephardi Jewish man in Havana writes the Ottoman chief rabbi in hopes of preventing his wife from remarrying; whether out of vengeance or respect for Jewish law is not clear.*

December 6, 1913, Havana
To his Eminence *Monsieur* Haim Nahum, Chief Rabbi of Turkey [Ottoman Empire], Constantinople [Istanbul].

*Monsieur* Rabbi,

I have the honor of bringing the following facts to your attention.

Five years ago I was married in Constantinople to Bella Adjiman of your city, of the Dağ Hamamı quarter. From this marriage we have a son by the name of Moise Bonomo, born here in Havana (Cuba).

Some time later, now three years ago, my wife abandoned me, taking my son with her. She left for Morocco, then spent time in France, and now I have learned that she is going to Constantinople in order to marry one of our coreligionists, saying that she is divorced.

I take the liberty of addressing Your Eminence in order to ask that you do not give her authorization to remarry because she is still my wife before God and before the world, according to our holy religion. It is inadmissible for her to marry another.

I would be much obliged if you would stop her as soon as she arrives in your city or demand of her a deposit to prevent her from leaving the city and keep me informed of what happens. In case she has not yet returned to your city, I would ask you that you do not allow her family (the Adjiman family) to know that you are trying to stop my wife, because they could give her warning and advise her to remain in France.

Thanking you in advance, I have the honor, *Monsieur* Rabbi, of presenting you my most respectful and sincere salutations.

Marco Bonomo

Letter from Marco Bonomo in Havana to the Ottoman Chief Rabbi Haim Nahum in Istanbul, December 6, 1913, The Central Archives for the History of the Jewish People (Jerusalem), HM2 9070.1. Translated from French by Devi Mays.

## 116. ALIMONY IN A TIME OF WAR: AN APPEAL TO ISTANBUL FROM THE PHILIPPINES [1914]

*Jewish men frequently emigrated in advance of their wives at the turn of the twentieth century. The era of mass migration raised an array of legal concerns for Sephardi women as for other Jewish women. In this letter a representative of Joseph Halfon, a Sephardi man from Istanbul residing in the Philippines, writes the American consulate to deny charges made against his client by Mrs. Halfon. Though Jewish law allows women to request an end to their marriage if the husband neglects his duties, it appears that Mrs. Halfon stopped short of demanding a divorce, placing the case outside the domain of religious authorities. Her position remained precarious, however, as her legal inquiry unfolded at a time in which women had virtually no protection under national or international laws.*

November 30, 1914

Your much valued letter of September 19 has reached us, and I hasten to inform you in response that Mr. Joseph Halfon is currently in Daet on a visit, but he resides periodically either in Naga or in Iriga in the province of Ambos Camarines. Please note that Mr. Halfon has never been in my service, as he occupies himself with his own affairs. He has occasionally purchased merchandise with credit from my company.

Concerning the allegations of Mrs. Halfon in regard to the promise that her husband made to send her £65 plus two pounds per month through my person, Mr. Halfon has told me that he never made such a promise. However he has said that upon leaving Constantinople [Istanbul] he promised Mrs. Halfon that he would send £2 per month without any consideration of the success or lack thereof of his affairs.

Mr. Halfon, fulfilling the sacred duty of a model spouse, has not only kept his promise but has exceeded it by sending the sum of £43, which has been sent by different routes as follows:

To Jacques Halfon, Joseph Halfon's nephew, who lives in Galata, Ali Han number 2, who has received £15, of which 12 francs were given to Mrs. Halfon, according to Jacques Halfon's letter of four months ago.

£4 sent directly to Mrs. Halfon, two pounds last March and the other two last September, the receipt of which was duly acknowledged by her.

A sum of £12 was sent to Mrs. Halfon by way of J. Landhi of Manila, Philippines, according to the letter of this past July 22.

A sum of £15, which constitutes part of the rent [she owes], has been given to Mrs. Halfon by Mr. Joseph Alfandari, the steward of my house in Hasköy,[4] according to his letter of this past October 12.

Given the above, it is clear that Mrs. Halfon has received the amount of £43 and not £2 as she claims. Therefore I kindly request you to summon Jacques Halfon and Joseph Alfandari and ask them in the presence of Mrs. Halfon if they have given her the money discussed above, for which I thank you in advance.

As for the wish expressed by Mrs. Halfon about her husband's return to Europe, the latter told me that in light of the European war, it would be impossible for him to go to Constantinople without risking his life. He expects an improvement in the situation, however, and meanwhile he will send his monthly payment to Mrs. Halfon.

Letter from Simon Lahana to the American Consulate in Istanbul, November 30, 1914, The Central Archives for the History of the Jewish People (Jerusalem), HM2.9073.2. Translated from French by Devi Mays.

## 117. HOW SHOULD ONE PRAY SOUTH OF THE EQUATOR? ARGENTINE IMMIGRANTS SEEK RABBINIC JUDGMENT FROM ISTANBUL [1914]

*The Sephardi immigrants who settled in Argentina in the late nineteenth and early twentieth century were drawn by various forces; some came as teachers for the Alliance Israélite Universelle; others joined agricultural colonies established by the Jewish*

---

4. A neighborhood of Istanbul.

*Colonization Association, an organization that facilitated the migration and tran-*
*sition of Ashkenazi Jews into agricultural labor. As was true in many New World*
*locales, Ottoman and Moroccan Jewish newcomers in Argentina faced a paucity of*
*Sephardi religious leadership. Reluctant to turn to Jewish communal leaders who*
*represented different traditions, Ottoman Jewish émigrés sent queries of a religious*
*nature to the chief rabbi in Istanbul. In this letter a man seeks judgment on a ques-*
*tion of observance unique to the Southern Hemisphere.*

Rosario, Argentina, June 16, 1914

Your Eminence,

Permit me to bother you in the name of the Jewish collective of
Rosario, because of a divergence of opinion arising between us, about
which we desire your guidance. I am referring to a verse in our daily
prayers, "Who causes the wind to blow and the rain and the dew to
fall."[5]

First I have the duty to remind you, as you will already know, that
the seasons in South America are the opposite of those of Europe; that
is to say that from Passover to Sukkot it is autumn and winter, and
from Sukkot to Passover it is spring and summer. As the abovementioned verse refers to the seasons from Passover to Sukkot, it is our
obligation to read the prayer inversely.

Permit me to express the reasons that are invoked in opinions contrary to the abovementioned one.

Some men say that, as we are Europeans who have always maintained the conviction of returning to our maternal land and who have
not encountered upon our arrival in the Republic of Argentina any
established community of Argentine coreligionists, and because we
ourselves have been the founders of this community, we must follow
the European custom.

The answer to these men is that it is not possible to ask Providence
for the dew and rain of the summer when here it is wintertime, just as
one cannot ask for the contrary.

One of our Arab coreligionists from Beirut tells me that we must
conform to the custom of those from Jerusalem, as we are always aspiring to the Promised Land, and this is proved by our motto, which
we never forget and which we repeat in every circumstance, "If I for-

_____

5. See Mishnah Berakhot 5:2.

get you, O Jerusalem, let my right hand wither[6]. . . . "Next Year in Jerusalem"[7]. . . .

I had to tell this man that this has nothing to do with history and that it pertains only to the divisions of the seasons. Each person must pray according to the zone in which he lives.

The third group invokes the reasoning that the holidays of Passover and Sukkot serve as the point of departure for these verses. The first heralds the summer and the second, the winter, and we must conform ourselves to them.

My response to them as well was that this is in conformity with the European seasons and not with the South American ones, and that doing as these men say would cause harm to our coreligionists, who are mostly grain traders, as well as to those of diverse nationalities who find themselves in Latin America.

As a result, while we maintain legitimate aspirations toward the state of our birth as well as toward our Promised Land, as long as we find ourselves in the Argentine Republic, we should ask that God give his natural gifts according to the South American seasons rather than the European ones.

Should it please your Eminence to deign to honor me with an answer to the address indicated, I offer the illustrious representative of our creed my highest consideration.

Your faithful servant,

David Pisanté

Letter from David Pisanté in Rosario to Haim Nahum in Istanbul, June 16, 1914, The Central Archives for the History of the Jewish People (Jerusalem), HM2 9072. Translated from Spanish by Devi Mays.

## 118. "SEPHARDI BUT NOT ORIENTAL": A POLEMIC IN NEW YORK (1914–1915)

*As they arrived on American shores from Ottoman lands, many Jewish émigrés announced themselves as Orientals who hailed from an Eastern empire. Such is the case of the first source reproduced below, which offers the words of the Levantine Jewish communal leader Joseph Gedalecia. (For more on Gedalecia see source 110.) Although*

---

6. Psalm 137:5.

7. A phrase traditionally recited at the conclusion of the Passover seder.

*Ottoman Jews initially registered their businesses, social clubs, and charitable associations under the rubric "Oriental," they soon discovered that the category was more commonly associated with East Asian and South Asian immigrants, who faced widespread legal discrimination and prejudice in the United States during this period. Seeking to avoid such treatment, and cognizant of widespread anti-Asian sentiment, various commentators advocated the adoption of the self-description "Sephardi" in lieu of "Oriental." By emphasizing their Iberian origins, new immigrant communities could claim a European rather than Eastern identity as they attempted to find a means of integration and advancement in their newly adopted country.*

[Testimony of Joseph Gedalecia]*

I believe "Oriental" is the appropriate term. I feel proud to be classed with Hindus and Chinese and Japanese and other Asiatics. Besides, the name reminds us of dear Turkey, to whom we owe so much gratitude and love for protecting us when the civilized countries were oppressing us. The word Levantine may be more accurate, but "Oriental" expresses the Turkish Jew, and we are nothing but Turkish Jews; although we have passed under the dominion of other countries, we still have the old characteristics. . . . The Oriental Jew never drinks; first as a Jew, and then as a Turk, he is forbidden; his ethical standard is both Eastern and Jewish, and this means something. In morals the people of the East are inferior to none.

[Letter sent by Ben-Sion Behar to the Ladino periodical of New York *La Amerika*]**

I have noticed the change of the word "Oriental" to "Sephardi" in the masthead of the latest issue of the journal [*La Amerika*], "Organ of the Judeo-Sephardi (and no longer Oriental) Colony of America." This change made a very deep impression on me.

The changed word is very small in content but very great in terms of its importance for the history of our Sephardi colony in America.

I have always asked myself why we designated ourselves, the Sephardim in America, with the name "Orientals," while the other immi-

---

* Quoted in David de Sola Pool, "Levantine Jews," *Jewish Charities* IV: 11 (June 1914), 29–30. Original in English.
** Ben-Sion Behar, "Sefaradim, ma no orientales," *La Amerika*, October 29, 1915, 2. Translated from Ladino by Devin E. Naar.

grant peoples from Turkey like the Greeks, Turks, Armenians, etc., do not call themselves Orientals.

By chance one night last week, having visited with my friends at the public school at 160 Rivington St., I listened with attention to a lecture that a professor gave about the life and customs of the Japanese and the Chinese. From the conclusion I understood clearly the great disdain that the Americans manifest toward the Japanese by labeling them with the name "Orientals."

Later I remembered the term "Oriental," which I have noticed is used to describe all our Sephardi brothers from Turkey. I became filled with disdain by this false name given to us without reason. I decided to make the following remarks concerning the difference between the words "Sephardim" and "Orientals."

According to my understanding, the word Oriental does not at all pertain to us Jews. Since the Jewish people was born and lived in the Orient (Palestine), it was known always by the name *'Am 'ivri* [Hebrew people], Israel, or *Yehudi* [Jew] and not *'Am mizrahi* [Eastern people].

The history of the European peoples shows us that the groups called German and Latin (English, French, etc.) were born in the center of Asia in ancient times and afterwards emigrated to Europe. Despite this, never have they been called Orientals even though they came from the Orient.

Before these peoples came to Europe, great Jewish communities could already be found in Europe, for example in Toledo (Spain) and in other cities. . . .

The celebrated historian Graetz, in all of his accounts of Jewish history during the period of exile, tells of the glorious acts of our ancient ancestors in Spain such as: Rabbi Judah Ha-Levi, Ibn Ezra, Rambam, ibn Gabirol, etc. [as well as those who lived during] the period of Jewish persecution in Spain and after, such as: Abravanel, Yashar mi-Kandia,[8] . . . Rahamal,[9] etc. (to whom [Graetz] attributes great importance); calling them the *Sephardim* ([lit.] "Spaniards").

Since then and until today in Turkey, Romania, Bulgaria, Serbia, etc., the Ashkenazim call us the *francos* ("Franks"), meaning Europeans.

The word Sephardi, which reminds us of the glorious history of our

---

8. Joseph Solomon Del Medigo.
9. Rabbi Moses Haim Luzzatto.

ancestors in Spain, is used in all the documents printed by our communities and chief rabbinates, with the words *'edat* or *rabanut ha-sefaradim*.

The word Sephardi brings us glory and a feeling of aristocracy. We can remark with pride that the history of the Jewish people in general, since Ramban,[10] singles out the names of our ancestors. This group, which is composed of two million people, has produced archaeologists, philosophers, astronomers, poets, rabbis, and politicians in the courts of various kingdoms. Still today, we descendants of Sephardim such as Luzzatto, Sonino, Natan, and many deputies in the parliament of Italy occupy important positions in various governments.

In Egypt the stock exchange and the business establishment are for the most part in the hands of the Sephardim. The signatures of Cattaui, Baron Menasho, Suares, etc., are valued around the world. In the important cities of India our Sephardim are the top businessmen, such as Lord Sassoon, etc. In Turkey officials who serve the government include Sephardi rabbis as well as lawyers, judges and other important government figures (even though our schools are in an inferior state). This demonstrates [the persistence of] our ancient abilities and intelligence. In Bulgaria as well as in all the lands of the Balkans, the important businessmen and government officials are our Sephardim. The greatest Jews of Holland are the Sephardim of Amsterdam.

With the word Sephardi we are honored because we were the first who formulated the idea of the return of the Jews to Palestine 400 years ago, since the time of Rambam [sic].[11] (Our brothers the Ashkenazim are new immigrants who have lived only seventy to eighty years in Jerusalem.)

This proves another point, that in the entire Hebrew world, the Sephardi pronunciation was accepted for the Hebrew language [and] is practiced in all schools and modern Hebrew seminaries.

With the word Sephardi we can also praise all of America, North and South, considering that it is our Sephardim who were the first Jewish immigrants to America who took an active part in all of the revolutions and wars for the liberty of the American flag, as is written

---

10. Moses ben Nahman (1194–1270), also known as Nahmanides or Ramban for short, was a rabbi, biblical commentator, kabbalist, and philosopher in Catalonia.

11. Moses Maimonides, or Moses ben Maimon (1135–1204), was arguably the most famous of Jewish philosophers and an important codifier of Jewish law.

in detail in the history of the Jews in America. In North America the first Jewish cemetery was built in New York in the year 1645 [sic] by the Spanish-Portuguese congregation "Shearith Israel."

In Brazil, South America, there exist until today various congregations and cemeteries that are more than three hundred years old and which honor those Sephardi Jewish immigrants from Spain who are highly respected by the authorities.

It is too much to bring more proof of our glorious past, like Menasseh ben Israel, who was the first (Sephardi) Jew to bring about the [re]settlement of the Jews in England, as well as Jacob Tirada of Amsterdam (Holland), among others.

Another difficulty presents itself with the name "Oriental," considering that in America there are thousands of Sephardim who have immigrated from Egypt, Algeria, Morocco, Holland, Italy, etc., whose prayers and customs, in our view, fit the Sephardi liturgy precisely. How can we distinguish ourselves from them and not recognize them as Sephardim like us, only because they do not come from Turkey?

As long as the Jewish people speaks a different language and has abstained from using its national language, Hebrew, despite the sad persecutions in Spain, we have been forced to continue to call ourselves Sephardim because our journals and books are edited in the Spanish language with Hebrew characters and because in all of our homes and businesses, we use the Judeo-Spanish language as our mother tongue.

The Spanish language and the land of Spain are not Oriental, and in Turkey the official language is not Spanish. We who came here as immigrants from Turkey were no more than guests for 400 years.

It is said that the entire Jewish people should speak their true language, Hebrew, in order to forget our past differences. However there actually exist two parties within the Jewish people—Judah and Israel, one of which speaks the Yiddish jargon and the other, Spanish—this division does not in the least lesson the aristocratic and glorious inheritance that the name Sephardi bestows upon us.

Ben-Sion Behar (*Sefaradi tahor*)[12]

---

12. Literally "pure Sephardi" or "pure Spaniard" in Hebrew, this term is often used as an aggrandizing term of self–description by Jews of Iberian origins. The expression appears to be a modern coinage based on a new interpretation of the Hebrew initials "samekh, tet," which Jewish authors traditionally appended to their signatures and writings as an abbreviation for "sofi tov" or "sofo tov," meaning "may I have a good end" or "may he have a good end."

## 119. CAN A SEPHARDI-ASHKENAZI ROMANCE
## SURVIVE? A RUSSIAN JEWISH WOMAN IN
## NEW YORK SEEKS ADVICE (1916)

*In early-twentieth-century New York City, as elsewhere in the United States, im-migrant communities of Yiddish-speaking Ashkenazi Jews and Ladino-speaking Sephardi Jews settled in the same neighborhoods. Many Yiddish-speaking immigrants had their first chance to meet Sephardim under these circumstances. Although young Sephardi and Ashkenazi immigrants often met on the street, in schools, and in the workplace, they spoke different languages, had different cultural mores and religious rites, and even pronounced Hebrew differently. As a result many Ashkenazim, who formed the vast majority of Jews in the country, had difficulties believing that their Sephardi neighbors were in fact Jews. Frustrated by their Ashkenazi coreligionists' refusal to recognize them as Jewish, more than one Sephardi man reported being driven to desperation and contemplating offering proof of his Jewishness to incredu-lous peers by demonstrating that he was circumcised. The following source, written in the form of an advice-seeking letter, a genre that first appeared in New York in the Yiddish-language newspaper* Forverts *of Abraham Cahan (1860–1951) during this period, describes the various tactics Sephardi immigrants employed to try to gain the recognition and acceptance of their coreligionists.*

To the editor of *La Bos del Pueblo*:

I am a Jewish girl born in Russia who came to America eight years ago. Although I am not remarkably well-educated, I have always wanted to marry a well-educated boy of the Jewish faith.

One of my girlfriends took me to the Oriental ball organized by *La Bos del Pueblo*, where I met a boy named Jack. . . .

At first glance I thought him Italian. The way he spoke, his counte-nance, and his gestures were like those of the Italians. But later, when we began seeing each other, he swore to me that he was a Spanish-speaking Jew.

Jack is well-educated, knows many languages, and has a good job. As he is in love with me, I too am in love with Jack, but my parents object to any union between us, since they do not believe that he is Jewish.

Now I beg you to tell me through your esteemed newspaper if it is possible that a Jew who doesn't speak Jewish [Yiddish] and doesn't look Jewish can nevertheless have a Jewish soul. I thought that in the case that Jack is Judeo-Spanish, there is no inconvenience in inter-marrying. I am certain that you will respond affirmatively, being that my love for Jack is so profound that I have begun to study the Spanish language and can even read your newspaper with difficulty.

Thanking you for your future kindness, I remain respectfully yours, Clara.

[The editors of *La Bos del Pueblo* respond:]

The paper on which this letter was written did not indicate that any special care was taken, but the composition of the letter in English was grammatically correct. This indicates the education and sincerity of a serious girl.

Despite this, we regret seeing that such a girl, having such an education, is still not up to par with her knowledge on Judeo-Spaniards in America. We would love to believe that this is not owing to her ignorance, but to the fact that New York, being a big metropolis, does not offer the possibility of teaching the population about all of its [residents'] classifications.

Yes, Clara, the boy who speaks Spanish, has Italian gestures, who can read our newspaper, is Jewish. The language that you speak is not the Jewish language. It is the Yiddish jargon, as ours is the Judeo-Spanish jargon.

No, we don't see any inconvenience in the intermarriage of the Sephardim with the Ashkenazim. There are many examples of Sephardim living with Ashkenazim in the greatest harmony. The important thing is that the two have the same level of education and that they be capable of adapting themselves to each other.

"Porke no?" *La Bos del Pueblo*, May 26, 1916, 6. Translated from Ladino by Aviva Ben-Ur.

## 120. A STOWAWAY'S JOURNEY FROM ISTANBUL TO MARSEILLE {1919}

*Following the Ottoman defeat in the First World War, British, French, and Italian troops occupied Istanbul. With the future of the city uncertain and the country ravaged by unprecedented losses on the battlefield and privations at home, many left the empire in search of a better future, never to return. Here we see the testimony of one such individual, a young Jewish boy from Tekirdağ, Thrace, who ran away from home and became a stowaway on a boat bound for France, before finally settling in Seattle.*

*In this selection Jack Azose (1901–1987), son of an itinerant rabbi, describes how a combination of luck, ingenuity, and knowledge of the French language allowed him to avoid detection as an undocumented migrant.*

It was a bright sunny morning when I was carrying my dad's luggage to a little steamship that would take him to Ada Pazar [Adapazarı], a little town in Turkey on the sea of Marmara.

I was nearly fifteen then. The date was August 19, 1919. On the way to the dock, my dad asked me to be good to my mother and find a job and take care of her until he would start sending money for our support. I promised just that.

About two hours later, I was in front of a huge four-funnel Russian steam ship, ready to leave for Marseille, France. I had a yearning for travel, which I still do. [I] went home, changed my underclothes and wore two sets, one on top of the other. My mother had two liras (Turkish dollars worth about 50¢) under the paper in the shelf, which she was saving for rent money. I took them and started towards the docks. I had a brother in the Turkish army and a brother in America. I made up my mind to come to America and France was my first stop over.

If I were to start taking steps towards securing the proper identification papers for my passport it would probably take me three months to get them at a cost of about forty liras, or twenty American dollars, something I did not have. So, without wasting any time, and without seeing my mother and my younger sister, I started toward the big Russian steam ship. When I arrived at the dock, the ship was getting filled up mostly with French soldiers going to France as heroes and conquerors, but there were quite a few civilians too.

When I reached the gangplank, there was a French sentry and a Turkish policeman asking questions. I passed through them in a hurry like I belonged to the ship and used only one French word to the French sentry—*Ça va?*—which in the French slang means—Is everything okay? By the time he answered in the affirmative, I was half way up the gangplank. By this time, my mother had come home from visiting a neighbor and recalling how many times I told her that I would stow away to France, found the necessary evidence—the money gone and my underclothes on the bathroom floor. She realized right then and there that I meant what I told her so many times about running away from home.

She took my younger sister with her and came to the docks looking for me. About three hours later she spotted me on the steerage rails watching the crowds down below. I saw them but I did not make any effort to try to talk to them for fear that the people next to me might start asking me questions and I wanted to avoid that.

Five minutes later I saw someone asking for papers or passports and I tried to get on the other side. The men stopped me and asked for my ticket in the French language. Being able to speak French, I told them I had my papers, tickets and passport in my suitcase, in my cabin. Then he called for a French sailor and asked him to come with me to my cabin to see if my papers were in order. We started to go down through those curved stairs, not knowing where, or how I was going to lose the French sailor, when suddenly an officer of the ship who seemed to be very mad stopped the sailor and started to bawl him out for something he was supposed to do and forgot to do. While the sailor was at attention I thought I found my chance to get away from there. I started to go up but the sailor shouted at me, "Hey, wait for me." I came back and was waiting for the sailor when the superior officer ordered him to go perform the task which he was supposed to have completed previously, right away, and off he went, leaving me there.

After the sailor was out of sight, I went downstairs and was looking for a place to hide. I saw five French soldiers who were sitting on top of an army blanket ready to start to eat. I approached one of them and told him that I was running away from Turkey and wanted to go to France. I begged him to help me and hide me, which they did. They put three suitcases, one on top of the other, leaving a small space between the wall and the suitcases and put two or three blankets on top of it, hiding me behind it. I stayed there for four hours until after the boat was 1,000 yards away from the dock. Then one of them came over and told me that it was safe to come out now because they combed the ship from one end to the other for stowaways. The ship was headed towards the Sea of Marmara and the Dardanelles. I was scared plenty, leaving all my folks behind and going towards a new world.

The five *Poilus*[13] had a meeting and agreed that if they could dress me up like one of them, no one would know the difference. So one

---

13. An informal term for a French infantryman during the First World War.

gave me a soldier's coat, another gave me a soldier's pants and belt and another gave me a soldier's hat, so I became a young soldier. On the first day out I met a young man from Istanbul, Turkey who was going to France, just like me, with the exception that he had all his papers in order and plenty of money with a rich uncle in Paris who[m] he was going to meet. I knew the young man from school but not well enough to ask him to lend me some money. He was only interested in how I was going to get away when we docked at Marseille.

As a soldier, I had certain privileges, like attending the dances at the main ballroom, which my friend could not attend. The whole trip was wonderful, good weather all the way through, but, as we all know, all good things must end sooner or later.

Six days later we docked at Marseille and my friends called me to one side and demanded my uniform, which belonged to them. They were afraid that I might get caught leaving the boat and get them in trouble. So I was a civilian again. My problem was to get off the ship without being caught. I went up on deck and watched how the soldiers were getting down over the side of the ship with ropes, sliding themselves down like acrobats. That gave me an idea. I told one of my friends that I was getting down of the side of the ship.

They gave me a drink of wine out of their tin can cups but I refused, because I was expecting the conductor to come and find me and deliver me to the police in the middle of the night in some strange city or town. Believe me I was plenty worried. Luckily, the train was an express train from Marseille to Paris without a stop. The next morning at 9:30 am we arrived at the French capital—Paris—the most beautiful city in the world. The train stopped at the Gare de Lyon. I got out of the train and was watching how the soldiers and passengers were getting out through the exit and saw one *gendarme* (French police) on each side of the conductors, collecting the passenger's tickets. I stood there watching the crowds for at least two minutes, then I began to worry how I was going to get out of there without being caught.

A little further down there was a baggage room. I saw an old man with a small cap pushing a car full of suitcases and trunks. The load was too much for him and I went over to lend him a hand. After we reached the other side of the station, without realizing it, I was free, and without too much effort on my part.

The old man tipped his hat in salutation, thanking me from the bottom of his heart for coming to his aid and I in turn, thanked him from the bottom of my heart for his help in getting me out of there. Of course, I did not say that aloud.

I turned around to see which way to go and there I saw the young man from Istanbul, waiting to see if I would be able to get out of the station without being caught. I went over and slapped him on the back of his neck and he turned around and saw me. He was very much surprised and said "how in the world did you get out?" I told him I had a first class ticket and got out ahead of him.

He had the address of his rich uncle in Paris and we asked a cab driver for directions and started for that address. When we reached out destination his uncle hugged him and kissed him and then asked about me. He introduced me as an old school acquaintance. Then turning to me, his uncle asked me a few questions as to relatives, or friends, if I had any money or passport and all the answers were answered in the negative. So he left his nephew in the [store] and took me to a restaurant down the street. He went and talked with the owner and then came and told me he would return for me later.

After I finished my meal I tried to pay for it but the owner would not take money from me. He said that he would write it off by nightfall. I realized the predicament I was in.

No one in Paris could rent a room in a hotel or rooming house without first obtaining a visa or a permit from the prefecture de police. The penalty was very severe if anyone would be caught on that offense so everyone was afraid to give me a place to sleep, knowing that I was a stowaway and that I did not have a permit. The young man from Turkey promised me to let me sleep in his room at the risk of being caught. We decided that, while he was talking with the landlady I would go up to the third floor and wait for him. I did this and so I spent my first night in Paris. The next day I went to the restaurant again and made some new friends. One of them had a good idea for me. He suggested for me to go to the Cité, meaning the Police Department, and tell them a lie—that I entered France legally and while I was waiting for the train at Marseille I feel asleep on one of the benches at the depot and while sleeping, a pick-pocket stole my wallet with my money and passport. Luckily I had my train ticket in another pocket, otherwise I would still be at Marseille instead of Paris.

I had no other way out so I went to the Police and lied about the whole thing. They asked me a few questions as to when I left Turkey, the name of the boat, the date it left Istanbul, my name, address and age. They gave me a temporary permit so I could get a room to sleep [in], with the warning that I shouldn't try to move to another address without first letting them know about it. I took a room in a cheap hotel, paid them for a week, and on the third day, someone gave me three addresses to go look for a job. One was a place which repaired carpets, second was a grocery store and the third was a restaurant. I picked the third one. . . .

I did not return to my hotel room again, which I should have done [to] give the hotel man my new address. After the [officers in the] Police Department gave me a temporary pass so I could get a room in a hotel, their intention was to check and double check my statements to determine whether I entered France legally or was a stowaway. They began by investigating at Istanbul through their representatives in the French Embassy. As you already might have guessed, all their investigations proved fruitless.

They sent word from Istanbul to Paris that in their opinion I was a spy and that I should be taken into custody right away. So the famous French secret police started on a search for me all over Paris. I did not learn of these happenings until much later.

Jack Azose papers, 1978, Accession No. 2795–001, University of Washington Libraries, Special Collections. Transcript of tape-recorded interview conducted by F. Roberts in February 1978, 1–7. Original in English.


## 121. A SEPHARDI COMMUNITY IS FOUNDED IN LOS ANGELES [1920]

*The dramatic expansion of the California economy in the mid-nineteenth century, spurred in great part by the Gold Rush, galvanized Sephardi as well as Ashkenazi Jews—immigrants and their first and second-generation American children—to move to the American West. Of all the Sephardi settlements in the region, Los Angeles soon became the largest, with its Judeo-Spanish population exploding in the early decades of the twentieth century as the city expanded geographically and demographically. The Sephardi Jewish immigrants of Los Angeles quickly formed a number of communal institutions, including the Peace and Progress Society, made up primarily of Jews from Rhodes. As Los Angeles's Sephardi community proliferated, its members thirsted for a single, unifying body. Out of this impulse was born "the Sephardic Community of Los Angeles" (otherwise known as* La Comunidad*), whose founding statutes are printed here.* La Comunidad *proved immensely appealing, long-lived, and culturally rich, while the synagogue eventually created by the community, the Sephardic Temple Tifereth Israel, served as a pivot of Los Angeles's Balkan, Middle Eastern, and North African community. As can be seen from the 1920 statutes, however, in its earliest years the community had a clearly Hispanic orientation. Although its members suggested that all Jews who practiced the Sephardi rite of Judaism were welcome within their sanctuary, they insisted that Spanish be used as the language of the community.*

The gentleman of the board as well as the others [in attendance] have signed the Statutes, thereby declaring themselves active members of the Sephardi Community of Los Angeles, and agreeing to pay the monthly due of $1.00 per person.

As can be seen in the Statutes, which have already been sent to press, the principal objectives of this community are religious and spiritual.

Additionally, when financial circumstances permit, [the board aims] to establish a synagogue, Talmud Torah, and recreational and literary center, with the aim of promoting the general intellectual and material wellbeing of our members.

Those who marry outside the Jewish faith are not admitted.

The Castilian language[14] has been unanimously accepted as the official language of the community. . . . This community is open to all Sephardi Jews without exception or regard to party, origin, or opinion. This applies equally to the descendants of Spain and Portugal and to the Jews of the Orient who still practice Judaism according to the true and original Sephardi rite, even though some among them do not speak the beautiful language of Cervantes, Maimonides, or Judah Ha-Levi.

The session was adjourned at 6 P.M., with all members departing cordially and in perfect accord.

Approved by Adolphe Danziger, President, and José M. Estrugo, Secretary and Vice President.

Actas y verbales de la Comunidad Sefardi de Los Angeles, Fundada Febrero 1, 1920, 3–4. Archives of the Sephardic Temple Tifereth Israel (Los Angeles). Translated from Ladino by Julia Phillips Cohen.

14. Modern standard Spanish. The Los Angeles community's decision to make Castilian rather than Judeo-Spanish the official language of their institution placed them firmly in the camp of those who sought rapprochement between Sephardi and Hispanic communities. (See also sources 68 and 134.)

## 122. A SEPHARDI ÉMIGRÉ ENCOURAGES LEVANTINE JEWS TO MOVE TO MEXICO (1922)

*Published in a Ladino periodical in New York City, the following editorial extolls the hospitality, customs, and climate of Mexico, suggesting that Ladino speakers in particular will find the Spanish spoken in the country close to their native tongue and its traditions compatible with their own. Although its author wrote of the many benefits Mexico had to offer, including its great economic potential, what he did not say may have been equally relevant to his plea. Written just a year after the United States began to restrict the entrance of newcomers from the southern and eastern regions of Europe, the author's attempt to convince his coreligionists to seek their fortunes on other shores may have constituted an implicit recognition of the growing nativist backlash against "undesirable" immigration in the United States during this period. Indeed, by 1924 a new immigration law severely restricted the flow of new immigrants from these regions into the U.S., leading increasing numbers of Ottoman and other émigrés to seek out Latin American destinations.*

It is a great pleasure for me to have this occasion, offered to me by the serial *La Luz*, to inform readers of the current situation in the Republic of Mexico, and to mention some of the reasons why the Sephardim should consider Mexico.

In all the countries in which I have traveled, no other has left me with such a good impression as Mexico, due to the favorable conditions that this country offers Sephardi Jews who might want to establish themselves here. There are many reasons for this.

The first is that the Sephardim will encounter no difficulties in understanding the language spoken there, adopting local habits, or accustoming themselves to Mexican food.

The Spanish that is spoken in Mexico, although it contains some Indian words, quite possibly resembles our Ladino more than the modern Spanish spoken in Spain, since—it should not be forgotten—contemporary Mexican society began to form at nearly the same time that the Jews were expelled from Spain. My opinion is that Sephardi Jews of today, with three months of studying and reading, would be able to speak Spanish better than some Mexicans of the interior regions.

As I have said, it will be easy to adopt local customs, or better put, to maintain many of them because they resemble the customs of the Levant (Turkey, Greece, etc.). The people do not hurry in business, everyone takes time to roam around aimlessly. What can be done tomorrow is not done today. They are never content with the government, although they always bear it no matter how bad it is. Put simply, the country is not in the state of perfection [reached by] the great nations of Europe and America, [yet residents of] these nations suffer more from the state of things than does the Sephardi Jew, who is already accustomed to such things from the country of his birth.

In addition I should mention other facts [of life in Mexico] that are very favorable. Social life is much more active than in the United States, people are much more pleasant, more hospitable and possess a courtesy that at times seems exaggerated. The Sephardi Jew will not have difficulty in attaining these qualities because they already form a natural part of his character. In regard to the climate, I should say that it is quite varied in Mexico, such that while it is cold in one city, in another city several kilometers away, it is very hot. Mexico City itself is never either very hot or very cold, but rather, has ideal weather that makes this city one of the healthiest in the world.

The potential wealth of Mexico is incalculable. Aside from the numerous oil wells that have made many American millionaires rich and the large mines of gold and silver, copper and zinc, etc, the importance of agriculture (wheat, corn, chickpeas, coffee, cocoa, vanilla, rubber, etc.) has always been great. The raising of livestock (hogs, sheep, cattle) is also progressing by the day.

The current situation of Mexico is somewhat poor, partially as a result of the global economic situation. In spite of this, Mexico is [economically] more secure than many European states, including both France and Italy; the immigrants that come from these countries find a means of earning a livelihood almost immediately.

I am convinced that the Sephardi youth who have a bit of self-confidence and, especially those who have the idea of establishing themselves there [will succeed], because I am sure that today this country will provide them with a better opportunity for improving their lives than any other country in the world.

Albert Avigdor, "Porke los sefaradim deven pensar en Meksiko," *La Luz*, February 5, 1922, 1. Translated from Ladino by Devi Mays.

## 123. "LET HIM BLESS US FROM BELOW THE EARTH": MOURNING A FATHER'S PASSING IN ISTANBUL
[1922]

*In 1922 a man by the name of Solomon Hasday addressed a letter from Istanbul to his brothers and sister-in-law in distant America. As he wrote Istanbul remained under the occupation of Allied forces following the Ottomans' defeat in the First World War, while the empire verged on collapse. Prompted by his own family's personal tragedy, Hasday put pen to paper to inform his brothers of their father's death. His words offer a rare glimpse into the intimate experience and religious worldview of a Sephardi Jewish man in the early twentieth century. Hasday not only spoke of their father's final moments, he was also adamant that the brothers owed their father a debt that included praying for his soul and performing the ritual rending of the clothes that forms part of Jewish tradition. He also counseled his siblings to send funds home in order to build their late father a proper tombstone, which would constitute his "eternal house in paradise." However they had fallen short in their role as sons during his life—presumably, as the letter hints, by remaining out of touch after settling abroad—this would give them an opportunity to honor their father in death.*

Constantinople, April 1, 1922

Dear sister-in-law and brothers Marco and Israel:

[This is the] second letter that we received from you this week. Each letter caused us great sadness, since your letters were so desired during the illness of our dear father, blessed judge of truth. After a short sickness our father now rests in paradise, beneath that tomb that covers him. At the last moments of his life father wanted to see his daughter and sons and pardon them for all of their sins.

My nerves and sadness do not permit me to write more. Cry a little, say a few prayers for our father. Pray a little so that his soul can rest in heaven. Today, sons and daughter, the duty to perform *kri'a*[15] and to pay him the honor he deserves is upon you. [Let us] come together and gather a sum of money so that the tomb that is his eternal home can be completed. Your money is the tombstone of which I speak. If in his life you could not support our old father you should [at least] please him in his death.

You, dear Marco. Cry and console yourself a little more, since in the hour of his death father had the coat you left him as a reminder

---

15. *Kri'a* refers to the ritual rending of garments during the period of mourning in Judaism.

[of you] before his eyes and wore it to comfort himself and make him happy [while thinking] of his son.

You, dear Israel, do not forget that your father died. Pray for him. Ask pardon before God and do your duty of building [him] an eternal house in paradise. Help [provide] the building and the roof for our father. Since we were unable to comfort him in his life, let him bless us from below the earth.

Letter of Solomon Hasday in Istanbul to his brothers Marco and Israel and sister-in-law in the United States, April 1, 1922. Private collection of Isaac and Dora Hasday. Translated from Ladino by Julia Phillips Cohen and Devin E. Naar.

## 124. AN ATTEMPT TO INHERIT THE ESTATE OF A TURKISH JEWISH WOMAN IN MEXICO CITY [1925]

*For many Ottoman Jewish immigrants of the early twentieth century, transoceanic travel was undertaken after hurried departures and in dire conditions. Even well-off travelers could lose papers, resulting in various legal problems en route or in their new homes. This selection details one such case of one family in Mexico City in the interwar period. Here the widower and children of a woman by the name of Sara Halfon de Lahana (d. 1925) struggled to prove their relation to their late wife and mother. Their case was complicated not only because they had lost the relevant birth certificates but also because Mexican law required documentation of a civil marriage, a practice that had not been required when the couple wed in the Ottoman Empire.*

Mexico City, September 12, 1925

Honorable Judge of the Third Civil Court,

I, Simon Lahana, by my own volition and in the intestate case of Mrs. Sara Halfon de Lahana, my deceased wife, respectfully come before you to say:

That upon her death my wife left behind four children—products of our marriage—two sons and two daughters, the first two having reached the age of majority and the last two minors.

That I can prove neither my marriage with Mrs. Halfon nor the birth of my children with authentic documents from the Civil Registry as Mexican law requires, because in the first case—that of marriage— [civil marriage] is not practiced in Turkey, and in the second—as regards birth—the documents have been lost due to our many travels.

That in order to prove our identities we do not have documents other than the register, passports, and other papers we have included here, [and which we have] duly translated.

That these documents prove that Mrs. Halfon was my wife, and also that Mr. Solomon and Isaac Halfon, and Fanni and Safira are my children with the deceased Mrs. Halfon.

In light of these facts, I ask you, Honorable Judge, if you would be so good as to accept this writing as submitted, ordering its recognition before the audience of the Public Ministry, and thereby recognizing my four children and myself as legitimate heirs to the estate.

Simon Lahana

Sección: siglo XX, serie: archivo historico, caja: 1902, folio: 344547, Archivo General de la Nación, Tribunal Superior de Justícia del Distrito Federal (Mexico City). Translated from Spanish by Devi Mays.

## 125.  HOW SEPHARDI JEWS CAN SERVE FRANCE (1926)

*A Salonican by birth, Sam Lévy (Shemuel Sa'adi a-Levi, 1870–1959) first made his name editing the French- and Ladino-language newspapers of his native city. By the time he penned this editorial in a French Jewish newspaper in Paris in the mid-1920s, he had been living in Western Europe for more than a decade. Here Lévy proposes that Ladino-speaking Jews have a special role to play in every country where they reside and that they make ideal citizens. Although he mentions it only briefly, Lévy's article agitates for the naturalization of tens of thousands of Ottoman Jews who had arrived in France before their empire had been dissolved and who had since become stateless after failing to register anew with the consulates of the Ottoman successor states of Greece and Turkey. (For more on Sam Lévy see sources 22, 67, 75, and 89.)*

Oriental Jews are of Turkish, Greek, Bulgarian, Serbian, Romanian, Italian, and even French nationality. What distinguishes them from their compatriots of other confessions is, above all, their mother tongue, Judeo-Spanish. There is also another factor we don't often take into account, which is of paramount importance. Greece, Bulgaria, Egypt, Syria, Palestine, and Romania were all places that formerly belonged to Turkey, which counted over a million Jewish subjects. These subjects were originally from Spain and had brought the dialect of Cervantes, as well as various useful skills, from Iberia. They work peacefully at their own affairs and ensure the economic development of the country. Never occupying themselves with politics, they cause no problems for the government, which holds them in high regard and harbors no suspicion towards them.

When the Balkan states asserted their independence, these Jews sincerely regretted the dissolution of the Turkish regime. Many emigrated to Turkey, Italy, England, France, the United States, and South and Central America. Those who stayed [in their old homes], complied loyally with the new laws and continued to occupy themselves with their own duties and affairs, constituting in each of these new countries a force of order, work, and progress. We must also recognize that all the Oriental governments, including the Romanian, pay homage to the economic activity of the Spanish Jews, and appreciate their absolute respect of law. They see no inconvenience in the fact that [these Jews] have maintained their mother tongue alongside the language of the country, because they know that Spanish, which is spoken by more than 140 million people, is an instrument of economic expansion, and constitutes a further asset for the nation.

This lengthy preamble was necessary to demonstrate that there is no anomaly in the grouping of "Spanish" Jews within one body residing in France, where they constitute, as in other countries, an element of order and productivity, that is to say of peace and progress. . . .

Jewish solidarity has been greatly praised. Perhaps it does exist among the Jews of the West, but Oriental Jews are more particularistic, or, to be more specific, they have more of a group mentality. For instance, Salonican Jews fraternize among themselves. They have their own benevolent societies and meeting centers; Jews from Constantinople have their own group and religious community; the Jews from Smyrna [Izmir] and the Jews from Adrianople [Edirne] have their own aid societies. It is a great mistake to scatter their efforts in this way. If they knew how to join together they would constitute a great moral force. It has also been said that Oriental Jews are very pious. They are not. They are simply traditionalists who respect the cult of memory. They enjoy finding themselves in temple once or twice a year in order to return to the past and to history, if only for a few hours; because the prayers and Jewish holidays recall to the "chosen people" the most notable acts of martyrdom.

Among the grievances previously lodged against Jews was their alleged cowardice. The Balkan campaigns have shown that Jews are men in all senses of the word. The success of the Balkan confederation was decided in 1913, the day of the victory at Kumanovo.[16] This victory—which the Serbians celebrate—was the work of the [Jewish] flag bearer Avramče, whose bravery, initiative, and decisiveness transformed a defeat...into a triumph.[17] There were countless Avramčes in the Balkan armies.

At the declaration of the Great War, 2,000 Oriental Jews volunteered their services to France, and 700 fell or were injured on the battle-fields. All the others conducted themselves just as courageously and were awarded honors for their service. I cite among the dead one name: that of Georges Raphael Carmona, who played an important part in the victory at the Battle of the Marne.

Let us conclude. At . . . [a recent] assembly in Nice, Mr. Charles Lambert, deputy from Rhône, demanded a new naturalization policy that would allow the government to assimilate honorable foreign elements more quickly and easily. This ambition is extremely judicious. The first foreign elements deserving naturalization are the Jews of the Levant. In addition to being law abiding and hard-working . . . they are productive and will give to this most hospitable land children who will serve their new nation with all their heart and devotion. Their commitment to hard work and loyalty, their love of France, their Latin origins—because they, themselves, are Latin—their service rendered in war, as well as other considerations, [all] militate in favor of the assimilation of these trustworthy individuals who will have one more reason to cherish France, the second home to all intellectuals, indeed, the most beautiful, noble and generous nation of all.

Sam Lévy, "Les Israélites sefardis en France," *L'Univers Israélite*, February 26, 1926, 95–96. Translated from French by Erin Corber.

---

16. The Serbian army defeated Ottoman forces in the Battle of Kumanovo, which took place in October 1912 (rather than 1913, as the author indicates) and prompted an Ottoman retreat from the region.

17. A reference to Abraham Pilesov of Niš, who distinguished himself during the Battle of Kumanovo.

## 126. WHEN SPANISH IS NO LONGER A JEWISH LANGUAGE: IMMIGRANT ENCOUNTERS ON THE STREETS OF NEW YORK CITY (1928)

*As a new generation of Sephardi Jews settled in the Lower East Side, Harlem, and other immigrant neighborhoods in New York City, they encountered other émigré communities, including Spanish-speaking non-Jews from Puerto Rico and elsewhere in Latin America. In part because Ladino and modern Spanish are mutually intelligible, these encounters sometimes led to personal relationships and cultural affinity. Tensions, however, also could attend the meetings of Spanish and Judeo-Spanish speakers in the "veritable Tower of Babel" of New York City, as is suggested by this pseudonymous letter by the Salonican-born Moise B. Soulam (1890–1967), editor of the Ladino newspaper* La Vara, *and author of its successful advice column.*

Dear *Vara* of my soul,

Wherever it may be, I am always hit in the face by a pet peeve, some vexation and angst, due to the misbehavior of certain of our women who still do not know whether they are in New York, in the city of the veritable Tower of Babel, where many languages are spoken, or whether they are living in the old Turkey, where our women used to speak not only shouting through the streets, but also moving their hands and feet.

Here it is the same with some of our women, who, without even knowing who is sitting by their side, in the car, elevated train, and subway, go around speaking to each other in Spanish, and shouting as if they were litigating.

If I write this to you, *Vara* of my heart, it is because on Monday, two Sephardi women living in . . . Harlem, were on the elevated, returning from downtown to their homes, speaking not only [by] shouting, but also gesticulating with their hands.

What was remarkable about the conversations that the women in question were having on the elevated was that one of them was speaking about matters between husband and wife. The woman speaking should have spoken to her friend either very softly or when they were alone in their homes.

Besides this they began to mock in Spanish a fat man who was sitting in front of them, and began to say things about him, both truths and untruths, ugly words that would make you want to block your ears.

Everything was going fine until the two women left the station at 116th Street, but as they walked down the stairs, they found themselves behind a Puerto Rican good-for-nothing, to whom they did not pay attention at first.

The women were walking on 116th Street, returning to their homes, and the Puerto Rican also continued to walk behind them.

The two ladies turned onto Park Avenue, when the Puerto Rican suddenly came to their side. After greeting them in Spanish, he invited the two to come to his house. . . .

You can well imagine that the two Sephardi women did not answer him, and the Puerto Rican continued to follow them. But seeing that he was not getting any response either to his greeting or to his inauspicious invitation, he ventured to speak a few dirty words to the two Sephardi women, who answered him brazenly, "What do you think we are? Get out of here before we call a policeman."

Upon hearing this the Puerto Rican told them:

"Excuse me, ladies, as I was sitting next to you on the elevated, I heard that you were speaking in Spanish some words that you will readily recall, and I thought that you two were———"

Thus saying, the Puerto Rican started walking rapidly or, better said, started running, before the two women could call a policeman. . . .

Don't ask me, dear *Vara*, how I came to know this, since my grandmother used to say, "do not pay money to learn a secret." This applies even more in this case because women cannot keep secrets. These two ladies told the story to their female neighbors, their female neighbors told their nieces, their nieces told their girlfriends, their girlfriends told their husbands, and before you could say "and the cat came and ate the kid, and the dog came and bit the cat,"[18] I also got a bite of this gossip. What I mean to say is that I came to know the matter and told it to you so that this may serve as a lesson for those women of ours who, finding themselves on the streets or in cars, on the elevated and in subways, be careful not to speak [by] shouting, because as I told you before New York resembles the Tower of Babel. Here there are peoples and individuals who speak various languages, and without knowing or thinking about it we can be heard, understood, and ac-

---

18. From Had Gadya, a song traditionally sung at the end of the Passover Seder.

cused by strangers, and the best thing of all is to behave yourself while talking.

Bula Satula (Moise B. Soulam), *La Vara*, November 30, 1928. Reproduced in Aviva Ben-Ur, "'We Speak and Write This Language Against Our Will:' Jews, Hispanics, and the Dilemma of Ladino-Speaking Sephardim in Early-Twentieth-Century New York," *American Jewish Archives Journal* 50:1–2 (1998): 136–38. Translated from Ladino by Aviva Ben-Ur.

## 127. MUSLIM PUPILS IN A JEWISH SCHOOL: A SEPHARDI TEACHER FROM THE EASTERN MEDITERRANEAN SETTLES IN TUNISIA [1931]

*Born in Edirne to a family of intellectuals and rabbis, Vitalis Danon (1897–1969) was educated in a traditional Jewish school until the age of eleven, at which point he was enrolled in the local Alliance Israélite Universelle school. Upon graduation Danon was recommended for admission to the École Normale Israélite Orientale, the AIU's prestigious teacher-training college in Paris and later sent to Tunisia to serve the organization. Danon remained in Tunisia for five decades, serving as a teacher and director of schools in Tunis, Sfax, and Hafsia, marrying a former pupil, and raising a family. During his time in Tunisia, he wrote exhaustively, contributing to journals including* L'Univers Israélite, *and penning various novels, a novella, a work of Jewish history for AIU pupils, and a sociological study of the Jews of the Jewish district (hara) of Sfax that was published in French, English, and Spanish. In the following letter, which Danon sent to the president of the Alliance Israélite Universelle from Sfax, he describes the matriculation of Muslim students into the local AIU school, a development Danon viewed with favor. During his time in Tunisia, Danon successfully petitioned for French citizenship, which he was granted on account of his work with the AIU.*

Sfax, October 7, 1931

Mr. President,

I have the honor to confirm my letter from the first of the month. As soon as I wrote it we reopened the school on Monday, October 5, as we are typically closed the day after Sukkot. This has been the best opening of the school year since I have been in Sfax. In previous years parents would bring their children some time during the first fifteen days of classes. Classes wouldn't be full and ready until the end of October. In 1930 the youngest class started with little more than four students. This year we already have fifty-four. Others will come later. Where will we put them all? . . . Regarding the Muslims, that day represented a storming [of the castle]. In front of the door, in the courtyard, one could see Arabs wearing fezzes, waiting patiently, because I didn't want to accept any of their children before accommodating our own and before knowing the number of available spots. Nearly all of them came accompanied by a Jewish notable, or armed with a letter of "warmest recommendation," an example of which I have attached here.

The president of the Charity Committee, Mr. Albert Sa'ada, recommended admitting two [Muslim pupils] and to follow up after the beginning of the school year. For many years he has opposed those who demanded the exclusion of Muslims. He has stated several times: I would like you to have enough space to admit as many Muslims as Jews. Shouldn't we be proud to have them coming to us Jews and trusting us with their children? This one here is a notary, that one a judge, and another a great landowner. They all recognize the high status of our school. This is a great tribute.

The very evening before school opened I saw a wealthy Arab accompanied by a former president of the Charity Committee enter my office. Imagine my surprise! He had presided over a committee opposed to admitting Arabs to our school. During his time [as president] you had written a beautiful response to this pretentiousness in your letter of November 3, 1924. And I saw before me this wealthy banker, hat in hand, begging me to take his protégé. May God pardon me if I committed the sin of pride in that moment! I swear that this comportment, this insistence on asking me for something, made me happy.

On the very first day of school, after I had sent away those whom I could not admit, I saw a member of the Great Council, a kind of deputy for us, approach. He asked only for one spot for his friend's son, nothing but one little spot, [imploring], "Put him on a stool, there, between two tables, in the back of the class. A school director must be flexible. You have such a good reputation in the Muslim world! You cannot refuse students, you must not!" . . .

We typically have 200 students, including twenty-five Muslims. To date we can count thirty-two of them distributed in the following manner: fourteen in the first class, three in the second class and nine in the third class. I ruthlessly refused to admit any of them to the fourth or fifth classes, reserving the available spots for the young Jews who had not come earlier in the month.

As you can see, there has been a happy reversal of opinion among the elite Jewish society of Sfax regarding Arab-Jewish relations.

Your devoted,
V. Danon

Letter by Vitalis Danon to the President of the Alliance Israélite Universelle, October 7, 1931. Archives of the Alliance Israélite Universelle (Paris), XII Tunisie E 50a. Translated from French by Alma Heckman.

## 128. ON THE NEED FOR AN AMERICAN SEPHARDI PRAYER BOOK (1934)

*Immigrant Jews reaching the United States from Southeastern Europe and the Middle East often organized themselves according to their city, region, or country of origin. Congregations and communities of Jews from Syria, Kastoria, Yanya (Ioannina), Monastir (Bitola), and Salonica each had their own synagogue rites. To militate against this fragmentation the Spanish and Portuguese Shearith Israel congregation of New York City welcomed new Sephardi immigrants into its High Holiday services in overflow spaces in the synagogue's basement. Yet the question of which liturgy the community would use continued to be a matter of debate for many decades. Would the prayer books of American Sephardim include English, or Ladino, or both? Would they follow the rites of the small community of Old Sephardim or of the much larger community of New Sephardim, or privilege one community of new immigrants over others? Here, Shearith Israel's president and rabbi, David de Sola Pool (1917–1984), speaks of the need to create a unified, English-language prayer book for all Sephardi Jews in the United States.*

The Union of Sephardic Congregations has recently put into the hands of the printer the manuscript of a work, which should bring blessing to the Sephardim of this country during the coming year. That work is the traditional Sephardic prayer book.

Without our own distinctive prayer book, we cannot hope to preserve our noble historic *minhag*.[19] Yet it has become increasingly difficult to obtain copies of our liturgy. The editions produced in Vienna are poorly printed on poor paper, and poorly bound, and these as well as the Italian and Palestinian editions do not have the English translation, which is essential if the prayer book is to be fully used as a book of devotion by

---

19. Custom.

the men, women, and children of our American Sephardic communities. The sumptuous edition published in London is so costly as to be virtually an edition *de luxe*, and the old American edition with English Translation is exhausted, and unfit to be reprinted because the type is so worn.

In this way a paramount need has grown up for an American edition of our prayer book, a need which must be satisfied if our Sephardic synagogues and religious schools are to be enabled to continue their work without grave hindrance. I emphasize that it must be an American edition, for only if we have a form of prayers that can be regarded as an American *minhag* shall we overcome the divisions within the synagogue among those who would insist on preserving in this country every fine point of local *minhag* which they have brought with them from Salonica or Rhodes or Monastir or Janina [Ioannina] or Aleppo or Jerusalem or Cairo or Mogador [Essaouira] or Gibraltar or London or Amsterdam or Jamaica or Curaçao, or any of the other places from which our American Sephardic communities are recruited. In addition, there is a Sephardic tradition of nearly three centuries that has existed in New York, and with very slight differences also Philadelphia and Montreal. To attain unity within the Sephardic synagogues of this country, all these *minhagim* must be merged and fused into one. The Sephardim in the United States are too few to allow themselves the luxury of trivial divisions on account of minor *minhagim*.

It is therefore a great source of rejoicing to announce that the edition of our prayer book which has now been given to the press by the Union of Sephardic Congregations not only has an English translation, but it also has the approval of the chief rabbi of the Syrian Jews of New York, leading *hazzanim*[20] of Oriental Jewish congregations in New York, and the rabbis of the old American Sephardic communities. May this prayer book to be published in the coming year 5695 bring to our scattered Sephardic communities a true inner unity, founded on a common spiritual heritage that shall be actively shared, and may the new edition of the prayer book bring to Sephardic Jewry a greater measure of knowledge and devotion to our ancient traditions.

David de Sola Pool, "Traditional Sephardic Prayer Book," *La Vara*, August 31, 1934, 8. Original in English.

_____

20. Cantors.

## 129. "A LETTER FROM THE LAND OF ISRAEL": A SALONICAN ÉMIGRÉ ON THE PALESTINIAN DISCOUNT BANK (1936)

*By the interwar period a substantial diaspora of Salonican Jews had established itself in centers across the globe, including New York, Paris, Haifa, Tel Aviv, and various Latin American cities. From their new homes many Salonican émigrés sent money back to the old country in support of their families, charitable causes, or both. In the eyes of those who stayed behind, the individuals who succeeded abroad gave Jews in Salonica reason to be proud. The following excerpt, published in a Ladino serial from Greek Salonica in the mid-1930s, extolls the innovations of a recently founded bank run by Jews of Salonican origin in British Mandate Palestine. Founded by Leon Recanati (1890–1945) in 1935, the Palestine Discount Bank was unique in several respects: it specialized in foreign trade, was open to individuals (rather than only to merchants and companies), and at the time of its founding was the only bank in Palestine run by Sephardi Jews. Commercial contacts and expertise were portable assets for many Sephardi émigrés during this period, even if the financial empire built by Recanati was unusual in its scale.*

A leak permitted me to learn that in the next general meeting of the shareholders of the Palestinian Discount Bank, a proposal will be floated to increase the [bank's] capital by issuing another ten thousand shares per lira, shares for which the demand is quite strong and can be considered henceforth as already purchased.

In publishing the balance sheet of the Palestinian Discount Bank, the Palestinian press has not failed to issue the most complimentary commentaries about the active leaders of this institution. Above all, *Haaretz*, in its special page on economic life in Palestine, dedicated to the bank in question a very sympathetic note revealing that the [bank's] leaders and founders are all Sephardi natives of Salonica.[21] Despite this fact, 90 percent of the bank's clientele are Ashkenazim, as Mr. Leon Recanati told me in the course of an interview he granted me.

We consider it interesting to announce on this occasion that the Palestinian Discount Bank has introduced an innovation that brings it great honor. Naturally we believe that [this example] will be followed in no time by the other Jewish banks established in Palestine. . . . Here it is:

Everyone is already aware that on the checks of the big banks there is a section in which one writes the name of the account holder and the

---

21. A Hebrew-language newspaper established in Palestine in 1918.

amount of the check, and in miniscule characters visible only under a magnifying glass can be found the printed name of the bank. All the Jewish banks here, from the Anglo-Palestine Bank to the Israel Bank, have [until now] printed straight lines, one next to the other, in these sections of their checks. A new series of checks [produced by] the Palestine Discount Bank [and] slated to be placed in circulation shortly [will become] the first in the Land of Israel to print, in small font, the name of the bank in Hebrew letters. Along the border of these checks, the very elegant new emblem of the bank—a work of true art—interlocks the ancient Jewish symbols of the Star of David and the menorah, while in the middle, [one finds represented] the four branches with which the bank occupies itself (construction, industry, commerce, and shipping), creating, all told, a completely original and uniquely Jewish assemblage.

We conclude by sending our best wishes for the continual development of the Palestinian Discount Bank, for the general wellbeing of the economy, and for the [strength of] the market in the Land of Israel. We address our most sincere congratulations to the exceptionally capable and active directors of the bank, Misters Recanati, Carasso, Burla, etc., who have succeeded in a relatively short period of time and have built their establishment on such strong foundations, despite our [recent] experience of a period of [economic] abnormality. They have thus brought great honor to Salonican Judaism, which is coming to be recognized and appreciated by our brothers from other countries, who find in us rare qualities that are being dedicated to reconstructing our old-new homeland.

Haim Toledano

Haim Toledano, "Un estabilimiento ke aze onor al djudaizmo salonikiote," *El Mesajero*, May 3, 1936, 2–3. Translated from Ladino by Devin E. Naar.

## 130. HONORING ATATÜRK IN A PARISIAN SYNAGOGUE (1939)

*In January 1939, Sephardi Jews gathered in a synagogue in Paris to commemorate the life of the first president of the Turkish Republic, Mustafa Kemal Atatürk (1881–1938), who died two months earlier. Many of the formerly Ottoman and*

*Turkish Jews who gathered on this occasion had left the eastern Mediterranean for France decades before. A significant portion of them no longer held Turkish citizenship—whether because they had failed to register with the proper authorities after the Ottoman Empire collapsed or because they had actively opted to become French citizens. Yet the celebrants' public declaration of their continued attachment to Turkey—and to the man they hailed as the "savior and reformer" of that country—remains striking. Their ceremony, which combined Turkish flags, speeches in Turkish, and the lionization of a foreign nationalist hero with French patriotic music and Jewish ritual, offers compelling evidence that Sephardi Jews in France believed that identification with their former homeland was compatible with their new allegiance to France.*

The Sephardi community performed a funeral service to the memory of Kemal Atatürk, savior and reformer of Turkey, at the Berith-Shalom Temple, Friday, January 13, 1939.

The temple was decorated for the occasion by the Lévi-Rivet company. Two Turkish flags veiled in black had been placed on the two sides of the ark. The portrait of Kemal Atatürk, loaned obligingly by the consul-general of Turkey, adorned the gallery.

The [Sephardi] chief rabbi N. J. Ovadia offered a funeral eulogy for the departed Kemal Atatürk; then, in the middle of a religious silence, the faithful stood and listened to Shiviti,[22] verses of a psalm chanted by the cantor José Papo; Mr. Robert Mitrani, secretary-general of the community, delivered a speech in Turkish exalting the memory of the deceased; the holy ark was opened briefly by Mr. Emmanuel Salem and prayers for France and Turkey were recited; the choir, which chanted "Adonai, ma Adam" and "Tehilat Adonai," closed the ceremony with the *Turkish March* and the *Marseillaise*.[23]

Among the people who took part in the ceremony, we noted the head of the office of the Ministry of the Interior, two delegates from the Turkish embassy, Consul-General Durry Bey, the honorary ex-consul Zia Bey, Mr. Basman, director of the Scholastic Office, accompanied by a few Turkish students, the vice-consul of Spain, Señor Gomez, a delegation from the Consistory of Paris, Mr. Berr, from the Prefecture of Police, Chief Rabbi of Paris Julien Weill, Dr. Alcalay, chief rabbi of

---

22. "I am ever mindful of the Lord's presence": Psalm 16:8–9.
23. "Adonai, ma Adam" ("God, what is man?"), Psalm 144:3–4, a traditional Jewish funeral chant about the fleeting nature of human existence; "Tehilat Adonai" ("Praise of the Lord"), a song composed of four verses from Psalms 145:21, 115:18, 118:1, and 106:2.

Yugoslavia, Señor Menahem Coriat, president of the Rabbinical Tribunal of Spain, representatives of La Fraternité, the Talmud Torah, the Jeunesse Sépharadite, the École Normale Orientale, the Hevra Kadisha,[24] and a delegation of veterans, Zionists, and Mizrahists.

The next evening, at 7:30 P.M., Radio Luxembourg broadcasted the speeches of the chief rabbi and M. R. Mitrani and the songs performed by Mr. José Papo.

"Un Service funèbre à la mémoire de Kemal Ataturk," *Samedi*, January 21, 1939. Translated from French and introduced by Ethan Katz.

## 131. A SEPHARDI PIONEER IN SEATTLE [1939]

*In the first decades of the twentieth century, Seattle emerged as the third largest émigré Sephardi community in the United States, after New York City and Los Angeles. Many of the earliest Sephardi settlers in the Pacific Northwest followed non-Jews to this port city, participating in the city's robust trade in fish and vegetables. The first Sephardi immigrants to Seattle, including Sam (né Solomon) Calvo (1908–1964), whom we encounter here, confronted a largely Yiddish-speaking, Ashkenazi Jewish community whose members did not immediately recognize them as Jewish. With time, however, Sephardim became a highly visible, well-organized, and influential segment of Seattle's Jewish population, integrating into the Jewish community generally. Calvo founded and owned the Western Fish & Oyster Co. (later Waterfront Fish & Oyster Co.) in Seattle's Pike Place Market, where many immigrant Sephardim maintained fish and produce stands.*

Mr. Sam Calvo was the first [of the] Sephardim to be inspired with the idea of coming to Seattle. . . . No Marmara Sephardim had ever gone to America and there was no talk among the Sephardim of the Near East of the "land of golden opportunity". . . .

Calvo's brother owned a clothing store in Galemi, a town near Marmara. One day while visiting his brother, Calvo came across a Greek family with whom he was acquainted. Upon chatting with the Greek lady of the family, Calvo was informed that she had a brother visiting from Seattle, Washington. She wanted Calvo to meet him. Shortly afterwards, the two men met; they began to chat about things in general and the Greek from Seattle impressed Calvo with descriptions of the

_____
24. Burial society.

business opportunities in the Pacific Northwest. Calvo had no idea where Seattle was but he felt as if he would like the city because it was situated in a salt water atmosphere with fresh water lakes surrounding its borders. The Greek lady urged Calvo to go to Seattle. She pointed out [that] he was not married, had no obligations and, besides, her brother was returning to Seattle and would be a companion for him. Calvo and his Seattle acquaintance went to a nearby tavern to discuss America over a bottle of raki. The Greek pointed out that when he first went to America he knew very little about the new country. But in spite of language difficulties he had earned enough money to return to the Near East for a visit. Now he was planning to return to Seattle; if Calvo wished to join him, he would be welcome. After a long conversation with the Greek from Seattle Calvo returned to the Greek residence of his friends. Again the Greek lady urged him to join her brother and, in reality, she was responsible for Calvo's decision.

That evening Calvo announced to his family that he intended to go to Seattle to seek his fortune. His family objected because they knew nothing of Seattle and were afraid to allow him to make such a long journey. After much discussion, Calvo was given consent. Before long, the entire community was excited about the proposed trip by one of their coreligionists to Seattle. Jacob Polichar (Sephardic), a friend of Calvo's, expressed a desire to join him in his adventure. They agreed to go together. The parents of these young Sephardim provided the necessary funds for the two young bachelors and wished them Godspeed.

Calvo and Polichar agreed to meet their Greek friend in Constantinople where they would purchase their tickets. They met their friend in Constantinople who had also brought his brother-in-law to join the party. These two Sephardim and two Greeks purchased tickets from Constantinople to Seattle. At Marseille, the Greek's brother-in-law became ill, so the party left him in France and continued the journey. Neither Calvo or Polichar could speak a word of English and their Seattle friend served as interpreter. The Greek himself was not very intimate with the English language but both Sephardim marveled at his command of the new language. When they arrived in New York they did not stop to visit the city; instead they started west as soon as possible.

They arrived in Seattle one evening in June of 1903. The next day their Greek friend brought them to another Greek who operated a fish market near the waterfront. Both Sephardim had brought their luggage with them because they were ready for any plans that might necessitate a change of residence. The owner of the fish market thought Calvo and Polichar were Greeks because they looked and spoke like Greeks. Both Sephardim pointed out they were Jews and then inquired as to the immediate prospect of finding employment. The proprietor told them he might be able to find work for them soon and asked both men to stay in his shop for the day.

That afternoon some Ashkenazic Jews stopped at this fish market to make some purchases. Knowing his customers were Jewish the Greek explained to them that Calvo and Polichar were newly-arrived Jews from Marmara. Then he turned to Calvo and Polichar and in Greek, told them his customers were also Jews. Both Sephardim were delighted to find there were Jews in Seattle, but the expression of joy was not to be seen in the Ashkenazic faces. Instead there was doubt and suspicion because Calvo and Polichar could not speak Yiddish and instead spoke in Greek. Calvo realized the Ashkenazim suspected him and his companion of being frauds so he quickly opened his valise and produced his phylacteries and Hebrew prayer books in order to impress them. This convinced the Ashkenazim, who later in the afternoon brought the two Sephardim to the home of Mr. and Mrs. Rickles.

Mr. Rickles was described as "a good Samaritan" and his home was always open to wandering Jews. He had an Ashkenazic friend from South America and through this man Mr. Rickles understood the full needs of Calvo and Polichar. Both Sephardim were invited to join the Rickles during the holiday of Shavu'oth. Calvo and Polichar lived in a hotel during their first week in Seattle but spent their afternoons and evenings at the Rickles' residence. Calvo and Polichar were very pleased to receive such kind hospitality amidst a strange gathering. Both Sephardim were introduced to Rabbi Genss, the spiritual leader of the Ashkenazic Bikur Holim and attended services at his synagogue. . . . By 1906 Calvo had his own fish market. He had saved his money and was ready to enter matrimony. An Ashkenazic wife was out of the question so he went back to Marmara to visit his family and find a spouse. He became engaged and married to Luna Levy of Marmara within a period of six weeks. Very shortly, Mr. and Mrs. Calvo returned to Seattle.

Albert Adatto, "Sephardim and the Seattle Sephardic Community" (M.A. thesis, University of Washington, 1939), 184–91. Original in English.

## 132. YIDDISH IMPRESSIONS OF SEPHARDI JEWS IN NEW YORK CITY (1941)

*Nineteenth and early twentieth-century Salonica has long fascinated a variety of observers, many of whom consider it the Jewish city par excellence due to its once large Jewish population, the affluence and influence a number of its Jewish residents achieved locally, and the reputation that Salonican Jews garnered abroad. Those who traveled to the Ottoman, and later Greek, port city during the modern period would often comment on the preponderance of Jews in Salonica. Others noted in awe that much of the city's trade came to a near standstill on the Jewish Sabbath. The excerpt that follows includes the impressions of a Yiddish journalist in New York, who wrote in 1941 that of all the Sephardi Jews living in his midst, only the Jews of Salonica captured his interest. Drawing a parallel to the Ashkenazi world his readers knew best, he suggested that the prominence of Salonican Jews equalled the respect that Jews from Vilna enjoyed among Ashkenazim. The final section takes a more somber tone, as it offers the author's premonition that under German occupation the once-great Jewish city he celebrated was under threat.*

I sit with a Sephardi *hakham*, [that is] with a Sephardi rabbi, and we talk about the Sephardi Jews in New York. From time to time my interlocutor groans about the fate of his brothers. Thirty thousand Sephardim, or Spanish Jews from the Near East and from the Balkan lands, live in New York today. But they are all spread across the great city, and it is a difficult thing to unite them. In the same manner as the Ashkenazi Jews—they all broke up into *landsmanshafts*.[25] And today they already have around fifteen of their own *landsmanshafts*. You have here Jews from the island of Rhodes and they have their own *landsmanshaft*; Jews from Monastir (a city in Yugoslavia) [today Bitola, Macedonia]—and they have their own *landsmanshaft*; Jews from Salonica, Jews from Turkey, Jews from Yanina [Ioannina], Greece, and

---

25. Mutual aid societies organized around place of origin.

so on, and all are great patriots only of their own synagogues, of their own clubs, of their own circles.

"And the Jews of New York are greatly mistaken"—the *hakham* continues to tell me—"if they think that the Sephardi community [of the congregation] Shearith Israel, where Rabbi David de Sola Pool is rabbi, is really composed of Sephardi Jews. This community has, throughout its existence, almost completely assimilated. Almost all members of Shearith Israel are today Ashkenazi Jews. Yes, the Sephardi Jews were the first Jews in New York, before the city took its current name. But of these Jews, of these Sephardim, nothing is left. The Sephardi community Shearith Israel has remained true only to its old name."

"We are true Sephardi Jews," the *hakham* said to me, "but should any one of us want to become a member of the Sephardi community Shearith Israel, God forbid he would be accepted there. Today it is a closed community of rich Jews, and if you're not rich enough, it means you sit at home". . . .

At this point the Sephardi Jews didn't interest me in general, as a group. From all these *landsmanshafts* that the *hakham* listed for me, only the Salonican Jews interested me. Why the Jews of Salonica? Whoever has been to the Land of Israel knows that the Salonican Jews there excel in their industriousness, their hard work and their poverty. Do the Salonican Jews also excel in these virtues in New York? In the Land of Israel the Salonican Jews excel as the best farmers, and with their persistence they developed the Jewish fish industry. What branch of work have they developed here? What have the Salonican Jews created in New York?

My first encounter with a Salonican Jew in New York was at the editorial office of the Spanish weekly *La Vara* on Rivington Street. *La Vara* is the only [Judeo-Spanish] newspaper published in the United States. They say that it's an understood fact that the editor of any newspaper for the Sephardi Jews in their mother tongue, Ladino, must be a Salonican Jew. In Jewish life in the Balkans and in the Near East, both with regards to Torah and also to the Jewish language Ladino—the Salonican Jews played the same role as the Jews of Vilna at one time played in Lithuania, in Russia. . . .

To find more details about the Salonican Jews in New York I needed to go to the Bronx. It is there that they are now mostly concentrated, and there, at 1220 Jerome Avenue, they have their Brotherhood, their fraternity, the Ermandad Sefaradi de Amerika (Sephardic Brotherhood of America). I went up to the first floor. [In] a large hall, the walls were covered with a large American flag and many pictures. On one side stands a large holy ark draped with a curtain. This is the locus of the Sephardi Jews. Here their club is located, and here is also their synagogue. . . . I was given some information here by a Salonican Jew, a *talmid hakham*, a Jew who graduated from a rabbinical seminary in Salonica over thirty years ago and here today he is an insurance agent. Here he insures men from death and homes from fire. And he makes a good living here. Although he is very occupied with his business, he finds time to learn, to study, and to devote himself to Jewish communal matters.

It will be interesting to get acquainted with the Salonican Jews in New York, [to learn] how they came here, how they live, what kind of jobs they hold. As my informer the above-mentioned *talmid hakham* and insurance agent told me:

"For the past thirty years, Jewish life in the Old Country has certainly changed, but not for those of us here in New York. We keep all of our old customs here, all of our old traditions, just like thirty years ago in Salonica. We further brought with us from our home our old *sidurim* and *makhzorim*,[26] and we maintain all the tunes and songs our parents taught us in our youth. If our parents could come down and look at how we live here as Jews, they would surely be pleased with us. For the Salonican Jews [it is of utmost importance to follow] *minhag avoyseyhe b-yadeyhem*[27] just as it is written.

"We have also kept to our old customs in family life. We are matched for marriage only among ourselves. . . . I love my brothers, I love the Ashkenazi Jews, but I am bound to the Sephardi Jews with stronger ties. The same [is true] for all Salonican Jews. Marriage with Ashkenazi Jews would make all of our old customs disappear, and we don't want that. We also want to live [our] family life just as our parents lived. We want to keep our language, our 'Ladino,' in our families. And we wouldn't know it [any longer] if we assimilate among other Jews". . . .

---

26. Jewish prayer books.
27. The practice of their fathers.

[The Yiddish correspondent's Sephardi informer continues]:

"Last week another great sorrow befell us, the fate of our brothers in Salonica, who have fallen in the hands of the bloodthirsty Nazis . . . under Hitler.[28] We have turned to the [American Jewish Joint Distribution Committee] to inquire whether it has received news from the Jews of Salonica. But the [committee] has until now received no word from that new Hell. For our part, however, we have directly undertaken an action to collect a sum of money for our now unlucky brothers in Salonica. The destruction of Salonican Jews has suddenly fallen upon us, and we must see straightaway to what extent they can be assisted. Salonica was a wonderful Jewish city. And what has become of it?"

H. Vital, "Saloniker yidn hobn khasene nor tsvishn zikh un getn zikh nit," *Forverts*, July 13, 1941, 1. Courtesy Forward Association. Translated from Yiddish by Michael Casper.

## 133. NOTES FROM LÉOPOLDVILLE: A JOURNEY FROM RHODES TO THE BELGIAN CONGO (1948)

*Arguably the most horrific manifestation of European colonial rule took shape in the Congo Free State, a corporate state formed in 1885 and privately controlled by King Leopold II of Belgium (1835–1909). Leopold's rule, which persisted until 1909, was motivated by the promise of profits from exploitation of copper, minerals, and especially rubber. It was also marked by extraordinary brutality, both of people and land. Lured by a colonial economy that offered great economic promise to Europeans, Sephardi Jews from Rhodes began to emigrate to the Belgian Congo in the early years of the twentieth century, building a community of some 2,500 at its peak in Elisabethville (Lubumbashi), with smaller numbers settling in Léopoldville (Kinshasa) around mid-century. In this source, a Sephardi traveler to Léopoldville, seemingly blind to the legacy of colonial brutality in the Belgian Congo, describes to Ladino readers in his native land the glories of the country, which he viewed as a "peaceful corner of Africa."*

I have just completed an intense and time-consuming journey, having made the enormous leap from the Near East to the African continent. My friends who learned of my decision were thoroughly surprised: they could not understand what prompted my decision at such an advanced age or why I sacrificed the proverbial cool climes of the "Pearl

---

28. German forces entered the city on April 9, 1941.

of the Islands," as we call Rhodes, for the tropical heat of Léopoldville, capital of the Belgian Congo. They even tried to dissuade me for my own sake, but in vain. The reasons for my resolve were as profound as they were complex.

Above all I could not resist the lure of an enchanting country where so many of my loved ones reside. I was unwilling to close my eyes for all eternity before embracing them one last time. Only those with sentimental spirits will understand the strong feelings and fascination [that drove me to make this trip]. I also felt compelled to take refuge in this important part of the world in order to preserve something I consider a precious treasure: my freedom! Here in this blessed country, which is administered with so much wisdom by the enlightened and democratic Belgians, people live under the jurisdiction of humane laws, as free and independent men, with a happy tranquility of spirit. Here one finds no trace of the nightmare that torments the peoples of the Orient, none of the mean and miserable politics; the spirit of fanaticism; the flagrant injustices that hound the most peaceable and unfortunate peoples of the earth! Moreover, having suffered during the recent World War . . . under the tyranny of a demagogue in a class all his own, I was unwilling to resign myself to the casualties of a new and terrible ordeal. I wanted to distance myself from such appalling sights by taking refuge in this faraway land, this peaceful corner of Africa.

Yet despite everything I feel isolated here and I suffer from nostalgia for the magical Orient. I am like a plant uprooted from its native soil and transplanted into a foreign and unsuitable land. I no longer breathe that pure and purifying air. I remain cut off from the invigorating and magical climate in which I was raised. All of this is to say that I feel far from so many loved ones and close friends. For this reason, I repeat the words of our great national poet Judah Ha-Levi, "If I am in the West, my heart is in the East." Though I find myself in the African Occident, my soul rests with my captivating memories of the distant East.

Hezekiah Franco, "Impresiones de viaje (a vuelo de pajaro)," *La Boz de Türkiye*, June 15, 1948, 368. Translated from Ladino by Julia Phillips Cohen.

## 134. "FORGE YOUR OWN PASSPORT": THE UNLIKELY RISE OF AN INTERNATIONAL AUTHOR AND DIPLOMAT [1949]

*Throughout the first half of the twentieth century, Jews from Ottoman and former Ottoman lands who settled abroad corresponded with individuals and communities in their erstwhile homes. Apart from trying to keep in touch with loved ones, they often asked religious questions or looked for documentation to secure their status in their new homes. In nearly all cases, correspondents wrote to resolve pressing issues of the moment. The following letter, sent from the son of the longtime Ladino journalist David Fresco (1853–1933) to the Turkish Jewish scholar Abraham Galante (1873–1961) is thus unusual in its orientation toward the past. Writing many years after his father's death, Mauricio Fresco attempted to piece his father's life back together with the help of a former colleague and scholar. In doing so he revealed intriguing elements of his own biography and literary work produced during a diplomatic career spent in many countries. (For more on David Fresco see source 71; on Galante see sources 70, 84, 88, 134-135, and 147.)*

April 26, 1949

Dear Mr. Galante,

Frankly I doubt you will remember me or the fact that during my youth I had the pleasure of seeing you often in the office of my father, David Fresco, where he worked so hard to publish his journal *El Tiempo* under conditions that can rightly be described as tragic, since he sacrificed his life, and that of our family, to this journal.

[Though] I am the youngest of the family, I worked with my father. It was during this time that I had the pleasure of meeting you. That was at least twenty-nine years ago. Although much time has passed, I still have fond memories of those who collaborated with and loved my father, because I must confess I am proud to be his son.

I have since worked in America as a journalist. I have published many books, and contributed to dozens of newspapers and journals in various languages.

You may have learned from my father that I have also involved myself in the world of diplomacy, and that I have spent time in many places around the world. I have witnessed major events in Manchuria and the war in Shanghai, spent time in Russia, and experienced the occupation of Paris (in a diplomatic post) as well as the city's liberation—in short, [experiences] too long to recount [here]. At present I am preparing a book, *Forge Your Own Passport*, which will no doubt cause me great trouble but in which I seek to prove the stupidity of passports, visas, nationalities, races, etc. With the experience of eighteen years of service in consular and diplomatic positions, I will bring to light many examples that prove how humanity is exploited. Certainly everyone [engages in exploitation], but this does not mean that one should abstain from denouncing it.

I came by your address through a young man who spoke to me of you, without knowing that I knew you many years ago. If it is possible I would be very much obliged if you could respond to me by airmail, in order to tell me whether you have ever published anything about my father.

The reason I ask is that, although I have all the love and admiration in the world for my father, I was unfortunately too young and naive to be able to inquire or know much about my father's past [while he was still alive]. I now feel it is my duty to write something about my father, even if only a small pamphlet.

Although I realize that it is unlikely, I wonder if you could tell me whether anyone has written anything about him? If so I would be very grateful if you could give me all of the available information on this subject.

The same young man who spoke to me of you has given me an issue of *La Boz de Türkiye* (which should be written *La Voz*, as in Spanish). Reading it causes the impression that it is filled with errors, because the differences between Ladino and Spanish have the effect of distracting the reader . . . rather than allowing him to grasp the meaning of the article. I am of the opinion that the editor of the journal should gradually begin to correct this, while also teaching his readers Spanish. If I am not mistaken, my father followed this approach.

Dear Mr. Galante, do me the kindness of sending me information about my father—that is, whatever you may have written about him. I hope it pleases you to know that I remember you fondly.

Mauricio Fresco

Letter from Mauricio Fresco in Mexico City to Abraham Galante in Istanbul, April 26, 1949, The Central Archives for the History of the Jewish People (Jerusalem), Galante papers, P-112/58. Translated from French by Julia Phillips Cohen.

## 135. "MY SON PLAYS TENNIS AT WIMBLEDON": A GLOBALLY-CONNECTED TURKISH JEW ENTERS ANGLO-JEWISH HIGH SOCIETY [1951]

*The United Kingdom, like the United States, was home to a well-established, highly acculturated and largely affluent community of Jews of Spanish and Portuguese origin who were long settled in the country by the time Ottoman Jewish newcomers began arriving in the nineteenth century. Although in many cases the differences between the communities remained stark, in rare cases Levantine Jews succeeded in establishing themselves as part of British high society, as evidenced in the following letter. Here the author, a Jew who was originally from Ottoman Rhodes and had passed through Istanbul and Rhodesia before settling in London, describes his success in business, his acceptance into the communal leadership of Anglo-Jewry, and his sons' elite education and training. Despite the author's rapid integration into elite circles in his adoptive city, it is striking that he also speaks of his belonging to a worldwide network of Jews from Rhodes who remained connected, from California and London to Rhodesia and the Belgian Congo.*

My dear Abraham,

Recently Mr. Nissim Benbassat from Argentina called on me to bring me greetings from Haim from Rhodesia, and at the same time he mentioned that he had been to see you, and I was delighted to learn that you are in good health.

I thought of writing you this letter to tell you of my present where-abouts as well as of my pilgrimages since I last saw you in Istanbul in 1915.

I was most grateful to you when you came to see me at the Taşkışla Hospital together with Şükri Bey, one of my teachers of the Idadiye of Rhodes.[29]

After I left Istanbul, I went to Makri via Kutakye [Kütahya] and Denizli. During my stay in Makri, because the only existing chemist died, I was appointed by the civilian authorities to be the chemist of that town, and I fulfilled my engagements very satisfactorily for the duration of the war. I was also at the same time the military telegraphist at the District Head Office.[30]

Of course, after the war was over due to the flow of emigration I

---

29. Although the letter was typed in English, the author included the words "Taşkışla Hastahanesi" (a major hospital of Istanbul) and "Şükri Bey" in the Arabic script of Ottoman Turkish.

30. The original, "Mintika Kumandanlık," translates roughly to the head office of the district or precinct and was also included in Arabic script by the author's own hand in this letter.

packed up and went to S[outhern] Rhodesia where I met Haim. I
lived there for five years, and then came to Europe.

Since 1930 I have been settled in this country, and I am very pleased
to say that I have made a success of my enterprises. My friends, Mr.
and Mrs. Ashkenazi, who are taking this letter to you, both originate
from Istanbul, and will no doubt tell you quite a lot about me.

I have introduced a new industry into this country, and have two
very substantial textile factories not very far from London. I also have
a factory in the north of England producing chemicals. Recently I
purchased a farm not very far from London, where we are producing
lime for agricultural purposes, and this new venture is progressing very
satisfactorily.

Apart from this I have other companies, wh[ich] export and import
from all parts of the World; China, Japan, India, and all the continental
countries, so you will note that I am a very busy man, and I consider
that my success can be compared very favorably with any of the more
successful *Rodislis*.

Of course, I am very happily married to a very charming lady; both
my friends will tell you how charming my wife is, and I have been blessed
with two very nice sons. My elder son, Michael, has just taken his degree at Oxford University, where he has had a very successful career.
He is a very good historian, and at the same time has produced reviews
and plays whilst at Oxford. He is twenty-one years of age. My younger
son, David, is now doing his military service, and is a pilot officer in the
R.A.F.[31] He is a very athletic young man, and is one metre eighty-six
cm. tall. He played tennis at Wimbledon last week in a R.A.F. Tourna-
ment. We are very happy in the two very nice sons we have, and both
my wife and I hope that they will become very useful world citizens.

In spite of my multifarious occupations I have also been able to
take part in some of our social and communal affairs. I am enclosing a
little slip circularized by our congregation, from which you will note
that I was a member of the British Board of Deputies, and I will be
elected again.

My son, Michael, has already finished at university, and will be joining my business within the next month or two, and I am also looking

---

31. An acronym for the British Royal Air Force.

forward to my younger son joining me when he leaves the R.A.F. in eight months time, and then I will be planning to make a trip to Turkey, and I hope to visit you.

I travel extensively all over the world, but it is on business and there is not much time for anything else. I have not visited Turkey since I left in 1920. I must tell you, by the way, that the pharmacy I ran during the 1914–1918 war belonged to Salih Zeki Bey, who was a great friend of Yunus Nadi, who was a member of parliament and most probably a contemporary of yours.

My sisters are scattered all over the world, most of them in California, USA, where I have visited them twice since the war. My younger sisters are in the Belgian Congo.

I get regular visits from all the *Rodislis* who come over here from all parts of the world. I had a visit the other day from Asher Alhadeff and his wife, Jeanette. Somehow it seems that there is a tremendous solidarity amongst all the *Rodislis*, and I can assure you that it gives me very great pleasure to be visited by all our friends when they pass through London.

My wife, although a lady born in London, has already learned quite a lot of Ladino. Our friends, Mr. and Mrs. Ashkenazi, will no doubt tell you quite a lot about us.

Well, Abraham, I have told you quite a lot about us, and I am wondering whether you will find time to write and tell me all your news.

I correspond with Haim[32] in Salisbury, but unfortunately it is almost a one-way correspondence as he is very lazy and does not write often; my letters are always answered by verbal messages which I receive from the Rhodesians when they come to visit me.

I look forward to hearing from you, and trust that this letter will find you in good health.

Yours very sincerely,

Haco

Letter from I. A. [Haco] Cordon in London to Abraham Galante in Istanbul, August 7, 1951, The Central Archives for the History of the Jewish People (Jerusalem), Galante papers, P-112/60. Original in English.

---

32. Galante's brother.

# VI.  THE EMERGENCE OF
## SEPHARDI STUDIES

## 136. FROM SPAIN TO SYRIA: A JEWISH SCHOLAR FROM ALEPPO STUDIES HIS FAMILY HISTORY [1787]

*Raphael Solomon ben Samuel Laniado (d. 1793) hailed from a family of leading Jewish scholars and judges whose ancestors fled Spain following the expulsion, passing through Edirne and Safed before settling in Aleppo in the sixteenth century. While he apparently learned of his ancestral ties to the Iberian Peninsula through family lore, Laniado pieced together the rest of his family's history after consulting the publications and manuscripts of various rabbinic authors. His reasons for compiling this family history were at once personal and political. Motivated by the desire to see his son Ephraim (d. 1805) succeed him in his position as chief judge of the Jewish community in Aleppo, Laniado sought to prove both the eminence of his lineage and the permissibility of his forebears' practice of ruling as sole judge rather than serving alongside at least two others, an approach his contemporaries suggested was the only proper way to uphold Jewish law. For Laniado, as for subsequent generations of scholars of Sephardi studies, interest in the field was often piqued by personal experiences that prompted authors to investigate the history of their own families and communities.*

According to what we have heard and what our ancestors have told us, our family can be traced to those who left during the expulsion, although we do not know to which of the expulsions this refers nor do we know [the names] of the elders of our family or which of them was a rabbi. [However] we have found evidence [of our family history] in the responsa of the sage Re'em[1] of blessed memory, volume one, chapter fifty-two . . . proving that Samuel Laniado of blessed memory was a great Torah scholar, so much so that Re'em of blessed memory called him "the Rabbi of Our Rabbis." And who among us is greater than Re'em? We do not know of any other [Laniados] living at the time, although we have heard that they were here in [Aram] Tsova [Aleppo] may God preserve it; and that they were the holy [people] of Erets.[2]

These were the formidable, resolute, reverent, and devout rabbis, the two great brothers. [One was] the magnificent rabbi who was filled with God's honor, our esteemed rabbi and teacher Samuel Laniado of blessed memory, the rabbi who was [known as] Possessor of the Tools, [because of] his publications *Keli Paz* ["A Golden Tool"], *Keli Yaqar*

---

1. An acronym for Rabbi Elijah ben Abraham Mizrahi (d. 1526), a leading rabbi, author, and adjudicator of Jewish law in Istanbul.

2. Abbreviation for Aram Tsova.

["A Precious Tool"], and *Keli Hemda* ["A Delightful Tool"]. He also authored other guides of various sorts on all twenty-four books [of the Bible] from Jeremiah to the end of Chronicles, which were not printed but are still in existence. It is also known that he wrote another book, *Keli Golah* ["A Diasporic Tool"], which was not published and has disappeared; we do not know what it was about. The aforementioned rabbi [Samuel Laniado] was the cornerstone, a rabbi and a judge and a head of a vast land [Aleppo]. [In this capacity] he issued judgments for the people of this city.

And the second [rabbi], his brother, was the distinguished rabbi, our esteemed rabbi and teacher Isaac Laniado of blessed memory. . . . It also seems that the rabbi [known as the] Possessor of the Tools lived long through the days of Moharit,[3] of blessed memory, as he [Moharit] explained in part A of his responsa, questions 66 and 124. I have also seen this appear in [the] book *Shem ha-Gedolim*, which has been reprinted. There under the letter shin, section fifty-four, one reads that the rabbi [known as the] Possessor of the Tools was [living] at the time of our teacher Rabbi Moses ben Hayim Alsheikh, Moharhav [Morenu ha-Rav Hayim Vital], and Mahrimat [Joseph Mitrani]. From all this it appears that [Samuel Laniado] had a long life and that he lived from the time of Maran until the time of Moharit. . . .

Rabbi Abraham, the son of the rabbi [known as the] Possessor of the Tools, had six bright sons. Of these, two were [noteworthy]: one was the rabbi who was greater than fortitude, our esteemed rabbi and teacher Solomon Laniado of blessed memory. He inherited the crown of his father and sat on the thrown of justice and served as a judge for the people of Israel in this city as he was [Rabbi Abraham's] first born. [Solomon's] brother was our great and esteemed rabbi and teacher Levi Laniado of blessed memory, who became a rabbi in Neve Amon [Thebes], may God preserve it. There, he was the head and the officer of the city. Of equal eminence to him, his son, our significant and esteemed rabbi and teacher Samuel Laniado of blessed memory, eventually inherited his father's crown in Na [Neve] Amon and became a rabbi and judge there.

---

3. Also Maharit. This could be an acronym for several different rabbis but most likely refers here to Joseph ben Moses Mitrani, who was of the generation of Joseph Caro and served as a chief judge in Safed.

When our teacher Rabbi Solomon, who was a rabbi here in Aleppo, passed away without any male children, the rabbis [of the city] consulted among themselves, and with the elders of the people and the ministers who were the great and magnificent masters, elected as the chosen among the fathers my father, the wonderful rabbi who was full of God's respect, our esteemed rabbi and teacher Samuel Laniado of blessed memory, as he was a descendant of the father and a fifth generation to the rabbi [known as the] Possessor of the Tools. And they appointed him to be the head and the judge, and he presided over [the people of] Israel [in Aleppo] for fifty years. When he passed away, just like Rosh [Asher ben Yehiel], of blessed memory, he left five ordained scholars: I, the eldest, inherited his crown. I have thus been presiding over monetary laws as a sole judge for about forty years, as this was the custom of the elders, the Rishonim,[4] to preside over monetary laws as a sole judge. And there were a few of them at the time of the Rishonim, rabbis before and after who were the strongest in the world, righteous, and greater than lions [who presided solely over monetary issues]. And nowadays too, there are many righteous and strong [who do so] and no one speaks up or even wonders whether such matters should not be decided by one alone. This is because these were the practices of the Rishonim from the times of our forefathers, as I have already mentioned. And [in our city] everyone accepted happily and wholeheartedly that the rabbi of the city would preside over cases as a sole judge.

Yet despite all my work I have faced poverty, as the people are in great need and they turn to me [for counsel] day and night. Furthermore, the hands of the ministers and their deputies have all been involved in embezzling. Therefore, due to the demands of the ministers of the country, and because I am also old and frail, and "Joseph could no longer control himself before all his attendants,"[5] I have for years trained my dear son Ephraim, the perfect sage, the excellent judge, may God protect him, to replace me. Now it is time for him to teach and judge, as he has reached his standing through his education, wisdom, and age, thanks to God's glory. Then, on a full-moon day, one *talmid hakham* [Torah scholar] stood up to Ephraim and challenged

---

4. Great rabbis of the eleventh through fifteenth centuries.
5. Genesis 45:1.

him like a man, saying that according to what we read in *Mishnat Hasidim*, one shall not issue rulings by himself, as no one except the One [God] has the right to serve as a sole judge. [The *talmid hakham* continued by suggesting that] we learn from this that if there are fewer than three [judges] at the tribunal, the ruling is not binding and a person may do as he pleases. He [the *talmid hakham*] was babbling to himself about this issue wherever he went, but no one informed me about it. He himself did not talk to me directly, and I was busy studying Torah. Then I learned that his intention was not [to please] God but rather to annoy and vex [us] due to his baseless hatred and his jealousy. Jealousy is the anger of men, and his problem was not with my son but rather with me, as I had issued, as a sole judge, a ruling that affected him. [Yet] this is my reward—a father is rewarded with a son, so that my son can replace me as [judge]. Therefore he [Ephraim] is entrusted with my duties and he accepts them. All we do is act justly and judge righteously.

I have thus decided to write this account in order to testify that I have ruled justly, that I have been rewarded justly, and that I have compelled people involved in a dispute to follow my orders in a just manner. May God help me speak the truth. Amen.

Raphael Solomon ben Samuel Laniado, *Sefer Kise Shelomoh* (Jerusalem: S. Tsukerman, 1900), 1: a–b. Translated from Hebrew by Yaron Ayalon.


## 137.  AN ENLIGHTENED EXCHANGE ACROSS THE MEDITERRANEAN [1851]

*Samuel David Luzzatto (1800–1865), known also by his Hebrew acronym, Shadal, was an Italian Jewish poet, scholar, and grammarian who authored a great number of works in Hebrew and Italian on critical approaches to the Bible, among other topics. Luzzatto began a correspondence with the Salonican scholar Judah Nehama (1826–1899) in the early 1850s, intrigued by Nehama's sympathies with enlightenment thought, knowledge of the Sephardi world, and enormous private library, then one of the largest and most important of the Levantine Jewish world. It is striking that in his letter to Nehama, included below, the Italian scholar speaks of learning of his Ottoman peer through a fellow maskil, or proponent of the Jewish Enlightenment (Haskalah), named Israel Stern, then residing in Algiers, an illustration of the remarkable interconnectedness and trans-hemispheric nature of the nineteenth-*

*century Jewish world of letters. It was not long until word of Nehama's erudition reached other eminent Jewish authors. In the years that followed, Nehama also corresponded with the Galician Jewish enlightener Solomon Judah Leib Rapoport (1790–1867) as well as a founder of the Wissenschaft des Judentums, the historian Leopold Zunz (1794–1886), among others.[6]*

The wise Israel Stern, a man tender in years but mature in wisdom (may God preserve him), came to me and informed me of your greatness, of your love of wisdom and scholarship, and [told me] that your soul yearned to enlighten me with your correspondence.[7] I therefore rushed and did not tarry to inform you that this is also my [chosen] path and my virtue. I am a friend to all lovers of Torah and wisdom and my only desire and my complete salvation rest in disseminating the sources of the Torah in order that the earth will be full of the knowledge of God. Because of this, I teach and, in the process, I have learned that there are ancient books and especially manuscripts scattered around the whole Jewish diaspora, particularly in the countries of the East. No doubt there are valuable treasures that remain in darkness and there is no demand or request [for them]. I hope to God that you will be able to aid me and all lovers of the study of Jewish history by providing me with a list of the precious ancient books that are in your hands or those of your friends.

Above all, my soul has yearned to know the truth of the matter concerning what I have heard about your glorious city where there remain a few small [Jewish] communities that preserve their own special prayer book and rite whose liturgy is neither Sephardi nor Ashkenazi. I would like to know each and every one of these communities and the characteristics of their prayer books.

You should also know that I have seen a printed prayer book of the Romaniot rite (published first in Venice and later in Constantinople), which I showed to certain wise men from your country who told me

---

6. Wissenschaft des Judentums ("Science of Judaism") was a movement that emerged in the early nineteenth century among German Jews who were committed to the critical study of Jewish history, literature, and culture. (For more on this historical school see source 140.)

7. Israel Jacob Stern, the man who brought Luzzatto and Nehama together, maintained an extensive correspondence with both men over the course of many years from an impressive number of locations. At the time of Luzzatto's writing, Stern was traveling in Algeria. One year later, in 1852, he received Luzzatto's mail in Salonica. By the following decade Stern had also penned letters to Nehama from Belgrade, Vienna, and Galicia.

that they had never seen such a thing and that this rite is no longer practiced anywhere.

And now, may God bless you, make me rejoice in your letters, either as a respondent or as an inquirer, and may God bless you with everything you do and may you know only happiness, along with your family and the household of your glorious and wise father-in-law, may he live long, and your soul as well, and the soul of the signatory here today in Padua, 12 Av 5611 [August 10, 1851].

Your friend, Shadal

Letter of Samuel David Luzzatto of Padua to Judah Nehama of Salonica, August 10, 1851, in Samuel David Luzzatto, *Igrot Shadal*, vol. 7 (Kraków: Y. Fisher, 1891), 1110–11. Translated from Hebrew by Julia Phillips Cohen.

## 138. THE FIRST JOURNAL DEVOTED TO THE SEPHARDI PAST APPEARS IN EDIRNE (1888)

*Born and raised in Ottoman Edirne, Abraham Danon (1857–1925) was a committed Jewish enlightener, rabbi, and scholar. Trained in Hebrew and Aramaic, he taught himself French, German, Greek, Latin, Ottoman Turkish, Persian, and Arabic, and published extensively in French, Hebrew, and Ladino. What follows is Danon's Hebrew introduction to a scholarly bilingual Hebrew-Ladino journal he founded in Edirne in 1888 under the title* Yosef Da'at/El Progreso. *Although the publication was short-lived, Danon remained intellectually active throughout his life. In 1891 he established a modern rabbinical seminary in Edirne, which he transferred to Istanbul in 1898. After the revolution of 1908 displaced octogenarian Chief Rabbi Moshe Halevi (ca. 1827–1910) Danon competed for the position, which he lost to his son-in-law Haim Nahum. (On Halevi see source 43; on Nahum see sources 43, 44, 53, 75, 115, and 117.) Danon stayed on in his capacity as head of the Istanbul Jewish seminary until it closed in the midst of the First World War. He subsequently moved to Paris, where he became a professor of Hebrew at the École Normale Israélite Orientale. Danon's call for the collection and preservation of rare documents of the Ladino-speaking world resonates with parallel developments among Yiddish-speaking Eastern European intellectuals of the same period.*

For the past six years I have yearned for and dedicated myself to one great passion and desire, devoting to it all my youthful efforts. And now at last, in spite of all obstacles in its path, it has arrived. Never had we dared hope to see Hebrew letters in our city, but here they are, brought here by the Society of the Proponents of Wisdom that was founded in Adrianople [Edirne], the offspring of the Society of the Seekers of Enlightenment. In keeping with the society's goals, it is my intention to publish a bimonthly journal, half of it in Hebrew and the other in Spanish, about the history of the Jewish diaspora in Turkey, and all that happens to our people living under the gracious rule of the Ottoman sultans. Our nation's history is a neglected field, overgrown with thorns and thistles, but within its sphere we have chosen this fertile and fruitful corner, which we will cultivate and protect. And even if our hands may recoil at times from unearthing dark mysteries, at the very least we can hope to gather together these fragmented reports and distribute them among our brethren living in the land of Turkey. I believe they have much to gain from this effort, since in the vineyard of our Oriental histories, precious treasures lay hidden: we do not know much of the habits and traditions of the various communities, nor of their relations with the venerated government and with the other nations living under its protection. If we tend to this vineyard with the plough of inquiry, many questions that have gone unnoticed would find an answer. There are ever so many manuscripts, books and documents, lying hidden among people's possessions, or buried in the communities' archives. These texts could shine a light on issues long forgotten. The riddles of the past would be elucidated.

I will not talk excessively about the nature of our revolution—this first issue and the articles it features will exemplify the new spirit animating our endeavor. The educated will see that truth and science guide our way. The daily news or spiteful quarrels among writers will not enter this house. But its doors stand open for any eloquent article, in Hebrew or in Spanish that sheds light on one of the corners of our history or destroys the shroud that covers the face of a man, a community, or a book, and conceals from us their habits and ways. Let our wise men rise up, let each one search in his own place or town of residence for the memories of his brothers and neighbors. Let them call to the hidden manuscripts: come out! And to our ancient Turkish histories: reveal yourselves! They should send the fruits of their research to this journal, which will gratefully circulate them among the people.

"El ha-kore," *Yosef-Da'at/El Progreso*, March 13, 1888, 2. Translated from Hebrew by Shir Alon.

## 139. A CALL FOR THE CREATION OF A SEPHARDI SOCIETY FOR THE STUDY OF JEWISH HISTORY AND CULTURE (1892)

*Mercado Joseph Covo (1870–1940), a teacher by profession, was also a historian who prepared studies of the Jewish communities of Serres, his native town, and Salonica, where he spent the final decades of his life. In the following excerpt, written in 1892, Covo argues that Jews must write their own histories, reasoning that doing so would help them correct the biased approach of outsiders while also providing them with insights into the persecution their ancestors had faced over centuries. Making reference to new Jewish historical scholarship developed in Germany and France, Covo called upon Ladino readers to create their own literary and scientific society devoted to the study of post-biblical Jewish history. He was not alone in proposing this program: just months after he issued his call, the Alliance Israélite Universelle introduced post-biblical history lessons into its classrooms across North Africa and the Levant. These pedagogical developments formed part of the proliferation of a self-conscious field of Jewish studies.*

If there is one branch of study that is entirely neglected in our schools it is the history of our forefathers from the time of their dispersion across the globe until the present. . . . [True,] our educational institutions offer lessons in biblical history. . . . Yet, we have for the most part been unable to go any further. Why is this? . . . . It is because we lack scholarly works offering a post-biblical history of the Jews, or an account of the accomplishments of our people following the construction of the Second Temple in Jerusalem through the present day. This history is known only by scholars but not by the youth: they lack the [proper] books.

Is it really necessary to ask? Does the history of our nation among the nations not have its merits? . . . Are we not obliged to examine the facts, seeing that they offer a thousand examples that bear the truth on every page of [our] history? Of which [other] history can this be said? How to bring these truths to light, and to lift the veil that renders our history invisible to so many of our brothers in Turkey? It is for this reason that we are in need of a literary and scientific society that can undertake various projects, including the publication of a well-written and easily comprehensible history of the Jewish people. Before all else we should begin with a history that will cover the period of the fall of our nation through the present, because we lack historical facts about this era. That which has been written on the topic is largely the work of Christian authors who were naturally inclined against us. A Jew interested in offering a faithful account of our past must therefore turn to the great historical works published in France, and particularly in Germany, by Jewish writers such as Theodor Reinach, Lambert, Munk, Schornstein, Dr. Graetz, Zunz, Albert Cohn, Léon Halévy, Schwab, Astruc, Abraham Cohen, Salvador, Frankel, Jost, and de Rossi. . . .[8]

By studying the Jewish past we will learn the secrets of antisemitic persecutions and the hateful calumnies that are invented against us. . . . Surveying Jewish behavior during the long period of persecutions will uncover the admirable conduct of a weak flock that braved the tortures of the auto-da-fé, exile, and misery . . . all in order to stay true to their one God and to follow divine law even amidst the temptations of fate and while living at the mercy of powerful kings. It will similarly make clear that wherever a small gust of liberty has blown, the Jew has occupied important positions in science, letters, and the arts. . . .

It is our hope that the Jewish youth of Turkey, and particularly of Salonica, will take up the task [of studying our history]. It is true that [this task] is onerous, but its utility and urgency are undeniable.

Dear friends of progress, do you want to hear my advice? Get to work. There is no time to lose!

Mercado Joseph Covo, "Korespondensia de Sheron: una reforma menesteroza," *La Epoka*, May 31, 1892, 2–3. Translated from Ladino by Julia Phillips Cohen.

## 140. A BLIND SPOT OF WISSENSCHAFT DES JUDENTUMS SCHOLARS: "SPANISH JEWS IN THE ORIENT" (1911)

*The Wissenschaft des Judentums movement, founded by a small group of German Jewish intellectuals in the early nineteenth century, aimed to promote the scholarly, critical investigation of Jewish history and culture. The scholars of the Wissenschaft school evinced an interest in the intellectual and cultural achievements of Jews in medieval Iberia, when Islamic rule allowed Jews to ascend to the elite ranks of society*

8. The scholars Covo references here include Theodor Reinach (1860–1928), Lion Mayer Lambert (1781–1863), Salomon Munk (1803–1867), David Schornstein (1826–1879), Heinrich Graetz (1817–1891), Leopold Zunz (1794–1886), Albert Cohn (1814–1877), Léon Halévy (1802–1883), Moïse Schwab (1839–1918), Élie-Aristide Astruc (1831–1905), Joseph Salvador (1779–1873), Zacharias Frankel (1801–1875), Isaac Markus Jost (1793–1860), and Azariah de Rossi (ca. 1513–1578), hailed by nineteenth-century Jewish scholars as a forerunner of modern Jewish historiography.

*and to partake in cultural pursuits shared by their Christian and Muslim neighbors. However, the Wissenschaft writers spared little ink on post-exilic Sephardi Jewry. In this selection the Salonican author Morris Isaac Cohen condemns the Wissenschaft circle for this lacuna, suggesting that it has rendered modern Sephardim a people without a history. His solution was to compose his own ethnographic study of the "Jewish woman of the Orient," for, he wrote, history was "not only the chronological narration of remarkable events" but also an account of the everyday lives, practices, and traditions of the communities and individuals under study.*

The history of the Spanish Jews since their expulsion from Spain has yet to be written. Neither Graetz nor Kayserling succeeded in giving us a complete and coherent description of the life of our ancestors from the time of their settlement in the Ottoman Empire through the present.[9] Nowhere do we find a study of their traditions and customs, of their successes and failures. . . . [Instead] what we find written in the chronicles and annals treats [only] certain important periods, or better put, certain remarkable episodes or events, such as the history of Don Joseph, prince of Naxos, Doña Gracia his mother-in-law and sister, the tragicomic epic of the famous messiah Shabbetay Sevi, the Carmona-Farhi tragedy of Constantinople [Istanbul], and perhaps a few other more or less important incidents.[10] A complete history of the life of our ancestors is still lacking. Only God knows if it will ever be possible to write [such a history] and whether a historian will be found to fill this void.

We are thus a branch of the tree of the people of Israel that lacks a history for a very important period of our existence. As if abandoning all desire to survive, we have not judged it necessary to document our existence or leave any traces behind. They say that we, the Jews of the Orient, are a family of mutes, a group of people without a language or literature. We add to this double negation yet a third: we have no history. . . .

History is not only the chronological narration of remarkable events, however, . . . [but] much more: it is the study of life, the search

---

9. Heinrich Graetz (1817–1891), mentioned in the previous source, and Meyer Kayserling (1829–1905) were distinguished Jewish scholars from Central Europe.

10. Don Joseph Nasi, who was a duke, not a prince, of Naxos, as this source suggests, and Doña Gracia Nasi were wealthy dignitaries in sixteenth-century Istanbul, where they settled after fleeing the Iberian Inquisition. Shabbetay Sevi was the seventeenth-century self-proclaimed Jewish messiah from Izmir (on which see sources 5 and 53); the "Carmona-Farhi tragedy" refers to the execution of Jewish notables Chelebi Behor Carmona and Haim Farhi in the early-nineteenth-century Ottoman Empire under the reign of Mahmud II (r. 1808-1839).

for truth, the analytical description of traditions and customs according to the manner in which they present themselves before the eyes of the observer and according to the manner in which they are painted in the imagination of the historian.

Morris Isaac Cohen[11]

Morris Isaac Cohen, "La mujer ande los djidios espanyoles de oriente" (Salonica, 1911). Reproduced in Beatriz León, "Dos conferencias sobre el papel de la mujer," in Beatrice Schmid, ed., *"Sala de pasatiempo": textos judeoespañoles de Salónica impresos entre 1896 y 1916* (Basel: Romanisches Seminar der Universität, 2003): 131–32. Translated from Ladino by Devin E. Naar.

## 141. WHY JEWISH READERS NEED TEXTS IN SERBIAN [1914]

*Rabbi Isaac Alcalay (1882–1978) served at various times in his life as the chief rabbi of Serbia, chief rabbi of Yugoslavia, and vice president of the World Sephardi Federation. A tireless activist for his coreligionists, he traveled across Europe to raise funds for Serbian Jews, who suffered greatly—along with Serbians of other faiths—during the First World War. In the following excerpt, written just a month before the war began, Alcalay expressed his desire to protect his community in another respect. Responding to Serbian Jews' rapid integration into their non-Jewish surroundings in the decades following their emancipation in 1888, he advocated for the production of Jewish texts in the Serbian language in the hope that it would provide the Jews of his country with "spiritual food" and ensure that they remained connected to their history and community. (For more on Alcalay see sources 52, 82, and 130.)*

Our people desperately need Jewish texts in the Serbian language. Apart from Daničić's translation of the Bible (Old Testament) and those few novellas by Davičo, there is hardly a single book of literary value that would supplement those provided by the school and the synagogue, [serving] as spiritual food.[12] Our coreligionists do not know their own history. Because of that, I have spent long hours translating

---

11. The author of this text may have been Moïse Cohen (1883–1961), the Ottoman Jewish author and activist who later became a vocal proponent of Turkish nationalism and adopted the Turkish name Munis Tekinalp (on whom see source 85). It was common practice among Jews in the Ottoman Empire and elsewhere during the period to adopt a non-Jewish version of their given, biblical names in public forums. In this case, Morris may have been the non-Jewish correlate of Moïse (French for Moses).

12. The Orthodox Christian Đura Daničić (1825–1882) was a prolific scholar, historian, and linguist of Serbian and Croatian; Hajim Davičo (1854–1918), was a Jewish novelist and playwright who wrote in Serbian.

[works of] Jewish history and [also] published a book that is meant to be used in schools as a textbook. A new popular edition is now needed. [Such a work] could first publish systematically, in slim issues of three to four printer's sheets, biographies of notable people from the Jewish past, and then gradually old and medieval literature, and finally belles-lettres and literature of our famous religious and lay poets from the past and the present. It would also be of great use for those among us who are interested in what is going on in the community and beyond, if a journal were to be published periodically. Such a journal could print the majority of texts in Serbian but also some Spanish as well, so that Jews from the new regions could use it and draw closer to us.

Isaac Alcalay, "Religiozno stanje jevrejskih građana u Beogradu," June 29, 1914, RG-31.037M, reel 1, United States Holocaust Memorial Museum Archive (Washington, D.C.). (Original in Fond 497, opis 1, sprava 23, Central State Historical Archives of Ukraine, Lviv.) Translated from Serbian by Emil Kerenji.

## 142. A LEADING SCHOLAR OF SEPHARDI JEWRY ELUCIDATES HIS SOURCES [1913]

*A banker, school director, and Jewish communal leader in Salonica throughout much of the twentieth century, Joseph Nehama (1881–1971) was also a dedicated and prolific chronicler of the Jewish past of his native city. He contributed dozens of essays on Jewish history, commerce, and health to the presses of Salonica and Paris, compiled the seven-volume* Histoire des Israélites de Salonique, *and labored for some forty years on a French-Ladino dictionary that offered an unparalleled window into the Judeo-Spanish dialect of Salonican Sephardim. In this document Nehama seeks reading matter from the central office of the Alliance Israélite Universelle in Paris for his historical research into the history of the Jews of Salonica. Like so many Sephardi intellectuals of his day, Nehama looked to the AIU as a source of professional and personal support.*

April 4, 1913

I am in the process of preparing a rather copious work on Salonica, its past, and its present. The history of the [Jewish] community has given me quite a headache. I have gone through a pile of responsa and various obscure writings, including a collection of unedited *haskamot*[13]

13. Rabbinic decisions; literally, "agreements."

from the Talmud Torah going back to the first years of the sixteenth century. I still need a few more documents that I cannot procure here. Could I ask you to send them to me for a few days? They must exist in the Alliance library.

Here is the list:

1. *Revue des Études Juives*, volume 40 (Danon's article)
2. (Capsali) *Tana Deve Eliyahu*
3. *Divre Yosef Sambari*
4. Nicolai—*Histoire des Emigrés d'Espagne et du Portugal* (I'm not sure of the title)

There are also three citations that I would like to verify, or better still, have copied. I do not dare write to Mr. Théodore Reinach, a great authority on the matter

1. Diehl—*Études byzantines*, page 247
2. Virgil's mention of the Jews of Therma
3. Flavius Josephus has also mentioned them in his *Antiquités juda-ïques* (on this last point M. Julien Weil[1], translator of Josephus, can teach me more as well.) If I weren't worried about imposing upon Mr. T. Reinach, I would ask him to tell me what he knows about the Jews of Salonica from their origins until their exile from Spain. Do you think I could write to him?

There must be some interesting documents on Salonica and its past in the Alliance archives, among them a work by R. Judah Nehama [which should have been] sent [to the library] by Dr. Moïse Allatini.[14] I would be very much obliged if the Alliance could send the dossier to me for a few days. I would look after it as if it were the pupils of my eyes.

So there it is—too many requests already. May I ask for an immediate response? My work is quite far along and I would like to publish it as soon as possible.

Thank you in advance and best wishes,

Jos. Nehama

Letter by Joseph Nehama in Salonica to Alliance Israélite Universelle Inspector Sylvain Bénédict, in Paris, April 4, 1913. Archives of the Alliance Israélite Universelle (Paris), XVI E 202a. Translated from French by Alma Rachel Heckman.

---

14. Moïse Allatini (1809–1882) was a banker and industrialist in Salonica who helped usher in reformist education and politics in the city's Jewish community.

400 The Emergence of Sephardi Studies

## 143. HAYIM NAHMAN BIALIK LAUDS A COLLECTION OF SEPHARDI FOLKSONGS [1921]

*Famously known as "Israel's national poet," Hayim Nahman Bialik (1873–1934) was a teacher, translator, essayist, publisher, literary critic, and Zionist activist as well as one of the most important poets of the Hebrew revival. After leaving his native village of Radi in the Volhynia region of the Russian Empire at the age of six, Bialik spent his early life between Zhitomir, Volozhin, Sosnowiec, Odessa, and Warsaw. In 1921, Bialik left Russia for Berlin, stopping en route in Istanbul, where he encountered the collection of Ottoman Jewish songs described below. As the excerpt makes clear, Bialik considered the "eastern melodies" and Hebrew lyrics of the Ottoman Jewish maftirim repertoire more "authentic" than the Yiddish folk poetry of Ashkenazi Jews. His interest in publishing the work of the Sephardi author Benjamin Raphael ben Joseph was therefore an outgrowth of both Bialik's interest in the revival of "Hebrew song" and his romanticized view of Sephardi traditions.*

18 Tamuz 5681 [July 24, 1921], Constantinople [Istanbul]

A fine idea occurred to the qualified and honored Rabbi Benjamin Raphael ben Joseph to publish this selection of the songs of our brethren from eastern lands. He compiled 500 songs—the majority collected from manuscripts and the minority from previously published books—that are sung aloud by our brethren from eastern lands. When in Constantinople I was told of the lovely custom of the Jews of Adrianople [Edirne] to gather young and old alike, on the Sabbath, religious holidays, and other days of leisure in groups called *maftirim* in order to sing these songs. They would sing the works of their favorite poets put to popular melodies. The esteemed publisher of this anthology collected these songs, ordered them according to the type and style of melody, and annotated the words and choruses as they are regularly sung. From this perspective these songs must be cherished as folk songs. Even when they lack liturgical value the popularity of the melodies and lyrics is sufficient reason to compile and publish them. We can only pray that the esteemed publisher will complete his work by printing the songs with their full musical notation, either alongside the songs themselves or in an addendum at the end of the book. This will be a vast improvement on the primitive style of notation currently included at the bottom of each page, which only hints at the melody. When he has published this addendum, his compilation will be complete and fully valued as a part of our folklore. As is widely known, our Ashkenazi brethren have been collecting folk songs with their musical notations in their spoken language [Yiddish] and are working assiduously towards their publication. Let not the place of [these] Hebrew folk songs be overlooked, as they are without all doubt superior to the [Yiddish] folk songs mentioned above. Their eastern melodies, despite being borrowed, are still closer in spirit to Hebrew song than folk songs in a jumbled language [Yiddish] borrowed from the nations of the North and West.

If Hebrew song is destined for revival, there is no doubt that it will turn first to, and draw its strength from, the vast well of eastern music. All those who hope for the revival and renewal of Hebrew folksong must congratulate Raphael ben Joseph for a job well done!

Hayim Nahman Bialik, Introduction to Benjamin Raphael ben Joseph, *Shire Israel be-Eretz ha-Kedem* (Istanbul: Benjamin Raphael ben Joseph, 1921/1922), 6–7. Translated from Hebrew by Shira R. Jaret.

## 144. AN ETHNOGRAPHY OF BOSNIAN SEPHARDI WOMEN (1931)

*Laura (Luna) Levi Papo, also known as Bohoreta (1891–1942) was born in Sarajevo, Bosnia, but moved to Istanbul as a young girl. After attending an Alliance Israélite Universelle school in that city, she became interested in Sephardi customs, proverbs, and ballads. Returning to Sarajevo as a young woman, she published her first work of ethnography in the form of a response to an unfavorable description of Sephardi women by the Croatian female author Jelica Bernadzikowska-Belović (1870–1946) in the serial* Bosnische Post. *Subsequently Papo dedicated herself to collecting Judeo-Spanish ballads, short stories, and proverbs from her community, publishing some in local Jewish newspapers. She became aligned with Sarajevo's Sephardi socialist group, Matatia, with whose members she staged several of her own plays at the Sarajevo National Theater and Belgrade's Jewish Cultural Center, among other places. Papo continued her research on Sephardi women in a study entitled "The Sephardi Woman in Bosnia," a selection of which is presented here.*

Tourists visiting Bosnia admire our picturesque country, with its beautiful colors, traditional outfits, turbans, and fezzes. Among the various items they notice are the *tokados*, small hats shaped like little boats, . . . [yet] these are growing rarer and will soon disappear altogether.[15]

---

15. A tokado or tukado was a headdress worn by married Sephardi women in the region.

Foreigners soon notice all this, but they hardly suspect that the women dressed in this fashion are the daughters of the Spanish Jewish branch of Israel, victims of Tomás Torquemada and the Dark Ages.

I do not want to burden the reader of this essay with historical details. I have chosen a much lighter topic for my short book. My aim is merely to shed light on [the lives and customs of] Sephardi women in Bosnia, and nothing more.

I started working on this topic quite by accident, in the winter of 1917, in the midst of an intense polemic with Ms. Bernadzikowska, who had brazenly maligned Sephardi women in her article "Sephardi Women in Bosnia." I proved her wrong. With well-reasoned arguments I demonstrated the true nature of our women. It was at this moment that this small book was born. With the guidance of Dr. Patsch, currently the chair of the Archeology Department at the University of Vienna and then director of the National Museum in Bosnia, I prepared the book in German. I have since translated the book into my mother tongue upon the suggestion of Dr. Vita Kajon, a man who encourages his coreligionists to write about Sephardi folklore in the Spanish vernacular we speak in our homes.

Spain, now a republic no longer ruled by clergy, is opening its doors to us and calling upon us, inviting us to establish new homes [within its borders]. Do Sephardim have enough strength to believe [the Spaniards] after suffering so much [at their hands]? The Spaniards claim that we belong to the Iberian family tree [and that] the best proof for this can be found in our customs, proverbs, traditional clothing, food, songs, and *romansas*.

Yet our branch put down roots in other countries where, thank God, we now live. Old trees should not be replanted. Yet neither should old customs be forgotten. It is for this reason that I have written this work.

I have set myself the task of describing the Sephardi women of the past whose lives are not remembered or celebrated as they deserve to be. . . . My dear mother, Esther Levi, has provided me with rich material for this book. She is the archetype of her generation and a spokeswoman of the recent past who stands between the present and the unknown future. It was my mother who encouraged me to tell the story of these women, true living relics, before they disappear before our very eyes. . . .

I have attempted to write in as clear a manner as possible, in a popular tone, so as to be understood by the majority [of Ladino-speakers]. I use a phonetic style, writing as I speak in order to make [my work] accessible to anyone who knows how to read Latin characters and because this is now the habit of the Ladino newspapers of the Orient.

For all of these reasons I hope that my readers will receive the book kindly, and that they will not expect my modest work to offer the last word on the topic.

Bohoreta, Sarajevo, winter 1931

Laura Papo Bohoreta, "La mujer sefardi de Bosna," manuscript dated December 18, 1931, Collection of the Historijski Arhiv (Sarajevo). Translated from Ladino by Ramajana Hidić Demirović.

## 145. A YOUNG SEPHARDI SCHOLAR INTERVIEWS A NATIVE OF ISTANBUL IN SEATTLE {1920–1938}

*Emma Adatto Schlesinger (1910–1997) immigrated to Seattle from her native Istanbul as a young girl in 1912, joining a young Sephardi community that would prove the third largest in the United States. At the insistence of their mother, Anna Perahia Adatto, both Emma and her brother Albert—who are pictured as young children on the cover of this book—attended the University of Washington as undergraduates and went on to write some of the first master's theses in the field of Sephardi studies to be written for an American university. (Emma Adatto's thesis, completed in 1935, was titled "A Study of the Linguistic Characteristics of the Seattle Sefardi Folklore.") In the following essay Adatto describes how her interest in the Sephardi community of Seattle was sparked by the cultural vibrancy she witnessed in her own home, which she described as a social hub of the larger Sephardi community. Adatto's interest was particularly drawn to the community's immigrant members, including a woman she fondly remembered as her "aunt from Istanbul" (La Tía Estambolía), a lively storyteller who despite her nickname was of no biological relation to the young Adatto. In the following selection Adatto recounts her earliest interviews with this woman and other members of the community, whom she interviewed with the help of University of Washington faculty in a campus recording studio. (On Emma Adatto see source 42; on Albert Adatto see sources 42 and 131.)*

There was little in her appearance that made an immediate impression. A rather short woman, she was neither fat nor thin, neither ugly nor pretty. Her gray hair was combed smoothly and ended in a small bun.

She often wore a *toca*, a filmy scarf, which may have been a token hair covering in lieu of the wig worn by other Orthodox women. I can't remember the color of her eyes, they might have been green. Her features and the color of her skin were not unusual. Madame Veisí [La Tía Estambolía] was always dressed in a well-made dress, carefully pressed with every hook and eye in its proper place. She wore the finest cotton stockings and shoes with Cuban heels. We never saw her without her diamond earrings dangling from her pierced ears. Sometimes she would wear a *colana*, a long gold chain, and on formal occasions she would wear her gold bracelets and diamond rings. Except on the Sabbath, she always held a cigarette between the yellowish thumb and forefinger of her left hand. On Saturdays, she carried a *tespil*, a string of amber beads used mostly by men, as a rosary by the Mohammedans and by the Greeks for comfort and solace. Because of her age, it was considered proper for a woman to play with the *tespil*.

I was about ten years old when she first visited our home and remember seeing my father rush to greet her and lead her to the honored place at the sofa. At a time when I was taught to serve the men first, it amazed me to watch him offer her a cigarette and light it for her with a flourish. My mother ordered me to prepare the Turkish coffee at once, but before it was to be served, I was to bring the *dulce*, the sweet that was offered as soon as a guest entered the house.

As the eldest daughter, I had been trained in my duties. I took out a large silver tray and placed a dish of sweets in the center. Usually it was strawberry preserves, but that day it was *cidra*, candied grapefruit rind, a delicacy served on special occasions. On one side of the *cidra*, I placed a crystal dish containing long-handled spoons made by the silversmiths of Constantinople [Istanbul], and on the other side, an empty glass dish on which the used spoons were to be placed. Then I placed glasses of fresh water on the tray before passing it to each guest, always beginning with the men. When my mother passed the tray, there was always a blessing in Hebrew, but when I did, there was an additional prayer: *novia*, may you marry.

As time went on and the Americanization process began to set in, the men began to tease about "ladies first" and the style was slowly accepted. If the rabbi was visiting, he was the first one served, then the older women and men, and finally the younger women. On the day that Madame Veisí came, my father took the tray from me and served her himself. She was quick to recognize the honor. After that I soon learned to serve her the demitasse with the thickest *kaymak*, the cream of foam that surfaced to the top of the cup when the Turkish coffee was carefully poured. Sometimes, if Madame Veisí had had a dairy dinner, we would put real cream in the cup for her. It was never done for anyone else.

Madame Veisí was a popular guest because of her wit and her charm. Her fame as a storyteller began to follow her wherever she went. In the days before television, when even radios were scarce, storytelling was live entertainment for those who could not speak English. Everyone loved the movies, where the piano music and the pantomime were an international language, but nothing could compare to a storyteller who had a repertoire of tales that could be altered to suit the mood of the narrator and the audience. Madame Veisi came to be called La Tía de Estambol, in keeping with her reputation as a Scherezade. Older women were often referred to as *tías*, aunts, but she became so well-known that everyone recognized her as the Tía from Estambol, as Constantinople was then called by the Sephardim. It didn't take long for the ear and the tongue to elide it to La Tiastambolía. There were some who never did know that her real name was Vida de Veisí.

In spite of her witticisms, ranging from plays on words to stories with sexual overtones, La Tía Estambolía always maintained a dignified air, bordering on snobbishness. She was like a grand actress making sure the scene was properly set. One could never ask her to tell a story. After the sweets, the coffee, and the small talk, the host would begin with such blessings upon her as may she have a long life, may she live to see all her nieces and nephews married, and may she see Jerusalem. Then she—always addressed in the third person, never in the second person—would be begged to tell a tale. Immediately, someone would light her cigarette; she would puff for a while while everyone remained quite still. This ritualistic appeal was always repeated three times before she would tilt her head to one side and ask, "What story would you like to hear?"

Then she would begin, *avía de ser*, there was once. With these magic words, we heard about the clever orphan girl whose intelligence and beauty enabled her to marry a handsome, wealthy man who had been cuckolded; the man with the blue umbrella who played such an important role in the life of an abandoned wife and her seven daughters; the princess who was kept in a tower but flew on the back of a parrot to meet an enchanted prince; the king's son who was exiled by his father for his kindness to a fish and married a maiden out of whose mouth came snakes. The plots were most often of Greek, Turkish, or other origins, but all the characters, except for those in one tale, were distinctly Jewish: Avrams and Rajels who observed the traditions of marriages, circumcisions, Sabbaths, kindness to strangers and the needy. The fascination was as much with their way of life as with the development of the plot. To this day I remember the Sabbath feast described in one of the tales. Every detail was complete: the embroidered cloth, the silver candelabra, the fish baked in lemon sauce, the roasted chicken, the rice cooked with tomatoes sauteed in oil, the psalms sung by the man of the house. . . .

She was about eighty years old when my mother and I went to see her to beg her to allow me to write down some of her tales for a collection of folk material of the Seattle Sephardim for my Master's thesis at the University of Washington. We found La Tía seated at one end of the *minder*, the stiff sofa found in every Turquina's [Turkish woman's] kitchen. The white gas and coal stove glistened, the linoleum floor was scrubbed, the starched white curtains were immaculate. Estreya, her niece, wiped the clean chairs for us to sit on.

"Estreya is so fussy, cleaning and scrubbing, scrubbing and cleaning," complained La Tía.

The slender Estreya just smiled and greeted us in Ladino, asking me in Spanish-accented English, "How are you, Emma?"

We had our *dulce* and *cafe con leche*, coffee with milk, and *bizcochos*, cookies. My mother, La Tía, and Estreya were exchanging news when I nudged my mother.

"May you live long, Vida," began my mother, "would you please tell Amada [my name in Ladino] one of your stories for her to write down?"

"What do you want them for?" asked La Tía.

Before I could answer, Mama told her, "They will put you in the books of the university."

I thought it might be a waste of time to explain a university to a woman who had never had a formal education. La Tía must have read my thoughts, for she said instantly with pride, "Mademoiselle, in case you don't know, we have universities, museums, concerts and clothes from Paris in Estambol, better than there is here in Seattle."

I spluttered an apology for my unspoken thoughts and said, "You are the best storyteller in Seattle, and I would like to write the stories down exactly as you tell them."

La Tía seemed somewhat mollified. She looked at my mother and then at me and commanded, "Take out your pencil and paper."

And she began to recite one of her tales as I wrote down her words as fast as I could. She was very patient with me and would wait if I needed more time to write. Sometimes I would read back to her what I had written, and she would make a few corrections. Sometimes she didn't want to be bothered. Occasionally she would say, "I have no *kef*, I'm not in the mood."

I soon learned to defer to her moods even when it seemed to be a wasted afternoon. She reminded me now and then that she was doing this out of great affection for my mother. I never went to La Tía's without my mother since she constantly encouraged us and frequently saved me from making a *faux pas*. . . .

The afternoons continued, and my notebooks were being filled when Dr. George Umphrey, head of the Spanish Department at the University of Washington, told me that the University of Washington Broadcasting Studio would be available to us through the courtesy of the Departments of English and Anthropology. Since I was a teaching fellow in Spanish at the university, I was eligible to receive such a service. The folksongs and tales were to be recorded on aluminum discs for a permanent collection.

There were about nine women from four or five areas of Turkey and the Island of Rhodes who were invited to come. Dr. Melville Jacobs of the Anthropology Department made the arrangements not only for the recording sessions, he also chauffeured the women to the studio. The women liked his black hair and dark eyes and his friendly, encouraging manner—he seemed like one of their sons. They put on their best dresses and sprinkled themselves with rosewater for this important occasion. Since only a few spoke English, I was the interpreter, and we managed very well except when some of the more personal remarks were too embarrassing for me to translate.

It was difficult for most of the women to sing the *romanzas* in an alien environment without the inspiration of an occasion such as an engagement party, a holiday, an important visitor. As they became accustomed to the room and the equipment, they began to relax, and the singing became less strained as the ballads of King Tarquino, Turunja, the Three Sisters, the Little Moors, the Three Doves, and the King of France were sung in the slow deliberate style that had been taught from generation to generation since the expulsion from Spain in 1492.

La Tía was totally unimpressed, but she behaved like a professional, waiting quietly for her turn. Her voice is recorded asking during an interruption if the light went out, referring to the electrical connection of the machine, and should she cut short her story; she continued the recitation without a break in the thread of the tale. . . .

The last time I saw La Tía was on a Saturday, just before she left for Los Angeles to live with relatives who had moved there. Except for a more pronounced shaking of her head, she hadn't changed much. She was seated in her favorite corner of the *minder*. I could see her eyes glittering behind her glasses. There was little that escaped her attention. I was always grateful to her for not asking me why I was not married. She knew I was teaching Spanish in Olympia and asked me how my work was coming along.

Estreya and the other women were putting finishing touches to the big *desayuno*, what we now call a brunch. I think it was Succoth, but since it was raining we were in the kitchen instead of the *Succah* in the backyard. We had to wait for the men to return from the *Kehillah*. The table was covered with a white linen cloth. On it were placed plates of salted raw fish, white cheeses, ripe olives, tomatoes, *fila* pastries filled with cheese, potatoes, spinach, eggplant, hard-boiled eggs, rolls covered with sesame seeds, cookies with a raki flavor and a large *pan de españa*, sponge cake, a sweet reminder of a bitter experience. . . .

There was not much conversation during the meal except for complimenting the cooks, *bendichas manos*, blessed hands, or a teasing *te afitó el horno*, the oven was in good form. After the final blessings, the men sang *pizmonim* and told tales from the Midrash. The women were busy with the serving of the meal and they listened more than they talked. La Tia remained seated in her favorite corner and took out her *tespil*. She knew her place and the conversation around her was concerned with tidbits of local gossip. The men would bring the news exchanged at the *Kehillah*, relating it with relish. The dishes were scraped as unobtrusively as possible since the actual dishwashing could be done only after dark, at the end of the Sabbath.

When it was time to leave, I thanked Tanti Estreya, as I called her and the other ladies who were close friends of my mother even though they were not my aunts. I kissed and embraced La Tía.

"My, my," said my mother, "we don't kiss the hand anymore, do we. We are living in modern times. There is not the same respect. Our grandchildren will never know how we lived. It will seem like fairy tales to them."

Everyone was quiet at this observation. "Don't say that, Anna," said La Tía. "Didn't you tell us that our customs will be preserved by scholars and put in books? Isn't Amada doing all her work to keep these memories?"

I couldn't help but kiss her again for having understood and her faith in me.

"*Ya basta*, that's enough," she said softly, "*Aide, novia*, it is time for you to marry."

We lost touch with each other, and in 1940, the year after I was married, my mother wrote me the sad news that La Tía had died in California of pneumonia, following an accident.

I put aside my Sephardic studies for 30 years and when *la hora buena*, the right time came, I opened up my collection of folktales that were not included in my thesis. As I reread La Tía's tales, I had a most unusual experience. She had been tucked away in the cells of my memory, completely intact. She was as alive, as charming, as interesting, as I had left her in 1938.

Emma Adatto Schlesinger, "La Tía Estambolía," in *Sephardic-American Voices: Two Hundred Years of a Literary Legacy*, ed. Diane Matza (Waltham, MA: Brandeis University Press, 1997), 72–79. © University Press of New England, Lebanon, NH. Reprinted with permission. Original in English.

## 146. A SEPHARDI STUDIES PROGRAM IS FORMED BY THE HISPANIC INSTITUTE OF COLUMBIA UNIVERSITY (1936)

*During the 1930s, Maír José Benardete (1895–1989), a recent Ph.D. from Columbia University, established a Sephardi studies program under the umbrella of Columbia University's Hispanic Institute. At that time the Columbia program was the only formal academic unit devoted to the study of Sephardi culture in the world, created just seven years after Salo Baron assumed the first chair in Jewish history in the American academy, also at Columbia. As director of the program Benardete sponsored lectures, wrote articles for the institute's Revista Hispánica Moderna, published a bilingual Ladino/Spanish study on the medieval Spanish-Jewish poet Judah Ha-Levi, and staged plays in Ladino. As a report on one such production from 1936 attests, members of the institute believed that programs on Judeo-Spanish culture would be of interest to a global community of "Spaniards, Hispanic Americans, and North American Hispanists" who were coming to consider Sephardi language and literature as part of their historical patrimony. (For more on Benardete see sources 114 and 149.)*

With the aim of . . . [supporting] the scientific investigations and publications that the [Sephardi] section is currently pursuing, a theatrical society has been formed. It has begun its work with a representation of Racine's biblical tragedy "Athalie," translated into Ladino (Judeo-Spanish) with the title "Athalie's Punishment." The play has been performed twice with great success.

In the Sephardi section of this journal, which will be published beginning with the next issue, we will offer a detailed description of this theatrical performance. Concerning its relevance to the work of the institute, the director wrote the following in a letter directed to his colleagues:

> Saturday April 18, the Institute will offer a theatrical performance that is unique in many respects.
>
> The celebration was organized by the Institute's Sephardi Studies Section, which is directed by Mr. Benardete. This section works actively to study Judeo-Spanish culture, which has produced great poets, philosophers, and scientists and today preserves highly valuable Spanish traditions. It proposes, furthermore, to reintegrate into the Hispanic spiritual community those Spaniards who, for historical reasons, have remained separated from Spain for more than 400 years. In addition to its intrinsic value, the theatrical work to be represented

offers us a unique opportunity to hear the Spanish language as it was spoken by Spaniards during the period of the Catholic monarchs and the discovery of America.

We have faith that Spaniards, Hispanic Americans, and North American Hispanists alike will look favorably upon this work of the institute and that they will contribute to the material and moral success of this performance.

"Sección de estudios sefarditas," *Revista Hispánica Moderna: Boletín del Instituto de las Españas* 2:4 (July 1936): 371–72. Translated from Spanish by Julia Phillips Cohen.

## 147. AMERICA'S FIRST CHAIR OF JEWISH HISTORY CONTACTS A PREEMINENT TURKISH JEWISH SCHOLAR [1936]

*Among the best-known scholars of Ottoman and Turkish Jewish history, Abraham Galante (1873–1961) was a historian, educator, professor, journalist, linguist, and activist. He authored more than sixty books and one hundred articles, many of which are weighted with translations of rare documents from Hebrew, Ladino, Ottoman and modern Turkish, French, and German. The following source, culled from Galante's personal archives, offers testimony to the wide-reaching effect of his scholarship. Here we see two letters that the eminent Jewish historian Salo Baron (1895–1989) addressed to Galante in 1936, requesting a number of the Turkish Jewish scholar's publications and offering his own works in exchange. Baron later integrated the research Galante and various other Ottoman Jewish scholars of Sephardi studies produced in his influential eighteen-volume* A Social and Religious History of the Jews. *(For more on Galante see sources 70, 84, 88, and 134–135.)*

February 13, 1936

Dear Professor Galante:

I am writing this letter in order to establish a contact with a colleague working in the same field at some distance. I am particularly anxious to have information concerning some of your publications which are not available in this city.

May I ask you to let me know at your earliest convenience where and when your studies on Don Joseph Nasi and Esther Kyra have appeared?[16]

---

16. Esther Handali, also known as Esther Kyra (d. 1590) was a Jewish woman who had influence at the sixteenth-century Ottoman palace.

I have seen your *Histoire des Juifs de Rhodes* announced for publication in 1935. Has it actually appeared and what is its full title? Also your book on *Rôle economique des Juifs de Constantinople* would be of great interest to me, as would be all the works listed as "in preparation" in your reprint of *Les Pacradounis*, 1933, which I have before me.

It seems to me that the best way would be if you sent me a complete list of your publications, indicating their prices and the bookseller from whom they may be [obtained], so that I may interest a library here to acquire the whole set. Personally I would also like to read quite a number of items. I wonder whether you would [be] interested in establishing a mutual exchange of reprints, in which case I should gladly offer you some of those which I still possess. For example, my Judenfrage auf dem Wiener Kongress (213 pp.); Azariah de Rossi's Attitude to Life (41 pp.); La Methode Historique d'Azariah de Rossi (61 pp.); I. M. Jost the Historian (26 pp.); Ghetto and Emancipation (12 pp.); The Jews and the Syrian Massacres of 1860 (29 pp.); Okhlose Israel be-yeme ha-melakhim (61 pp.); Teshuba be-safah italkit me-et r. Abraham Graziano (16 pp.) and the Historical Outlook of Maimonides, which just appeared (109 pp.).[17] Please indicate which of these would be of special interest to you.

Hoping to obtain from you a speedy affirmative answer to my proposal and the list for the library, I am,

Very truly yours

Salo W. Baron

April 24, 1936

Dear Professor Galante:

I have received your letter of 26 March and soon after followed your books and reprints, which you were kind enough to send me. Some of them were familiar to me, others I could not find in any of the libraries in this city. I have already had the opportunity to make use of some of the extensive information assembled in your works on the Jewries of the Eastern Mediterranean. I hope that you will continue sending me your publications in any phase of Jewish history and literature as soon as they appear. . . .

---

17. All titles appear here as in original.

During my forthcoming visit to Europe and Palestine in 1937 I may stop for a short time in Constantinople [Istanbul] and it shall give me great pleasure to make your personal acquaintance.

With kindest regards, I am,

Sincerely yours,

Salo W. Baron

Letters of Salo Baron in New York to Abraham Galante in Istanbul, February 13 and April 24, 1936. The Central Archives for the History of the Jewish People (Jerusalem), Galante Papers P-112/45. Original in English.

## 148. HISTORY AS ELIXIR: AN INTERWAR STUDY OF SALONICAN JEWISH HISTORY (1936)

*In 1923 the Jewish communal council of Salonica sent Isaac Samuel Emmanuel (1896–1972) to study at the Jewish Theological Seminary in Breslau (now Wrocław, Poland). Although the community's expectation was that he would return to his native city of Salonica to serve as a rabbi upon completing his training at the seminary, Emmanuel remained in Europe for more than a decade, earning his Ph.D. in history in 1936 from the University of Lausanne. That same year he published the first volume of his extensive study of the early centuries of Jewish life in Ottoman Salonica. Although Emmanuel had already pursued this history into later centuries, his choice to publish only the portion of his work that focused on Salonican Jewry's "Golden Age" coincided with his view that history could serve as an elixir for a community in crisis. As his coreligionists faced social and political exclusion as well as physical violence throughout the 1930s, Emmanuel believed that learning the history of their once-great community could "uplift the spirits of the Jews of Salonica," infusing them with a new sense of pride.*

In 1923, during my first stay in Germany at the rabbinic seminary of Breslau, I was touched by the importance scholars in that country attached to the past of their communities, especially of their institutions. At that time I understood that a similar study of the Jewish community of Salonica, Mother City in Israel,[18] would offer an important contribution to scholarship. I would add to it my filial fondness and affection. It was then that I decided to write this work, the first part of which appears today.

---

18. 2 Samuel 20:19.

Starting in 1924, my research in Berlin, Paris, London, and Oxford allowed me to consult and study a great number of documents that are usually overlooked. I used rare manuscripts and books, a few hundred collections of rabbinic responsa, sermons, eulogies, periodicals, and a great number of booklets that are not always easy to obtain.

Together with my brother, H. S. Emmanuel, I undertook thorough research in the Jewish cemetery of Salonica. Patiently and despite fatigue, we copied around 3,000 epitaphs. These are the sources on which I based this volume.

At the same time, I published in Hebrew 500 epitaphs from the Salonican Jewish cemetery that I found interesting for the history of the community and Jews in general. . . . The reader will find the texts of these epitaphs dated 1500–1660 and the biographical notes, which I added as a supplement to this volume.

The limited scope of this work and various other circumstances have not allowed me to include as much as I would have liked, although I have in manuscript form all sections of the work that I have not published here. As it is, I have had to overcome great difficulties of all kinds to have this volume printed. It is only my affection for the community of which my family has been a member since 1497 that gave me the courage and energy to achieve this outcome. That is why I ask the respected reader to judge this work not according to the importance of its subject but according to how much one can expect from the contribution of a single person. . . .

It is my hope that these pages will be useful for Jewish history and will serve to uplift the spirits of the Jews of Salonica, who have had to suffer so much in recent years. As in the past, they will continue to be proud of their two-thousand-year-old community.

Lausanne, May 26, 1936

Isaac Emmanuel, *Histoire des Israélites de Salonique: histoire sociale, économique et littéraire de la Ville Mère en Israël* (Paris: Librairie Lipschutz, 1936), vol. 1, 9–10. Translated from French by Olga Borovaya.

## 149. COMPARING LADINO AND YIDDISH:
## A SCHOLARLY EXCHANGE IN NEW YORK [1937]

*Maír José Benardete (1895–1989) immigrated to New York from Çanakkale in 1910, pursued an education at the University of Cincinnati, received a Ph.D. from Columbia University, and came to serve as professor of Spanish at Brooklyn College and Hunter College in New York City. In 1913 Benardete helped conduct a sociological survey of the Sephardi community of Cincinnati (on which see source 114). He went on to collect ballads from Sephardi Jewish residents of New York City, submitting his findings in a 1923 master's thesis. Benardete later developed the Sephardi studies program at Columbia University under the auspices of the university's Hispanic Institute (on which see source 146). Here Benardete corresponds with the distinguished historian and librarian Jacob Shatzky (1893–1956), chair of the Historical Section of the YIVO Institute for Jewish Research and author of more than one thousand studies of modern Jewish history and thought, most of which were written in Yiddish and focused on Poland.*

August 4, 1937

My dear Mr. Shatsky,

Mr. Morris Starkman has just written me to acknowledge my letter of inquiry about certain possible parallels between Yiddish and Judeo-Spanish folklore. He considers you "the greatest authority in the U.S. on the Yiddish folklore [and] on the Yiddish ballads." From other people too I heard you were the very depository of the information I am after.

I am in the midst of writing a book on the Spanish ballads that have survived in the Sephardi tradition of the Levantine and Moroccan Jews. I want to establish the presumption that the Jews were the participants of the *zajal* and *muwashshah* types very current in Andalusia.[19] Arabic scholars here and abroad have demonstrated that the Provençal lyric has its model in the *zajals* invented in Spain. Through my very imperfect knowledge of Hebrew I have discovered for myself that our great Hispano-Hebrew poets wrote some of their fine poems in the *muwashshah* scheme. For example, [see] poem forty-six in Yehudah Halevi [Judah Ha-Levi]'s anthology (Philadelphia, 1928). You will notice that it begins with a refrain, and the quatrains have their first three verses in the same rhyme [whereas] with the fourth we see the rhyme

19. The zajal ("melody") and muwashshah ("ode") were forms of Arabic strophic poetry developed in medieval Iberia.

of the refrain. Al-Makkari establishes that there were Andalusian Hebrews who wrote *muwashshahs* in Arabic. [Question 1)] Has this type of poem been conserved in Yiddish folklore?

Incidentally, when I was a boy I use[d] to sing with my boy friends in the synagogue (Dardanelles, Turkey in Asia) on the Saturday before Purim, the lyric ballad of Judah Ha-Levi on the story of Esther. After each quatrain we would give the translation, in a cantilatory fashion, of the quatrain in Ladino.

2) Was this poem sung in the Ashkenazi congregations?

3) Did the custom exist in the Ashkenazi tradition of singing in Yiddish the translations of the liturgy?

And now to a more definite problem:

The Spanish ballads preserved in the Sephardi tradition belong to the fifteenth century. The majority of them are of a chivalric nature, with very scanty interpolations of a Jewish nature. We have also a Biblical cycle in the ballads—Abraham's conversion to the true religion, the sacrifice of Isaac, the crossing of the Red Sea, Tamar and Amnon, etc. How about the Yiddish tradition?

4) Have many ballads of the German lands survived in Yiddish folklore?

5) Were ballads of an exclusively Jewish character written on the model of the German balladic pattern?

6) Have ballads of Russian and Polish origin entered the Yiddish folklore, transmuted in the Germanic mold? Or were the Slavonic ballads the starting point for new verse forms in Yiddish?

Your expert knowledge in the field ought to enable you to answer my perplexing questions. I was told too that you have made [a] study of Sephardi folklore. If the information I received is correct, will you please let me know what you have written on this subject?

If I can be of any help to you I should be more than glad to reciprocate.

¡Shalom!

M. J. Benardete

P.S. ¡Another parallel in Yiddish literature!

Thanks to the cooperation of Ashkenazi scholars I have been able to procure this valuable information.

The Spanish ballad was so overwhelmingly popular in the sixteenth century among the exiles living in the Ottoman Empire that at least three poets who wrote original Hebrew poems received inspiration from the ballads. For example Israel [ben Moses] Najara of Damascus placed above some of his poems this notice. "To be sung to the melody of such and such Spanish ballad."[20] His enemy, Menahem [ben Judah] de Lonzano, and Joseph Ganso followed the same tradition. By reading the inscriptions of their composition I was fortunate in collecting the first lines of about one hundred popular ballads among the Sephardim in the sixteenth century.

Was this custom current among the Hebrew poets of the Ashkenazi tradition? Did they request their readers to sing their original compositions to the tune of the then popular Yiddish songs and ballads?

Have you been able to garner in the responsa of the Ashkenazi rabbis references to the singing of Yiddish songs?

Finally are there any Yiddish songs with Sephardi themes? Any ballads on Hispano-Jewish history?

Sincerely,

M. J. Benardete

Letter from Maír José Benadete in New York to Jacob Shatsky in New York, August 4, 1937. YIVO Institute for Jewish Research (New York City), RG 356, Folder 2. Original in English.

## 150. DOCUMENTING THE DESTROYED JEWISH LIBRARIES OF SALONICA (1947)

*As they undertook the systematic extermination of Jewish populations across Europe during the Second World War, the Nazis and their non-German accomplices also targeted Jewish artifacts and libraries for destruction. Salonica, home to one of the richest assortment of Jewish manuscript and book collections in the Sephardi world, was impacted deeply by these efforts. In this text, written shortly after the war's end, historian Joseph Nehama (1880–1971) attempts to document the extent of this confiscation.*

---

20. Israel ben Moses Najara (1550–1625) was a rabbi and scholar of Iberian origin who lived in Safed, Damascus, and Gaza and was well known for his liturgical poetry.

Ever since the exodus from Spain, Salonica has been the true city of books and printing. Throughout the ages, from the end of the fifteenth until the middle of the eighteenth century, Iberian immigrants brought countless manuscripts and printed books of great value with them in their baggage. Biblical and Talmudic Hebrew, Arabic, and Latin appear within these treasures that include Masoretic exegesis, the *Gemara*, religious philosophy, medicine and natural sciences. Moreover, wealthy Salonican Sephardim continued to have the honor of enriching their libraries through frequent acquisitions made in the great cities of the East, as well as Venice, Livorno, Amsterdam, and the main Polish publishing centers. They often had scribes in their employ who worked without interruption to copy the most precious manuscripts on parchment prepared expressly for this purpose with particular care.

In this manner all the wealthy families came to own rich book collections. Catastrophic fires often destroyed Jewish quarters. The libraries there perished along with other riches. But as soon as homes were raised from the rubble, the appetite for knowledge and the sacred respect for a moldy letter would bring every wealthy Jew to reconstitute his small spiritual treasure. Purchases were made in the cities of the countryside and abroad, while copyists and printing presses were set to work. [Collectors] would scarcely hesitate to consecrate a portion of their assets to this end: they were as proud of a collection of books as of a golden coffer, a case of jewels, or a set of carpets or fabrics of great value. For among Sephardim, knowledge has always had an edge on temporal goods, and a well-stocked library was considered by all an incontestably noble prerogative.

Three libraries, famous throughout the East, disappeared in the disastrous fire of 1545: those of Abraham Benveniste, Samuel Benveniste, and Perahia the Italian. True treasures of jurisprudence and medicine were lost in the fires of 1620, 1734, 1759, 1877, and 1890. In the fire of August 18, 1917, one of the worst that has ever afflicted the old city, a great number of priceless libraries were devoured, belonging to rabbinical seminaries (*yeshivot*) and to rich individuals. Taking a random sample, among the most important [libraries destroyed] included that of the Boyana seminary, Haimucho Covo, Chelebi Elie Hacohen, Yacovachi Covo, Asher Simha, Shalom Saias, and Sabetai Hasid. Countless historical and encyclopedic works perished in Judah Nehama's house, in the building of the Kadima Society, and the home of the astronomer Saul Amariglio.

Luckily many incunabula and rare works were purchased in Salonica by the bibliophiles Ephraim Deinar[d] and Elkan Adler, who visited the city during the first years of the nineteenth century.[21] Their precious acquisitions can be found sheltered in New York and in London.

All that remained of the books, manuscripts, illuminated *megilot*, archives, Torah scrolls, and synagogue ornaments (*mapot, parashiyot, rimonim*, etc.) were systematically confiscated by the Nazis, starting with the first days of the invasion in April and May 1941. Under the Rosenberg Commission, teams assembled for this task carefully packed in well-cataloged and labeled crates all of the valuable libraries whose existence the fifth column had thoroughly registered long before the war. Mr. Joseph Nehama's library had the sad honor of being the first to be rounded up. Aside from abundant encyclopedic material and a trove of historical works, it included works of sociology and general philosophy as well as complete collections of Jewish reviews and publications. The plunder was accomplished quite rapidly: community and private libraries were transported to Germany within just a few weeks.

The library of the Bet Din, which boasted 1,500 volumes, a great number of which had been purchased in Palestine after 1917, included, among other things, various editions of the Talmud, Turim, works by Maimonides, Joseph Caro and, above all, the complete collection of 600 quartos devoted to the responsa of local rabbinic legal experts. It constituted the most important and varied source base for the city's Jewish history since the dawn of modern times, and a testament to the exuberant spiritual vitality of Salonican Jewry.

Works of a similar nature graced the shelves of the following libraries, which also fell prey to the Rosenberg Commission:

1. That of Judah Nehama, which had been donated to the Jewish

---

21. Ephraim Deinard (1846–1930) was an American Jewish bibliophile who traveled the globe in search of exemplars of early Hebrew printing. Elkan Adler (1841–1946), the son of Nathan Marcus Adler, chief rabbi of the British Empire, spent his life amassing an enormous library of Jewish manuscripts and books, which were eventually dispersed among libraries in London, New York, and Cincinnati.

community of Salonica. It included an assorted collection of works in the new Hebrew of the post-Mendelssohnian Haskalah.[22]

2. Those of the teachers of the community's schools, numbering 500 volumes, many of which were reference works. A few shelves were reserved for a modest but well-chosen collection of historical works (Graetz, Dubnov, etc.) and neo-Hebraic literature.

3. That of Dr. Zvi Koretz, numbering 1,000 volumes, most of which were reference works. It included one of the most beautiful editions of the Babylonian Talmud and collections of German publications on Judaism.

4. That of Rabbi Saul Amariglio, reconstructed at great expense after the fire of 1917. It contained more than 500 volumes and included, aside from an important collection of responsa, a number of important works on Jewish history, as well as a significant assortment of works of contemporary Hebrew authors.

5. That of Rabbi Haim Habib, which numbered about a thousand volumes, most of which concerned questions of jurisprudence and rare exegetical texts. It included a collection of original editions on synagogue ritual as well as old family records accumulated over many generations.

6. That of the Monastir synagogue. Exclusively rabbinical and legal in nature, it was a gift of the patron Jacob Israel of Monastir [Bitola], in which he had invested most of his fortune and, finally

7. That of about ten rabbinical seminaries (*yeshivot*) numbering in their entirety 3,500–4,000 volumes including Talmudic works, responsa composed by Salonican authors, and biblical exegesis.

Following the arrival of German troops in Salonica, the Rosenberg Commission also made off with two archival repositories:

1. That of the Jewish community and

2. That of the Union Bank of Salonica, in which they no doubt hoped to discover some valuable evidence in favor of the Nazi thesis concerning the occult power of international Jewish finance

---

22. Moses Mendelssohn (1729–1786) was a German Jewish enlightener in eighteenth-century Berlin whose philosophical writings were influential in non-Jewish and Jewish circles. Mendelssohn is often hailed as having inaugurated the *Haskalah*, or Jewish Enlightenment, which, by the nineteenth century, counted among its principal preoccupations the renaissance of the Hebrew language.

as well as certain elusive details concerning the shadowy plot of the Jewish plutocrats who schemed against poor Germany.

About 150 Torah scrolls were seized from the synagogues. A small number were sent to Germany. The rest were ripped apart and burned.

The confiscation of all these learned works was organized and directed by Dr. Hans Heinrich of the Rosenberg Commission. The crates in which the plunder was sealed bore the initials G.S.V.

The circulating libraries of the former students of the Alliance Israélite (2,500 volumes), B'nai B'rith (1,500 volumes), former students of the Mission laïque française (2,000 volumes) and a few others consisting of encyclopedias and literary and historical works in various languages, notably French, escaped the Nazi plundering, but were scattered and ended up for the most part in the hands of the city's secondhand booksellers or in the dispensaries where paper bags are made for the common grocery store.

Juridical and cultural works from the various *yeshivot* that remained undetected by the Nazis were likewise scattered and squandered. The two most important [such collections] are the result of the munificence of the benefactor Haimucho Covo and included treasures of responsa from all eras and all the countries of the diaspora, midrashic, rational, and mystical commentaries as well as histories, compendia, sermons, and funerary speeches. One of these repositories was the seminary on Ménexé Street; the other was the seminary on Queen Olga Street. Together they originally comprised three thousand volumes, but generous donations from individuals [in Salonica] as well as from the communities of Thrace, Macedonia, and Thessaly, particularly the precious collection of Mair Nahmias of Larissa, were added to the collection [over the years].

At the moment the Jewish community of Salonica, which drew its glory from its spiritual riches accumulated over the course of half a millennium, is without books. With its fifty thousand martyrs deprived of any burial, the shroud of memory envelops the prestige of its vast erudition and its fervent worship of knowledge.

Joseph Nehama, "Les bibliothèques juives de Salonique détruites par les Nazis," *Cahiers Séfardis*, March 15, 1947, 134–36. Translated from French by Alma Rachel Heckman.

## 151. YITZHAK BEN-ZVI FOUNDS A CENTER FOR THE STUDY OF "EASTERN JEWS" IN JERUSALEM (1948)

*Born in the Russian Empire, Yitzhak Ben-Zvi (1884–1963) attended the Galatasaray imperial high school and pursued a law degree in Ottoman Istanbul before moving to the United States and ultimately settling in Palestine. An ardent Zionist, Ben-Zvi was among the signatories of the Israeli Declaration of Independence. In 1948 he created and assumed leadership of the Institute for the Study of Jewish Communities in the East, later renamed the Ben-Zvi Institute (Yad Ben-Zvi), under whose auspices he carried on research on the history and religious practices of Mediterranean, Middle Eastern, and North African Jewry. From 1952 to 1963, Ben-Zvi served as president of Israel. In this document he articulates the aims of the institute, and calls for assistance in gathering archival material that would abet future scholarship in the field.*

The Institute for the Study of Jewish Communities in the East was established in 1948 with the aid of three bodies: the General Organization of the Workers in the Land of Israel, the National Committee, and the Committee of Workers in America.

The aim of the institute is to assemble information and official documents from institutions and from private persons concerning the living conditions of the Jews in the Middle East. The research will focus on their economic, cultural, and external political conditions as well as their [intra-communal] organization and their customs, beliefs, and lore. The material will be collected and arranged systematically in order to enable its publication.

*The Framework*: The subject of the research is, as stated above, the Jewish collectives that live around the Mediterranean. Three big units and four smaller ones can be discerned in the Middle East. The main characteristic that defines them and differentiates them from one another is their spoken language, notwithstanding the one and only national language [Hebrew] that is shared by the whole Hebrew nation.

The large units [of analysis] are (1) "Arabophone Jewry" (those who speak Arabic), which is in turn divided into eight branches: the Jews of Iraq, Syria, Lebanon, Yemen and Aden, Egypt, Libya, Tunisia, and Algeria and Morocco; (2) the Ladino (*Spaniolit*) speakers of Anatolia, the Balkans (*Rumelia*), and other areas; (3) the Persian-speaking Jews (in Persia, Afghanistan, Bukhara, and Dagestan). The four small units are the Aramaic-speaking Jews (Kurdistan), the Turkic-Tatar-speaking

Jews (Russia and parts of Turkey), the Georgian speakers (North Caucasia)[sic] and the Berber-speakers (*Shlokh*, in North Africa). To these should be added the research on more remote collectives of far-flung Jews in India, China, Abyssinia, and the isolated communities in the Western and Eastern parts of the globe.

Each of these units possesses not only a distinct history, but also a unique folklore and character in the present day. They maintain a tremendous cultural treasure orally as well as in written forms. These riches, most of them as yet unstudied, are gradually being forgotten and are sometimes completely invisible. Traditions and customs previously unknown [to scholars], which were maintained for hundreds of years, are nowadays vanishing rapidly. There are two causes for this process. The first is national agitation directed mainly against minorities and especially against the constantly persecuted Jewish minorities. These persecutions, which are also aimed at other religions and other people, have wrought particular damage upon Jewish uniqueness. To this should be added the battle against Zionism, which has lately assumed the form of a battle against all Jews. It should be taken into consideration that during this process, vast cultural treasures and whole communities will be damaged and perhaps even vanish, God forbid.

The second cause is the natural tendency towards cultural change and *'aliyah*.[23] This tendency has climaxed with the reestablishment of the state of Israel, which has opened hitherto unknown paths of *'aliyah* and salvation to those remote communities dispersed in the exiles of Ishmael.[24]

Newcomers from all corners of the East have already gathered. There is hardly any community in the Diaspora from which newcomers have not arrived in the Land of Israel. Many have brought with them living traditions from their places of origin. The land of Israel can [therefore] become a central site for the research of Eastern [Jewish] communities.

It is only natural that here in this country the process of the unification of these tribes into one nation has begun. It is here that the

---

23. *'Aliyah*, literally "ascent" in Hebrew, refers here to Jewish migration to the biblical Land of Israel and, later, to the modern state.
24. A reference to Muslim lands.

unique characteristics of each tribe are blurring and disappearing. There are several reasons for this. The first one is negative—that is, assimilation. The second one is positive, and it is *'aliyah* and national cohesion. In any case [we are witness to] the dissolution of traditions and even to their total erasure. There is thus an urgent need to start gathering the sparks of culture and lore for research purposes while they are still live.[25] Bringing these sparks to our land bears national significance as well, especially in these days in which we are on the verge of redemption.[26]

The Institute for the Study of Jewish Communities in the East exists under the auspices of the Hebrew University, which has appointed a special committee to monitor its activities. The committee is composed of three deputies: the chair of the Institute for Jewish Studies, the chair of the Institute of Near Eastern Studies and a third member who represents the executive management of the university. The signateur listed below and his assistant, Dr. A. Hirschberg, a research fellow at the Hebrew University, stand at the head of the institute.

We hereby call upon all institutions and people who are interested in the history of their nation and are concerned about its destiny, to help us by sharing any kind of material relating to Jewish life in the East. We are especially interested in manuscripts and printed material such as accounts, regulation, originals or reliable photocopies that may serve the institution's research and publishing purposes. Among other publications we intend to publish a special bulletin that will include extracts of this significant material. The bulletin will be published in Hebrew and include appendices in English and French.

Yitzhak Ben-Zvi, "Ha-Makhon le-heker ha-'Edot ha-Yehudiyot ba-Mizrah ha-Tikhon," *Davar*, April 7, 1949, 2. Courtesy The Pinhas Lavon Institute for Labor Movement Research (Tel Aviv). Translated from Hebrew by Miriam Frenkel.

---

25. Here Ben-Zvi draws on the kabbalistic (Jewish mystical) teachings of the mystic Isaac Luria (1534–1572), who called on Jews to gather together the sparks of God's light that had been scattered in the course of creation.

26. According to a kabbalistic tradition, *tikun 'olam*, the healing of the world, is achieved when Jews gather up and redeem these sparks.

## 152. TEACHING HEBREW IN MADRID: THE EMERGENCE OF SEPHARDI STUDIES IN SPAIN (1949)

*In the following selection, Abraham Shalom Yahuda (1877–1951) looks back with ambivalence on his time during the early part of the twentieth century as a professor of Semitic studies at the University of Madrid. A polymath and prolific scholar, Yahuda's trajectory and allegiances spanned the globe. Of Baghdadi origin, he was born in Jerusalem, studied at the Universities of Strasbourg and Heidelberg, and served as lecturer at Berlin's Hochschule für die Wissenschaft des Judentums before moving to Spain. Even after assuming his new position in the Spanish academy, Yahuda insisted on keeping his British citizenship—a status members of his family had obtained after traveling from Baghdad to Calcutta. In the following source, he emphasizes his role in promoting Jewish studies at the University of Madrid during the early twentieth century. Although he received extensive support from various quarters in Spain, Yahuda suggested that the continued opposition he faced from conservative Catholic circles eventually drove him to leave his post.*

My lectures on the great Jewish luminaries of Spain generated much interest among the [Spanish] newspapers; all of them—except for two Catholic extremist publications—urged the government to establish a chair for me at the university. This was no easy task. I did not want to relinquish my British citizenship as required by law, and the government had to propose a new law to the Senate allowing it to appoint foreign citizens as professors. A feat like this was difficult to achieve. Therefore the government researched and identified a law from 1836 that allowed a foreign national to become professor of a foreign language, if [the language in question] was a spoken one—and so it had to be proven that Hebrew was a living language. Two professors were entrusted with this task, and they brought forward evidence in the form of instructional manuals and translated books that [demonstrated that] Hebrew was a spoken language in the Land of Israel. [Hayim Nahman] Bialik's translation of *Don Quixote* clearly tipped the scales in favor of viewing Hebrew as a living language. But this did not end the matter. It had to be confirmed by the philosophy faculty, by the High Council of the Ministry of Education, the Academy of History, and the Academy of the Spanish Language that I was qualified for the position—and it was the latter that had to decide whether Hebrew could be considered a living language, since it was spoken by only a portion of the people of Israel. I provided all of the material required by the academy, not only to attain the chair, but also to obtain from the committee of scholars authorized by the government . . . a public declaration that Hebrew was alive in the mouths of the Jewish people. The decision pivoted on the fact that Hebrew dominated all [levels of] instruction as well as scientific fields and disciplines in all the [Jewish] schools in the Land of Israel and in many [Jewish] schools outside it, from kindergarten to the highest grades. As such it confirmed once again that "from the mouths of infants and sucklings you have founded [your] strength."[27]

The decision to recognize Hebrew was accepted by a great majority of academy members, among them world-renowned scholars and writers in literature and the sciences. However some devout Catholics abstained. . . .

This victory, which was achieved with much effort during the course of an entire year, reinforced my desire to bring about a second triumph for Hebrew at the university. Upon being appointed chair I explicitly stipulated that Hebrew be considered obligatory, as was Arabic, by the philosophy department, and that each student who wanted to obtain a doctorate in Hispanic culture also had to pass a Hebrew exam. And so it was that Madrid's university was the first and only one in the world where Hebrew was considered an obligatory subject. Two of the more religious newspapers loudly protested, saying among other things, "How did it come to this, poor Spanish people, that it has become impossible to be crowned with a doctorate without knowledge of the Hebrew language?"

When King Alfonso XIII asked me why I insisted on these terms, I explained that Hebrew culture had once been important in Spain because it grew and flourished there, reaching new heights and impacting Spanish learning, much as had Arabic culture. The Hebrew program in the university was a great success and many students persevered with voracity and diligence in their studies. They were all Catholics, among them priests and female students whom they called *las rabinas* ["women rabbis"]. Many students specialized in Hebrew, and two of them, Manuel Casas and Ignacio González Llubera, acquired sufficient

---

27. Psalm 8:3.

knowledge to become very good professors in their own right. Students from other fields as well as important persons from outside the department attended my lectures on biblical literature and our poetry in Spain. Doctor Nordau, who was living in Spain during the First World War, often attended my talks.[28]

For six years I served as the head of the Hebrew Department at the university, and at the same time I also taught Hebrew and other Oriental languages at the Centro de Estudios Históricos. This was basically a seminar for advanced students working on different subjects, such as the relationship among Semitic languages or the remnants of Hebrew inscriptions in Toledo, Barcelona, Tarragona, and other cities in Spain. We compiled complete bibliographic material of everything that was written in Spain about the Jewish communities in various cities. We also prepared a Hebrew-Spanish, Spanish-Hebrew dictionary with the help of Doctor [Hayim] Bograshov, the high school teacher in Tel Aviv who lived in Madrid during the First World War. But the purpose of our work was to lay the foundation for gathering all the existing sources from different archives about the history of our people in Christian Spain and in particular, the Inquisition and its schemes. All these efforts were left incomplete, however, and the years of labor amounted to nothing because of [the interference of] people who wanted only to hinder our work. I must say, however, that the government, whether conservative or liberal, always helped us, and great scholars such as [Ramón] Menéndez Pidal, and influential persons in political circles, such as Gumersindo Azcárate, vice rector of the university, and Senator Ángel Pulido, the first propagandist to advocate for the return of Spanish Jews, worked hard to make sure the government was supportive. But there were also professors and politicians who strove to undermine us, while two clerical newspapers used every opportunity to publish articles full of accusations against me. Together they worked to destroy everything I had built. They issued false and unimaginable statements about me until I finally had enough of it and resigned from my position. . . .

The subject of my resignation was taken up by all the newspapers, university circles, and the government, where it made a powerful im-

---

28. Max Nordau (1849–1923) was an influential Zionist leader, author, and physician.

pression. On that very same day Professor Elías Tormo, head of the Philosophy Department, delivered an explosive speech in the Senate against the agitators: Minister of Education and Culture Natalio Ribas followed and promised to convince me to revoke my resignation. The king also got involved and invited me to discuss the matter. The minister [Ribas] came to visit me and said that if I didn't change my decision he too would resign from his position. Out of respect I responded to him, but I saw that my labor had been in vain, and I left Spain with sadness and a heavy heart after seven years of fruitful and productive work. The chair, which had been founded for me, was no longer.

The study of Hebrew [in Spain] was revived twenty [years] later— seven years ago—when an Institute for Hebrew Literature was founded in Madrid upon the initiative of the erudite José María Millás [Josep Maria Millàs Vallicrosa], an old Catholic who understands our language and literature very well; he spent time in Israel and attended classes for one or two years learning Hebrew. Several young scholars work under his supervision, and he publishes a review called *Sefarad*, which is dedicated to the literature of Israel, especially to the writings of our people and poetry in Spain during the Middle Ages; it also contains important research and critical reviews about Jewish topics from around the world. His books on R. Judah Ha-Levi and R. Solomon ibn Gabirol have earned him renown, and there is hope that this Institute will develop and continue to bear more fruit with time. However, my name is not mentioned in connection with the Institute. Even the fact that I was the one to lay the foundation for the study of Hebrew in Spain is forgotten.

A. S. Yahuda, "Perakim mi-Zikhronotai," *Hed ha-Mizrah*, August 5, 1949, 8. Courtesy of the Historical Jewish Press Website, National Library of Israel and Tel Aviv University, http://jpress .org.il. Translated from Hebrew by Allyson Gonzalez.

## 153.  A SEPHARDI DOCTORAL STUDENT IN MEXICO ISSUES A PLEA FOR THE STUDY OF LADINO [1952]

*Born in Harlem to Ottoman Jewish immigrant parents, Denah Levy Lida (1923–2007) was among the first American Sephardi Jews to write master's and doctoral theses on Sephardi culture and history. In 1952 she submitted a Ph.D. dissertation to the Universidad Nacional Autónoma de México (UNAM) in Mexico City in which she appeals to young Sephardim in the Americas to study the Ladino spoken by their parents' generation before it disappears.*

The small number of Sephardim in America, as well as the attitude of those who reside there, signal the death of their dialect. It disappeared from public life when *La Vara*, the last Sephardi periodical in New York, ceased publication. Thirty years ago there were many such journals in this city but the number of readers has been reduced to such a degree that even this one single organ could no longer sustain itself. . . .

The Sephardi colony still has some social life, yet it is one that continues to lose its distinguishing features. . . . Thus the regional characteristics are lost, substituted for a common jargon in which certain elements of old Spanish can be discerned but which lacks all of the personality of a Romance language. The mind of its speaker is that of an Anglo-Saxon,[29] which affects his manner of speaking even in another language.

The fact that Sephardim continue to maintain their own particular way of life remains the only hope for conserving their dialect. The nucleus that still has some life left and that guards the spirit of our culture must recognize its responsibility and accept it with pride. Because the majority of this group is unaware of the historical value of the language of their parents, it is necessary to teach them—to give them a collective consciousness of that which is their own. We must disabuse them of the idea that the language they hear at home is merely a poorly spoken form of Spanish that is incorrect and shameful to speak. Instead we should teach them the linguistic value of their dialect and the importance of studying it now in order to conserve what remains of it, as well as to allow it to enter the realm of history with dignity. This job must be undertaken by young Sephardim. We can hardly expect

---

29. Here a native speaker of English.

430 The Emergence of Sephardi Studies

academic work from the older generation as they are people with little education, a working people that came to the New World in search of what they did not have. . . . They set themselves to creating a better life for their families, something their children now enjoy.

It is therefore to my contemporaries that I direct my plea. They are the ones who must cultivate the fertile ground.

Denah Levy [Lida], "El sefardí esmirniano de Nueva York" (Ph.D. dissertation, Universidad Nacional Autónoma de México, 1952), 1–5. Translated from Spanish by Julia Phillips Cohen.

# Index

431

CPSIA information can be obtained
at www.ICGtesting.com
Printed in the USA
JSHW061558030822
28854JS00001B/20

9 780804 791434